MARTIN NOTH

EXODUS

THE OLD TESTAMENT LIBRARY

General Editors

G. ERNEST WRIGHT, The Divinity School, Harvard University
JOHN BRIGHT, Union Theological Seminary, Richmond, Virginia
JAMES BARR, Princeton Theological Seminary
PETER ACKROYD, University of London

MARTIN NOTH

EXODUS

A Commentary

The Westminster Press
Philadelphia

Copyright © 1962 S.C.M. Press, Ltd.
Translated by J. S. Bowden from the German
Das zweite Buch Mose, Exodus
(Das Alte Testament Deutsch 5)
published 1959 by Vandenhoeck & Ruprecht,
Göttingen

Library of Congress Catalog Card No. 62-7940

Sixth Printing, 1974

TYPESET IN GREAT BRITAIN
PRINTED IN THE UNITED STATES OF AMERICA

CONTENTS

5

CONTENTS

6

TRANSLATOR'S NOTE

THE ORIGINAL COMMENTARY was based on the author's own translation of Exodus. This English edition prints the Revised Standard Version, with italic type to distinguish JE from P and square brackets enclosing material which Professor Noth regards as secondary. Where differences between his text and the RSV are such as to affect the commentary, this has been indicated in the notes.

I

INTRODUCTION

1. THE CONTENTS OF THE BOOK

IN THE EXTANT manuscripts of the Greek translation of the Old Testament, the so-called Septuagint, the 'Second Book of Moses' has been given the title 'Departure (from Egypt)' = *exodos* (*Aigyptou*), and accordingly it has been called *Liber Exodi* in the Latin Vulgate. This title indicates an important part of the contents, the historical events narrated in the first part of the book. It is customary to refer to the book as 'Exodus', whereas in the original Hebrew it is described by the first words of the text (*weʾēlleh šemōt*) '(These are) the names', following a usage widespread in the ancient East.

The book comprises only a limited extract from a larger whole, the complex of the 'Five Books of Moses', the so-called Pentateuch.* It begins at a very clear and very important turning point in the Pentateuchal narrative. In the first book, Genesis, the patriarchal history has been told up to its conclusion; the second book, Exodus, presupposes the existence of a people Israel in Egypt. Whereas Genesis is concerned with distinct individual figures, from the beginning of Exodus onwards the subject is Israel as a collective entity. It is true that the names of the 'sons of Israel' (= sons of Jacob) are related once again in Ex. 1.1 ff. to form a link with the patriarchal history that has gone before, but neither these individual names nor, as a rule, the individual tribes play any further part in subsequent events—Israel is treated as a whole. There is, moreover, a considerable lapse of time between the end of Genesis and the beginning of Exodus over which the narrative passes almost imperceptibly, the whole period of the sojourn of Israel in Egypt, which according to the

*On this see G. von Rad, *Genesis*, ET 1961, pp. 13 ff.

9

late tradition of Ex. 12.41 was of considerable length. Of this the Old Testament tradition has no more to tell us. Here we have the largest gap in time which is indicated by the Pentateuchal narrative in the form in which it has been transmitted. It was therefore quite appropriate for a new book to begin at just this point when, at a time unknown to us, the great literary work of the Pentateuch was first divided into five books or rather was apportioned between five separate rolls. The ending of the book is a different matter; here the continuity of a coherent narrative is interrupted quite abruptly. The theme of the instructions received by Moses on Sinai and of the way in which they are carried out is by no means exhausted at the end of the book; it continues through the whole of the third book, Leviticus, and into the beginning of the fourth book, Numbers. The practical aspects of a division into five approximately equal parts caused the interruption of the continuity at this point and only by later additions was the last chapter of Exodus made to look like some sort of a conclusion.

It therefore follows that Exodus must be understood as part of a larger whole. In view of what has been said, this is true not only of its relationship to the following 'books' but also—in spite of the break which is caused by the transition from one theme to another—of its relationship to Genesis. For the whole complex of the Pentateuchal tradition already had the essential elements of its structure at the stage of oral tradition before it began to be fixed in writing, a development whose results we have today in the 'Five Books of Moses'. This tradition was enshrined in cultic confessions of faith through which on certain occasions the mighty acts of God in the prehistory and early history of Israel were celebrated.* These confessions were rooted in particular circumstances in which the action of God had been made manifest, circumstances which are still clearly recognizable as distinctive themes even in the narrative form of the whole as we have it in the transmitted text.

The Book of Exodus deals with the central events of the Pentateuchal tradition. The first part of the book describes the Exodus from Egypt. It was always a fundamental expression of Israelite faith that 'Yahweh brought up Israel out of the land of Egypt'. In this event Yahweh had by a decisive act demonstrated for Israel that he was at work in history and at the same time quite clearly took Israel to himself. The climax of the divine action in these happenings

*For details see von Rad, *loc. cit.*

comes in the miraculous rescue at 'the sea',* and wherever the Exodus from Egypt is discussed the first thought is always of the wonder
at the sea. Even the narrative form, existing as it does now in a
number of variants, builds up to this peak, although it first deals in
considerable detail with the subject of the plagues and the repeated
negotiations with Pharaoh. This part of the story probably originates
in the Passover tradition, which is concerned with the protection of
the first-born in Israel, both man and beast. These were guarded by
the Passover sacrifice against the onslaught of the 'destroyer', whereas
in Egypt the 'destroyer' could carry on with his work of annihilation
and in so doing bring in the last and most terrible plague. In addition,
the story of the birth, youth and call of Moses has been inserted into
the beginning of the story of the 'Exodus from Egypt'.

The second main theme of the book is the theophany and the
making of the covenant on Sinai. This element of the tradition has
had a separate history; it was probably recited at certain central
cultic festivals in Israel in which the making of the covenant between
God and people was regularly re-enacted. Remarkably enough it
appears to have been incorporated only at a relatively late stage into
the summary credal confessions of the mighty acts of God towards
Israel, and doubtless at first had its own special place in the cult. It
was however already included in the complex of Pentateuchal
tradition before the development of the fixed literary form which we
now possess and quite properly formed the central point in this
complex. For Israel the making of a covenant is connected by no
means indispensably but at least appropriately with the subject of
'the Law', with the result that the Law in its most varied forms now
plays a most important part in the narrative of the theophany and
the making of the covenant. This whole theme is by no means concluded in Exodus, but the book contains the most important features,
namely the narrative describing the theophany on the mountain and
the making of the covenant between Yahweh and Israel. The additions to this theme in the following books fall under the subsidiary
heading 'law' (in the wider sense), which is elaborated in great detail.

Between the two main topics which have already been mentioned
there are further narratives which belong to the separate subject of
Israel's wanderings in the wilderness, i.e. the period during which

---

*[This term will be used throughout in place of the traditional 'Red Sea',
which is not an accurate translation of the Hebrew text and has a confusing effect
on any discussion of the route of the Exodus. Cf. further ch. II. 8, p. 102. Tr.]

God led Israel through the desert between Egypt and Palestine. They in fact form a link between the Exodus and the Entry into the Promised Land. These narratives comprise a loose juxtaposition of episodes from nomadic life in the wilderness, a life whose characteristic features were still at a later date familiar to the tribes of Israel, bounded as they were by the desert. But this theme does not serve merely to give a graphic description of a particular period in the pre-history of Israel; behind it stands the tenet of Israelite faith that it was in fact 'in the wilderness' that Yahweh had shown his concern for Israel (cf. Hos. 13.5; Jer. 2.2; 31.2). The theme of the wanderings appears once again in the Book of Numbers. If we look at the Pentateuch as a whole, it forms a frame round the Sinai theme and in its turn is framed by the two matching themes of the Exodus from Egypt and the Entry into the Promised Land. Thus, although there is at first sight a bewildering abundance of such different individual narratives, the Pentateuchal traditions have been arranged under a clear pattern which holds this unusual work together and makes it clear that the individual books—and among them Exodus—are just members of a greater whole.*

2. THE LITERARY COMPOSITION OF THE BOOK

The present final form of the Book of Exodus, as indeed that of the whole Pentateuch, has been found to be the result of a very complicated process involving the evolution of traditions as well as literary development. The intensive work on the Pentateuch which has been carried on by scholars for many generations has shown that the completed Pentateuch, as it now stands in the Old Testament, cannot be explained as the work of one 'author' and that the attribution of the Pentateuch to Moses as author, of which we find traces only after the Old Testament period, does not hold true. Viewed as one large entity, the Pentateuch seems remarkably consistent, but the individual details betray a multitude of differing concepts and styles which compel us to posit quite a long process of literary development. The most probable solution of the literary riddle of the Pentateuch has proved to be the hypothesis that the present Pentateuch is the result of a working together of different, originally independent

*For a thorough treatment of this cf. G. von Rad, *Das formgeschichtliche Problem des Hexateuchs*, 1938, = *Gesammelte Studien zum Alten Testament*, 1958, p. 9–86; M. Noth, *Überlieferungsgeschichte des Pentateuch*, 1948.

'written sources', each of which, in a separate literary work, had fixed the material of the Pentateuchal tradition in writing. This hypothesis, which at first was tested and confirmed chiefly on Genesis, is quite evidently well supported for Exodus also. Accordingly, here too we have the written sources of the 'Jahwist' (J) the 'Elohist' (E), and the 'Priestly writer' (P).* Of these sources the two first-named belong quite closely together as the 'older sources', whereas the Priestly writing is a comparatively late work with its own peculiar approach. In Exodus, it is true, the literary relationships are rather more complicated than in Genesis. The reason for this is the content of the book. In the first part, which tells of the Exodus from Egypt and the beginnings of Israel's wandering in the wilderness, the interchange between the contributions of the different sources is still much the same as in Genesis. The narrative of the events on Sinai, on the other hand, reveals a different state of affairs. As the Old Testament Law was understood to have its basic roots in the covenant on Sinai, different corpora of Law were inserted into the Sinai narrative. These sit too loosely to their context to show any signs of having once belonged to one of the narrative sources mentioned above. It must therefore be supposed that they were at first independent entities and were placed in their present position at some stage of the literary development which we can no longer ascertain. This is the case both with the '(Ethical) Decalogue' and the 'Book of the Covenant', but not on the other hand with the so-called 'Cultic Decalogue' of ch. 34, which is firmly established in the context of the J narrative. The insertion of these passages of other origin considerably disturbed the firm structure of the three narrative sources, especially as the passages inserted seem to have brought with them still further accretions which served as a framework to them. To this we must add that the central events of the theophany, the making of the covenant and the giving of the 'Law', have clearly attracted all kinds of supplementary expansions and elaborations, so that the literary situation at this point has become unusually complicated. The position is further changed in the Sinai narrative, as the P stratum now comes very markedly into the foreground. Hitherto P has provided a summary survey of history as a framework and has only changed to a more detailed description at important individual events which are crucial for its theology (the Creation, the Flood and the Covenant with Noah, the Covenant with Abraham). Now,

*See von Rad, *Genesis*, pp. 23 ff.

however, it has reached its real goal, the description of how the cultic community formed of the twelve tribes of Israel was constituted by divine commandment, with a cult and cultic apparatus regulated down to the last detail. P therefore now expands to its full extent and for long sections forces the old sources right into the background. But at the same time this P material has also received a particularly large number of secondary additions. This is understandable, as the design for the legitimate sanctuary with all its apparatus, as given by P, was of fundamental significance for the post-exilic Jerusalem cult. It was therefore obvious, indeed necessary, that everything in the actual practice of the post-exilic sanctuary which deviated from or went beyond the P design should be introduced at least as a secondary element into the P narrative. The narrative was in the main left unaltered, but in this way underwent considerable expansion.

As a result of all this we must reconstruct the literary development of Exodus in roughly the following way. Credal summaries of the fundamental acts of God in the prehistory and early history of Israel, including the Sinai theme, assisted greatly in the construction and arrangement of the whole within the framework of the general Pentateuchal tradition. In addition, a great deal of narrative material, certainly first handed down by oral tradition, served to give the description of the events a concrete and living form. Beyond these general statements we can say hardly anything really certain about the state of things at the pre-literary stage.

We can only recognize clearly the literary compositions which literary-critical analysis has made it possible to disentangle from the interwoven form which they subsequently had and so to view them in isolation. We can form a particularly clear picture of the work of the 'Jahwist', as both in Genesis and in Exodus it has been inserted into the main narrative largely in its original language and original order and has therefore been preserved. The 'Jahwist', i.e. the anonymous author of this particular narrative stratum in the Pentateuch, is probably to be dated in the time of David or Solomon. At any rate he belongs to the beginnings of the transformation of the Pentateuchal tradition into literature and is for us the chief representative of the older sources. His work, which spans all the Pentateuchal narrative material from the Creation to the Conquest, has two main characteristics. First, J preserved the older narrative material which had either come to him in the framework of the already existing pattern or had been inserted by him into that framework exactly as it had been preserved, fresh and alive, and frequently with its grandeur of conception, and by his great narrative skill gave it a definitive form. Secondly, he presented the great compilation of traditions which had been produced in this way in the light of a salvation-history theology, the programme of which is formulated in particular in Gen. 12.1–3. By doing this he did not, it is true, let the cultic origin of the traditional themes and also of many of the individual items disappear completely, but he let it fade very much into the background. In important points he spiritualized and rationalized the older traditions. The best illustration of this in the Book of Exodus is his description of the making of the covenant in 34.1–28. Here there is no cultic element, and the decisive action consists in a revelation of the divine will in much the same way as that in Gen. 12.1–3. For J not merely the cultic sphere but the whole of history is the province of the divine action. It would seem an obvious assumption that the time of David, which involved Israel in a train of events which led to far-reaching commitments in 'foreign policy', did not fail to influence the theology of the Jahwist, and that at the same time the necessary conditions arose for the Pentateuchal tradition to be made into literature. The result we possess in the work of J.

We obtain a much less vivid picture of the 'Elohist', whose contribution can also be distinguished in Exodus, though much less clearly than in Genesis. Nevertheless here too E proves to be a continuous work which runs parallel to J but arose independently of it. At some now unascertainable time, but before the Priestly writer was involved in the literary development of the Pentateuch, the work of E was incorporated into the parallel work J, apparently in such a way that E was not preserved in its original entirety but only in those elements which seemed essential. The question whether J or E is the earlier is disputed; E is usually taken to be the less ancient, but this cannot be proved for certain. In any case E in fact stands much nearer to the pre-literary stage of the Pentateuchal tradition than J, at whatever date the work may have been set down in writing. The E narrative of the making of the covenant (Ex. 24.9–11), with its marked cultic presentation, surely belongs to an earlier stage of the history of the tradition than the corresponding J narrative which has been mentioned earlier. It is often assumed that E may have had a special affinity with 'prophecy'* but we can gain no certain

*Cf. von Rad, *op. cit.*, pp. 25 f.

indication of this from Exodus. If this were in fact the case we should think of an early stage in the history of prophecy and certainly not of 'classical prophecy'.

The 'Priestly writing' (P) is of a completely different character from the older sources J and E. Its author lacks any direct connection with a narrative tradition that is still fresh and alive. Instead he knows this tradition only at second hand from the combined work JE, now in literary form, which clearly served as a model. He has taken over the construction and arrangement of the whole from this model, but has little interest in a description of the course of history as such. In general he is content with summary indications of the sequence of events. His attention is entirely devoted to the divine ordinances and instructions which are for him of eternal validity. These ordinances and instructions have indeed been promulgated at definite moments of history—P always makes this concession to the experience of faith that God has acted in history—and could there-fore be treated only within the framework of a historical description, but the stress lies on these ordinances and instructions in themselves, and their content, once they have been given, no longer appears dependent on historical suppositions. This characteristic of P emerges clearly even in the Book of Exodus. After a few remarks which serve as a transition and an introduction, P describes the call of Moses, his negotiations with Pharaoh and the 'plagues' of Egypt (in chs. 6–11*). But the description has lost all the tension which is built up in the narrative of the older sources, in which the reaction of Pharaoh on each occasion and the further course of events seems completely uncertain from episode to episode. In P, everything is played out to a divine plan which has been previously determined and, moreover, already divulged. The description given by P sud-denly becomes much fuller, however, at the last plague (ch. 12*), for now we have the instructions for the Passover sacrifice which is to be observed thenceforward. These are given in full detail. Re-marks about the Exodus from Egypt are followed by a description of the miracle at the sea (ch. 14*) and then the story of the manna (ch. 16*). In P this last story is in fact told in some detail, but not so as to give a lifelike description of the plight of Israel in the barren wilderness. It is intended to reveal to Israel the ordinance, made at Creation, that there shall be rest on the seventh day, and to enjoin

*Parts only of these chapters belong to P. For details see the text of the chapters in question.

the keeping of a jar of manna as a lasting remembrance. In the description of the stay at Sinai too there is no indication that Israel experienced an overwhelming encounter with God. P no longer talks of a theophany or the making of a covenant. Israel appears at Sinai so that Moses may receive on the mountain detailed instructions for making the sanctuary and the things it is to contain as well as for establishing the legitimate cult. This is indeed a fundamental event for P, whose whole description leads up to it and virtually comes to a conclusion with it. For, according to P, in this event Israel received the all-embracing ordinance by which the people were to live from then on wherever they might be—at first still in the desert, later in the cultivated Promised Land. If we are to find a date for P, the *terminus a quo* is primarily the end of the Judaean kingship of the line of David in 587 BC, as the 'High Priest' in P has already taken over insignia and cultic functions of the Jerusalem king. Moreover it is apparent at various points that P is also later than the reform pro-gramme in Ezek. 40 ff.

Ezek. 40.1 dates this to the year 571 BC, but the section is not a unity and no certain dating can be made of its different strata. P calls for a date late in the Exile or after the Exile, thus showing itself to be in any case some centuries later than the older sources in the Pentateuch and—a more important factor—to derive from a com-pletely different situation. Israel's loss of independence and the collapse of her old institutions had made it necessary for her to have a new organization on the basis of a common cult in Jerusalem which since the enforcement of the Deuteronomic demand for unity had been the only legitimate sanctuary. This explains P's interest in the one legitimate sanctuary and in the ordinances which were valid for Israel. It is difficult to give a more exact date for P. There is much to suggest that P with its instructions for the sanctuary belongs to the period before the rebuilding of the Jerusalem temple and the full restoration of the cult there, i.e. sometime before 515 BC, when the rebuilt temple in Jerusalem was solemnly consecrated. In that case it would have become necessary to alter the design in P by secondary additions for it to conform to the actual circumstances in the temple. We cannot, however, produce definite proof for such a dating, as we have also to reckon with the possibility that in the final shaping of the P text some alterations have in the course of time crept in to ensure conformity with the sanctuary that actually existed.

3. THE FINAL FORM OF THE BOOK

After the P narrative and its additions had been expanded by the incorporation of the already combined JE narrative, the literary development which produced Exodus in the form in which it has been handed down was virtually complete. There remain just a few completely secondary elements which were added later. The corpora of law, which cannot be assigned to any of the sources (see above p. 13), had already been included in the JE narrative at some earlier stage.

Exegesis of the book is concerned with its final form. Even its literary history can only be discovered by a literary-critical analysis of this final form. Such exegesis cannot however be carried out without constant reference to the individual stages of this literary development. In its present state the book is as it were a fabric, skilfully woven from a series of threads, and the only satisfactory way of analysing a fabric is to keep firmly in sight the threads of which it is made up and the material of which the threads themselves are composed. Each thread belongs to the pattern of the whole, and none is without its own importance. The path from the living narratives of the oldest literary strata, still recognizably rooted in the formative period of oral tradition, to the rationalizing theology of ordinances which is advanced in the latest writing is a significant one, whose course has left its traces in the final form of the book in a number of decisive moments. It is a path which even within the Book of Exodus leads us into central concepts of the faith of the Old Testament.

II

THE EXODUS FROM EGYPT

1.1 – 15.21

1. THE BEGINNINGS OF EGYPTIAN OPPRESSION:
1.1–22

1¹ These are the names of the sons of Israel who came to Egypt with Jacob, each with his household: ² Reuben, Simeon, Levi, and Judah, ³ Issachar, Zebulun, and Benjamin, ⁴ Dan and Naphtali, Gad and Asher. ⁵ [All the offspring of Jacob were seventy persons;] Joseph was already in Egypt. ⁶ Then Joseph died, and all his brothers, and all that generation. ⁷ But the descendants of Israel were fruitful and increased greatly; they multiplied and grew exceedingly strong; so that the land was filled with them.

8 *Now there arose a new king over Egypt, who did not know Joseph.* ⁹ *And he said to his people, 'Behold, the people of Israel are too many and too mighty for us.* ¹⁰ *Come, let us deal shrewdly with them, lest they multiply, and, if war befall us, they join our enemies and fight against us and escape from the land.'* ¹¹ *Therefore they set taskmasters over them to afflict them with heavy burdens; and they built for Pharaoh store cities, Pithom and Raamses.* ¹² *But the more they were oppressed, the more they multiplied and the more they spread abroad. And the Egyptians were in dread of the people of Israel.* ¹³ So they made the people of Israel serve with rigour, ¹⁴ and made their lives bitter with hard service, in mortar and brick, and in all kinds of work in the field; in all their work they made them serve with rigour.

15 *Then the king of Egypt said to the Hebrew midwives, one of whom was named Shiphrah and the other Puah,* ¹⁶ *'When you serve as midwife to the Hebrew women, and see them upon the birthstool, if it is a son, you shall kill him; but if it is a daughter, she shall live.'* ¹⁷ *But the midwives feared God, and did not do as the king of Egypt commanded them, but let the male children live.* ¹⁸ *So the king of Egypt called the midwives, and said to them, 'Why have you done this, and let the male children live?'* ¹⁹ *The midwives said [to Pharaoh],*

*'Because the Hebrew women are not like the Egyptian women; for they are
vigorous and are delivered before the midwife comes to them.'* [20] *So God dealt
well with the midwives; and the people multiplied and grew very strong.* [21] *And
because the midwives feared God he gave them families.* [22] Then Pharaoh
commanded all his people, 'Every son that is born to the Hebrews
you shall cast into the Nile, but you shall let every daughter live.'

[1–7] The introduction of the great theme 'The Exodus from
Egypt' is connected briefly and loosely to the theme of the Patriarchs
which has preceded it in the Book of Genesis. We now have this
connection only in the late formulation by P (vv. 1–7); the numerical
detail in v. 5a refers back to the secondary P section Gen. 46.8–27,
which is perhaps an indication that it too is secondary. The older
sources too would originally have had a similarly brief connection
with the stories of the Patriarchs. In this connection the great step is
taken from the history of the family of the Patriarchs to that of the
people of Israel. The expression *b*enē *yisrā'el*, which in v. 1 still means
the 'sons of Israel', i.e. 'sons of Jacob' (on this cf. Gen. 35.10 P), from
v. 7 onwards consistently describes the 'Israelites' who now form the
object of the divine action in history. This transition is achieved by
the simple statement that after the generation of the sons of Jacob
had died (v. 6) an unspecified period of time had elapsed during
which the descendants of Jacob had increased so greatly that they
had now become a 'people' (v. 9) living in the midst of Egypt.

[8–14] Here we have an immediate motive for the Egyptian
oppression of the 'people of Israel'; Israel, who had increased in
number and had thus become strong, seemed so undesirable to the
Egyptians that a new Pharaoh, who by this time knew nothing of
Joseph's former good offices to the Egyptian administration, which
had under an earlier Pharaoh led to a ceremonial invitation of the
whole of Jacob's family to Egypt (cf. Gen. 45.16 ff.; 47.1 ff.), saw
himself compelled to take counter-measures. These counter-
measures consisted first in a restriction of freedom by the general
conscription of Israelites for forced labour in building and agricultural work, and later in the brutal slaughter of their male children.
The following chapters deal chiefly with the first of these two counter-
measures, and in the narrative description of the oppression of Israel
in Egypt the forced labour is to be the primary theme. This corresponds with an actual historical situation. Egypt had long been an
autocratically ruled land in which virtually all work was done by an

enslaved subject people in the service of the king.* This situation was well known to the Old Testament tradition (cf. Gen. 47.13–26). Even alien elements of the population were subject to this system. It often happened that people living in the neighbourhood of the fertile Nile country, especially those with no settled dwelling from the area to the north-east of Egypt which borders on Asia, would come into Egypt like the 'Bedouin tribes of Edom' who were admitted into the land on the eastern border of the Nile delta by an Egyptian frontier official of a time about 1200 BC.† It was the custom in the ancient Orient of the second millennium BC to describe such people, who were deprived of the rights of the old-established inhabitants of the land, as 'Hebrews'. This description is used in the Old Testament narrative of Israel's dwelling in Egypt both by the Israelites and the Egyptians, at least in Ex. 1, in so far as the latter talk of 'Hebrew women'. The word 'Hebrew', when used in the Old Testament, often sounds as though it were the name of a people. But in the Old Testament the Israelites are only called 'Hebrews' in particular situations, such as the sojourn in Egypt, and in this we can still see the special significance of the word 'Hebrew'. The Egyptian tradition also knows of such 'Hebrews' (the word is transcribed ʿpr in the Egyptian hieroglyphic script which can only be written in consonants). There are several Egyptian texts which describe the employment of such 'Hebrews' as building workers.‡ A passage from an administrative letter of the time of Pharaoh Raamses II (1292–1225 BC), preserved on a Leiden Papyrus, is particularly remarkable. It discusses the question of providing corn for 'the people of the host' and 'for the ʿpr, who are drawing stones for the great gateway of . . . (name of the building) . . . of Raamses, the beloved of Amon'. . . . This information brings us to a period of history in immediate proximity to the narrative in Ex. 1. Not that the 'Hebrews' mentioned in the papyrus must have been identical with the oppressed Israelites of Ex. 1; for the Egyptian as for the whole of the oriental world at that time 'Hebrew' was quite a comprehensive term which included far more than just the Israelites in Egypt. But

---

*Cf. A. Erman and H. Ranke, *Ägypten und ägyptisches Leben im Altertum*, 1923, p. 55 f.

†Cf. the report of this official preserved on a papyrus. [J. B. Pritchard, *Ancient Near Eastern Texts*,² 1955, p. 259, gives an English translation of the passage in question. Tr.]

‡They are collected in K. Galling, *Textbuch zur Geschichte Israels*, 1950, pp. 30 f.

the story of the oppression does in fact show the Israelites in the position of such 'Hebrews' ('*pr*) and indeed particularly in the time of the Pharaoh Raamses II. The very concrete information in v. 11, according to which the Israelites had to help in the building of the cities of Pithom and Raamses, is an indication of this. Both towns lay in the eastern Nile delta, Pithom on the site of the present hill ruin of *tell er-reṭābe* in the fertile valley *wādi eṭ-ṭumēlāt* which stretches from the eastern arm of the Nile to the neighbourhood of the Bitter Sea in the middle of the Isthmus of Suez, Raamses slightly further north in the north-east part of the delta. Raamses was the delta residence of the Pharaohs, built by Raamses II, and its full Egyptian name runs *Pr-Rʿmssw-mry-'Imn* = 'House of Raamses, the beloved of Amun'; Pithom, in Egyptian *Pr-'Itm* = 'House of Atum', was also built by Raamses II who was particularly interested in the eastern delta. The narrative material of the Egyptian oppression thus includes some accurate historical features which are important for the understanding and dating of the Israelite stay in Egypt. They were presumably passed on from the beginning with the narrative tradition of the theme of the 'Exodus from Egypt'.

To Egyptian eyes all this would have been a picture of what had once been customary in Egypt, but in ancient Israel, to whom the autocratic Egyptian state was and remained something foreign, it was seen as a hostile measure which had been specially directed against an Israel which was looked upon with mistrust. The report of the Egyptian oppression occurs in this simple form in the latest literary narrative, P (vv. 13 f.). The older literary narratives have gone further and explain the hostile attitude of the Egyptians which is presupposed in the tradition from the start as caused by fear in the face of an Israel now grown extremely numerous. Here the main thought of the narratives may have been that it was the Egyptian aim to keep down the now powerful Israelites by forced labour and to prevent them by a rigorous slavery from developing their strength (so in essentials vv. 8–11 J). Only then would there arise the further thought that the Egyptians wished to put a check to any further increase in Israelite numbers by means of this forced labour and limit or even completely prevent the growth of another generation (cf. vv. 10a, 12). Here in fact it remains questionable whether the imposition of forced labour could be a suitable means for this end. Perhaps the part of the story which is concerned with the danger to Israelite posterity in Egypt was only grafted on to the tradition of forced labour afterwards and has been developed for originally independent reasons.

[15–22] Pharaoh's quite brutal command to his people to throw all newborn Israelite boys into the Nile appears in v. 22. It is not said whether this order was to be carried out by brute force or by some underhand trick and whether in fact it was really carried out at all for any length of time. In its present context this command appears just as Pharaoh's most extreme measure after his failure with the midwives which has already been mentioned, but in fact in v. 22 on the one hand and vv. 15–21 on the other we are dealing with different literary strata in which the circumstances which endanger the new-born Israelite boys have been treated each in a different way. This is indicated by the fact that v. 22 speaks of Pharaoh, while in vv. 15–21 we have 'the king of Egypt' (the remark 'to Pharaoh' in v. 19 may be an addition). As the word 'God' and not the divine name Yahweh is used in vv. 15–21 we must regard v. 22 as part of the J narrative (joining on to vv. 8–12), whereas the passage vv. 15–21 is to be taken as a fragment of E which, as a special piece of the Elohistic tradition, was already incorporated in the formation of the literary unity of the older Pentateuchal material (JE), and thus eventually found a place in the completed Pentateuch. According to vv. 15–21 the king of Egypt wanted to be sure of preventing any further growth of Israel by surreptitiously doing away with the boy children of the Israelites as soon as they were born, in some way of which we are not told. This assumes that the Israelites lived very close together in Egypt, and had not yet grown so excessively numerous that two midwives were insufficient to help at all Israelite births. The two midwives, who have been given the decorative Hebrew feminine names 'Beauty' and 'Splendour', are expressly described as 'Hebrew women', and in this story the king of Egypt is under the impression that these two Hebrew women will comply with his wishes. It is not even said that he had promised them any form of reward for their action. Of course he is mistaken here, and his artfulness is surpassed by the artful remarks of the two midwives (v. 19). Clearly too the midwives may be sure that they are under the protection of their God in their passive resistance to the mighty king of Egypt. The E fragment is the only part of Ex. 1 in which God is mentioned. The midwives' fear of God proves to be a real factor in history, and God afterwards gives express and visible confirmation to the midwives that this fear of God was the right course, and that he stands with those who fear him against all earthly power, by 'dealing well' with them (v. 20a). Thus God helps Israel in Egypt invisibly yet effectively by means of the midwives. After the concluding v. 20, which states this explicitly, v. 21 looks like a secondary addition and in fact adds nothing new; it seems to be a later attempt to substantiate in rather more detail the very general remark that God 'dealt well' with the midwives.

We must ask whether the part of the narrative which describes the danger to the new-born Israelite boys did not in fact come into the tradition from the following story of the birth of Moses, which presupposes this danger. It would then at a secondary stage have been incorporated into the theme of the forced labour in Egypt so that this forced labour looked as though it was meant to prevent any increase of the Israelites (cf. vv. 9b, 10a), an application which is hardly to be understood as its original purpose. In the older sources, of which in fact only J is still at all recognizable in its original shape, this attempt on the new-born male Israelites appears as a second more drastic measure since the forced labour had failed as a means of diminishing Israelite numbers (v. 12). P could later dispense with a description of this second measure, and his short description of the forced labour (vv. 13 f.) could also omit the aim to reduce Israelite numbers, as he did not intend to include even the story of the birth of Moses in his work. In so doing P returned to quite an old state of the tradition.

2. THE BIRTH OF MOSES: 2.1–10

2 ¹ *Now a man from the house of Levi went and took to wife a daughter of Levi.* ² *The woman conceived and bore a son; and when she saw that he was a goodly child, she hid him three months.* ³ *And when she could hide him no longer she took for him a basket made of bulrushes, and daubed it with bitumen and pitch; and she put the child in it and placed it among the reeds at the river's brink.* ⁴ *And his sister stood at a distance, to know what would be done to him.* ⁵ *Now the daughter of Pharaoh came down to bathe at the river, and her maidens walked beside the river; she saw the basket among the reeds and sent her maid to fetch it.* ⁶ *When she opened it she saw the child; and lo, the babe was crying. She took pity on him and said, 'This is one of the Hebrews' children.'* ⁷ *Then his sister said to Pharaoh's daughter, 'Shall I go and call you a nurse from the Hebrew women to nurse the child for you?'* ⁸ *And Pharaoh's daughter said to her, 'Go.' So the girl went and called the child's mother.* ⁹ *And Pharaoh's daughter said to her, 'Take this child away, and nurse him for me, and I will give you* *your wages.' So the woman took the child and nursed him.* [10] *And the child grew, and she brought him to Pharaoh's daughter, and he became her son; and she named him Moses, for she said, 'Because I drew him out of the water.'*

The style of this brief story is smooth, but the story is not in itself a complete unity. The introduction indicates that the boy was the first-born child of his parents. We are therefore surprised at the sudden appearance in v. 4 of an elder sister, who has not only not been introduced earlier but according to v. 8 is already a grown girl. Of course this state of affairs does not drive us to assume several 'sources' from which the narrative has been composed, as no continuous succession of doublets is discernible in the narrative. It is much more likely that a simple basic story was afterwards embellished, to heighten the tension for the hearer or reader, by the addition of the special point that the boy was nursed by his own mother. The whole story, including this expansion, belongs to the old Pentateuchal narrative material and may be assigned to J.

[1] No names are given to the parents of the child; it is only a late tradition which was acquainted with the names of Moses' parents (Ex. 6.20; Num. 26.59). The sister, subsequently introduced, is also unnamed; here likewise it is only a later tradition which says that Miriam was the sister of Moses (see pp. 122 f. below). It is merely remarked that the parents were 'of the house of Levi'. What, however, the original tradition means by 'the house of Levi' remains extremely questionable—later it was natural to think of the 'priestly tribe of Levi'; indeed in view of Ex. 4.14 (see pp. 46 f. below) we must even ask whether a more accurate translation might not be 'from the house (the family) of a Levite' or even 'from a Levitical house, i.e. a Levitical family'. In any case there is something special about this descent. The life of a new-born 'Hebrew child' (cf. v. 6) is threatened; this presupposes not so much the story of the midwives in 1.15–21 as the general command of Pharaoh in 1.22. [2] The child can be successfully hidden for only a short time from the Egyptians who wish to carry out the order of Pharaoh; then—this may be the meaning—it will betray its presence by loud crying. [3] So it is put by its mother in a concealed spot somewhere among the reeds on the banks of the Nile. Perhaps someone will find it and take it home without realizing that it is a Hebrew child. In any case it seems better to expose the healthy, 'goodly' child to an uncertain

fate than to leave him to a quite certain death. This 'uncertain fate'
—as the story with all its later developments intends us to understand—in fact means Yahweh, but this is said neither explicitly nor
obviously.

[5] The arrival of Pharaoh's daughter, which now follows, and the
way in which she acts, are portrayed in a naïve way reminiscent of
a folk-tale. A daughter of Pharaoh—in Hebrew she is described as
'*the* daughter of Pharaoh' because she is the only one concerned in the
present story—comes with her maidens quite unceremoniously down
to the Nile to bathe. In contrast to her brutal father she takes pity on
the boy although fully realizing that he is a Hebrew. [4, 7–10a] According to the elaboration of the story she even allows the boy to be
nursed by a Hebrew woman and gives her wages. [10b] She adopts
the boy, as though a daughter of Pharaoh could perform such a legal
action on her own initiative. She gives the boy a name which is explained from the Hebrew language as though Hebrew were the tongue
spoken by her; in fact the explanation does not quite fit the story as
the boy was not really 'drawn out of the water'. The explanation of
the name Moses given here belongs to the popular etymology of
names which is frequent in the Old Testament. The derivation of the
name Moses (*mōšeh*) from the verb *māšāh*—'draw out' (here the name
could in form be an active participle whereas the explanation
properly requires a passive) was perhaps current in ancient Israel
in connection with a story of the wonderful rescue of the child Moses.
It might even be that such a story arose as an aetiology of the
name. Ancient Israel did not know that Moses is in reality an Egyptian name, that it is a shortened form of Egyptian names like
Ahmosis, Thutmosis, etc. The narrator of Ex. 2.1–10 did not know
this either; otherwise he would hardly have missed the opportunity
of explaining the strangeness of the name by the adoption and
naming of the child by a daughter of Pharaoh.

We would be closing our eyes to well-known facts if we were un-
willing to recognize that the elements in the story of the birth of
Moses are themes which occur frequently in legendary stories.* The
world of the ancient East provides the legend of the birth of King
Sargon of Akkad who was an important ruler in Mesopotamia in the

---

*See the material in A. Jeremias, *Das Alte Testament im Lichte des alten Orients*[4],
1930, pp. 400 ff.; cf. also H. Gressmann, *Mose und seine Zeit*, 1913, pp. 7 ff.

second half of the third millennium BC.* According to this, when
Sargon was born he was put by his unnamed mother in a little box,
made of reeds and sealed with pitch, and was then set afloat on the
Euphrates. A peasant saw him and adopted him, and finally the god-
dess Ishtar grew fond of him and made him a great and powerful
king. This motif is also well-known from the Cyrus legend which is
told in Herodotus (I 108 ff.). A ruler seeks the life of a child whom he
fears as a future opponent and has it exposed, but the child is rescued
in a miraculous way and later gains the victory over the ruler and
himself becomes a great king. It can hardly be doubted that such
stories were known in the world of ancient Israel and had their effect
on the development of the story of the birth of Moses. Although the
individual details of these legends are developed in completely different ways, there is common to them all the basic thought that great
figures, both rulers and benefactors, had stood from the beginning
of their lives under the special working of a divine providence which
had proved itself effective in the face of all the attacks directed
against them by worldly despots. The mythical element which
frequently emerges in comparable legends is completely lacking in
the Old Testament story of the birth of Moses, whose particular point
is that it is the daughter of the despot himself who rescues the future
antagonist and allows him to grow up in the immediate surroundings
of the despot. The story certainly only arose once the historical figure
of the man Moses had taken a firm place in the ancient Israelite
tradition.

3. MOSES IN MIDIAN: 2.11–4.23

11 *One day, when Moses had grown up, he went out to his people and
looked on their burdens; and he saw an Egyptian beating a Hebrew, one of his
people.* 12 *He looked this way and that, and seeing no one he killed the Egyptian
and hid him in the sand.* 13 *When he went out the next day, behold, two Hebrews
were struggling together; and he said to the man that did the wrong, 'Why
do you strike your fellow?'* 14 *He answered, 'Who made you a prince and a
judge over us? Do you mean to kill me as you killed the Egyptian?' Then
Moses was afraid, and thought, 'Surely the thing is known.'* 15 [*When Pharaoh
heard of it, he sought to kill Moses.*]

   *But Moses fled [from Pharaoh, and stayed in] the land of Midian; and
he sat down by a well.* 16 *Now the priest of Midian had seven daughters;
and they came amd drew water, and filled the troughs to water their father's
flock.* 17 *The shepherds came and drove them away; but Moses stood up and
helped them, and watered their flock.* 18 *When they came to their father [Reuel],*

*[There is an English translation of this legend in Pritchard, *Ancient Near
Eastern Texts*, p. 119. Tr.]

he said, 'How is it that you have come so soon today?' [19] *They said, 'An Egyptian delivered us out of the hand of the shepherds, and even drew water for us and watered the flock.'* [20] *He said to his daughters, 'And where is he? Why have you left the man? Call him, that he may eat bread.'* [21] *And Moses was content to dwell with the man, and he gave Moses his daughter Zipporah.* [22] *She bore a son, and he called his name Gershom; for he said, 'I have been a sojourner in a foreign land.'*

23 In the course of those many days the king of Egypt died. And the people of Israel groaned under their bondage, and cried out for help, and their cry under bondage came up to God. [24] And God heard their groaning, and God remembered his covenant with Abraham, with Isaac, and with Jacob. [25] And God saw the people of Israel, and God knew their condition.

3 [1] *Now Moses was keeping the flock of his father-in-law, [Jethro,] the priest of Midian; and he led his flock to the west side of the wilderness, and came to [Horeb,] the mountain of God.* [2] *And the angel of the* LORD *appeared to him in a flame of fire out of the midst of a bush; and he looked, and lo, the bush was burning, yet it was not consumed.* [3] *And Moses said, 'I will turn aside and see this great sight, why the bush is not burnt.'* [4] *When the* LORD *saw that he turned aside to see, God called to him [out of the bush], 'Moses, Moses!' And he said, 'Here am I.'* [5] *Then he said, 'Do not come near; put off your shoes from your feet, for the place on which you are standing is holy ground.'* [6] *And he said, 'I am the God of your father, the God of Abraham, the God of Isaac, and the God of Jacob.' And Moses hid his face, for he was afraid to look at God.*

[7] *Then the* LORD *said, 'I have seen the affliction of my people who are in Egypt, and have heard their cry because of their taskmasters; I know their sufferings,* [8] *and I have come down to deliver them out of the hand of the Egyptians, and to bring them up out of that land to a good and broad land, [a land flowing with milk and honey, to the place of the Canaanites, the Hittites, the Amorites, the Perizzites, the Hivites, and the Jebusites].* [9] *And now, behold, the cry of the people of Israel has come to me, and I have seen the oppression with which the Egyptians oppress them.* [10] *Come, [I will send you to Pharaoh] that you may bring forth my people, the sons of Israel, out of Egypt.'* [11] *But Moses said to God, 'Who am I that I should [go to Pharaoh, and] bring the sons of Israel out of Egypt?'* [12] *He said, 'But I will be with you; and this shall be the sign for you, that I have sent you: when you have brought forth the people out of Egypt, you shall serve God upon this mountain.'*

[13] *Then Moses said to God, 'If I come to the people of Israel and say to them, "The God of your fathers has sent me to you," and they ask me, "What is his name?" what shall I say to them?'* [14] *God said to Moses, I* AM WHO I AM.' *And he said, 'Say this to the people of Israel, "I* AM *has sent me to you."'* [15] *God also said to Moses, 'Say this to the people of Israel, "The* LORD, *the God of your fathers, the God of Abraham, the God of Isaac, and the God of Jacob, has sent me to you": this is my name for ever, and thus I am to be remembered throughout all generations.* [16] *Go and gather the elders*

of Israel together, and say to them, "The LORD, *the God of your fathers,* [*the God of Abraham, of Isaac, and of Jacob,*] *has appeared to me, saying, 'I have observed you and what has been done to you in Egypt;'* [17] *and I promise that I will bring you up out of the affliction of Egypt,* [*to the land of the Canaanites, the Hittites, the Amorites, the Perizzites, the Hivites, and the Jebusites, a land flowing with milk and honey*].' " [[18] *And they will hearken to your voice; and you and the elders of Israel shall go to the king of Egypt and say to him, "The* LORD, *the God of the Hebrews, has met with us; and now, we pray you, let us go a three days' journey into the wilderness, that we may sacrifice to the* LORD *our God."* [19] *I know that the king of Egypt will not let you go unless compelled by a mighty hand.* [20] *So I will stretch out my hand and smite Egypt with all the wonders which I will do in it; after that he will let you go.* [21] *And I will give this people favour in the sight of the Egyptians; and when you go, you shall not go empty,* [22] *but each woman shall ask of her neighbour, and of her who sojourns in her house, jewelry of silver and of gold, and clothing, and you shall put them on your sons and on your daughters; thus you shall despoil the Egyptians.'*]

4 [1] *Then Moses answered, 'But behold, they will not believe me or listen to my voice, for they will say, "The* LORD *did not appear to you." '* [2] *The* LORD *said to him, 'What is that in your hand?' He said, 'A rod.'* [3] *And he said, 'Cast it on the ground.' So he cast it on the ground, and it became a serpent; and Moses fled from it.* [4] *But the* LORD *said to Moses, 'Put out your hand, and take it by the tail'—so he put out his hand and caught it, and it became a rod in his hand*—[[5] *'that they may believe that the* LORD, *the God of their fathers, the God of Abraham, the God of Isaac, and the God of Jacob, has appeared to you.'*] [6] *Again, the* LORD *said to him, 'Put your hand into your bosom.' And he put his hand into his bosom; and when he took it out, behold, his hand was leprous, as white as snow.* [7] *Then God said, 'Put your hand back into your bosom.' So he put his hand back into his bosom; and when he took it out, behold, it was restored like the rest of his flesh.* [[8] *'If they will not believe you,' God said, 'or heed the first sign, they may believe the latter sign.* [9] *If they will not believe even these two signs or heed your voice, you shall take some water from the Nile and pour it upon the dry ground; and the water which you shall take from the Nile will become blood upon the dry ground.'*]

[10] *But Moses said to the* LORD, *'Oh, my Lord, I am not eloquent, either heretofore or since thou hast spoken to thy servant; but I am slow of speech and of tongue.'* [11] *Then the* LORD *said to him, 'Who has made man's mouth? Who makes him dumb, or deaf, or seeing, or blind? Is it not I, the* LORD? [12] *Now therefore go, and I will be with your mouth and teach you what you shall speak.'* [[13] *But he said, 'Oh, my Lord, send, I pray, some other person.'* [14] *Then the anger of the* LORD *was kindled against Moses and he said, 'Is there not Aaron, your brother, the Levite? I know that he can speak well; and behold, he is coming out to meet you, and when he sees you he will be glad in his heart.* [15] *And you shall speak to him and put the words in his mouth; and I will be with your mouth and with his mouth, and will teach you what you shall do.* [16] *He shall speak for you to the people; and he shall be a mouth*

for you, and you shall be to him as God.] [17] *And you shall take in your hand this rod, with which you shall do the signs.'*

18 *Moses went back to Jethro his father-in-law and said to him, 'Let me go back, I pray, to my kinsmen in Egypt and see whether they are still alive.' And Jethro said to Moses, 'Go in peace.'* [19] *And the* LORD *said to Moses in Midian, 'Go back to Egypt; for all the men who were seeking your life are dead.'* [20] *So Moses took his wife and his son[s] and set them on an ass, and went back to the land of Egypt; and in his hand Moses took the rod of God.*

[21 *And the* LORD *said to Moses, 'When you go back to Egypt, see that you do before Pharaoh all the miracles which I have put in your power; but I will harden his heart, so that he will not let the people go.* [22] *And you shall say to Pharaoh, "Thus says the* LORD, *Israel is my first-born son,* [23] *and I say to you 'Let my son go that he may serve me'; if you refuse to let him go, behold, I will slay your first-born son."* ']

The reports of the flight of Moses into the land of Midian (2.11 ff.) and of his return from there to Egypt (4.18 ff.) make a frame round the whole of this section and separate it both from what goes before and from what comes after. In essentials, the section describes how Moses encountered God in the land of Midian and how as a result he was commissioned with a message from God to the Israelites in Egypt. The content of his proclamation was to be that God would now free the Israelites from their subjection and lead them out of Egypt. This subject not only takes up the greatest amount of space within the section but must also have formed the kernel of the tradition from the beginning of its history, for no other starting point can in fact be found for a historical tradition of a stay of Moses in the land of Midian to which the story of the encounter with God might perhaps have been attached in a secondary manner. The action taken by Moses against the unjust assault on a 'Hebrew' in Egypt which compelled him to flee from Egypt (2.11–15) is as little an independent element of the tradition as the exemplary readiness to help which he displays in the scene at the well in the land of Midian (2.16–20). These are just explanations by the narrator of how Moses came out of Egypt and how he came to be connected with the household of a Midianite priest. It is indeed a very old element of the tradition that Moses was connected by marriage with Midian, but even this hardly seems likely to have given rise to the contents of the entire section; in view of the tradition of a later meeting between Israelites and Midianites (cf. Ex. 18) it would not have been necessary to go to the length of letting Moses at some previous time stay for a while with the

Midianites. The primary tradition therefore was clearly that Moses experienced his first encounter with God on the mountain of God in Midian.

This is most remarkable. In the old historical narrative tradition of the Old Testament the Midianites appear as the dreaded foes of an Israel which has meanwhile become settled in Palestine. They are the oldest camel nomads known to us,* who from time to time used to invade the settled land (cf. Judg. 6.1 ff.). They are, moreover, occasionally mentioned alongside Arabian tribes and tribal associations (Gen. 25.4). In later times the area of their pasturage lay in north-west Arabia on the east side of the Gulf of Elath, the Gulf of *el-'aqaba*, where according to the evidence of the geographer Ptolemy (second century AD) of Eusebius-Jerome (in the *Onomastikon*) and of medieval Arabian geographers, perhaps even as early as that of the Jewish historian Josephus (first century AD) there was a place 'Madian' in a neighbourhood rich in oases not far from the southern end of the gulf mentioned above. This was evidently named after the Midianites. This would take us from Egypt out into a district which was quite some distance away and separated from Egypt by the whole of the Sinai peninsula. It is impossible to say whether such a distant location for the Midianite territory is inconsistent with the part played by the Midianites in the Old Testament traditions of Moses, but on the other hand we must reckon with the possibility that the Midianites of Old Testament times, who as camel nomads were quite mobile, at least for a while had had their camping places and watering spots even to the west of the gulf of *el-'aqaba* and the *wadi el-'araba* and were thus on the Sinai peninsula and in particular in its northern part, the so-called wilderness of Sinai. There is absolutely no certain indication in the Moses stories for fixing the neighbourhood in which tradition has it that Moses meets the Midianites. It cannot be assumed with any degree of certainty that in his flight Moses was aiming for the near neighbourhood of Egypt and hence the eastern delta, as the theme of the flight merely serves the narrator's purpose of leading Moses to the Midianites and is secondary in comparison with the primary element of tradition that Moses first encountered God in the land of Midian. This implies at the same time that even the locality of the 'mountain of God' in Midian can no longer be fixed. It makes a further appearance in Ex. 3.1 and yet again in Ex. 18.5. The context of this last appearance

*Cf. M. Noth, *History of Israel*, ET², 1960, pp. 160 f.

is a meeting between Moses, who now brings the people of Israel along with him, and the priest of Midian; it is thus evident that it belongs firmly to the complex of the tradition of the meeting between Israel and Midian. In Ex. 3.1 this mountain of God is called Horeb, but the name occurs at the end of the passage in such a lame way that it must quite certainly be regarded as an explanatory addition which later attempted to define more precisely the originally un-named 'mountain of God' in Midian. In the deuteronomistic litera-ture the mountain of the great theophany, the covenant with God and the proclamation of the Law is customarily described with the name Horeb (e.g. Deut. 1.2, 6, 19), whereas elsewhere in the Old Testament and particularly in the special Sinai tradition it is called Sinai. The glossator of Ex. 3.1 therefore evidently wanted to identify the mountain of God in Midian with Horeb/Sinai. In doing so he made an equation which was certainly already very old. True, we must ask whether the mountain of God in Midian, left so strikingly without a name, which was traditionally the place of a meeting between Israel and Midian and of a connection between Moses and the family of the Midianite priest during the time that Israel was wandering in the wilderness,* was originally identical with Sinai (= Horeb). But probably this equation already lay behind the rise of the story of Moses' first encounter with God in the land of Midian.

This story can hardly belong to the oldest part of the tradition. Moses here does not receive the decisive commission of a proclama-tion to the Israelites in the land of their slavery, Egypt. Of course the Israelites stand under the care and protection of their God even in Egypt. But this land was still not worthy of becoming the scene of a direct theophany to Israel; this takes place only in the wilderness. Perhaps the special Sinai tradition lies behind this idea. Now if Moses in the wilderness is sent by God as a messenger to Israel while they are still living in Egypt so that a connection between God and people may be established not by means of a direct theophany on Egyptian soil but in Moses' status as messenger, we are led to assume a basis in a combination of the Sinai tradition and the Exodus tradition. Such an idea was not present in the tradition from the very beginning, but was only conceived in the course of the development of the tradition.†
At this stage in the formation of the tradition, however, the starting point was probably the equation of the unnamed mountain of God in Midian, which originally belonged to a special element of the

*Cf. pp. 147 f. below on Ex. 18.   †Cf. von Rad, *Genesis*, p. 20.

tradition, with Sinai (= Horeb). Then the experience of Moses in
Ex. 3.4 was a prelude to the future experience of Israel. As Israel
'fled' (Ex. 14.15a) from Egypt, eventually witnessing in the wilderness the appearance on the holy mountain of Sinai (= Horeb) of
their God (Ex. 19), so too at an earlier time Moses had once been
forced to 'flee' from Egypt (Ex. 2.15b) to be astounded by a theophany on the 'mountain of God' in the wilderness (Ex. 3.1 ff.). We
cannot explain why the story in the latter context does not simply
speak of Sinai (= Horeb) but is associated with the tradition of the
unnamed mountain of God in the land of Midian, identified with
Sinai (= Horeb). Perhaps at the same time we are to find here the
basis of the affinity of Moses to the Midianites, who at one time
belonged with 'the mountain of God'.

Although the story of how Moses was sent as a messenger to the
Israelites in Egypt after God had appeared to him at a place in the
wilderness belongs to a relatively late stage in the history of the
tradition, it is nevertheless part of the older material of the Pentateuchal narratives fixed in literary form and is represented in both
the old narrative strata J and E. P later passed over this story and
unthinkingly has Moses receiving his commission in Egypt (Ex.
6.2 ff.). In our section P appears only in 2.23abb–25 with a brief
remark about the groaning and crying of the Israelites in bondage in
Egypt and how this is heard by God. If this passage is detached, the
remaining narrative material is obviously not a literary unity but
shows clear traces of the juxtaposition of two originally independent
threads of narrative which have subsequently been woven together.
At the conclusion, the twofold report of the return of Moses to
Egypt is particularly clear. Whereas in 4.18 as a result of his encounter with God Moses immediately makes up his mind to return to
Egypt and therefore asks, and receives, permission from his father-
in-law, according to 4.19–20a it is Yahweh who orders him to return,
apparently some time after Moses has had his encounter with God
and when the danger to his life in Egypt has passed (v. 19b), a
command with which Moses immediately complies. As the divine
name Yahweh occurs in v. 19,* vv. 19–20a must be assigned to J and

*[The RSV, for reasons which are given in the Preface, translates the Tetra-
grammaton with the English word LORD printed in capitals, whereas Noth in the
body of this commentary, following a usage now universal among Old Testament
scholars, uses the more accurate name Yahweh of the God of Israel. For the sake
of clarity I have retained this latter usage throughout so that 'Yahweh' in the
commentary will in each case correspond with 'the LORD' in the RSV text. Tr.]

therefore v. 18 to E, to which might also be added v. 20b, as the 'rod of God' seems to have played a special part in E (cf. p. 47). The connecting verses 21–23 which anticipate the following narrative in an unusual way can hardly have belonged to the original story. As the divine name Yahweh appears in them, they are perhaps to be regarded as an addition to the J narrative, if they were not first added to the JE narrative after it had already been combined.

The results which we have obtained from the concluding passage —the juxtaposition of J and E and the secondary additions—are confirmed by the large central section 3.1–4.17. We can see how the passage 3.1–16 is formed from both J and E by the strikingly abrupt changes between the divine name Yahweh and the word 'God'. An examination of the details leads to the following division: J: 3. 1ab*a*, 2, 3, 4a, 5; E: 3.1b*b*, 4b, 6. At the same time it becomes clear that the E variant has not been preserved in all its entirety, as at least its introduction is no longer intact, having been partially suppressed by elements from the J narrative. In what follows, 3.7 f. and 3.9 ff. are again clearly doublets; the divine name Yahweh shows that 3.7 f. belong to J, while the repeated occurrence of the word 'God' in 3.9–15 is a feature of the Elohistic narrative. From 3.16 onwards no further explicit doublets are conspicuous; from now on a single strand of the tradition, which is certainly that of J, predominates, though there are various secondary additions which will be commented upon in the exegesis of individual passages. Only the remark in 4.17, where Moses is presented with the wonder-working 'rod', appears quite abruptly and has no connection with what has gone before. It seems to belong to the E narrative. The abrupt occurrence of this verse also serves to show that here too the E narrative was incorporated only fragmentarily into the combination of the old Pentateuchal narrative material and that an Elohistic section, now no longer extant, must have stood between 3.9–15 and 4.17.

The introduction, 2.11–22, offers little scope for literary-critical considerations. In essentials the narrative follows a smooth course, apart from a number of secondary additions which will be noticed later. Only the subordinate clause 2.23a*a*, which hangs in the air in a strange way, offers any difficulty. The following P passage cannot be its original conclusion as the contents do not correspond at all with what has gone before. In view of 1.15–21 the phrase 'the king of Egypt' in 2.23a*a* is reminiscent of E, and in fact the whole clause is best understood in the context of the E narrative. According to

4.19 J only lets Moses return to Egypt at the express command of
Yahweh in which the reason given is that the hostility in Egypt which
endangered Moses' life is now past. According to E, however, Moses
returned to Egypt of his own accord immediately after his encounter
with God (4.18). It is not said anywhere in this latter narrative that
the encounter with God in the wilderness only took place once the
'king of Egypt' had died. This presupposes that E too had a passage
no longer extant, parallel to the J narrative, according to which
Moses had for some reason fled from the 'king of Egypt' into the
land of Midian. Thus as E now stands there is a gap between 1.15–21
and 2.23a*a* similar to that between 2.23a*a* and 3.1b*b* and between
3.9–15 and 4.17.

The conclusion to be drawn from all this is that apart from the
very short summary observations by P the first chapters of the book of
Exodus to a large extent contain the wording of the old narratives J
and E; of these, as far as we can see, J is preserved in a complete and
continuous form, whereas only fragments of E have been incorporated
into the combined narrative work to expand the variant given by J.
It is clear, however, from what still remains of the E narrative that its
original content was very similar to that of J.

[2.11–22] The connection between 2.11 and the story of the birth
of Moses which precedes it is loose; it is assumed that Moses had not
hitherto lived among his fellow countrymen and had not shared their
hard lot. He had to 'go out' to them from the surroundings of the
royal court in which he had grown up. In the meanwhile he had
become a grown man; according to Acts 7.23 he would by then
already have been 40 years old, whereas the Old Testament narrative has pictured him as still being quite a young man (P's information about Moses' age in Deut. 34.7 was still unknown to the old
narrators). The Old Testament tradition has nothing to say about the
time spent at the Egyptian court; it was only at a later date that this
gap in the tradition was filled with the observation that he 'was
instructed in all the wisdom of the Egyptians' (Acts 7.22). At the
court of the king of Egypt Moses did not forget that he belonged with
'his people', a fact of which he became aware in some way. This he
immediately proves at the first opportunity with an act which, in
spite of all the circumspection employed, is none the less resolute.
The incident also goes to show to what a pitch the bondage of the
Israelites had by this time come; for some apparently trivial reason
an Egyptian can kill an Israelite on the spot (the verb *hikkāh* must

surely have the same meaning here as it doubtless has in the following verse and thus means 'kill' and not just 'beat'). Moses did not see how 'his people' were faring on just one occasion out of curiosity; from now on they are to be his concern and so he 'goes out' to them on the following day, only to discover that his action against the Egyptian has already become common knowledge, at least among 'his people', and that the atmosphere is not so much one of joy over his championing the oppressed as mistrust of his person and his prompt action.

Once his act has become known Moses is compelled to flee. Sufficient reason for his flight is given by v. 14b.; once the Israelites know about the affair it will not remain long hidden from the Egyptians, who will then take steps about it. Moses withdraws at the right time. The reference to Pharaoh in v. 15 looks like a variant to vv. 13 and 14 and probably represents a secondary addition to the narrative. No reason is given for Moses' choice of the land of Midian as his goal. An examination of the history of the tradition explains this choice. The land of Midian was chiefly known as the scene of Moses' first encounter with God, and the story of the flight from Egypt is intended to allow Moses to reach just this place. The scene by the well in Midian follows a pattern frequent in Old Testament stories when a foreigner is to be brought into contact with the people of the land (cf. Gen. 24.11 ff.; 29.2 ff.). This pattern comes straight from real life. Watering places are the usual spots for meeting people, especially in a neighbourhood where there are no fixed dwellings, as it is from them that water must be drawn every day and to them that animals, especially the flocks of sheep and goats, must be brought to drink. Quite often disputes arise at them over the precious water. Whoever is first there or is able to have his own way guarantees himself a considerable share of the water supply, which is perhaps scanty. The watering places therefore give a strong and upright foreigner the opportunity to stand up for the weaker ones in the struggle for water. The womenfolk especially are such weaker ones, as they have to cope with shepherds whenever they wish to draw water for their houses and their flocks. In the present instance there are seven daughters of the priest of Midian who have to pasture the flock for their father and lead it down to the watering place, because according to this particular story the priest has no sons at all (Num. 10.29 differs). They have already drawn water up the well-shaft in their buckets and have filled the troughs from which the flock is to drink. Then the shepherds come along with their flocks and themselves want to make use of the water which has been drawn by the womenfolk. At this stage Moses, who is recognizable as an Egyptian in a foreign land by his clothing, has the opportunity to interfere. In so doing he makes the acquaintance first of the daughters of the priest and later of the priest himself, remains as a protected guest (in Hebrew *gēr*) in the house of the priest of Midian, becomes his son-in-law and has a son by his daughter. Verse 18 gives the name of the priest as Reuel, a name which is given to him only once elsewhere, in Num. 10.29: in Ex. 3.1; 4.18; 18.1 ff. his name is Jethro. Now in the text of Ex. 2.18 the name Reuel looks very much like an addition, but when this addition was made—and this presumably happened at quite an early stage—the Midianite father-in-law of Moses was known in certain Israelite circles by the name Reuel. The difference in names shows that the oldest tradition of Moses' relation by marriage with Midian gave no name for his father-in-law, who was originally described merely as the 'priest of Midian'. This is still the case even in the present text when he is introduced for the first time in Ex. 2.16. It is impossible to discover the origin of the different names given to the priest at a later date. Tradition names the priest's daughter married to Moses as Zipporah; this name means 'bird' (feminine) and is certainly to be regarded as just a girl's name which was not uncommon in old times. It was given to the Midianite wife of Moses as the story became more concrete. Zipporah was probably never the subject of special traditions. Gershom, the son of Moses, is however a different matter. This name cannot be separated from the eponym of the priestly family at the sanctuary of Dan, who according to the original text of Judg. 18.30 went back beyond their ancestor Gershom to Moses, and that at a relatively early period before it was customary to derive all priests, including the 'Gershonites' (cf. Num. 3.17 ff.), from Aaron. Thus Gershom, the son of Moses, comes from the Danite priestly tradition and we have the rare occasion of an element of north Israelite tradition finding its way into the Pentateuchal narrative. Gershom was the only son of Moses known to the J tradition. It was quite appropriate to introduce him at this stage of the story, where the tradition of Moses' kinship with a Midianite priest emerges for the first time, and in this way he has a Midianite woman for a mother, which can hardly have been intended in the Danite priestly tradition. As usual in folk tales, his name is explained by Moses' situation as *gēr* in the land of Midian (see above).

[3.1–6] The story of Moses' decisive encounter with God which now follows is made up of two elements, the narrative of the theophany at a particular place in the wilderness and the narrative of the sending of Moses. In the E version of course the former narrative element has faded away completely; God just suddenly calls Moses by name (v. 4b) and no descriptive details are given either of the surroundings or of how this calling takes place.* After Moses has replied to the calling of his name with the customary 'Here am I', the one who calls reveals himself as 'God of the Fathers' (v. 6), whereupon Moses hides his face, presumably by wrapping it in his mantle (cf. I Kings 19.13), in fear of the sight of God. The wording suggests that God is thought to have appeared in some visible way. The place where this happened was the 'mountain of God' (in the land of Midian). The passage in which this is given (v.1b*b*) certainly belongs to the E version. The word 'God' in the term 'mountain of God' could possibly have occurred in J also, but the mention of the 'mountain of God' in Ex. 18.5 E suggests that here too the expression comes from the E narrative. It remains uncertain whether there is anything else in v. 1 as it has been transmitted which goes back to the E version. The chief question concerns the name Jethro, as it also appears elsewhere in E contexts (4.18; 18.1 ff.) and is in any case not to be derived from J (see above on 2.18). If the name Jethro here is not simply an addition occasioned by later occurrences of the name and if therefore E is to be given some no longer definable part of the statements in v. 1a, then E, like J, would have had Moses pasturing the flock of his Midianite father-in-law and at one stage of his wanderings from pasturage to pasturage would have had him going off into the distance. In doing this Moses would reach a 'mountain of God', apparently unknown before, on which he would be called upon by God in an astounding way to receive his commission.

The wanderings of Moses in a land still unknown, as he tends the flock of his father-in-law, which lead to his finding of the place in the wilderness at which he was addressed by Yahweh, appear more clearly in the J version as a special element of the tradition. Moses discovers this place and is told that it is 'holy ground' (v. 5) to which no man may 'come near' and whose surroundings may be trodden only by naked feet, i.e. feet left in their natural condition. In pattern

---

*[In his own translation of the text Noth encloses the words 'out of the bush' (3.4b) in square brackets without comment, thereby implying that they are a later (secondary) addition. Tr.]

this story recalls many of the patriarchal narratives, especially the story of the discovery by Jacob of the sanctuary of what is later to be the cult centre of Bethel (Gen. 28.11–22 JE). It is therefore probable that here too we are dealing with an original local tradition to which the 'holy ground' concerned was still known as such at a later period. The narrative offers no clues towards fixing it in a more definite locality. All that can be inferred from the context into which this tradition has been introduced is that the place was in the wilderness, in particular in the wilderness which lay between Egypt and the cultivated land of Palestine. This place, which was presumably still known to later Israelites, at least to those who passed on caravan trains through the wilderness which spread to the south of their dwelling-places, was marked out by a 'burning bush'. As no specific account is given for this phenomenon, although it is assumed to be the permanent feature of the place in question, we must look for an explanation of it. The favourite explanation of exegetes has been a manifestation similar to St Elmo's fire, and in fact we must imagine something of this sort; we cannot, however, regard this as a certain explanation. It is understandable that such a phenomenon was regarded as something awesome, as a sign of divine presence. H. Gressmann is able to produce a whole series of parallels from Syria–Palestine of stories of bushes which burn yet are not consumed.* This local tradition of the holy place of the burning bush in the wilderness has now entered the Israelite tradition to give a concrete background to the story of Moses' first encounter with God. We may ask whether J, who can hardly have known the wilderness of the south from his own experience, and perhaps even the oral tradition which was handed down to him, did not look for the holy place of the burning bush, originally independent, on Sinai. The Hebrew word for 'bush' (s'neh) which is used here certainly had nothing to do with the name 'Sinai' originally; in many Semitic languages it is the recognized description for a particular kind of thorny shrub, and in Arabic, in the form sinā, it refers specially to the thorny shrub Cassia obovata which can be found today in Palestine in the neighbourhood of the Dead Sea. If then there is a concrete local tradition in the background, the word appears in Ex. 3 because a particular kind of bush is to be described which can be given this name and only this name in Hebrew. There is no intention of any sort of mysterious allusion to the name Sinai. It is however possible that when the story was

*Moses, pp. 26 ff.

later incorporated into the framework of the Moses tradition the
word s^eneh was felt to contain an allusion to the name Sinai, with the
result that the scene was subsequently transferred to Sinai. This could
also be the reason for the phenomenon of the fire, which is reminiscent of the features which accompany the theophany on Sinai.
Perhaps J was already thinking of this as a prelude to the subsequent
great theophany on Sinai in which Moses took part. First of all he
has the 'angel of the Lord' (Hebrew *mal'āk Yahweh* = Greek *angelos
Kyriou*), a heavenly messenger, acting as the mediator of the divine
power on earth, who is described rather vaguely, appearing to Moses
in the fire of the bush. Later, however, when we have a personal
address to Moses and are dealing no longer with the 'appearance' of
God but with his 'speech', it is Yahweh himself who acts.*

[3.7–17] Both in actual fact and in the history of the tradition it is
the divine commission to Moses which forms the real nucleus of the
story of Moses' stay in the land of Midian as told by the old sources
of the Pentateuch. At the same time, this commission is formulated
in the two sources in rather different ways. In J Moses hears Yahweh
announce that he will lead Israel up out of Egypt (vv. 7 f.) and is
ordered to proclaim the divine purpose to the Israelites in Egypt
(vv. 16 ff.). Here Moses is quite simply the messenger of God who
receives the news of what Yahweh intends to do and has to pass on
this news to Israel, in the form of a proclamation in which the
messenger represents the one who sent him and speaks for him in the
first person (vv. 16b, 17). This is reminiscent of the prophets known
to us from a later time, but with the difference that here a redemptive
act of Yahweh is to be proclaimed, whereas the later prophets are
concerned primarily and predominantly with an impending divine
judgment. J formulated the commission to Moses long before the
appearance of 'classical' prophecy; thus at this early stage the arrival
of a messenger of God who was sent to precede an imminent divine
action was not unknown in Israel. For E too Moses is an 'envoy';
three times in this connection it is said that God 'sends' Moses
(vv. 10, 12, 13), and here the same word is used which is to be
employed later by the prophets to describe their office (cf. Jer.
26.12, 15). At the same time however Moses is in E given the command to 'bring forth' Israel out of Egypt (vv. 10, 11, 12) whereas
according to J it is Yahweh himself who will 'bring up' Israel out of
Egypt (vv. 8, 17). Of course this is an insignificant difference, as it is

*Cf. Gen. 16.7 ff. and von Rad, *Genesis, ad loc.*

certain that E too understands that in the Exodus Moses is no more
than an instrument of the divine action. But the difference is none
the less there. The J description should therefore be regarded as the
more original, as we have in it the narrative development of the
primitive confession of Israel that 'Yahweh has led Israel out of
Egypt'. In contrast E presents us with an interpretation of the work of
Moses which has already become a shade more substantial. In both
cases, however, the sole initiative in the events which now begin
clearly remains with Yahweh himself.

According to J (vv. 7 f., 16 ff.) Yahweh's speech to Moses is simple
and—in its original form—short. Yahweh has already begun to act.
Not only has he heard the *ṣᵉ'āḳāh* of the Israelites, i.e. the cry for help
of the helpless oppressed (v. 7); he has also already 'come down'
(v. 8). J says quite clearly and unconcernedly that Yahweh comes
down from his dwelling place in the highest heaven to do something
on earth (cf. also Gen. 11.5, 7 J). The 'Promised Land' is indicated
as the immediate goal of the Exodus, albeit by the passing reference
to a 'good and broad land' (further remarks made about this land
may be secondary additions). Moses is now to report his encounter
with God to the 'elders' of Israel, i.e. probably the heads of the great
families as the representatives and spokesmen of the whole (v. 16),
with the explicit information that Yahweh who appeared to him is
none other than the 'God of the fathers' of the patriarchal tradition
who is now beginning to fulfil the promise of land which he made to
the Patriarchs. Moses is to deliver to them the divine proclamation
that the 'Exodus' is now imminent. In its original state the J narrative probably reached only as far as v. 17a*a*. In what follows then
probably not only is the stereotyped description of the Promised
Land (v. 17a*bb*) a later addition but also the detailed description of
the events of the Exodus in **3.18–22**. Here the divine proclamation
at this early stage strangely anticipates the later narrative by predicting the details of coming events, predicting them moreover with
some verbal borrowings from the later narrative (for v. 18 see 5.3;
for v. 21 see 11.3; for v. 22 see 11.2). With these additions the
proclamation of God receives a predictive element whereas originally
it contained only a short announcement of the mighty act of God.

[3.9–15] In E, where between v.6 and v. 9 perhaps only the
introduction to the divine speech of v. 9 ff. is lacking, Moses receives
the commission to 'bring forth' Israel since God has let the cry of the
people of Israel come before him (v. 9 is parallel to v. 7; the phrases

'I will send you to Pharaoh', v. 10, and 'go to Pharaoh', v. 11, somewhat destroy the smooth flow of the narrative and are perhaps expansions). When Moses asks anxiously how he is to achieve this great work
he receives the promise that God will 'be with him' and as confirmation of his divine commission a 'sign' is presented to him. This is
strongly reminiscent of the stories of charismatic leaders in the time of
the 'Judges', and the wording is in part the same. There is for example
the story of Gideon who in the same way 'is sent' to perform an
action (not merely to pass on a divine proclamation) and who also
receives for himself the promise that God will 'be with him'. He too
requests and receives a 'sign' as confirmation of his mission (Judg. 6.
14 ff.). The promise 'I will be with you' means quite literally that
God will be present. Now of course the 'sign' promised to Moses is not
named, as v. 12 has obviously been transmitted in a fragmentary
state. This is evident from the mere fact that the word 'God' appears
in the third person in the context of a speech made by God and from
the unjustifiable transition from the singular address made to Moses
to the plural address to the Israelites.* The last clause of this verse
apparently contains something which Moses is to say to the Israelites
and in it 'this mountain' is the 'mountain of God' of v. 1. Now this
future 'serving on this mountain' can hardly be the sign intended in
this context, as it will only take place when the Exodus has already
been accomplished; the sign must therefore originally have stood
after v. 12a. We are as little able to tell what may originally have
been in the gaps now existing in v. 12 as whether the gaps themselves
arose accidentally in the transmission of the text or whether something contradictory to the J source was omitted by the redactor.
After Moses has been assured by the 'sign' of the divine commission
he still requires some proof to give to the Israelites. This proof would
consist in the fact that he is able to tell them the name of the one who
sent him. For in ancient Eastern thought the name of the person
who existed was a necessary part of his existence and one knew of a
reality only if one was able to pronounce its 'name'. In the same way
Moses will only be able to make the Israelites believe in the reality of
his encounter with God if he is able to tell them the name of the God
who appeared to him. This presents no problem for J, as he has made
use of the divine name Yahweh right from the beginning of his narrative and has also at least from Gen. 4.26 onwards presumed that this
name is known among men upon earth. In his narrative, Moses need

*This transition is of course not so clear in the English version.

only mention this familiar name (v. 16). E, who usually uses the
* word 'God' instead of this name, is in a different position. In his
narrative the God who appeared to Moses had first appeared without
a name or just as 'God of the fathers' (v. 6, cf. v. 13); the question
about his name therefore has some point. By letting the 'God of the
fathers' answer the question about his name and thus give Moses the
proof he needed for the Israelites E now allows the name Yahweh to
be known, at first only in Israel. In so doing he presumably remained
nearer to historical reality, for in some way the rise of the cult of
Yahweh in Israel in particular is connected with the process of Israel's
becoming a people before the conquest of Palestine. The giving of the
name follows in vv. 14 f., first and foremost through the mysterious
sentence *ehyeh 'ᵃšer ehyeh*, 'I am who I am', from which the catchword
ehyeh 'I am' is taken as the name of the God who appeared to Moses
(v. 14). This name unmistakably hints at the divine name Yahweh
in so far as an Israelite ear could immediately understand the transition from *ehyeh* to *yahweh* merely as a transition from the first to the
third person (in which the *w* of *yahweh* in place of the *y* of *ehyeh* may
have been felt as dissimilation after the initial *y*) so that the name
Yahweh would be understood to mean 'he is'. Verse 15 explicitly
puts forward this connection by inserting the name Yahweh for the
ehyeh of v. 14. We cannot of course completely escape the impression
that there is some overcrowding in vv. 14 f. The threefold introduction to God's speech does not look original; this unusual repetition is
stressed rather than explained by the little word 'also' at the beginning of v. 15. If then we have both primary and secondary material
in these verses, we must hold the simpler expression to be the original
and thus should not understand v. 15 to be a secondary expansion of
v. 14 in the sense of being an explicit interpretation of the *ehyeh*
(*'ᵃšer ehyeh*) through the name Yahweh, especially as v. 14 could
hardly have been in need of such an express interpretation. Instead
we should regard the simple giving of the name in v. 15 as an original
answer to the question at the end of v. 13, in the same way as the
sentence in v. 15b, 'this is my name for ever', will then take up the
question 'What is his name?' in v. 13. Verse 14a would then have
been added subsequently as an explanation of the name Yahweh and
would have been inserted into the context by means of 14b which
verbally anticipates the following clause. In this way the insertion of
the little word 'also' at the beginning of v. 15 would eventually commend itself. Should v. 14a(b) then be a secondary literary element

in the material of the E narrative the addition could still be quite old and could go back to a perhaps still older tradition of the explanation of the name Yahweh. Be this as it may, v. 14a(b) however old it is is of great significance as the only explanation of the Old Testament name for God which has actually been handed down in the Old Testament. Thus we can leave aside the question whether the divine name had had a history before it was used in Israel, perhaps in conjunction with a pre-Israelite or non-Israelite cult on the 'mountain of God' (or Sinai), and likewise the further question whether the explanation in v. 14 rightly defines the original meaning of the name. We may just observe that the name Yahweh is in fact probably to be derived from the stem *hwh*, frequent in the Aramaic and Arabic dialects, which corresponds to the Hebrew root *hyh* 'be'.* It is an important fact that within the framework of the Old Testament tradition the divine name has been understood in the way in which it is explained in v. 14. How far this understanding, alongside which the Old Testament hands on no other possibility of interpretation, was widespread in Israel we have no means of telling. There is scarcely any reference to this understanding elsewhere in the Old Testament except for the strange *ehyeh* of Hos. 1.9, which seems once again to allude to the interpretation of the name Yahweh in Ex. 3.14. There therefore the divine name is explained to mean 'He of whom the saying "I am who I am" is true'. This saying is not simply interchangeable with the short 'I am'. For in view of what has been said earlier, v. 14b, in which the *ehyeh 'ašer ehyeh* of v. 14a appears shortened to a simple *ehyeh*, is presumably just a redactional transition to v. 15 and in no way an authentic interpretation of v. 14a. Thus the sentence *ehyeh 'ašer ehyeh*, 'I am who I am', must be self-explanatory. It allows of various interpretations between which a firm decision is hardly possible. It is, however, hard to maintain that this sentence either refuses an answer or gives an evasive answer to the request for the name. For not only does the wider context lead us to understand that the name Yahweh is disclosed to Moses as a real divine name and not merely as the disguising of a divine name, especially if v. 14a(b) should be a secondary addition to v. 15; in addition, the sentence v. 14a does not give itself to be understood in

*The form *yahweh* in vv. 14 f. is apparently understood as a verbal form, which indeed it can be (= 'he is'). But perhaps it was originally a matter of a noun derived from the root *hwh* and formed by the prefix *ya* being added = 'the being one' (cf. L. Koehler, *Die Welt des Orients* I 5, 1950, p. 405).

this way—if it did it would have to run not 'I am who I am' but 'I am called whatever I am called'. The sentence construction *ehyeh* '*ašer ehyeh* can also be translated as a future, 'I will be who I will be', without making any essential difference, as it is said of the God who now means to act in the history of Israel. In either event it is according to Hebrew linguistic usage meant to express something which cannot be defined more closely.* Here perhaps the meaning is less one of pure indefiniteness ('I am someone or other') than of that kind of indefiniteness in which something definite is envisaged but is not meant to be expressed ('I am something, but it will only turn out later what I am'). Most likely, however, that kind of indefiniteness is expressed which leaves open a large number of possibilities ('I am whatever I mean to be'). Though these different nuances in the short sentences may be held together and each of them be read out of it according to circumstances, it is in any case important to note that the verb *hyh* in Hebrew does not express pure 'being', pure 'existing' but an 'active being'; and in the present instance this certainly means an 'active being' which does not take place just anywhere, but makes its appearance in the world of men and primarily in the history of Israel. This perhaps is what is expressed in Ex. 3.14a to explain the name Yahweh. We must be on our guard against wanting to read more out of this interpretation than its wording permits.

[4.1–9] In J as well as in E Moses, entrusted with a divine message to the Israelites, requires some means of authenticating himself to those to whom the message is addressed; this he receives in a twofold way by being given the power to do two 'signs' which he will be able to make use of in case of need. Is it a feature of the picture of a messenger of God here presupposed by J that he be able to show that he has received the divine commission by the exercise of miraculous 'power'? We may allow this question all the more as Moses afterwards never comes into the pressing situation of having to make emphatic use of this twofold authentication before the Israelites (cf. on 4.30 f.). Only in the later P narrative does the theme of the rod transformed into a serpent make a further independent appearance (7.9–12), apparently on the basis of an old tradition, but in another context, namely in front of Pharaoh. Can J then in 4.1 ff. be said merely to have rounded off the picture of Moses as divine messenger which was present in his mind? The connection in 4.1 ff.

*On this see especially T. E. Vriezen, "*Ehje* '*ašer* '*ehje*', *Festschrift Alfred Bertholet*, 1950, pp. 498–512.

is not completely smooth. Verse 5, with its verbal repetitions of what has gone before, is not only superfluous, but is inserted into the narrative so carelessly, without any new introductory formula for the divine speech, that it can only be regarded as an addition. But what can be said of v. 5 can also be said of v. 8 and at the same time of v. 9 which is reminiscent of the 'plagues' (cf. 7.14 ff.). Here Moses is empowered to give as it were a prelude to these plagues, but the gift of 'power' does not correspond with the two gifts of power mentioned earlier, in so far as in this case Moses cannot immediately perform the 'miracle' as a test. [4.10–12] After the messenger of God has received his commission and the means of proving himself, we find in vv. 10 ff. that although he has been equipped in this way he nevertheless objects, objects moreover with an excuse (v. 10) which conceals the anxiety of man before a task given by God. Later prophecy too knows the same thing (cf. Jer. 1.6). Moses is taught by Yahweh that he, Yahweh, is the Creator and thus the real Lord over man and his facilities for perception and expression (v. 11), that he can therefore let man serve him with his natural aptitudes and will give him whatever is necessary to fulfil the task in hand, in this case by 'teaching', by showing him what he must say at the decisive moment. This too recalls the later 'classical' prophets, who did not usually have the content of their message prepared beforehand, but in each instance received the 'word' which they were to say on any occasion (cf. especially Jer. 28.11 ff.). It is surprising that after this divine promise Moses has the audacity to repeat his refusal in a still more brusque way (v. 13), and quite astonishing that the divine wrath, which thereupon quite understandably flares up (v. 14aa), neverthe-less immediately leads to a further promise, that Aaron shall be a companion for Moses (vv. 14abb–16). Yahweh, who means to do a great work in which Moses is to serve as his messenger, shows con-siderable forbearance towards Moses' human weakness. Now it is of course true that the section vv. 13–16 represents a secondary addition, made in any case during the transmission of the tradition and per-haps even at the literary stage within the J narrative work, which has the aim of bringing Aaron into the story and uses the repeated (and heightened) theme of the objections by Moses to form the link. Here and in what follows the mention of Aaron does not seem to fit the original form of the narrative. If we have to understand the word 'brother' in v. 14 in the narrow sense and not as a general term 'kinsman', Aaron appears in this section as Moses' physical brother;

this was not the meaning of the oldest tradition to be fixed in writing (cf. on 15.20). Nevertheless this addition was made at quite an early stage, as is shown by the ancient use of the description 'the Levite' in v. 14, which in fact is perhaps older than the use of the name Levi in 2.1. For alongside the designation 'your brother', the description 'the Levite' is hardly to be understood as giving us information about his descent; it rather seems to assign to Aaron a function which Moses himself does not have. Apparently in *lēwī* we have here an old technical term. That Yahweh is already leading 'the Levite Aaron' to Moses at the same time as he is speaking to Moses (v. 14b; cf. v. 27) is a sign that his work is not limited by space. Altogether the subsidiary section vv. 13–15 presents a picture of the messenger of God reminiscent of the later 'classical' prophecy. Aaron will now be the real messenger and in contrast to him Moses, who will tell him what to do, will take the place of God (v. 16b*b*). Moses will 'put the words in his mouth' (v. 15a) in the same way as God does with the prophets (cf. Jer. 1.9b) and Aaron will serve Moses as a mouthpiece (v. 16b*a*) just as the prophet is the 'mouth of God' (Jer. 15.19). Moses' silence after v. 12 (v. 16) shows that he is now ready to obey the divine command.

[4.17] The 'rod' appears quite abruptly in v. 17. Moses is to use it to 'do the signs'. This remark does not fit at all well with vv. 1 ff. according to which Moses will need his rod only for one of the two signs. Verse 17 thus certainly comes from the E version, in which Moses is apparently given not merely one 'sign' (cf. 3.12a) but a number of signs. In view of the parallel J version, however, the E tradition has been preserved only in fragments.

[4.18–23] To carry out his task Moses returns to Egypt, as is reported in two variants (cf. pp. 33 ff. above). According to J (vv. 19, 20a) he took his wife and children with him; according to E (vv. 18, 20b) he apparently returned alone (cf. 18.2 ff.) but had with him the 'rod of God' (cf. v. 17) with which to perform the signs, as is here expressly stated. Yahweh's speech to Moses in vv. 21–23, which still presupposes the situation before his departure (cf. on the other hand v. 20a), is to be assessed in the same way as the section 3.18–22 (see above p. 41). It already hints at the last of the plagues and with regard to this describes Israel as the 'first-born son' of Yahweh, whose violation Yahweh will avenge on the 'first-born son' of Pharaoh in accordance with the *ius talionis*. Israel is also named Yahweh's 'son called out of Egypt' in Hos. 11.1.

4. THE RETURN OF MOSES AND HIS FIRST MEETING WITH PHARAOH: 4.24–6.1

24 *At a lodging place on the way the* LORD *met him and sought to kill him.* 25 *Then Zipporah took a flint and cut off her son's foreskin, and touched Moses' feet with it, and said, 'Surely you are a bridegroom of blood to me!'* 26 *So he let him alone. Then it was that she said, 'You are a bridegroom of blood,' because of the circumcision.*

[27 *The* LORD *said to Aaron, 'Go into the wilderness to meet Moses.' So he went, and met him at the mountain of God and kissed him.* 28 *And Moses told Aaron all the words of the* LORD *with which he had sent him, and all the signs which he had charged him to do.*] 29 *Then Moses [and Aaron] went and gathered together all the elders of the people of Israel.* 30 *And [Aaron] spoke all the words which the* LORD *had spoken [to Moses], and did the signs in the sight of the people.* 31 *And the people believed; and when they heard that the* LORD *had visited the people of Israel and that he had seen their affliction, they bowed their heads and worshipped.*

5 ¹ *Afterward Moses [and Aaron] went to Pharaoh and said, 'Thus says the* LORD, *the God of Israel, "Let my people go, that they may hold a feast to me in the wilderness."'* ² *But Pharaoh said, 'Who is the* LORD, *that I should heed his voice and let Israel go? I do not know the* LORD, *and moreover I will not let Israel go.'* ³ *Then they said, 'The God of the Hebrews has met with us; let us go, we pray, a three days' journey into the wilderness, and sacrifice to [the* LORD] *our God, lest he fall upon us with pestilence or with the sword.'* ⁴ *But the king of Egypt said to them, '[Moses and Aaron,] why do you take the people away from their work? Get to your burdens.'* ⁵ *And Pharaoh said, 'Behold, the people of the land are now many and you make them rest from their burdens!'* ⁶ *The same day Pharaoh commanded the taskmasters of the people [and their foremen],* ⁷ *'You shall no longer give the people straw to make bricks, as heretofore; let them go and gather straw for themselves.* ⁸ *But the number of bricks which they made heretofore you shall lay upon them, you shall by no means lessen it; for they are idle; therefore they cry, "Let us go and offer sacrifice to our God."* ⁹ *Let heavier work be laid upon the men that they may labour at it and pay no regard to lying words.'*

10 *So the taskmasters [and the foremen] of the people went out and said to the people, 'Thus says Pharaoh, "I will not give you straw.* 11 *Go yourselves, get your straw wherever you can find it; but your work will not be lessened in the least."'* 12 *So the people were scattered abroad throughout all the land of Egypt, to gather stubble for straw.* 13 *The taskmasters were urgent, saying, 'Complete your work, your daily task, as when there was straw.'* 14 *And the foremen of the people of Israel, whom Pharaoh's taskmasters had set over them, were beaten, and were asked, 'Why have you not done all your task of making bricks today, as hitherto?'*

15 *Then the foremen of the people of Israel came and cried to Pharaoh,*

'*Why do you deal thus with your servants?* [16] *No straw is given to your servants, yet they say to us, "Make bricks!" And behold, your servants are beaten; but the fault is in your own people.'* [17] *But he said, 'You are idle, you are idle; therefore you say, "Let us go and sacrifice to the* LORD." [18] *Go now, and work; for no straw shall be given you, yet you shall deliver the same number of bricks.'* [19] *The foremen of the people of Israel saw that they were in evil plight, when they said, 'You shall by no means lessen your daily number of bricks.'* [20] *They met Moses [and Aaron], who [were] waiting for them, as they came forth from Pharaoh;* [21] *and they said to [them], 'The* LORD *look upon you and judge, because you have made us offensive in the sight of Pharaoh and his servants, and have put a sword in their hand to kill us.'*

22 *Then Moses turned again to the* LORD *and said, 'O* LORD, *why hast thou done evil to this people? Why didst thou ever send me?* [23] *For since I came to Pharaoh to speak in thy name, he has done evil to this people, and thou hast not delivered thy people at all.'* **6** [1] *But the* LORD *said to Moses, 'Now you shall see what I will do to Pharaoh; for [with a strong hand he will send them out, yea] with a strong hand he will drive them out of his land.'*

[4.24–26] The brief note about an incident on Moses' return to Egypt is very obscure in several respects. Why does it appear at all in this place? As it deals with the theme of circumcision we would rather expect to find it connected with the description of Moses' marriage or even the birth of his son. A definite locality evidently plays some part here. At a solitary, mysterious place in the wilderness Moses was fiercely attacked by Yahweh, who here displays a 'demonic' character and, perhaps in the course of the Old Testament transference of all supernatural workings to the one God, has taken the place of the local demon who would originally have been meant in this passage. For this reason the scene has been inserted here where Moses, with his wife and child, for the first time wanders through the desolate wilderness on his return to Egypt. When the tradition arose, did it still know the definite 'lodging place' in the wilderness at which this strange incident took place? Or did it merely have a quite general impression of the uncanny atmosphere of the wilderness by night? The wilderness locality with its demon however only forms the background for a brief narrative which has been transferred to it and linked up with it, an aetiological narrative of some kind. It is expressly said at the conclusion, in v. 26b, that the reason is given for the expression 'bridegroom of blood', a term which it was customary to use 'because of the circumcision', i.e. in the case of those who were or had just been circumcised. The way in which v. 26b is written certainly suggests that this expression was for the narrator an ancient one, no longer current in his time, but still known from an earlier period. This expression 'bridegroom of blood' indicates a connection between circumcision and marriage, and the story which explains the expression understands circumcision as an apotropaic act which keeps away a nocturnal threat—and here the wedding night may originally have been envisaged. Some obviously very old customs and ideas associated with circumcision appear in the story. No reason is given why in the face of the threat Zipporah should resort to the act of circumcision in particular; the aetiological aim of the narrative requires this spontaneous action by Zipporah. Zipporah carries out the act with a 'flint', just as in Josh. 5.2 f. 'flint knives' serve to effect the circumcision; such a primitive sacral act called for the use of an old and not a 'modern' implement. As Moses is the person involved at the beginning and the end of the story, the appearance of his son on the scene is completely obscure; it also leaves uncertain to whom the remark 'touched his feet' refers.* One is tempted to assume that the part played by the son is to be regarded as an addition to the tradition which was occasioned by the later custom of child circumcision, whereas the original material still dealt with the older adult circumcision, and that by 'touching the feet' the act of circumcision would appear to have been effected symbolically upon Moses. But these are only vague hypotheses on a section which in this brief form is quite inexplicable.

[4.27–31] After the nocturnal interlude in the wilderness Moses reaches Egypt and there fulfils his commission by delivering his message. To do this he gathers together the elders of Israel (v. 29b) which was apparently possible without any difficulty as the Israelites in Egypt lived quite near to one another (cf. above on 1.15 ff.). The 'people' represented by the elders also hear the message and believe it willingly (v. 31a); they bow themselves in worship before their God who has taken them to himself, and thereby show themselves ready for whatever God has prepared to happen to them (v. 31b). Of course the wonderful signs of 4.2 ff. are done before the people (v. 30b) but it is not said that they would really have been necessary.

*[The rendering 'Moses' feet' given in the RSV begs the question; the Hebrew text has merely an ambiguous third person suffix which is accurately translated in AV and RV. 'Feet' is of course here a euphemistic expression, as elsewhere in the Old Testament. Tr.]

There is no hint of an initial unbelief which had to be overcome; the wonderful signs are done because they happen to be what was provided for the authentication of the messenger of God. The passage is connected with 4.13–16 by the introduction of Aaron and the mention of him alongside Moses. Here too, in 4.27 ff., the appearance of Aaron betrays itself quite clearly as a secondary addition (see above pp. 46 f.). According to the present wording of v. 30 Aaron did the wonderful signs before the people. This is unexpected in view of what has gone before; according to 4.13–16 Aaron is to represent Moses merely as a 'spokesman', and according to 4.2 ff. the 'power' to do the wonderful signs is given to Moses alone. Thus Aaron has only subsequently been introduced as a spokesman into v. 30a and Moses was originally the subject in the whole of v. 30. Then too only Moses would originally have been mentioned in v. 29. Accordingly the passage vv. 27 f. must also be regarded as secondary; in fact this does not fit at this point anyhow. Once again it goes back to the 'mountain of God' (v. 27b) although in the meantime Moses has already been a long time on his journey from the land of Midian to Egypt. Even if we wish to leave out of consideration the nocturnal incident in the wilderness described in vv. 24–26 as a special passage which does not concern the larger context, according to vv. 18–20—and moreover in both the narrative versions, J and E—Moses would already have returned to his father-in-law from the place where he had his encounter with God and in any case would be on the point of starting off for Egypt. Moreover, it is striking that in v. 28 Moses says nothing to Aaron about the special commission with which according to 4.13–16 he has specially been entrusted. Here we already get the impression that the subsequent introduction of Aaron is not the result of a systematic and well-considered redaction, but that Aaron has been inserted into each of the old Moses stories as opportunity offered while Moses has been pushed to one side.* In what follows, therefore, it is generally tacitly assumed that the mention of Aaron alongside Moses is occasionally secondary.

[5.1–6.1] After the Israelites in Egypt have heard the message from God brought by Moses, the initiative is placed in their hands with the

*If we ascribe the use of the expression 'mountain of God' to the E version (cf. above p. 38 on 3.1) we shall have to see a mixture of J and E elements in the language of this verse, as the divine name Yahweh is mentioned in vv. 27 f. In that case we must assume that the addition which introduces Aaron was made to the JE narrative after it had been combined, at least in the case of individual parts of the addition, which is probably not a unity in itself.

first negotiations with Pharaoh to attempt to secure from him their release from Egypt. As they are in Egypt as forced labour in the royal service, only a decision from Pharaoh can free them from their immediate situation unless they are ready and willing to resort to force or to deception. Thus the request to Pharaoh and the negotiations with him are the obvious move. Thanks to a simple way of thinking it is here supposed that the Israelite labour force was able to speak directly to the Egyptian ruler through their representatives. The first negotiations turn out very much to the disadvantage of the Israelites. An appeal to the 'God of the Hebrews' (v. 3)—this means the God of Israel, whose people describe themselves quite appropriately to the Egyptians (see p. 21 above) as a people of 'Hebrews'—of course makes no impression at all upon Pharaoh, who worships the great gods of his country. He diagnoses their request for release as unwillingness to work (vv. 8, 17), and as a punishment lays increased quotas of work upon the Israelite forced labour, which he requires for his building plans and understandably does not mean to set free. The individual details are described very clearly in a broadly executed narrative style; we are told how the 'taskmasters'—i.e. the Egyptian officials who had to organize and supervise the forced labour—received Pharaoh's command not as previously to supply the Israelites with the straw necessary to mix with the clay for making wind-dried bricks, and how readily they complied with this command; how the Israelite 'foremen', i.e. overseers who were responsible to the Egyptian officials for the fulfilment of the temporarily harsh quota of work, attempt in vain to secure from Pharaoh the withdrawal of the increased requirements and how in so doing they submissively describe the Israelites not merely as 'servants of Pharaoh', but—if another reading* of the text of v. 16b is the right one—in their present situation as 'people of Pharaoh', though of course at the same time they quite boldly point out to Pharaoh that with such harsh treatment he does wrong to this 'his people'.

At first sight this vivid narrative gives the impression of being complete and a unity. A closer examination, however, gives rise to a number of questions. Few, indeed, are of a literary nature; from this point of view the section 5.1–6.1 runs quite smoothly. Only v. 4

---

*[This other reading, which is rendered by Noth in his translation, is that of an emendation considered probable in R. Kittel, *Biblia Hebraica*,³ 1945, and supported by the LXX and the Syriac. In translation it would run '. . . your servants are beaten. And (in so doing) you do wrong to your people.' Tr.]

appears strange as it clashes with the following v. 5. This verse speaks of a thought which came to Pharaoh. This does not of course appear from the wording of the introduction to the verse, as the Hebrew wrote 'Pharaoh said' even if he meant 'Pharaoh thought'. But the content of v. 5a can only be meant as one of Pharaoh's thoughts which he does not express to the Israelites, if we follow the reading of the Samaritan Pentateuch in place of the barely understandable Massoretic text.* Pharaoh then means that the Israelites, who have already grown far too numerous, must be kept under by hard labour (cf. on 1.11). We can even suppose that the original wording of v. 5b was 'And am I to grant them a rest from their burdens?'† Verse 4 is not completely appropriate before this thought, as it anticipates a decision which Pharaoh only makes as a result of his thought in v. 5. Now as v. 4 speaks of the 'king of Egypt', whereas in the previous and subsequent verses the word 'Pharaoh' is consistently used, we may see v. 4 as a fragment of E which has been inserted in the context of the J narrative which otherwise runs from 5.1 to 6.1. Of course this does not explain why this single not very important verse should have been taken from the E tradition which, though no longer preserved here otherwise, must also have reported the negotiations with the king of Egypt and have been added to expand the J variant.

It is more important to notice that in the negotiations with Pharaoh Moses quite remarkably is put in the background. The intensification of the work quotas required of the Israelites by Pharaoh after their request for release leads the Israelite 'foremen' to call upon Pharaoh in the name of their kinsmen (vv. 15 ff.), and in vv. 20 ff. we are surprised to learn that in the meantime Moses has been waiting outside so as to find out the result of the negotiations with Pharaoh and to receive the rebukes of the foremen. These complain that Moses' desire has resulted in their gaining a still worse reputation with Pharaoh and his officials (v. 21ba) and has given Pharaoh just one more pretext for still harsher and more murderous treatment (v. 21bb). At this stage Moses now becomes Israel's spokesman before Yahweh and passes on to Yahweh the rebukes which he

*[This is followed by the RSV. The reading which Noth prefers may be translated: 'And Pharaoh thought, "They are now more numerous than the (native) people of the land." ' Tr.]

†Then originally the reading would have been w*hisbattīm*; the 'ōtām would only have been added subsequently when the consonantal text was read falsely as w*hisbattem*.

has received (vv. 22 f.). Yahweh for his part draws the attention of
Moses to the imminent miraculous divine actions which will lead to
Israel's release from Egypt (6.1). Now what is astonishing is not only
Moses' unexpected reappearance in v. 20, but also his almost imper-
ceptible retreat in v. 3. After Moses has required the release of the
people in the name of the God of Israel and has been refused by
Pharaoh (vv. 1 f.), a first person plural suddenly appears in the
speech in v. 3 which can only refer to the Israelites as a whole or to
their representatives. In the text as it now stands this direct transition
is less striking, as in v. 1 Moses and Aaron were named together. But
in view of the content of v. 3b these two cannot originally have been
meant to speak in the first person plural, as it is their intention to take
all the people out into the wilderness to sacrifice to their God. In v. 3
we also have quite clearly a new contribution to the negotiations from
the Israelites, who begin by explaining that their God has met with
them. These several factors force us to the conclusion that underlying
5.13–19 is a piece of narrative in which the Israelites deal collectively
with Pharaoh, perhaps through some such group of representatives
as the 'elders', just as later, in vv. 15 ff., the 'foremen' of the Israelites
present their case to Pharaoh. We cannot make a literary division
between this passage and its present surroundings; not only does it
form the basis of the further narrative in vv. 20 ff. in which Moses
appears once again, but vv. 1 and 2 which lead up to it and in which
Moses is the chief spokesman to Pharaoh are already connected with
what follows by the mention of a (pilgrimage) feast 'in the wilderness', similar to the sacrifice 'in the wilderness' envisaged in v. 3. We
shall therefore have to assume that a tradition about the commence-
ment of negotiations with Pharaoh, in which the Israelites as a body
appeared as taking part in the discussion, has found a place in the J
tradition which is complete in itself. It may be asked why in his
literary work J did not smooth out the tensions which arose in this
way, as this would have been possible without excessive manipula-
tion; to this we can reply that not only did J generally preserve a
conservative attitude towards the individual narrative traditions
which came his way, but in the present instance the essential content
of the scene of the first negotiations with Pharaoh was already so
stereotyped during the process of oral tradition that J incorporated it
into his work as an erratic block. At the same time, it becomes clear
that although there is general agreement about the basic material in
the tradition of the great events at the Exodus, the individual details

of this tradition have been narrated in a number of variant forms which did not arise only when they were given fixed shape in various literary works, but were already present in the previous stage, that of oral tradition. The passage 5.3–19, in which Moses is not mentioned, appears in the literary work of J as an element incorporated from an older tradition, and it is not outside the bounds of possibility that we have here a piece of a version of the narrative description of the Exodus theme which occupies an even earlier place in the history of the tradition. In any case, in contrast with the later version, which in general occupies the forefront in the literary sources and gives a prominent place to Moses, this passage had no knowledge of Moses' presence at the beginning of the negotiations with Pharaoh.

It is also evident, from a discrepancy between this and the preceding narrative of the call of Moses, that a special and probably very old form of the tradition lies at the back of Ex. 5. At the call of Moses no mention was made of a feast which was to be held to Yahweh three days' march into the wilderness.* Therefore in the present context the request to Pharaoh in 5.(2), 3 to be allowed to do this appears as a false pretext; but we can hardly assume that this was the original intention in putting forward this request. After the story of his call, Moses—as in J—was sent to the Israelites with a message from Yahweh, after which they were to wait for what their God would do for them; or he was appointed—as in E—as a charismatic leader for the Exodus and would now have to carry out his task in a corresponding way. But in 5.3 it is said that the 'God of the Hebrews' has met with the Israelites = 'Hebrews'. This statement can hardly originally have been meant to refer to the meeting with God in which Moses alone took part; only the present context requires this forced meaning. So from this point too we are driven to the conclusion that a special and presumably extremely old narrative version underlies 5.3–19, which began its story of the Exodus from Egypt with the God of Israel meeting with his people in Egypt and summoning them to a feast in the wilderness. We have no further information about how this 'meeting' took place, as 5.3–19 is just a fragment of an older tradition which has been amalgamated with the tradition of the call of Moses in the land of Midian. By 5.1 f. J has created a transition passage which starts off with an interview between Moses and Pharaoh, but

*We can hardly quote the isolated remark in 3.12b*b* E in this connection, even if we disregard the fact that it does not belong to the context of the J source which underlies 5.1 ff.

which at this early opportunity bases the request for release on the feast in the wilderness which derives from what follows. And from v. 20 onwards J again lets Moses enter the chain of events as a mediator between God and people. After his remonstrances he eventually obtains the promise of imminent miraculous and powerful divine aid in accordance with the divine message with which he was sent to the Israelites at the time of his call (3.16 f.). 'With a strong hand', i.e. 'with power', Israel, according to this promise, will be 'sent' out of Egypt; thus Pharaoh will be driven not merely to give up his opposition to the departure of Israel but even to long for this departure and forcibly demand it. In the way in which the clause 6.1b has been written, the expression 'with a strong hand'—'with power' cannot refer to the action of Yahweh which would compel Pharaoh to restrain himself against his real wishes, but to the future action of Pharaoh. Yahweh will prove himself so powerful that Pharaoh will 'send Israel out', indeed he will even 'drive them out with a strong hand'. The double form of the subordinate clause in 6.1b does not look original; in view of the catchword 'let go' in 5.1 f., a secondary variant which repeats this word* has been placed before the clause in which the phrase 'drive out' is used.

5. ANOTHER CALL OF MOSES: 6.2–7.7

2 And God said to Moses, 'I am the LORD. 3 I appeared to Abraham, to Isaac, and to Jacob, as God Almighty, but by my name the LORD I did not make myself known to them. 4 I also established my covenant with them, to give them the land of Canaan, the land in which they dwelt as sojourners. 5 Moreover I have heard the groaning of the people of Israel whom the Egyptians hold in bondage and I have remembered my covenant. 6 Say therefore to the people of Israel, "I am the LORD, and I will bring you out from under the burdens of the Egyptians, and I will deliver you from their bondage, and I will re-deem you with an outstretched arm and with great acts of judgment, 7 and I will take you for my people, and I will be your God; and you shall know that I am the LORD your God, who has brought you out from under the burdens of the Egyptians. 8 And I will bring you into the land which I swore to give to Abraham, to Isaac, and to Jacob; I will give it to you for a possession. I am the LORD".' 9 Moses spoke thus to the people of Israel; but they did not listen to Moses, because of their broken spirit and their cruel bondage.

*[In both 5.1 and 6.1b forms of the same Hebrew verb šālaḥ are used; this similarity is obscured by the RSV rendering which uses two completely different words. Tr.]

10 And the LORD said to Moses, 11 'Go in, tell Pharaoh king of Egypt to let the people of Israel go out of his land.' 12 But Moses said to the LORD, 'Behold, the people of Israel have not listened to me; how then shall Pharaoh listen to me, who am a man of uncircumcised lips?' 13 But the LORD spoke to Moses and Aaron, and gave them a charge to the people of Israel and to Pharaoh king of Egypt to bring the people of Israel out of the land of Egypt.

14 These are the heads of their fathers' houses: the sons of Reuben, the first-born of Israel: Hanoch, Pallu, Hezron and Carmi; these are the families of Reuben. 15 The sons of Simeon: Jemuel, Jamin, Ohad, Jachin, Zohar, and Shaul, the son of a Canaanite woman; these are the families of Simeon. 16 These are the names of the sons of Levi according to their generations: Gershon, Kohath, and Merari, the years of the life of Levi being a hundred and thirty-seven years. 17 The sons of Gershon: Libni and Shimei, by their families. 18 The sons of Kohath: Amram, Izhar, Hebron and Uzziel, the years of the life of Kohath being a hundred and thirty-three years. 19 The sons of Merari: Mahli and Mushi. These are the families of the Levites according to their generations. 20 Amram took to wife Jochebed his father's sister and she bore him Aaron and Moses, the years of the life of Amram being one hundred and thirty-seven years. 21 The sons of Izhar: Korah, Nepheg, and Zichri. 22 And the sons of Uzziel: Mishael, Elzaphan, and Sithri. 23 Aaron took to wife Elisheba, the daughter of Amminadab and the sister of Nahshon; and she bore him Nadab, Abihu, Eleazar, and Ithamar. 24 The sons of Korah: Assir, Elkanah, and Abiasaph; these are the families of the Korahites. 25 Eleazar, Aaron's son, took to wife one of the daughters of Putiel; and she bore him Phinehas. These are the heads of the fathers' houses of the Levites by their families.

26 These are the Aaron and Moses to whom the LORD said: 'Bring out the people of Israel from the land of Egypt by their hosts.' 27 It was they who spoke to Pharaoh king of Egypt about bringing out the people of Israel from Egypt, this Moses and this Aaron.

28 On the day when the LORD spoke to Moses in the land of Egypt, 29 the LORD said to Moses, 'I am the LORD; tell Pharaoh king of Egypt all that I say to you.' 30 But Moses said to the LORD, 'Behold, I am of uncircumcised lips; how then shall Pharaoh listen to me?' 7¹ And the LORD said to Moses, 'See, I make you as God to Pharaoh; and Aaron your brother shall be your prophet. 2 You shall speak all that I command you; and Aaron your brother shall tell Pharaoh to let the people of Israel go out of his land. 3 But I will harden Pharaoh's heart, and though I multiply my signs and wonders in the land of Egypt, 4 Pharaoh will not listen to you; then I will lay my hand upon Egypt and bring forth my hosts, my people the sons of Israel, out of the land of Egypt by great acts of judgment. 5 And the Egyptians shall know that I am the LORD, when I stretch forth my hand upon Egypt and bring out the people of Israel from among them.' 6 And Moses and Aaron did so; they did as the LORD commanded them. 7 Now Moses was eighty years old, and Aaron eighty-three years old, when they spoke to Pharaoh.

It is immediately obvious that here the narrative theme of the call of Moses, which has already formed the content of the section 3.1–4.16, is repeated, and moreover with essentially the same elements of the story. The only difference which catches the eye is that in 6.2 ff. the call of Moses, in marked difference from what we find elsewhere, is clearly thought to take place in Egypt, whereas according to 3.1 ff. it happened in the land of Midian. The real substance of the narrative is not, however, affected by this difference. But no reason at all is given for a further call of Moses, which in fact contains nothing new. Now the section 6.2–7.7 displays all the linguistic, stylistic and conceptual characteristics of the Priestly source (P) of the Pentateuch, so that there can be no doubt that in 6.2 ff. we have the P version of the same incident as appeared in the JE version in 3.1 ff. As in the P version the call of Moses took place in Egypt, the Pentateuchal redactor who combined the old sources JE with P allowed the call of Moses in the land of Midian which led up to a first conversation with Pharaoh to come before the P version of the call of Moses. The result is that within the sequence of events in the Pentateuch as a whole the latter call now appears in connection with the promise of 6.1 as a confirmation of the commission given to Moses and an invitation to make new demands of Pharaoh. The wording, however, shows that originally this was an independent treatment of the theme of the one call and commissioning of Moses. Within the section, in **6.13–30**, we have a great secondary insertion, of which the external distinguishing mark is the almost literal repetition of v. 12 in v. 30, which is preceded in vv. 28 f. by a summary reference to the call of Moses and the commission formulated in v. 11. The passage 28–30 thus serves to pick up the threads of the narrative at the very place where they had been let drop in v. 12, before the insertion. The insertion stands immediately before the first mention of Aaron and serves to introduce Aaron as the elder brother (in P's view) of Moses. It is introduced in v. 13 by the observation that Yahweh did not speak to Moses alone, but to Moses and Aaron, and that it was to both of them that he gave the charge to bring Israel up out of Egypt. This introduction has its counterpart at the conclusion in vv. 26 f. The insertion goes back a considerable way to introduce Aaron; it begins by enumerating the sons of Jacob and the families who stem from them according to the list in Gen. 46.8 ff., which on its part derives from Num. 26.5 ff. But only the information about Reuben and Simeon is given. These two are followed by Levi in accordance with the traditional form of the twelve tribe system. From now on the insertion confines itself to a genealogy of the Levites. For the sons and grandsons of Levi this genealogy follows in v. 16 ff. the division of Num. 3.17 ff. The only difference is that in Ex. 6 a secondary addition has been made of different, but not consistent, details about the ages. The insertion achieves its real purpose in v. 20 where Moses and Aaron make their appearance within the framework of the Levitical genealogy in the third generation from Levi. The name of their mother, which else-where occurs only in Num. 26.59, is mentioned at the same time. To make the genealogy complete, however, mention is made of some further Levites of the same generation, a number of whom appear only here (vv. 21 ff.), and in v. 23–25 further details are given about the family of Aaron and his cousin Korah, some of which, as for example the list of the sons of Aaron, are also known elsewhere (cf. Num. 26.60 etc.) and some of which occur here only and certainly derive from post-exilic expansions and elaborations of the Levitical genealogy.

[6.2–12] The basic P-narrative begins with a lengthy speech from God to Moses (vv. 2–8). In a sequel to the last previous piece of the P narrative (2.23a*b*b–25) which told how God was concerned for the Israelites in Egypt and 'made himself known to them',* we are briefly told, without more details about the circumstances, that God spoke to Moses, whose well-known figure was not deemed by P to need any special introduction. Moses is simply presumed to be living among the Israelites in Egypt and the place of this encounter he has with God is thought of as being anywhere in Egypt. At the beginning of the speech God makes himself known and straightway uses the divine name 'Yahweh', uses it moreover, as the following verse goes on to explain, as a name which is now given for the first time. The detailed narrative element of the revelation of the name of God to Moses in 3.13–15 E appears in P in this simple form. Whereas even after 3.13–15 E now goes on to use the word 'God' in the narrative, P quite consistently changes the divine title at Ex. 6.2 and from this point on uses in the story the divine name Yahweh which has now been revealed. At an earlier time, in the age of the Patriarchs—so v. 3 says—God had been called 'El Shaddai'. According to Gen. 17.1 P this

---

*[The Hebrew in 2.25b, translated by the RSV 'and God knew their condition', is strange and should perhaps be emended in accordance with the LXX, as Kittel's text suggests. There is virtually no consonantal change and the resultant text reads as the translation above. Tr.]

title of God had been revealed to Abraham in a similar form of disclosure to that which we have in Ex. 6.2 with the name Yahweh. Apart from the passage cited, Gen. 17.1, the solemn divine name 'El Shaddai' occurs in P only in Gen. 28.3; 35.11; 48.3 (and in 43.14 in a context where the source is doubtful) on special occasions. There is evidence of it elsewhere in the Old Testament only in Ezek. 10.5. The shorter name for God, 'Shaddai', which is connected with it, occurs more frequently, partly in very old parts of the Old Testament (Gen. 49.25; Num. 24.4, 16), partly in late Old Testament writings (especially in the Book of Job), but in the latter clearly as a mysterious and archaic name for God. There can be no doubt that we have here a very old divine title. In the full form 'El Shaddai' it is comparable with other compositions with the word 'El' (= 'God') as they occur in the old patriarchal tradition as divine names at Palestinian sanctuaries which are occasionally well defined (cf. Gen. 14.18–20; 16.13; 21.33; 33.20; 35.7). The title 'El Shaddai' too certainly comes from the group of these old Palestinian divine names, though there is no cult place mentioned in the tradition at which it originally had its home. In P it serves as *the* divine title of the patriarchal period instead of the large number of titles evidenced in the old sources. Many different hypotheses have been advanced to explain the name 'Shaddai', but none of them is really convincing. The LXX usually rendered 'Shaddai' by *Pantocrator*; following this the Vulgate translated it *deus omnipotens*, which is a forerunner of the translation 'God Almighty' in all the English versions. We may ask whether P still knew the significance of this divine title which had already been handed down over a long period. In any case this significance was hardly very important for him. More important was the fact of a name unknown to the Patriarchs but now newly revealed to Moses and thus to Israel; and, as a name could not be just empty sound, a new name necessarily also represented a new revelation. In Ex. 6.2 ff. P refers to the promise made by God as 'El Shaddai' to Abraham in Gen. 17.1 ff. The promise of land confirmed by a covenant (cf. Gen. 17.8a) is expressly guaranteed (vv. 4, 8) and the explanation of the firm association between God and people which is given with the 'covenant'-formula to Abraham for himself and his posterity (cf. Gen. 17.7b, 8b) is likewise repeated (v. 7a). But the new thing which the new divine name signifies is this, that God now means to fulfil the promises which are still outstanding by acting in history in the Exodus from Egypt (vv. 6, 7b), indeed that he has

already made a beginning in so far as he has already heard the
sighing of the Israelites and has remembered his covenant (v. 5). The
divine name Yahweh is bound up with this great historical action
which now begins as a new revelation of God. Moses is sent as a
messenger from God to proclaim this action to the Israelites (vv.
6 ff.).

Moses delivers his message from God, but finds no response from
the Israelites whom P excuses because of their very straitened situation. Moses is then addressed a second time by God (v. 10) and in
addition to the task of messenger of God, which he had been
originally as in J (3.16 f.), now receives the further task of engineering
the Exodus of Israel from Egypt in person by requiring the release
of Israel from Pharaoh (cf. 3.10 E). In the face of this difficult task
Moses, to avoid the new charge and with reference to the failure of
his proclamation to the Israelites which has already occurred, objects
that he is unskilled in speaking (v. 12). In this context P uses the
drastic expression 'of uncircumcised lips' in which the word 'uncircumcised' bears the transferred meaning 'incompetent'. [7.1–7]
At this point Aaron is given to him as a spokesman, just as in the
secondary section 4.13–16, and here too, just as in 4.16, the relationship of Aaron to Moses is explained as that of a prophet to God
(7.1). Aaron is introduced as Moses' brother, but is nevertheless
clearly supposed to be as well-known a figure as is Moses himself in
6.2. The prediction of the stubbornness of Pharaoh serves to announce the great divine signs and wonders (7.3) which will eventually be followed by the great act of God against the still stubborn
Pharaoh, the Exodus of Israel (7.4 f.; cf. 3.18 ff.). The details about
the ages of Moses and Aaron (7.7) fit in with P's special interest in
chronological information of this sort. The age given for Moses is in
complete harmony with the details in Deut. 34.7 according to which
Moses finally died at the age of a hundred and twenty, after forty
years' wandering in the wilderness. The ancestor of the priesthood,
Aaron, was known to the later Priestly tradition as the elder brother
of Moses (cf. also 6.20 in the secondary insertion examined above);
he is here made three years older in age.

The content and language of the P section 6.2–7.7 raise the question of its relationship to the description given in the older sources in
3.1–4.17. The affinities are so close that it can hardly be doubted
that P knew the older narratives, knew them moreover when they
had already been interwoven and had been expanded by secondary

additions. For P, as has been demonstrated in detail above, has in his composition included elements not only from J and E but also from the additions in ch. 3 and 4. P collected together the older material and simplified it, but still reproduced the essential content in his own language. There is a notable deviation in the fact that in P we have the introduction of Aaron without any derogatory remark being made about Moses (not so in 4.13–14aα).

6. DIVINE SIGNS AND WONDERS BEFORE THE STUBBORN PHARAOH: 7.8–10.29

8 And the LORD said to Moses and Aaron, 9 'When Pharaoh says to you "Prove yourselves by working a miracle," then you shall say to Aaron, "Take your rod and cast it down before Pharaoh, that it may become a serpent."' 10 So Moses and Aaron went to Pharaoh and did as the LORD commanded; Aaron cast down his rod before Pharaoh and his servants, and it became a serpent. 11 Then Pharaoh summoned the wise men and the sorcerers; and they also, the magicians of Egypt, did the same by their secret arts. 12 For every man cast down his rod, and they became serpents. But Aaron's rod swallowed up their rods. 13 Still Pharaoh's heart was hardened, and he would not listen to them; as the LORD had said.

14 *Then the Lord said to Moses, 'Pharaoh's heart is hardened, he refuses to let the people go.* 15 *Go to Pharaoh in the morning, as he is going out to the water; wait for him by the river's brink,* [*and take in your hand the rod which was turned into a serpent*]. 16 *And you shall say to him, "The* LORD, *the God of the Hebrews, sent me to you, saying, 'Let my people go, that they may serve me in the wilderness; and behold, you have not yet obeyed.'* 17 *Thus says the* LORD, *'By this you shall know that I am the* LORD: *behold, I will strike the water that is in the Nile* [*with the rod that is in my hands, and it shall be turned to blood*], 18 *and the fish in the Nile shall die, and the Nile shall become foul, and the Egyptians will loathe to drink water from the Nile.'" '*

19 And the LORD said to Moses, 'Say to Aaron, "Take your rod and stretch out your hand over the waters of Egypt, over their rivers, their canals, and their ponds, and all their pools of water, that they may become blood; and there shall be blood throughout all the land of Egypt, both in vessels of wood and in vessels of stone." '

20 Moses and Aaron did as the LORD commanded; [*in the sight of Pharaoh and in the sight of his servants,*] he [*lifted up the rod and*] struck the water that was in the Nile, [*and all the water that was in the Nile turned to blood*]. 21 *And the fish in the Nile died; and the Nile became foul, so that the Egyptians could not drink water from the Nile;* and there was blood

throughout all the land of Egypt. [22] But the magicians of Egypt did the same by their secret arts; so Pharaoh's heart remained hardened, and he would not listen to them; as the LORD had said. [23] *Pharaoh turned and went into his house, and he did not lay [even] this to heart.* [24] *And all the Egyptians dug round about the Nile for water to drink, for they could not drink the water of the Nile.*

[25] *Seven days passed after the* LORD *had struck the Nile.* **8** [1] *Then the* LORD *said to Moses, 'Go in to Pharaoh and say to him, "Thus says the* LORD, *'Let my people go, that they may serve me.* [2] *But if you refuse to let them go, behold, I will plague all your country with frogs;* [3] *the Nile shall swarm with frogs which shall come up into your house, and into your bedchamber and on your bed, and into the houses of your servants and of your people, and into your ovens and your kneading bowls;* [4] *the frogs shall come up on you and on your people and on all your servants.' " '* [5] And the LORD said to Moses, 'Say to Aaron, "Stretch out your hand with your rod over the rivers, over the canals, and over the pools, and cause frogs to come upon the land of Egypt!" ' [6] So Aaron stretched out his hand over the waters of Egypt; and the frogs came up and covered the land of Egypt. [7] But the magicians did the same by their secret arts, and brought frogs upon the land of Egypt.

[8] *Then Pharaoh called Moses [and Aaron], and said, 'Entreat the* LORD *to take away the frogs from me and from my people; and I will let the people go to sacrifice to the* LORD.' [9] *Moses said to Pharaoh, 'Be pleased to command me when I am to entreat, for you and for your servants and for your people, that the frogs be destroyed from you and your houses [and be left only in the Nile].'* [10] *And he said, 'Tomorrow.' Moses said, 'Be it as you say, that you may know that there is no one like the* LORD *our God.* [11] *The frogs shall depart from you and your houses and your servants and your people; they shall be left only in the Nile.'* [12] *So Moses [and Aaron] went out from Pharaoh; and Moses cried to the* LORD *concerning the frogs, as he had agreed with Pharaoh.* [13] *And the* LORD *did according to the word of Moses; the frogs died out of the houses and courtyards and out of the fields.* [14] *And they gathered them together in heaps, and the land stank.* [15] *But when Pharaoh saw that there was a respite, he hardened his heart, and* would not listen to them; as the LORD had said.

[16] Then the LORD said to Moses, 'Say to Aaron, "Stretch out your rod and strike the dust of the earth, that it may become gnats throughout all the land of Egypt." ' [17] [And they did so;] Aaron stretched out his hand with his rod, and struck the dust of the earth, and there came gnats on man and beast; all the dust of the earth became gnats throughout all the land of Egypt. [18] The magicians tried by their secret arts to bring forth gnats, but they could not. [So there were gnats on man and beast.] [19] And the magicians said to Pharaoh, 'This is the finger of God.' But Pharaoh's heart was hardened, and he would not listen to them; as the LORD had said.

[20] *Then the* LORD *said to Moses, 'Rise up early in the morning and wait for Pharaoh, as he goes out to the water, and say to him, "Thus says the* LORD,

'Let my people go, that they may serve me. [21] Else, if you will not let my people go, behold, I will send swarms of flies on you and your servants and your people, and into your houses; and the houses of the Egyptians shall be filled with swarms of flies, and also the ground on which they stand. [22] But on that day I will set apart the land of Goshen, where my people dwell, so that no swarms of flies shall be there; that you may know that I am the LORD in the midst of the earth. [23] Thus I will put a division between my people and your people. By tomorrow shall this sign be.' " ' [24] And the LORD did so; there came great swarms of flies into the house of Pharaoh and into his servants' houses, and in all the land of Egypt the land was ruined by reason of the flies.

25 Then Pharaoh called Moses [and Aaron,] and said, 'Go, sacrifice to your God within the land.' [26] But Moses said, 'It would not be right to do so; for we shall sacrifice to the LORD our God offerings abominable to the Egyptians. If we sacrifice offerings abominable to the Egyptians before their eyes, will they not stone us? [27] We must go three days' journey into the wilderness and sacrifice to the LORD our God as he will command us.' [28] So Pharaoh said, 'I will let you go, to sacrifice to the LORD your God in the wilderness; only you shall not go very far away. Make entreaty for me.' [29] Then Moses said, 'Behold, I am going out from you and I will pray to the LORD that the swarms of flies may depart from Pharaoh, from his servants, and from his people, tomorrow; only let not Pharaoh deal falsely again by not letting the people go to sacrifice to the LORD.' [30] So Moses went out from Pharaoh and prayed to the LORD. [31] And the LORD did as Moses asked, and removed the swarms of flies from Pharaoh, from his servants, and from his people; not one remained. [32] But Pharaoh hardened his heart this time also, and did not let the people go.

9 [1] Then the LORD said to Moses, 'Go in to Pharaoh, and say to him, "Thus says the LORD, the God of the Hebrews, 'Let my people go, that they may serve me. [2] For if you refuse to let them go and still hold them, [3] behold, the hand of the LORD will fall with a very severe plague upon your cattle which are in the field, the horses, the asses, the camels, the herds, and the flocks. [4] But the LORD will make a distinction between the cattle of Israel and the cattle of Egypt, so that nothing shall die of all that belongs to the people of Israel.' " ' [5] And the LORD set a time, saying, 'Tomorrow the LORD will do this thing in the land.' [6] And on the morrow the LORD did this thing; all the cattle of the Egyptians died, but of the cattle of the people of Israel not one died. [7] And Pharaoh sent, and behold, not one of the cattle of the Israelites was dead. But the heart of Pharaoh was hardened, and he did not let the people go.

8 And the LORD said to Moses and Aaron, 'Take handfuls of ashes from the kiln, and let Moses throw them toward heaven in the sight of Pharaoh. [9] And it shall become fine dust over all the land of Egypt, and become boils breaking out in sores on man and beast throughout all the land of Egypt.' [10] So they took ashes from the kiln, and stood before Pharaoh, and Moses threw them toward heaven, and it became boils breaking out in sores on man and beast. [11] And the magicians

could not stand before Moses because of the boils, for the boils were upon the magicians and upon all the Egyptians. [12] But the LORD hardened the heart of Pharaoh, and he did not listen to them; as the LORD had spoken to Moses.

13 *Then the* LORD *said to Moses, 'Rise up early in the morning and stand before Pharaoh, and say to him, "Thus says the* LORD, *the God of the Hebrews, 'Let my people go, that they may serve me.* [[14] *For this time I will send all my plagues upon your heart, and upon your servants and your people, that you may know that there is none like me in all the earth.* [15] *For by now I could have put forth my hand and struck you and your people with pestilence, and you would have been cut off from the earth;* [16] *but for this purpose have I let you live, to show you my power, so that my name may be declared throughout all the earth.*] [17] *You are still exalting yourself against my people, and will not let them go.* [18] *Behold, tomorrow about this time I will cause very heavy hail to fall, such as never has been in Egypt from the day it was founded until now.* [19] *Now therefore send, get your cattle and all that you have in the field into safe shelter; for the hail shall come down upon every man and beast that is in the field and is not brought home, and they shall die.' " '* [20] *Then he who feared the word of the* LORD *among the servants of Pharaoh made his slaves and his cattle flee into the houses;* [21] *but he who did not regard the word of the* LORD *left his slaves and his cattle in the field.*

22 And the LORD said to Moses, 'Stretch forth your hand toward heaven, that there may be hail in all the land of Egypt, upon man and beast and every plant of the field, throughout the land of Egypt.' [23] Then Moses stretched forth his rod toward heaven; *and the* LORD *sent thunder* [*and hail*], *and fire ran down to the earth. And the* LORD *rained hail upon the land of Egypt;* [24] *there was hail,* [*and fire flashing continually in the midst of the hail,*] *very heavy hail, such as had never been in all the land of Egypt since it became a nation.* [25] *The hail struck down everything that was in the field throughout all the land of Egypt, both man and beast; and the hail struck down every plant of the field, and shattered every tree of the field.* [26] *Only in the land of Goshen, where the people of Israel were, there was no hail.*

27 *Then Pharaoh sent, and called Moses* [*and Aaron*], *and said to* [*them*], *'I have sinned this time; the* LORD *is in the right, and I and my people are in the wrong.* [28] *Entreat the* LORD; *for there has been enough of this thunder and hail; I will let you go, and you shall stay no longer.'* [29] *Moses said to him, 'As soon as I have gone out of the city, I will stretch out my hands to the* LORD; *the thunder will cease, and there will be no more hail, that you may know that the earth is the* LORD'S. [30] *But as for you and your servants, I know that you do not yet fear the* LORD *God.'* [[31] (*The flax and the barley were ruined, for the barley was in the ear and the flax was in bud.* [32] *But the wheat and the spelt were not ruined, for they are late in coming up.*)] [33] *So Moses went out of the city from Pharaoh, and stretched out his hands to the* LORD; *and the thunder and the hail ceased, and* [*the rain*] *no longer poured upon the earth.* [34] *But when Pharaoh saw that the rain and the hail and the thunder had ceased,*

he sinned yet again, and hardened his heart, he and his servants. [35] So the heart of Pharaoh was hardened, and he did not let the people of Israel go; as the LORD had spoken through Moses.

10 [1] *Then the* LORD *said to Moses, 'Go in to Pharaoh; for I have hardened his heart and the heart of his servants, that I may show these signs of mine among them,* [2] *and that you may tell in the hearing of your son and of your son's son how I have made sport of the Egyptians and what signs I have done among them; that you may know that I am the* LORD.'

[3] *So Moses [and Aaron] went in to Pharaoh, and said to him, 'Thus says the* LORD, *the God of the Hebrews, "How long will you refuse to humble yourself before me? Let my people go, that they may serve me.* [4] *For if you refuse to let my people go, behold, tomorrow I will bring locusts into your country,* [5] *and they shall cover the face of the land, so that no one can see the land; and they shall eat what is left to you after the hail, and they shall eat every tree of yours which grows in the field,* [6] *and they shall fill your houses, and the houses of all your servants and of all the Egyptians; as neither your fathers nor your grandfathers have seen, from the day they came on earth to this day."'* [7] *Then he turned and went out from Pharaoh.*

[7] *And Pharaoh's servants said to him, 'How long shall this man be a snare to us? Let the men go, that they may serve the* LORD *their God; do you not yet understand that Egypt is ruined?'* [8] *So Moses [and Aaron were] brought back to Pharaoh; and he said to [them], 'Go, serve the* LORD *your God; but who are to go?'* [9] *And Moses said, 'We will go with our young and our old; we will go with our sons and daughters and with our flocks and herds, for we must hold a feast to the* LORD.' [10] *And he said to them, 'The* LORD *be with you, if ever I let you and your little ones go! Look, you have some evil purpose in mind.* [11] *No! Go, the men among you, and serve the* LORD, *for that is what you desire.' And [they] were driven out from Pharaoh's presence.*

[12] Then the LORD said to Moses, 'Stretch out your hand over the land of Egypt for the locusts, that they may come upon the land of Egypt, and eat every plant in the land, all that the hail has left.' [13] So Moses stretched forth his rod over the land of Egypt, *and the* LORD *brought an east wind upon the land all that day and all that night; and when it was morning the east wind had brought the locusts.* [14] *And the locusts came up over all the land of Egypt, and settled on the whole country of Egypt, such a dense swarm of locusts as had never been before, nor ever shall be again.* [15] *For they covered the face of the whole land, so that the land was darkened, and they ate all the plants in the land and all the fruit of the trees which the hail had left; not a green thing remained, neither tree nor plant of the field, through all the land of Egypt.* [16] *Then Pharaoh called Moses [and Aaron] in haste, and said, 'I have sinned against the* LORD *your God, and against you.* [17] *Now therefore, forgive my sin, I pray you, only this once, and entreat the* LORD *your God only to remove this death from me.'* [18] *So he went out from Pharaoh, and entreated the* LORD. [19] *And the* LORD *turned a very strong west wind, which lifted the locusts and drove them into the Red Sea; not a single locust was left in all the country of Egypt.* [20] *But the* LORD *hardened*

Pharaoh's heart, and he did not let the children of Israel go.
21 Then the LORD said to Moses, 'Stretch out your hand toward heaven that there may be darkness over the land of Egypt, [a darkness to be felt*].'²² So Moses stretched out his hand toward heaven, and there was thick darkness in all the land of Egypt three days; ²³ *they did not see one another, nor did any rise from his place for three days; but all the people of Israel had light where they dwelt.* ²⁴ *Then Pharaoh called Moses, and said, 'Go, serve the* LORD; *your children also may go with you; only let your flocks and your herds remain behind.'* ²⁵ *But Moses said, 'You must also let us have sacrifices and burnt offerings, that we may sacrifice to the* LORD *our God.* ²⁶ *Our cattle also must go with us; not a hoof shall be left behind, for we must take of them to serve the* LORD *our God, and we do not know with what we must serve the* LORD *until we arrive there.'* ²⁷ But the LORD hardened Pharaoh's heart, and he would not let them go. ²⁸ *Then Pharaoh said to him, 'Get away from me; take heed to yourself; never see my face again; for in the day you see my face you shall die.'* ²⁹ *Moses said, 'As you say! I will not see your face again.'*

This section on the 'plagues of Egypt' is a formal entity. It is built up in a most symmetrical way and represents an independent whole even in content. It begins with Moses—after a number of passages in which he is accompanied by Aaron—coming before Pharaoh to require by order of his God the release of Israel from Egypt and confirming this demand by divine signs and wonders. This does not however lead to any concession from the stubborn Pharaoh. Thus the same events repeat themselves several times in a similar way, and at the close the situation is the same as it was at the beginning. The negotiations are broken off; this is stated expressly in 10.28 f. In addition, an anticipatory reference is made to 11.9 f., where once again a retrospective survey of the divine wonders in Egypt is given and it is finally asserted that the heart of Pharaoh remained hardened, just as it had been from the beginning. But it is not the case that the demands and the miraculous signs from God which Moses advanced at the behest of Yahweh were unable to achieve their purpose because everything foundered on the evil will of Pharaoh. Rather is it Yahweh himself who again and again brings about Pharaoh's unwillingness so as to display his wonderful power in Egypt and to the Egyptians in manifold ways. True, Pharaoh's unwillingness is expressed in different ways. Where the 'hardening' of Pharaoh's heart is mentioned it means on the one hand that

*This last phrase is no longer intelligible.

'Pharaoh's heart was hardened' (7.13, 22; 8.19; 9.35) and on the other that 'Yahweh hardened Pharaoh's heart' (9.12; 10.20, 27). Both formulae are thus used without differentiation, though there is an increasing tendency of the second to take precedence over the first. As, however, it had already been announced in 7.3 that Yahweh meant to 'harden' (with another Hebrew verb) Pharaoh's heart, we shall have to assume the narrator to mean that right from the beginning it was only Yahweh who was really at work. Wherever 'stubbornness'* is mentioned we have a similar case. First of all it is sometimes said that 'the heart of Pharaoh was stubborn' (7.14; 9.7) sometimes that 'Pharaoh made his heart stubborn' (8.15, 32; 9.34), but in 10.1 it is emphatically stated that Yahweh hardened the heart of Pharaoh and his servants. It is improbable that by this most inconspicuous change of formula the narrator had meant to express that what was at first human resistance was eventually followed by stubbornness caused by God as a punishment which brought about destruction. Rather does he still mean that from the beginning the divine demands and wonders stand opposed by the unwillingness of Pharaoh which is also caused by God. Pharaoh is thus as much a tool of the divine action on the one side, by acting with it without realizing this while following the dictates of his will (cf. Rom. 9.17), as is Moses on the other; all this happens so that many wonderful signs may take place in Egypt (10.1 f.; 11.9).

While it is now clear that the plagues form the subject of a section of the narrative complete in itself, it is less so that they are the contents of a single independent element of the tradition. True, they presuppose in general just the bondage of the Israelites in Egypt and the refusal of the Egyptian ruler to let them go. This supposition formed part of the Exodus theme from the beginning. But the story of the plagues has no real purpose; it ends with Moses' final departure from Pharaoh without any change in the situation. The story is directed exclusively towards the account of the Passover night and makes no sense without it. But the account of the Passover night is a separate independent piece of tradition (cf. pp. 88 ff. below), and not merely just the last section in the series of plagues. This is already clear from the fact that the preceding story of the plagues is clearly rounded off (10.28 f.; 11.9 f.) and that the account of the Passover

---

*[By using the rendering 'harden' throughout, the RSV obscures the fact, brought out here by Noth, that two different Hebrew roots are used in this expression. Tr.]

has quite a different construction, no longer following the very symmetrical scheme of the plague narrative. This situation leads us to the conclusion that the account of the Passover night occupies a primary place in the tradition in comparison with the plague narrative. In the Passover night Israel is freed from Egypt by the miraculous intervention of its God. The reason for this event being preceded by plagues which were shown before Pharaoh, who had been made stubborn by Yahweh himself, is that Yahweh wished to 'multiply' his 'signs and wonders' in Egypt. This is said expressly in 7.3 and is repeated once again in 11.9 in the retrospect over the plague narrative. Whenever in the Old Testament summary references to the mighty deeds of God at the beginning of the history of Israel speak in an apparently stereotyped phrase of the 'signs and wonders' at the Exodus from Egypt (Deut. 4.34; 6.22; 7.19; Pss. 105.27; 135.9, etc.) it is the plagues that they primarily have in mind.

The plague narrative is not a literary unity. At least two different narrative threads may be clearly distinguished. The mere fact of the juxtaposition and interweaving of two different expressions for the same idea which has been indicated above leads us to conclude that in the form in which the narrative has been transmitted a number of literary strata are present. We can even recognize two different narrative frameworks running alongside each other. According to one of these, which chiefly occurs in a compact narrative sequence in 18.16–19 and 9.8–12, Moses and Aaron from time to time initially receive instructions from God to perform certain actions which by virtue of the divine power result in plagues. These plagues, however, make no impression on the heart of Pharaoh, which remains 'hardened'. The other framework, of which the only compact example can be found in 8.20–32, has as a characteristic element the constant negotiations between Moses, the spokesman of his God, and Pharaoh. Each section of the narrative is made to begin with a demand from Moses to Pharaoh by order of Yahweh that Israel should be released, and with the announcement of the plague which is in store should Pharaoh not comply. The beginning of the plague is followed by a hasty recall of Moses and the request of Pharaoh that he should entreat with his God for the ending of the plague; but although this regularly happens the heart of Pharaoh again and again remains 'stubborn'.

With the help of the characteristics which have been mentioned, the two original narrative sequences can quite easily be separated one from the other; in accordance with their linguistic usage the former should be assigned to P and the latter to J. The literary critical question only becomes difficult right at the end of the plague narrative, from 9.13 on. It is clear that for the most part we have here the J narrative. But not only does the catchword 'harden' occur several times (9.35; 10.20, 27) but so does the scheme of introducing the narrative sections which is elsewhere characteristic of P (9.22 f.; 10.12 f., 21 f.); the difference is that in these cases the complete P narrative is no longer preserved, and so we must suppose that, when the strata were put together, in an unusual way preference was given to the J narrative over the P narrative. It has been popular to think of E in the narrative elements in question, but as the divine name Yahweh regularly occurs in them (9.22, 35; 10.12, 20 f., 27) this assumption has little probability. A special problem is the occurrence of the double expression 'God Yahweh' in 9.30. But whether this completely isolated word 'God' ('*lohīm*) appearing *alongside* the name 'Yahweh' can be used to prove the presence of E elements in the plague narrative seems very doubtful, especially as the textual tradition is not in full agreement at this point. The general state of the plague narrative speaks more for the hypothesis that only the sources J and P are to be detected in the plague narrative.

In this case we must assign to P: 7.8–13, 19, 20 a*a*, 21b, 22; 8.5–7, 15a*b*b, 16–19; 9.8–12, 22, 23a*a*, . . . 35; 10.12, 13a*a* . . . 20–22, . . . 27; 11.9 f. All the rest is substantially to be assigned to the J narrative.

In both literary strata the individual plagues belong together in a sequence and there can be no doubt that right from the beginning of the tradition 'many' divine signs and wonders were mentioned. Nevertheless we may ask whether in the course of what was primarily oral tradition the number of signs and wonders has not been further increased. In any case, towards the end of the narrative a number of discrepancies are revealed in the fact that occasionally something is destroyed in one plague which had already fallen victim to an earlier plague. Now and then attention is drawn to this discrepancy within the narrative itself, without the discrepancy being done away with. It remains doubtful whether from the beginning the narrative had suffered such discrepancies without paying any special attention to them, in the interest of a large number of signs and wonders, or whether the discrepancies first arose along with a gradual development of the plague theme. There is a further difficulty in the fact that the plagues which extend over the whole land of Egypt must also affect the Israelites in Egypt, which is hardly the real intention of the narrative. P generally pays no attention to this difficulty in his summary narrative. In J it is occasionally expressly said that the Israelites or their dwelling-places were excepted from the plagues through a further wonderful act of God (8.22 f.; 9.4, 26) but even in J this difficulty is not noticed consistently. It is thus evident that even the set of plague stories is not a well considered literary product but is derived from living oral tradition of the mighty acts of God towards his people. It is intended to lay special stress on the fact that it was the wonderful power of Yahweh alone which was at work in the Exodus from Egypt without Israel having to, or even being able to, do anything of itself.

[7.8–13] In an introductory passage 7.8–13 P reports the first demonstration of the wonderful power of Yahweh before Pharaoh. It is the first meeting between Moses and Aaron and Pharaoh which is explicitly mentioned within the P narrative. According to 6.11, at his call Moses received the charge to go to Pharaoh and require the release of Israel; in answer to his objection (6.12) Aaron was given to him to help to carry out this commission (7.1 ff.). If 7.6 narrates that Moses and Aaron 'did as Yahweh commanded them', this perhaps presupposes that they had already appeared before Pharaoh with their request for release, but of course without success. Be this as it may, they are now sent to Pharaoh and at the same time equipped with the power to carry out a miracle (7.8 f.). Pharaoh will require one if he is to believe them. Although it is not said in the extremely brief P narrative, this supposes that they are to put or repeat the request for release. In the old Pentateuchal narrative Moses was vouchsafed to change his rod into a serpent to authenticate himself as a messenger from God before the Israelites (4.1 ff.). P has transferred this element of the tradition into the context of the negotiations with Pharaoh, and has allowed Aaron to take over the action from Moses. The performance of this charge has the surprising result (7.10) that at the request of Pharaoh the Egyptian magicians who have been summoned are able in their turn to do the same miracle (7.11–12a). The Egyptian magicians—the word *ḥartom* which is rendered 'magician' in the RSV is perhaps a loan word from the Egyptian—of course have this power only by their secret arts, but nevertheless they have it. Here then is granted the reality of supernatural miracle-working among the 'heathen' which can be achieved through 'secret arts', i.e. 'magic', and which on occasion can be just the same as the effects produced by the wonderful power of the God of Israel. True, there is a basic difference in the source of the power, but this difference does not reveal itself outwardly and can only be believed and thereafter expressed. For Israel there is only the God who is experienced in history, from whom alone all working of miracles stems, and who places his working of miracles at the service of his actions in history. The miracle-working effected by 'secret arts' has moreover—though this of course is a practical and not a funda-mental difference—definite limits to its potentialities. The legitimate miracle-working of God is superior to it. This is evident both from the fact that according to the present section of the narrative the serpent produced from Aaron's rod is able to devour the serpents produced by the Egyptians (7.12), and also from the fact that in the continua-tion of the P narrative the Egyptian magicians can only just keep pace with the divine wonders. In this respect P has constructed his narrative quite methodically and systematically. In the first two plagues, which now follow, the Egyptian magicians can still act in the same way as Moses and Aaron do in the name of their God (7.22a; 8.7a), which produces the remarkable effect that the Egyptian magicians repeat the miracle despite the fact that it has already been performed and cannot possibly be repeated at that moment and despite the fact that they themselves seem to be spreading the plague in question over Egypt. At the next stage they are no longer in a position to emulate Moses and Aaron and must expressly recognize that 'the finger of God', i.e. the effective working of God (cf. Ps. 8.3), has a hand in their work and that therefore Moses and Aaron, as it might at first have seemed to outside eyes, are not for their part working with magic arts. As the Egyptian magicians could not attribute to Moses and Aaron a greater magic power than they themselves have at their disposal they cannot in the end but speak the truth (8.19). Finally the Egyptian magicians themselves are affected by the last plague and must retreat from the scene, never again to make an appearance (9.11).

[7.14–25] In the first real plague we have the tainting of all the water in Egypt so that it is no longer drinkable—a dreadful blow for all living beings, who need a daily supply of water. Here there are two different detailed descriptions of the plague, one alongside the other. According to one the water in the Nile, which is *the* source of Egypt's water supply, is made foul by a sudden, general death of fish, while according to the other all the water in the waterways of Egypt is turned to blood. The latter idea occurs in the shorter P version (vv. 19, 20a*a*, 21b, 22); in this great importance is attached to the statement that *all* the water in Egypt was made foul, hence the fairly long enumeration in v. 19 and the remark about the water 'in the trees and in the stones'* which can only refer to the sap of trees and the springs which rose from the rocks on the edge of the Nile valley. In the rather more detailed J version both ideas appear inter-connected. But the idea of the changing of water into blood was clearly only inserted from the P narrative into the J narrative at a subsequent time. Verse 17 in particular shows that all is not well in the transmitted J text by making a direct transition from a speech of Yahweh to a speech of Moses. It is moreover the case that in the formula of proclamation in which a 'Behold, I . . .' is followed by a Hebrew participle, elsewhere Yahweh always appears as the subject of the thought and the action (cf. 8.2; 8.21; 9.18; 10.4). Verse 17 therefore was originally worded in such a way that Yahweh remained the speaker right until the end. In that case then v. 20a*bb* also has been subsequently altered; in this part of the verse Yahweh would originally have been mentioned as the active subject. Now it is just these two verses, in which in a J context the water is said to have been changed to blood, which have demonstrably been altered and expanded at a later date. As the original conception in J spoke of Yahweh's 'striking' the water of the Nile, which may have been meant quite generally as a destructive action in a transferred sense, the secondary introduction of the narrative element of the 'striking' rod would easily commend itself with the difference that in the con-text of the J narrative, which makes no mention of Aaron, the rod is placed in Moses' hand with reference to 4.2–4 J. In connection with this narrative element reminiscent of P, the changing of water into blood was also taken over from P.

The original J narrative begins with the affirmation of the 'stubbornness' of Pharaoh, which according to J has already displayed itself in the first negotiations (5.1–6.1). Thereupon in v. 16 explicit reference is made with quite literal repetition to the demand from God which has already been made to Pharaoh in 5.1, a demand moreover which regularly appears in J whenever the plagues are next announced. It is not said why Pharaoh used to go out to the

*[This is a literal translation of the Hebrew text; there is no justification for the addition of the words 'vessels of' in RSV. Tr.]

water on the Nile bank every morning (so again in 8.20). Could the Israelite narrator have thought that Pharaoh used to wash himself every morning in the Nile (on this cf. 2.5 J)? It is immediately assumed that Pharaoh remained 'stubborn' at his meeting with Moses and therefore the plague is announced without conditions (not so in subsequent cases). In this way the plague begins, which from the beginning was intended to last for seven days (v. 25). This first time Pharaoh allows it to pass silently over himself and over Egypt by defiantly going 'into his house' (v. 23) and remaining stubborn. In their desperation the Egyptians meanwhile try to dig for water, but according to the narrator with scant success, so that it was a very serious plague.

Some have wished to derive the idea of the poisoning of the Nile water and the changing of it into blood from the polluted appearance of the Nile and the reddening of its rising water as a consequence of the various alluvial deposits which it carries along. But this was a process which repeated itself once a year and which, as even the Israelite far removed from Egyptian life would certainly have known, did not make the water of the Nile in any way undrinkable and did not kill the fish in the river. Rather do we have here a unique divine wonder which is specially related to the situation in Egypt only in so far as the Nile and its water are of decisive significance for the whole of Egyptian life. Moreover, the state of the tradition suggests that in Israel the story was chiefly told in the version in which the Nile was polluted by a great death among the fishes (so J). In this case any connection with the yearly rise of the Nile seems most improbable. The P version, with the change of all the water in Egypt into blood, which heightens the miracle and the plague still further, presumably rests only on a literary process; for as P in 7.8–13 once referred back to the old narrative 4.1 ff. he presumably allowed himself to be guided in his description of the first plague by the thought of the story in ch. 4, which was already known to him with its secondary expansions, and in v. 9 of which the theme of the changing of water into blood appears.

It is not considered that the pollution of the Nile water must necessarily also have affected the Israelites in Egypt.

[8.1–15] The plague of frogs is connected with the first plague in so far as it once again derives from the Nile or from all the waters of Egypt. In fact it appears less serious than the first plague; it is just very disagreeable and inconveniences daily life and activity. This plague too fits the special circumstances of Egypt, as the frog is an extremely well known phenomenon in an Egypt made humid through the overflowing of the waters of the Nile, and also plays a part in Egyptian mythology as an embodiment of life-giving power.* In the Palestinian homeland of Israel, on the other hand, it had no significance. The word 'frog' occurs in the Old Testament only in connection with the Egyptian plague (apart from the present passage only in Pss. 78.45; 105.30). Of course, the fact that the frog, instead of appearing as a representative of the renewal of life, becomes a fearful plague through its prevalence and its penetration into all the places in the land is a unique divine miracle. Here too we hear nothing of how the Israelites in Egypt fared during the plague.

Here too in accordance with his scheme P tells the story quite briefly (8.5–7, . . . 15a*b*b). The usual note about the 'hardening' of Pharaoh's heart is omitted from the closing remark 15a*b*b in view of more explicit information about the 'stubbornness' in J (v. 15a*a*). In J it is explicitly announced (8.2–4) that if Pharaoh refuses to accede to the divine demand the plague will follow. The scene is not a meeting on the bank of the Nile, but takes place in Pharaoh's palace, where Moses has been instructed to present himself (8.1) after an interval of seven days, as Pharaoh had withdrawn into the palace in the face of the first plague. The announcement of the plague vividly describes the impending infiltration of the frogs right into the most remote rooms of the houses and into the furnishings and utensils of everyday life; indeed they will even come up on men, among whom even Pharaoh himself is included, so that he suffers the greatest personal inconvenience from the disagreeable plague. In view of the P section 8.5–7, J's customary remark that 'Yahweh did' as he had threatened which elsewhere occurs at this point is omitted; it is in any case assumed that Pharaoh persisted in his refusal although this is not expressly stated. The plague of frogs, which Pharaoh has to endure with everyone else, in this instance causes him for the first time—and thereafter again and again in J—to have Moses summoned while the plague is happening (the name Aaron has in view of the P narrative been subsequently inserted in many places, but not absolutely consistently, into the J text) and to ask him to entreat Yahweh to end the plague (8.8) .Thus Pharaoh indirectly acknowledges that Yahweh, whom he had in the first negotiations still boasted that he did not know (5.2), is the paramount author of the

*Cf. H. Bonnet, *Reallexikon der ägyptischen Religionsgeschichte*, 1952, pp. 198 f.

plagues and thus is the only one who can put an end to them, and that as the spokesman of Yahweh Moses must therefore be effective as an intercessor before Yahweh. He supports his request by a promise to let Israel go (8.8b) which is neither meant seriously nor regarded by Moses as being meant seriously. Nevertheless Moses declares himself ready to accede to the request, for the ending of the plague will be just as much a sign of the power of God as the beginning of the plague. And so it happens. To make matters quite clear, Moses allows Pharaoh to give him a time at which he is to make his intercession (8.9 f.). Pharaoh will then recognize that, at the exact moment when Moses makes the agreed intercession, the plague will cease all at once through the sudden death of countless frogs, and it will in this way become clear to him that the death of the frogs did not happen by chance but was the work of the all powerful God who has none to equal him (8.10b). The death of the frogs then comes about as was foretold, and we now get a further glimpse of the extent of the plague from the fact that the dead frogs everywhere have to be gathered together in heaps (8.14). As soon as the plague ceases, Pharaoh immediately tacitly withdraws his forced 'permission' for Israel to depart; he remains 'stubborn' (8.15a*a*).

[8.16–32] Next there follows a fearful plague of insects. Here too the two versions P and J appear alongside one another. Each of the two uses a different word for the insects which come in tremendous numbers throughout Egypt. P speaks of 'gnats', whereas J uses a word which perhaps just has the general meaning 'insect', but which was understood as early as in the old Greek translation of the Old Testament to have the special meaning 'horse-fly', and is often understood in this way today. It is clear that we have here mere variants on one and the same subject. When, however, the redactor came to join the two strands of the narrative together, the difference in the catch-words which are used to describe the two plagues led him to think that two different plagues followed one another, and therefore the two variants are not inserted one in another as was the case previously, but are placed side by side. The result is that here for the first time the two variants are preserved completely intact.

The P variant 8.16–19 has the usual terse form. On Yahweh's command Aaron strikes the dust of the earth with his wand and by the divine working this earth is changed into a swarm of flies. The word here rendered as 'dust' (*'āpār*) does not really mean what we understand by dust, but the countless particles in the soil. It is often used in the Old Testament as a picture for something innumerable (cf. Gen. 13.16; 28.14; Isa. 40.12 etc.) and such a thought certainly plays a part here. If the soil of the land is changed into gnats, the result must be an enormous number of these insects, and this in its turn must represent an unbearable affliction upon both man and beast. Even in this instance we have a connection with a well-known phenomenon of life in Egypt; flies and gnats have always been a particularly troublesome feature of the country and at that time of course they arose in such unprecedented numbers that it was an overwhelming catastrophe.

J (8.20–32) narrates the course of this plague in his usual manner; the only difference is that the negotiations with Pharaoh gradually become longer and longer. For the first time, when the plague is announced it is also said that the Israelites in the land will be exempt from the plague. No flies are to come near the 'land of Goshen' in which Israel is pictured as living together, separate from the Egyptians (8.22, 23a), and in this special exception of the 'land of Goshen' Pharaoh is to see particular proof of the miraculous power of Yahweh.* Now for the first time Pharaoh, whom Moses had this time once again met in the morning on the bank of the Nile to announce the plague (8.20), but who is certainly to be found in his palace on the next day, for which the coming of the plague is threatened (8.23b), enters into discussion with Moses who has again been summoned hastily once the plague has begun (8.25 ff.). True, Pharaoh's request 'Make entreaty for me' in v. 28 looks very abrupt (according to the usual Hebrew way of speaking we would expect at least an 'and now' before it), so that we are justified in asking whether the passage 25b–28a is not a later addition to the narrative which would then originally have been written in the same way as 8.8. But as the narrative theme of the negotiations with Pharaoh is clearly heightened as the J narrative continues, we must continue to maintain the originality of the passage in question in spite of the formal discrepancy. First of all Pharaoh puts forward the proposal that the Israelites should be granted the sacrificial feast for their God, for which they would need to have a few days' holiday from their labour; but this feast must be held within the land so that Israel does not escape against the will of Pharaoh (8.25). Moses makes the obvious objection to Pharaoh; the nomadic sacrificial customs of the Israelites would be 'abominable' to the Egyptians, i.e. something

*On the 'land of Goshen' see von Rad, *Genesis*, pp. 394 f.

which gave cultic offence, and would raise a spontaneous and highly dangerous excitement among the Egyptians. It is here supposed that the Egyptians would see the Israelite sacrifice, although the Israelites in fact live by themselves in the land of Goshen. The thought behind the narrative conceives of quite a narrow space within which the Israelites and Egyptians were side by side. What would be the 'abomination' to the Egyptians is not clearly stated. The way in which v. 26 is written leads one to think of the special nature of the kind of sacrifice offered. According to ancient nomadic custom the Israelites, maintaining this custom in spite of their stay in the agricultural land of Egypt, would offer chiefly animal sacrifice and especially that of beasts from their flocks. In Egypt the sacrifice of whole animals including sheep and goats was not completely unknown, although it was not very usual; by preference a vegetable offering was made along with poultry and pieces of meat.* The Israelite narrator may have been thinking of this usual kind of Egyptian sacrifice when he described the Israelite whole offering of animals from the flock as 'abominable' to the Egyptians. At the same time the Israelites for their part would certainly act contrary to the Egyptian ideas of cultic propriety in respect of the place of the cult and the sacrificial ritual, and it is quite rightly supposed that people are usually particularly susceptible in the case of any cultic ceremonies which are held in their territory. All this goes to suggest that during their stay in Egypt up till now the Israelites had not sacrificed to their God. Quite surprisingly, Moses does not object that the Israelites for their part could not offer sacrifice in Egypt as it was a cultically foreign land and therefore 'unclean' for them. Perhaps the narrator paid no attention to this point; perhaps too he does not let Moses speak of it either as it would have made no impression at all upon Pharaoh. In any case, in advancing this objection Moses rejects Pharaoh's offer and repeats the demand of 5.3 that Israel should be released for a three days' march into the wilderness to offer sacrifice (8.27). Pharaoh declares himself agreeable to this proposition with the proviso that they do not go too far away in case perhaps they do not come back again (8.28a). As the sequel to the discussion shows, the narrator to begin with does not take this offer to be meant seriously (as distinct from the first proposal by Pharaoh). Nevertheless, on this occasion too Moses complies with the request for entreaty (8.28b) and shows that he does not trust Pharaoh's promise by his warning

*Cf. Bonnet, *op. cit.*, pp. 548 f.

against any repeated deception on the part of Pharaoh (8.29). But in any case, his God will once again display his power in making an end of the plague of insects. It is once again agreed that entreaty shall be made the following day, and events follow the same course as they did in the previous instance.

[**9.1–7**] The story of the plague upon the cattle, which destroys all the beasts that are in Egypt, is told without variants in only one form, which is a literary unity. It displays the characteristics of the J description: the plague is announced as imminent should Pharaoh refuse, the Israelites are to be exempted from the plague—and this indeed happens as Pharaoh takes pains to discover through a special investigation (9.6, 7a), and despite everything Pharaoh's heart remains 'stubborn'. Now of course this section displays remarkable discrepancies and deviations from the narrative scheme of J. In the first words spoken by Moses there is an abrupt transition from the usual Yahweh-speech delivered by Moses as a messenger (v. 1) to a speech of Moses, so that in the announcement of the plague proper Yahweh is mentioned in the third person (vv. 3 f.). In what follows we miss the theme of the summoning of Moses while the plague is raging and the negotiations which lead up to a request for Moses to make entreaty. In connection with the latter, it may of course be said that once the plague had suddenly begun and had done its work it ended quite of its own accord. But it still remains striking that the element of negotiation with Pharaoh after the beginning of the plague is completely lacking. Add to this the formal discrepancies which have already been noted and we are forced to the conclusion that the section represents a secondary addition to the J narrative which, while making use of the customary J formulae, does not fit into the framework of the J narrative completely smoothly.

[**9.8–12**] The story of the boils is told only in P and in a way which is quite characteristic of P. Here Moses himself performs the action which leads to the plague; Aaron, whose rod has hitherto played some part, appears only as the assistant of Moses. The ashes from the kiln which Moses throws into the air spread out as 'dust' (here we have the proper word for what we call dust) all over Egypt and fall down on all living beings, causing boils and sores to erupt. Egypt has always been a land of many skin diseases (cf. Deut. 28.27). It may have been a popular idea that they were caused by 'dust'. Here the special feature is the general extent of the visitation. As elsewhere in P, we are not told how the Israelites fared, still less how Pharaoh himself fared, which is all the more striking as here for the last time in P the Egyptian magicians appear and are all smitten with boils. Within the P narrative it is quite understandable that even the animals were affected, but on looking at the narrative as it has now been compiled one may well ask how it comes about that there are still any beasts left in Egypt after the events narrated in 9.1–7 apart from the cattle possessed by the Israelites.

[9.13–35] The section about the plague of hail is quite extensive; the main part of it belongs to J, while in accordance with what has been said above on p. 70 P is only incompletely represented with the short sentences in 9.22, 23a*a*, . . . 35. These do however at least show that P too narrated the plague of hail. In the J narrative a great deal of space is taken up with the element of the negotiations with Pharaoh. Verses 14–16 are striking in connection with the announcement of the plagues. Its purpose is to explain why hitherto Yahweh has allowed the divine signs and wonders to have no effect on Pharaoh: it was Yahweh's will to display his 'power' to Pharaoh in ever new ways and with ever mounting effect, and thus to know that his fame was spread over all the earth, as men would still tell everywhere of the wonders which he did in Egypt. This reflection of course corresponds to the general meaning of the whole of the plague narrative, but in this position it appears too early, for we would now expect it to be followed by the final decisive act of Yahweh. This expectation is also aroused by the language at the beginning of v. 14; according to this Yahweh will now 'send all his plagues upon the heart of Pharaoh'. What this expression means is questionable. As the words 'all my plagues' can hardly mean 'the sum of my plagues' in the sense of 'the climax of the plagues' the emphasis should clearly be placed on the words 'upon your heart'; the meaning would then then be that Pharaoh should take all the plagues—those which have already happened and those which are now announced—to heart (an interpolator, who inserted the clumsily attached reference to the servants and the people of Pharaoh, already misunderstood it in this way). The secondary character of the passage is also shown in the reference to the 'pestilence' in v. 15, i.e. to the secondary section 9.1–7. But even if vv. 14–16 are cut out as secondary the announcement of the plague still remains unusually lengthy. This is because in a surprising way Moses goes on to recommend the Egyptians to take what precautions are possible against the destructive work of the plague which is announced for the next day. The threatened hail, which is to fall with unusual fulness and violence (9.18), will of course destroy the plants growing in the land, but this is not the chief object of the remark, as it goes without saying and no possible precautions can be taken. But men and beasts can be brought home for safety (9.19). That the narrative imagines that men would be able to take effective safety precautions throughout the whole of Egypt for themselves, their workpeople in the field and their cattle once again shows the narrow bounds within which events are conceived to take place. In this part of the story the narrator has the Egyptians themselves confronted with a test of their belief. As distinct from Pharaoh himself, who in the view of the narrator shows himself to be 'stubborn' even in this special instance, and from a number of his 'servants', there were also 'servants of Pharaoh' who took Yahweh's announcement seriously and followed the recommendations of Moses (9.20 f.). Here Pharaoh's 'stubbornness' shows him to be particularly stiff-necked. At the same time, in a very subtle way, the reason is given why there should still be cattle left in Egypt even after this plague, as is later supposed in the account of the Passover night. According to the present sequence of the narrative there should have been no cattle among the Egyptians even before the plague of hail; but as 9.1–7 proved to be secondary this discrepancy did not occur in the original J narrative. So the hail comes, accompanied by terrifying thunderstorms, particularly terrifying because this was something completely unknown in Egypt; once again the land of Goshen is not affected (9.23abb–26). At the onset of the plague Pharaoh unconditionally acknowledges himself to be guilty before Yahweh, who is in the right in that he has demonstrated with signs and wonders before Pharaoh that he is the only powerful God (9.27). At his request, supported by the promise to let Israel go, Moses declares himself ready to go out of the city, i.e. to the place where the Israelites are dwelling, as soon as he leaves Pharaoh—and not on the following day as hitherto—and make entreaty to bring the plague to an end. The fact does not of course escape him that even this time Pharaoh did not mean his promise seriously (9.29 f.). So this plague too comes to an end. A supplement put in at a somewhat unsuitable place (9.31 f.) goes on to remark that the late-ripening wheat and spelt had not come up far enough for them to be ruined by the hail. In this way there was still something left for the plague of locusts which now follows.

[10.1–20] A plague of locusts is one of the most feared of all catastrophes in the East; it usually destroys in the shortest time imaginable every green thing that grows, and results in dreadful famine. Such is the plague which in unparalleled degree (10.6*ab*, 14b) is inflicted upon Pharaoh and the Egyptians. In this section too fragments of a P variant occur again (10.12, 13a*a*, . . . 20) according to which the raising of Moses' (not Aaron's) rod at the divine command as in 9.22, 23a*a* lets loose the plague. The J narrative stands to the fore-front of the section; it is exceptionally detailed, as the element of the negotiations with Pharaoh is taking up more and more room. On this occasion Moses, on being ordered to go once again into Pharaoh's palace, is told right at the beginning that the reason for this is the 'stubbornness' of Pharaoh. This 'stubbornness' is the occasion of the ever-renewed miraculous signs which are afterwards to be handed down in Israel from generation to generation (10.1 f.). Now too for the first time, since hitherto J has always supposed that Moses' execution of the first command goes without saying and has there-fore made no special mention of it, we are told how Moses goes to Pharaoh. Also in this context we have the first report of the demand to which Pharaoh is to accede (10.3–6a) after which special mention is made of the departure of Moses from Pharaoh (10.6b). In this skilful way J has purposely effected a heightening of the plague narrative. The reproachful question at the beginning of the address to Pharaoh is also new. Moses' speech expressly refers to the previous plague of hail and thus notes that the hail had still left some of the growing plants and trees (10.5b, cf. also v. 15). Nothing was said of this in the original J narrative of the plague of hail. For the first time Pharaoh is advised by his servants to be reasonable, before the onset of the plague announced for the next day (10.7). Some of these 'servants' had already taken matters seriously as early as the plague of hail (9.20) and, although even the 'servants' are laid under the constraint of the stubbornness sent by God (10.1), they have not yet become so foolish after what has happened up till now as to have lost all common sense. So before the plague begins Moses is recalled once more for a discussion which in fact comes to nothing. For Moses can do nothing but request the release of all Israel with all the cattle they possess, as all the men and all the beasts must come along to 'hold a feast to the Lord' (10.9). Pharaoh refuses him roundly with a remark which is clearly meant ironically (10.10a) as he—not in-correctly—suspects that Israel purposes something which in his eyes is 'evil' (10.10b). He will at least—and this proposal is now meant quite seriously—keep back the families and cattle of the Israelite men to ensure their return. As Moses (though this is not explicitly said) naturally does not agree to this, he is sent away once again in dissension (10.11b). The tension is already reaching a climax. The plague comes and does its work of destruction with uncanny speed. So Pharaoh 'in haste' (10.16) recalls Moses yet again. Again Pharaoh acknowledges his guilt and 'only this once' requests pardon. He asks Moses to make entreaty for the ending of the plague without making any deceptive promise, and Moses as before is quite ready to accede to the request, in this case immediately. Thus this plague too comes to an end.

[10.21–29] The section about the plague of the 'darkness over Egypt' has been transmitted in a remarkably fragmentary way. Again we find elements of a short P version in 10.21 f., 27 which in this case may even have been preserved complete. In it the rod of Moses (not Aaron) once again plays a part; it is lifted up to heaven and thereupon brings complete darkness over Egypt for the space of three days. It has been supposed that the idea of 'darkness over Egypt' is connected with a phenomenon occurring in Egypt in early summer. The hot south-east wind comes and often for some days fills the air so strongly with dust that the atmosphere grows dark. In that case this plague would be envisaged as a rare heightening of a not altogether unusual happening. Of course this connection is not very probable. Perhaps we should rather think of darkness as representing calamity, as being the realm of evil powers of chaos, so that as the last in the series of plagues the 'darkness over Egypt' was a specially impressive and dangerous visitation even if we hear nothing of any material damage.

The J version is preserved only in part; its beginning has fallen victim to the amalgamation with P so that we can no longer establish how detailed it was in its original form. Perhaps the redactional omission of the beginning suggests that it was only brief, in which case after the noticeable heightening in the previous plagues J in this instance made his narrative quite brief so as to indicate that the possibilities of negotiation were now virtually exhausted. Verse 23 presupposes the announcement and the beginning of the plague, further details are given about the effect of the plague, and we are told that in a miraculous way the Israelites in their place were free from its effects. Pharaoh has Moses summoned to make a last request. As an advance on 10.11a he now expresses himself agreeable that all Israel shall depart; only the cattle of the Israelites are to be left behind to guarantee their return (10.24). Moses replies with a remark which is certainly to be understood ironically (10.25) and bluntly rejects this last offer of Pharaoh with the pertinent observation that sacrificial beasts will be necessary for the feast in the wilderness and that only at the place and time will the kind and number of the sacrificial victims be made known through the proclamation of the divine will. Thus Israel must have all the cattle they possess at their disposal and cannot look for sacrificial beasts first, take them along, and leave the rest of the cattle behind (10.26). Thereupon Pharaoh breaks off negotiations with a threat which is apparently meant seriously (10.28). A continuation of the series of plagues as hitherto now no longer appears possible. Now only a new way of divine action can continue.

7. PASSOVER NIGHT AND THE EXODUS: 11.1–13.16

11 ¹ *The* LORD *said to Moses, 'Yet one plague more I will bring upon Pharaoh and upon Egypt; afterwards he will let you go hence; when he lets you go, he will drive you away completely.* ² *Speak now in the hearing of the people, that they ask, every man of his neighbour and every woman of her neighbour, jewelry of silver and of gold.'* ³ *And the* LORD *gave the people favour in the sight of the Egyptians. Moreover, the man Moses was very great in the land of Egypt, in the sight of Pharaoh's servants and in the sight of the people.*

4 And Moses said, 'Thus says the LORD: *About midnight I will go forth in the midst of Egypt;* ⁵ *and all the first-born in the land of Egypt shall die, from the first-born of Pharaoh who sits upon his throne, even to the first-born of the maidservant who is behind the mill; and all the first-born of the cattle.* ⁶ *And there shall be a great cry throughout all the land of Egypt, such as there has never been, nor ever shall be again.* [⁷ *But against any of the people of Israel, either man or beast, not a dog shall growl; that you may know that the* LORD *makes a distinction between the Egyptians and Israel.* ⁸ *And all these your servants shall come down to me, and bow down to me, saying, "Get you out, and all the people who follow you." And after that I will go out.' And he went out from Pharaoh in hot anger.*] ⁹ Then the LORD said to Moses, 'Pharaoh will not listen to you; that my wonders may be multiplied in the land of Egypt.'

10 Moses and Aaron did all these wonders before Pharaoh; and the LORD hardened Pharaoh's heart, and he did not let the people of Israel go out of his land.

12¹ The LORD said to Moses and Aaron in the land of Egypt, ² 'This month shall be for you the beginning of months; it shall be the first month of the year for you. ³ Tell all the congregation of Israel that on the tenth day of this month they shall take every man a lamb according to their fathers' houses, a lamb for a household; [4] and if the household is too small for a lamb, then a man and his neighbour next to his house shall take according to the number of persons; according to what each can eat you shall make your count for the lamb. [5] Your lamb shall be without blemish, a male a year old; you shall take it from the sheep or from the goats; [6] and you shall keep it until the fourteenth day of this month, when the whole assembly of the congregation of Israel shall kill their lambs in the evening. [7] Then they shall take some of the blood, and put it on the two doorposts and the lintel of the houses in which they eat them. [8] They shall eat the flesh that night, roasted; with unleavened bread and bitter herbs they shall eat it. [9] Do not eat any of it raw or boiled with water, but roasted, its head with its legs and its inner parts. [10] And you shall let none of it remain until the morning, anything that remains until the morning you shall burn. [11] In this manner you shall eat it: your loins girded, your sandals on your feet, and your staff in your hand; and you shall eat it in haste. It is the LORD's passover. [12] For I will pass through the land of Egypt that night, and I will smite all the first-born in the land of Egypt, both man and beast; and on all the gods of Egypt I will execute judgments: I am the LORD. [13] The blood shall be a sign for you, upon the houses where you are; and when I see the blood, I will pass over you, and no plague shall fall upon you to destroy you, when I smite the land of Egypt.

14 'This day shall be for you a memorial day, and you shall keep it as a feast to the LORD; throughout your generations you shall observe it as an ordinance for ever. [15] Seven days you shall eat unleavened bread; on the first day you shall put away leaven out of your houses, for if any one eats what is leavened, from the first day until the seventh day, that person shall be cut off from Israel. [16] On the first day you shall hold a holy assembly, and on the seventh day a holy assembly; no work shall be done on those days; but what every one must eat, that only may be prepared by you. [17] And you shall observe the feast of unleavened bread, for on this very day I brought your hosts out of the land of Egypt: therefore you shall observe this day, throughout your generations, as an ordinance for ever. [18] In the first month, on the fourteenth day of the month at evening, you shall eat unleavened bread, and so until the twenty-first day of the month at evening. [19] For seven days no leaven shall be found in your houses; for if anyone eats what is leavened, that person shall be cut off from the congregation of Israel, whether he is a sojourner or a native of the land. [20] You shall eat nothing leavened; in all your dwellings you shall eat unleavened bread.'

21 *Then Moses called all the elders of Israel, and said to them, 'Select lambs for yourselves according to your families, and kill the passover lamb.* [22] *Take a bunch of hyssop and dip it in the blood which is in the basin, and touch the lintel and the two doorposts with the blood which is in the basin; and none of you shall go out of the door of his house until the morning.* [23] *For the* LORD *will pass through to slay the Egyptians; and when he sees the blood on the lintel and on the two doorposts, the* LORD *will pass over the door, and will*

not allow the destroyer to enter your houses to slay you. [²⁴ *You shall observe this rite as an ordinance for you and for your sons for ever.* ²⁵ *And when you come to the land which the* LORD *will give you, as he has promised, you shall keep this service.* ²⁶ *And when your children say to you, "What do you mean by this service?"* ²⁷ *you shall say, "It is the sacrifice of the* LORD's *passover, for he passed over the houses of the people of Israel in Egypt, when he slew the Egyptians but spared our houses."* '] *And the people bowed their heads and worshipped.*

28 Then the people of Israel went and did so; as the LORD had commanded Moses and Aaron, so they did.

29 *At midnight the* LORD *smote all the first-born in the land of Egypt, from the first-born of Pharaoh who sat on his throne to the first-born of the captive who was in the dungeon, and all the first-born of the cattle.* ³⁰ *And Pharaoh rose up in the night, he, and all his servants, and all the Egyptians; and there was a great cry in Egypt, for there was not a house where one was not dead.* ³¹ *And he summoned Moses [and Aaron] by night, and said, 'Rise up, go forth from among my people, [both you and the people of Israel]; and go, serve the* LORD, *as you have said.* ³² *Take your flocks and your herds, as you have said, and be gone; and bless me also!'*

33 *And the Egyptians were urgent with the people, to send them out of the land in haste; for they said, 'We are all dead men.'* ³⁴ *So the people took their dough before it was leavened, their kneading bowls being bound up in their mantles on their shoulders.* ³⁵ *The people of Israel had also done as Moses told them, for they had asked of the Egyptians jewelry of silver and of gold, and clothing;* ³⁶ *and the* LORD *had given the people favour in the sight of the Egyptians, so that they let them have what they asked. Thus they despoiled the Egyptians.*

37 *And the people of Israel journeyed from Rameses to Succoth, about six hundred thousand men on foot, besides women and children.* ³⁸ *A mixed multitude also went up with them, and very many cattle, both flocks and herds.* ³⁹ *And they baked unleavened cakes of the dough which they had brought out of Egypt, for it was not leavened, because they were thrust out of Egypt and could not tarry, neither had they prepared for themselves any provisions.*

40 The time that the people of Israel dwelt in Egypt was four hundred and thirty years. ⁴¹ And at the end of four hundred and thirty years, on that very day, all the hosts of the LORD went out from the land of Egypt. [⁴² It was a night of watching by the LORD, to bring them out of the land of Egypt; so this same night is a night of watching kept to the LORD by all the people of Israel throughout their generations.

43 And the LORD said to Moses and Aaron, 'This is the ordinance of the passover; no foreigner shall eat of it; ⁴⁴ but every slave that is bought for money may eat of it after you have circumcised him. ⁴⁵ No sojourner or hired servant may eat of it. ⁴⁶ In one house shall it be eaten; you shall not carry forth any of the flesh outside the house; and you shall not break a bone of it. ⁴⁷ All the congregation of Israel shall

keep it. [48] And when a stranger shall sojourn with you and would keep the passover to the LORD, let all his males be circumcised, then he may come near and keep it; he shall be as a native of the land. But no uncircumcised person shall eat of it. [49] There shall be one law for the native and for the stranger who sojourns among you.'

50 Thus did all the people of Israel; as the LORD commanded Moses and Aaron, so they did. [51] And on that very day the LORD brought the people of Israel out of the land of Egypt by their hosts.]

[**13** [1] *The* LORD *said to Moses,* [2] *'Consecrate to me all the first-born; whatever is the first to open the womb among the people of Israel, both of man and of beast, is mine.'*

3 And Moses said to the people, 'Remember this day, in which you came out from Egypt, out of the house of bondage, for by strength of hand the LORD *brought you out from this place; no leavened bread shall be eaten.* [4] *This day you are to go forth, in the month of Abib.* [5] *And when the* LORD *brings you into the land of the Canaanites, the Hittites, the Amorites, the Hivites, and the Jebusites, which he swore to your fathers to give you, a land flowing with milk and honey, you shall keep this service in this month.* [6] *Seven days you shall eat unleavened bread, and on the seventh day there shall be a feast to the* LORD. [7] *Unleavened bread shall be eaten for seven days; no leavened bread shall be seen with you, and no leaven shall be seen with you in all your territory.* [8] *And you shall tell your son on that day, "It is because of what the* LORD *did for me when I came out of Egypt."* [9] *And it shall be to you as a sign on your hand and as a memorial between your eyes, that the law of the* LORD *may be in your mouth; for with a strong hand the* LORD *has brought you out of Egypt.* [10] *You shall therefore keep this ordinance at its appointed time from year to year.*

11 *'And when the* LORD *brings you into the land of the Canaanites, as he swore to you and your fathers, and shall give it to you,* [12] *you shall set apart to the* LORD *all that first opens the womb. All the firstlings of your cattle that are males shall be the* LORD's. [13] *Every firstling of an ass you shall redeem with a lamb, or if you will not redeem it you shall break its neck. Every first-born of man among your sons you shall redeem.* [14] *And when in time to come your son asks you, "What does this mean?" you shall say to him, "By strength of hand the* LORD *brought us out of Egypt, from the house of bondage.* [15] *For when Pharaoh stubbornly refused to let us go, the* LORD *slew all the first-born in the land of Egypt, both the first-born of man and the first-born of cattle. Therefore I sacrifice to the* LORD *all the males that first open the womb; but all the first-born of my sons I redeem."* [16] *It shall be as a mark on your hand or frontlets between your eyes; for by a strong hand the* LORD *brought us out of Egypt.'*]

The Exodus from Egypt comes about as a direct consequence of the slaughter of the Egyptian first-born on the night of the Passover. 12.41 = 12.51 expressly affirms that in the view of the present narrative this happening was the decisive event of the Exodus. This section was attached to the preceding plague narrative because in the slaughter of the first-born we have the last plague, which now produces the intended result, the release of the Israelites from Egypt. Indeed the aim underlying the plagues which have so far been narrated is more than achieved; not only does Pharaoh now at last declare himself ready to let Israel go with all their cattle, but he drives Israel out of his land with the greatest speed—in the middle of the night—because the overwhelming power of Yahweh has been shown to him in the slaughter of the first-born, and he now has to fear something even more deadly if Israel remains in his land even a moment longer. Nevertheless the account of the Passover night and the Exodus is a special element of the tradition which does not simply continue and conclude the plague narrative. It is even a primary and independent element of the tradition in comparison with the plague narrative which forms the basis for the development of the plague narrative. The story has its own particular arrangement. In the original form of the story (on 11.7 f. see pp. 92 f. below) the slaughter of the first-born is not announced to Pharaoh this time in advance; it takes place, and of course once it has taken place it is hardly a time for negotiations with Pharaoh. It is announced to Israel alone, because this time Israel must take precautions so as to be spared from the destruction which is to go out over Egypt. The precautions are of a cultic nature; they are described with the term 'Passover'. Now such a 'Passover' is to be held every year in Israel in the future, and the present tradition points emphatically to this by joining to the instructions for the preparation of the 'Passover' on that particular Passover night in Egypt the ordinance that this cultic usage is to be repeated every year in the future for all time in Israel as a commemorative representation of what Yahweh had done in Egypt to deliver Israel (12.14, 24–27a). There can therefore be no doubt that the present narrative of the Passover night and the Exodus gained its shape in the context of the Passover, which was thereafter celebrated every year; and if we are to understand it properly we must also keep in mind the later cultic history of the Passover. 'Passover' describes a sacrifice made by night or alternatively the animal used in this sacrifice. The Old Testament speaks of preparing ('keeping') the 'Passover' (sacrifice) (12.48 etc.), of killing the 'Passover'* (12.21 etc.) and of the 'sacrifice of the Passover' (12.27 etc.), but not on the

*[The word 'lamb', supplied by RSV, is understood in the Hebrew. Tr.]

other hand of a 'feast of the Passover' (this expression occurs in the Old Testament in Ex. 34.25 only and is certainly secondary). Apart from the meal which is customary at a sacrifice, the chief feature of this sacrifice is the apotropaic, prophylactic rite with the blood, which had to be sprinkled on the entrances to the houses. At some time of which we can no longer be certain, but in any case only on the soil of the cultivated land of Palestine, the nocturnal Passover sacrifice was combined with the 'feast of unleavened bread' (Mazzoth) which belongs to a series of agricultural feasts which derive from the pre-Israelite tradition of the cultivated parts of Palestine (so Ex. 23.15; 34.18). This was a (pilgrimage) 'feast' in the proper sense and is consistently described as such in the Old Testament. This combination of the two customs, which is presupposed in the festal calendars of Deut. 16 (vv. 1–8) and Lev. 23 (vv. 5–8) may go back to a time when the Passover sacrifice and the feast of unleavened bread fell approximately together; there may also have been special impetus towards it from the fact that at the Passover sacrifice also it was usual to eat 'unleavened bread and bitter herbs' (12.8). In its oldest literary form the account of the Passover night and the Exodus probably itself stems from this combination of Passover sacrifice and feast of unleavened bread (cf. 12.21–23 and 39) but in such a way that the Passover sacrifice stands continually in the foreground. This sacrifice has its own special cultic prehistory independently of the feast of unleavened bread. It stems from a different sphere of life from the agricultural feast of unleavened bread; for originally it almost certainly belonged to the milieu of nomadic shepherds and thus without doubt goes back to the time before they settled in a cultivated region. In this region, where more or less settled possessors of flocks were a not unsubstantial element of the population, it was still celebrated and combined with the feast of unleavened bread.

The account of the Passover night and the Exodus now transfers the origin of the Passover sacrifice into the unique situation of Israel's Exodus from Egypt. For the meaning seems to be that then for the first time Israel was given instructions for a nocturnal rite, hitherto still unknown to them, which would serve to protect both themselves and their cattle. Even the name 'Passover' seems to be made known to Israel now for the first time, and its significance is explained (12.13, 23, 27). Of course this explanation is extremely obscure. It derives the term *pesaḥ* (more familiar in English in the adjective 'Paschal', formed from the New Testament word *pascha* which reproduces the Aramaic form of the word) from a verb *psḥ* whose meaning cannot be established with any certainty. Etymologically it could mean 'to be lame', 'to limp', and it does in fact occur in the Old Testament in this meaning in II Sam. 4.4 and perhaps also in I Kings 18.21 (26). It has therefore been popular to render the word 'limp past' or 'leap past' in the account of the Passover night.But this appears extremely strained, and the word 'past', which is really essential for the Passover account, is not in fact properly contained in the word. So we may have a verb which is to be distinguished from the root 'to be lame', 'to limp' but whose real meaning is now as hidden from us as the significance of the word *pesaḥ*. The translation 'pass over' in the RSV is hypothetical, as any rendering must be. The explanations of the meaning of the term Passover do not in fact imply that then alone the Israelites must have understood what the 'Passover' was; they occur here because now the Passover is mentioned for the first time. Some expressions sound as though the Passover was not something completely new for the Israelites at the Exodus and suggest that it was the case of their performing a rite which they already knew for a special reason on a special occasion (12.11b*b*, 21b*b*). In fact we must ask whether the Passover does not belong to an earlier period of history than the Exodus, and whether it did not have some origin which we can no longer discover in the primitive dwelling-places of wandering shepherds. For cultic celebrations which are repeated every year usually derive from the exigencies of a life lived in a regular rhythm, and any precise historical reference is as a rule added only at a later date. We can certainly prove this in the festal calendars of the Old Testament, with their agricultural feasts, and it is therefore at least probable that we can do the same with the Passover sacrifice. We can easily understand the details we know of the Passover sacrifice from the circumstances of the lives of the nomadic herdsmen who even today, as always, move out in the spring from their winter grazing-grounds on the steppes and in the wilderness to summer pastures which are either in the neighbourhood of or actually in the cultivated region. Here in the dry season of the year, after the reaping of the fields, nourishment can still be found for their flocks, and when the work of cultivation begins again in the autumn they return to their winter pasturage. The beginning of their travels with the accompanying dangers for man and beast, especially for the new-born of whom the first-born were particularly precious, must have been the occasion for a special animal sacrifice, primarily to keep away evil powers. The apotropaic significance of the Passover sacrifice then comes out very strongly even in the Old Testament tradition, where alongside the rite with the blood we have the Passover sacrificed by night, for night was necessarily to a special degree the season for the attack of evil powers which had to be kept away. The situation of an imminent departure, which is a presupposition of the Passover sacrifice, is easily understandable in this context. Here belongs the preparedness of the participants for the march which was maintained even when Israel had become a settled nation (12.11), and here too perhaps also belongs the eating of flat cakes of quickly baked unleavened bread with the sacrificial meat, for 'bread baked quickly was unleavened'.* According to Bedouin custom it would have been baked fast on hot stones or on glowing ashes without any baking utensil.

In view of all this we should assume that the Passover sacrifice was already known, in the time before Israel became settled and before the stay in Egypt, as a cultic ceremony performed before the spring departure to the summer pasturage. It then acquired a particular historical reference as a constantly repeated cultic representation of the one great 'departure', namely the departure from Egypt, with the result that at the same time the account of the Exodus as now handed down at the Passover sacrifice was shaped along the lines of the Passover rite. A particular example of this is the element in the tradition which portrays danger completely surrounding Israel, who were protected by the apotropaic action of the sacrifice, danger which threatens the first-born of both man and beast. The mere fact that although the danger is really directed only at human first-born in the 'houses' (12.23b, 30b) reference is made, of course incidentally, but nevertheless consistently, to the first-born of beasts as well (11.5b; 12.29b; 13.15a) shows that the independent Passover ritual has had some effect on the Exodus narrative. This is evident most of all in the figure of the 'destroyer' (12.23b and less vividly also 12.13b),† for whose appearance no reason is given and whose relationship to Yahweh remains obscure. As it is improbable that this 'destroyer' was only introduced subsequently to avoid attributing to Yahweh the act of destroying the Egyptians, since it is generally said quite unthinkingly that Yahweh himself 'smote' Egypt, we must

*G. Dalman, *Arbeit und Sitte in Palästina* IV, 1935, p. 53.
†[Hebrew 'blow of the destroyer' for RSV 'plague to destroy'. Tr.]

clearly regard the 'destroyer' as an old element, derived from the
thought-world of the Passover sacrifice, which has not been completely integrated with the remarks about Yahweh's personal action
against the Egyptians. Therefore 'destroyer' will have been the
original name for the demonic power which the Passover sacrifice had
the effect of keeping away. In this way the tradition of the slaughter
of the first-born in Egypt may have derived from the Passover ritual
and the ideas associated with it and may in its turn have formed the
basis for the plague narrative. It was the occasion of the Passover
ritual, the departure of the herdsmen with their animals, which led
to its association with the Exodus from Egypt.

The section 11.1–13.16 is not a literary unity. This is shown in particular by the juxtaposition of 12.1 ff. and 12.21 ff. which clearly
indicates the presence of doublets. In 12.1–20 we have the usual
linguistic characteristics of P, and this is directly preceded in 11.9 f.
by the conclusion of the plague narrative in the style of P. After
12.20 the language characteristic of P occurs again in 12.28 and then
once more in 12.40–51. In this last section the almost verbal repetition
of 12.41b in 12.51 is striking. Such a repetition leads us to assume that
what lies in between represents a later addition to P at the end of
which the P narrative is taken up again with its last sentence. The
contents of the passage 12.43–50 are also strange, as the passage
almost completely ignores the situation in Egypt and presupposes
the settlement of Israel in a cultivated area. The individual note
12.42 is also to be counted an addition to P as it falls lamely after the
closing formulas of 12.40–41. Alongside this P material there is also
an apparently older narrative which from its character is certainly
to be regarded as Yahwistic. In it we come up against all kinds of
inconsistencies. The difficulties begin immediately, in 11.1–8. Quite
surprisingly, in 11.4 we are not told to whom the divine message
delivered by Moses applies. According to the first clauses this
message can only be directed to Israel, but as it goes on the situation
imperceptibly changes; now 'Yahweh' and the 'Israelites' are
spoken of in the third person and Pharaoh is addressed (11.7–8a).
Thereafter, the closing observation 11.8b presupposes a further
conversation with Pharaoh which is in no way possible for Moses in
J after 10.28 f. So in any case we must regard 11.7 f. as an ill-
considered addition made without any regard to the narrative
context—that is, if the whole passage 11.4–8 is not itself perhaps a
whole set of additions; it does not form an indispensable link in the J

narrative. The passage 12.21 ff. in any case belongs to the J narrative. 12.21–23 is here followed in 12.24–27a by a section with such striking elements of deuteronomistic language that we must certainly assume it to be a deuteronomistic addition to the J narrative, all the more so as we can again trace the contribution of a deuteronomistic commentator in ch. 13. In 12.29–39 apart from a few individual additions we have the compact and virtually complete J account of the Exodus. Thus we must assign to the original J narrative 11.1–6; 12.21–23, 27b, 29–39. Ch. 13 displays a deuteronomistic style throughout and is a deuteronomistic addition to the old narrative of the Exodus, which in a loose connection with this narrative puts forward regulations for the eating of unleavened bread and the sacrifice of the first-born. It is easy to understand how in the *locus classicus* of the Passover and feast of unleavened bread all sorts of material for regulating the performance of these ceremonies should have found a place.

[**11.1–8**] To the report of the last meeting between Moses and Pharaoh J directly attaches the divine proclamation of the decisive blow against Egypt which will lead to the speediest possible release of Israel from Egypt. Nothing is said, however, in this context about what form the blow is to take (11.1). In connection with the preparations for this event there now first of all appears a subsidiary theme of the Exodus narrative, the account of the outwitting of the Egyptians, in themselves well-meaning (11.2 f.). At the divine command the Israelites are to obtain from the Egyptians, among whom they are here pictured as living in neighbourly community, precious articles* which may perhaps be imagined as vessels or even pieces of jewellery. As when this theme is taken up again later it is observed that in this way the Israelites 'despoiled' the Egyptians (12.36b), it is supposed that the Egyptians, who first had no inkling of the imminent Exodus and then would hardly have been thinking of their valuables amidst the shrieks of the night of the Passover and the Exodus, were originally of the opinion that they would get the precious articles back again. Thus the 'request' (11.2; 12.35 f.) is to be understood as asking for a loan. It is not said how this borrowing on the part of the Israelites is to be justified. The Israelites are not reported as having acceded to the divine demands, but this is presupposed in v. 3 where the success of this action is implicitly

---

*[While the Hebrew word *k'lī* can be used of jewellery, it is normally quite general in meaning and therefore the RSV rendering is perhaps too precise. Tr.]

E.–D

confirmed. At the same time the opportunity arises of throwing light on Pharaoh's exceptional stubbornness and malice towards Israel; this was by no means caused by a wicked and provocative attitude on the part of the Israelites, for in themselves the Israelites, supported by the appropriate working of their God, were well liked in Egypt, and the manly form of Moses ('the man Moses') was highly regarded even among the 'servants of Pharaoh', even though these last could not help supporting Pharaoh (but cf. 9.20; 10.7 J). The theme of the 'despoiling' of the trustful Egyptians, completely alien to our way of thinking, is to be derived from the delight of the Israelite narrator in the successful deception of foreigners. No judgment of the subjective conduct is even considered; the only fact involved is that at this time Egypt was a power hostile to Israel.* Otherwise it is just a matter of an explicit subordinate theme in the Exodus narrative.

Moses now announces—apparently to the Israelites—in the form of a divine message which he has received and is handing on that as a final blow all the first-born in Egypt will be slain on the very next night (11.4–6). If this passage is original in J it gives the reason for the instructions which then follow in 12.21–23. The addition 11.7 f. (see pp. 92 f. above) after the example of 8.22 f.; 9.4 (10.23b) promises a special action which will exempt Israel, but overlooks the fact that in this case Israel is to receive further instructions for special precautions against the plague, which after 11.7 would be super-- fluous.

[**11.9–12.20**] There now follows in 11.9–12.20 a great compact P section. After the final words of P in the plague narrative (11.9–10), in 12.1–14 detailed instructions are given for the preparation and performance of the Passover sacrifice. The reason for these instruc- tions is only given at the end. The breadth and comprehensiveness of the instructions envisages the Passover sacrifice as later celebrated each year in peaceful times in a cultivated land and takes scant consideration of the critical situation of Israel immediately before the Exodus. The introductory remark about the beginning of the year interrupts the connection between v. 1 and v. 3; it corresponds to the form of delivering instructions and laws through Moses or through Moses and Aaron which is elsewhere usual in P (cf. e.g. 25.1). It is certainly an addition and is intended to provide a definite ruling that the year begins in the spring, a custom taken over in Israel from Mesopotamia in the eighth or seventh century BC, instead

*Cf. Gen. 30.25 ff. and von Rad, *Genesis, ad loc.*

of in the autumn, as in ancient Israel (cf. 23.16; 34.22). Secondarily it provides a cultic justification for this by placing Passover and Mazzoth in what is now the first month of the year. The instructions given for the Passover in vv. 3 ff. presuppose accurate calendar dates (vv. 3, 6) which were usual for festivals and feast days in the post-exilic period; in the older time the dates were determined by the natural course of the year. 'This month' in vv. 3, 6, if v. 2 is not original, means the current month, and that was for P even without v. 2 the first month of the year beginning in the spring, corresponding to the month Abib in the old Israelite calendar (cf. 23.15; 34.18). For the Passover sacrifice young male animals from the flock, i.e. sheep or goats, without any blemish, were necessary (vv. 3, 5) and this doubtless corresponds with old sacrificial custom. Likewise the offering of the sacrifice by families also belongs to the original rite (vv. 3b, 4), perhaps because the flocks, whom the sacrifice was chiefly to protect, were a family possession. It was only temporarily interrupted by the Deuteronomic demand for the centralization of even this cultic custom (Deut. 16.2, 5–7) but was later reinstated on the grounds of the old tradition, as the present P text shows. The casuistic* instructions, giving the most accurate details possible for the numbers to share in each lamb, and the consequent joining together of two smaller neighbouring families which is in some cases necessary, leads one to think rather of peaceful circumstances than of the situation of the Israelites in Egypt. The same is true of the ordinance that the animal must be taken as early as the tenth day of the month (v. 3) and then is to be 'kept' until it is killed on the fourteenth day of the month (v. 6). Do we perhaps have in this a secondary 'fragmentation' of the cult act on the occasion of a difference in the dating, which may have arisen from the false co-ordination of a new calendar to the rhythm of a natural year (cf. the separation of the Day of Atonement, to be observed on the tenth day of the seventh month, from the Feast of Tabernacles, which begins on the fifteenth day of the seventh month according to Lev. 23. 27, 39)? On the evening of the fourteenth day there follows the killing which begins the nocturnal sacrifice. It is said that the whole 'congregation of Israel' takes part in this killing (v. 6b) in so far as all the families act at the same time. The mention of the 'congregation' again recalls the later (post-exilic) Israel, whereas in Egypt Israel was not really a cult community, even for P. In the present chapter the word

*On casuistic law see pp. 174 f. below.

'congregation' occurs for the first time in the Old Testament, in connection with an act of sacrifice reported by P, who by way of an exception allows it to take place even before the founding of the legitimate cult on Sinai. Elsewhere P knows of no cultic action before the giving of the Law on Sinai. True, in the present section P avoids the real sacrificial terminology which he usually employs, but he can hardly have failed to understand that the Passover was a sacrifice, even if according to the original custom it was celebrated in the houses of the families and not in a (central) sanctuary. The old tradition of the Passover night at the Exodus from Egypt was so important that P could not but take it up, even if it could not be made completely to agree with his ideas of the beginning of the legitimate cult in Israel. The stipulation that the Passover sacrifice may not be boiled in water but must be roasted on the fire without being cut up (v. 9) is in conflict with the Deuteronomic ordinance of boiling (Deut. 16.7). In this point too, as earlier in the question of the place where the Passover victim is to be killed, P goes back behind the Deuteronomic law to the doubtless original rite. The demand that any meat remaining over on the next day is to be burned so that it is not profaned (v. 10) also certainly belongs to this original rite, as does the demand that all should be ready to depart (v. 11).

After all the necessary instructions have been issued, the reason for them is given in vv. 12 f. 'This night' (v. 12), on which all the first-born in Egypt are to be smitten, means the Passover night which has been described in the preceding instructions. According to vv. 3 and 6 at least a further five days must elapse between the moment of the proclamation and 'this night'. This does not agree with the J narrative, which in its announcement means the night immediately following (11.4–6). P wanted all the requirements of the Passover ritual to be observed accurately even in the situation before the Exodus. Whether something special is imagined in the 'judgments' which Yahweh will on that fateful night 'execute on all the gods of Egypt' (v. 12), or whether it simply means that Passover night will prove the powerlessness of the Egyptian gods, we can no longer decide. In v. 13 the meaning of the Passover sacrifice is described by P in old, derived and very solemn formulas (cf. v. 23 J); even the 'destroyer' occurs here, though in the context of a very vague expression.*

*On this verse cf. pp. 91f. above.

On the basis of the later connection between the Passover sacrifice and the feast of Mazzoth, vv. 15–20 enjoin the eating of unleavened bread for seven days beginning with Passover night. It is of course hard to imagine how the Israelites in Egypt could have kept the commandment to eat unleavened bread quietly for seven days after the fateful night, especially with a cultic assembly on the first and seventh days (v. 16). This passage again visualizes the situation in Palestine as also appears from the formal phrase 'a sojourner or a native of the land' (v. 19b). According to cultic usage feast days are counted from evening to evening (v. 18) so that the Passover night coincides with the first half of the first day of Mazzoth. The chief days of the feast of Mazzoth are the first and the last, for which a rest from work is enjoined with a solemn cultic proclamation (v. 16). This does not hold for the days of the feast which lie in between, as they are singled out only by an extremely emphatic demand for the eating of unleavened bread (vv. 15b, 19). In origin the feast of Mazzoth was a cult feast in the agricultural tradition of Palestine at the beginning of the grain harvest, at which the first produce of the land was offered for the cultic consecration of the harvest and eaten still uncontaminated by the addition of leaven.

[12.28] P's long instructions about the Passover sacrifice and the eating of unleavened bread close with the brief remark in 12.28 that all was carried out. The remark at the same time implies that the Egyptian first-born were also killed as was announced in the divine proclamation as the reason for the Passover sacrifice (12.12 f.), a fact which is not once observed elsewhere in P.

[12.21–27] The J narrative begins again in 12.21. After the announcement of the decisive blow against the Egyptians which is to take place on the coming night (11.4–6), Moses assembles the elders as the men responsible for the action which is to be taken among the families (clans), to give them instructions for the Passover sacrifice (vv. 21b–23). These instructions are chiefly concerned with the apotropaic smearing of the entrances to the houses with the blood of the sacrificial victims and once again add the prohibition against leaving the houses in view of the nocturnal destruction which is being wrought outside. The silent and worshipful accepting of the instructions by the 'people' (v. 27b) tacitly presupposes that the instructions are handed on by the elders. The deuteronomistic supplement vv. 24–27a, within which v. 24b is demonstrably an addition because of its singular address, which does not fit the framework, requires the retelling of the story of the Exodus at the Passover sacrifice which is to be repeated every year and thus presupposes this custom.

[12.29–39] In contrast to P, J reports the Exodus of Israel in comparatively great detail. After Israel had complied with the instructions for Passover night (though this is not explicitly remarked in J), and after the first-born, as was announced in 11.4–6, had been killed (v. 29), Pharaoh and all Egypt with him were so overwhelmed with the fearful action of the God of Israel (v. 30) that despite the final breaking off of negotiations, which according to 10.28 f. he had desired, he now has Moses called once again, immediately and while it was still night (v. 31), not for further negotiations but to give him immediate permission to depart with all the conditions which he had required (vv. 31 f.). Indeed he even asks that Israel will procure for him the blessing of the God of Israel at the feast which they purpose in the wilderness and thus indirectly recognizes that up till now he has been under the powerful and effective curse of this God who has visited him with all the plagues right up to this last one. Now he can no longer say, as he had in 5.2, that he does not know Yahweh; he has come to know him in all his fearful reality. Does he expect even now that the Israelites will return and bring with them the blessing of their God? Perhaps not. But the blessing of the God who has power even over Egypt will in any case have its effect upon him and upon the Egyptians even without the presence of the Israelites. So far for the Israelites the way of departure is free and the Egyptians, who now no longer think of the valuables which they have lent (vv. 35 f.; cf. pp. 93 f. above), urge Israel to depart quickly in the fear that something even more dreadful might come upon Egypt (v. 33). But the Israelites were not prepared for the need to depart so quickly; they had not provided themselves with food for the journey, but on the Passover night had only prepared the dough which they would bake the next morning for their daily needs, as they were used to do day by day. So now in their sudden departure by night they had to take the bread with them in the kneading bowls (v. 34) before it had even been mixed with the leaven, and on the following day could only bake bread from that while they were on the way, bread which would only be unleavened cakes as they had no leaven to hand (v. 39). This is how J explains the combination of the Passover sacrifice and the feast of unleavened bread which follows. Here we are clearly concerned not with the perhaps very ancient custom of eating unleavened bread *at* the Passover sacrifice, but with the eating of Mazzoth *after* the Passover night. J too therefore begins from the later combination of the two originally independent cultic ceremonies of the Passover sacrifice and the feast of unleavened bread. Now his explanation is much more enlightening than that of P. Whereas in P there is no reason at all why the Israelites should continue to eat unleavened bread in Egypt for seven days after the Passover night and we are given no idea of how this was at all practicable, J gives a completely pertinent explanation of the historical situation. P was interested in the cultic ordinances as such, and even where he derived them from a definite event in history on the basis of an old tradition he still gave a complete formulation of these cultic ordinances as they were valid for his time, even at the cost of historical probability. J seems to have envisaged only one day of eating unleavened bread after the Passover night. This may correspond with the original and more ancient festal custom, in which case the extension of the feast to seven days is the result of a later development, in the course of which the cultic character of the ceremony was as in other feasts heightened and increased. We can no longer tell the origin of the number given in v. 37b for the departing Israelites, but in any case it exceeds enormously what is even in the slightest degree historically probable. We can no longer make out who the accompanying 'mixed multitude' are thought to be (v. 38; cf. also Num. 11.4). Perhaps at the root of it lies the quite correct idea that other elements besides the Israelites were customarily employed as forced labour in Egypt and that they now took the opportunity to escape in similar fashion. The departing Israelites began their journey from the neighbourhood of the town of Raamses (cf. on 1.11) and first went to Succoth (v. 37a). 'Succoth' represents the Hebraising of the Egyptian town-name *Tkw*. The ruins of this *Tkw* are to be found on the present *tell el-maskhūṭa* in the *wadi ṭumēlāt* east of Pithom (cf. on 1.11); it is therefore situated in approximately the middle of the isthmus between the gulf of *es-suwēs* and the Mediterranean Sea (cf. further 13.20 J).

[**12.40–51**] With 12.40 f. P concludes the account of the Exodus. The detail of the four hundred and thirty years for the stay of the Israelites in Egypt is probably connected with the whole chronological system of the Priestly writing and has been constructed on this basis.* Nearest to it is the mention of four hundred years in Gen.

*Cf. von Rad, *Genesis*, p. 67.

15.13b which is, however, an addition there and more probably is the result of the rounding off of the number four hundred and thirty. This figure does not fit in with the observation in Gen. 15.16 according to which the fourth generation would already have left Egypt;* moreover, the addition to P in Ex. 6.13-30 only counts on four generations from the sons of Jacob to Moses. From a historical point of view this last calculation, which gives us a period of round about a century, is certainly much nearer the truth than the estimate of four hundred years or more, which has all historical probability against it. Along with this chronological information P reports briefly and ceremoniously the 'Exodus from Egypt' without even hinting at the connection between this event and the happenings of Passover night (v. 41); the knowledge of this connection is tacitly assumed. 'That very day' can really only refer to the day last described in the preceding narrative, which would be the last day of the feast of unleavened bread—the twenty-first day of the month. In view of the earlier mention of the seven days of unleavened bread the reference of a remark such as 'that very day' is in fact obscure (so too the same expression in 12.17).

The addition about the 'night of watching' (12.42) surely means that on the Passover night—for this must be meant—Yahweh 'kept watch' to a special degree, as indeed he never either slumbers or sleeps, and that as a commemoration of this the Israelites afterwards kept this night every year as a night of 'watching'. This is evidently also meant to provide the explanation of an expression used at a later date, 'a watch for Yahweh', which certainly refers to the Passover night.

The additional Passover regulations, which are principally concerned with the question of admission to the Passover sacrifice, quite ingenuously presuppose the later situation of an agricultural community with the mention of 'natives of the land', 'sojourners' and 'strangers', and with the assumption that the Israelites had slaves and day labourers. Strangers staying in the land of Israel are to have the same rights as Israelites if they submit to the regulations about circumcision which apply to Israel. Bought slaves belong to the *familia* of their master; they are to be circumcised and then they too may take part in the Passover sacrifice. Foreigners, on the other hand, remain excluded, as do 'sojourners' and 'hired servants' whom we should think of as being primarily merchants and foreign workers.

*Cf. von Rad *ad loc.*, p. 182.

The domestic character of the Passover is stressed in v. 46, as is the necessity that the slaughtered and roasted Passover victim be left so whole and intact that not a bone of it is broken. John 19.36 refers to this last regulation, which also occurs in Num. 9.12.

[**13.1–16**] The deuteronomistic section 13.1–16 is hardly all of a piece, but has apparently been inserted gradually; this is clear from the division of the regulations for the first-born at the beginning and end of the section and from the appearance of a plural address in vv. 3 f. in the middle of a passage which is otherwise written in the singular. In connection with the eating of unleavened bread at Succoth (so J 12.39) it is ordained that every year unleavened bread is to be eaten in the month of the Exodus when in the future the Israelites live in Palestine (vv. 5–10). Unleavened bread is moreover to be eaten for seven days (as 12.15 ff. P) with a pilgrimage feast on the last day (12.16 requires rest from work on the first *and* last day). All is to serve as a 'memorial' of the Exodus and a re-enactment of its happenings (cf. 12.24–27a deuteronomistic). To explain the term 'remembrance', metaphorical language is used; 'a sign on the hand' and 'a memorial between the eyes' (v. 9). This would originally mean tattooing on the hand and jewelled ornaments which hung over the forehead down as far as the bridge of the nose. In v. 16 (as in the related passages Deut. 6.8; 11.18) the technical term *ṭōṭāpōt* is used to describe these ornaments; its root meaning 'drops' indicates the droplike shape of such articles. The original significance of these things, which has receded right into the background in the Old Testament narratives, is that they were the signs of membership of definite cults and were at the same time prophylactic amulets; later they were used only as 'signs of remembrance' of something, and in this sense Deuteronomy and the deuteronomistic literature occasionally speak metaphorically of them. Later Judaism once again understood this metaphorical language literally and based the custom of 'prayer bands' on hand and forehead upon the Old Testament passages which have been just cited. The passage with the plural address, vv. 3 f., gives the month of Exodus its old Hebrew name Abib (otherwise P in 12.[2], 18 with the numbering of the months), without however giving the exact day of the month for the eating of unleavened bread (otherwise P in 12.18). On 13.3–10 cf. especially Deut. 16.1–8.

The regulations about the first-born (cf. 34.19–20a and on this pp. 263 f. below), which are loosely attached to the narrative of the killing of the Egyptian first-born and hardly suppose that the Passover was really a sacrifice of the first-born, stem from the general clause (vv. 1 f.) that all first-born (from the mother's point of view) and in particular all male first-born (so expressly vv. 12, 15 and Deut. 15.19 with respect to the first-born of beasts) belong to God and are to be consecrated to God, not only the beasts, but also the men (cf. 22.28b). As with the fruits of the land, so too with living beings, each first produce is claimed by the deity who is the giver of the blessing which lies in fertility; originally it would have been intended that every first produce was to be sacrificed. There is no conclusive evidence that there was ever sacrifice of first-born humans in Israel which was regarded as legitimate. Instead, the sacrifice of the human first-born which was basically required of all men was replaced by a sacrifice of cattle and thus 'redeemed' (cf. 13b; on this see the traditional basis of Gen. 22). The special regulation for the corresponding redemption of the first-born sacrifice in the case of an ass rests on the fact that among the domestic animals the ass was not counted as a potential sacrifice (this is to be inferred from Lev. 11. 1 ff.; Deut. 14.4 ff.). In this case therefore a substitute offering had to be made, or otherwise the first-born of the ass, not being suitable for sacrifice but still claimed as the property of the deity, was killed and thus withdrawn from profane human use (v. 13a). The keeping of these ordinances about the first-born was again to be a 'memorial' of the divine action in killing the first-born of the Egyptians (vv. 14–16).

8. THE MIRACLE AT THE SEA*: 13.17–14.31

17 *When Pharaoh let the people go, God did not lead them by way of the land of the Philistines, although that was near; for God said, 'Lest the people repent when they see war, and return to Egypt.'* 18 *But God led the people round by the way of the wilderness toward the Red Sea. And the people of Israel went up out of the land of Egypt equipped for battle.* 19 *And Moses took the bones of Joseph with him; for Joseph had solemnly sworn the people of Israel, saying, 'God will visit you; then you must carry my bones with you from here.'* 20 *And they moved on from Succoth, and encamped at Etham, on the edge of the wilderness.* 21 *And the* LORD *went before them by day in a pillar of cloud to lead them along the way, and by night in a pillar of fire to give them light, that they might travel by day and by night;* 22 *the pillar of cloud by day and the pillar of fire by night did not depart from before the people.*

* Cf. Introduction, p. 11 n.

14[1] Then the LORD said to Moses, [2] 'Tell the people of Israel to turn back and encamp in front of Pi-ha-hiroth, between Migdol and the sea, in front of Baal-zephon; you shall encamp over against it, by the sea. [3] For Pharaoh will say of the people of Israel, "They are entangled in the land; the wilderness has shut them in." [4] And I will harden Pharaoh's heart, and he will pursue them and I will get glory over Pharaoh and all his host; and the Egyptians shall know that I am the LORD.' And they did so.

5 *When the king of Egypt was told that the people had fled, the mind of Pharaoh and his servants was changed toward the people, and they said, 'What is this we have done, that we have let Israel go from serving us?'* [6] *So he made ready his chariot and took his army with him,* [7] *and took six hundred picked chariots and all the other chariots of Egypt with officers over all of them.* [8] And the LORD hardened the heart of Pharaoh king of Egypt and he pursued the people of Israel as they went forth defiantly. [9] The Egyptians pursued them, all Pharaoh's horses and chariots and his horsemen and his army, and overtook them encamped at the sea, by Pi-ha-hiroth, in front of Baal-zephon.

10 When Pharaoh drew near, *the people of Israel lifted up their eyes, and behold, the Egyptians were marching after them; and they were in great fear.* And the people of Israel cried out to the LORD; [11] *and they said to Moses, 'Is it because there are no graves in Egypt that you have taken us away to die in the wilderness? What have you done to us, in bringing us out of Egypt?* [12] *Is not this what we said to you in Egypt, "Let us alone and let us serve the Egyptians?" For it would have been better for us to serve the Egyptians than to die in the wilderness.'* [13] *And Moses said to the people, 'Fear not, stand firm, and see the salvation of the LORD, which he will work for you today; for the Egyptians whom you see today, you shall never see again.* [14] *The LORD will fight for you, and you have only to be still.'* [15] The LORD said to Moses, 'Why do you cry to me? Tell the people of Israel to go forward. [16] Lift up your rod, and stretch out your hand over the sea and divide it, that the people of Israel may go on dry ground through the sea. [17] And I will harden the hearts of the Egyptians, so that they shall go in after them and I will get glory over Pharaoh and all his host, his chariots, and his horsemen. [18] And the Egyptians shall know that I am the LORD, when I have gotten glory over Pharaoh, his chariots, and his horsemen.'

19 *Then the angel of God who went before the host of Israel moved and went behind them; and the pillar of cloud moved from before them and stood behind them,* [20] *coming between the host of Egypt and the host of Israel. And there was the cloud and the darkness;* and the night passed without one coming near the other all night.*

21 Then Moses stretched out his hand over the sea; and the LORD drove the sea back by a strong east wind all night, and made the sea dry land, and the waters were divided. [22] And the people of Israel went into the midst of the sea on dry ground, the waters being a wall to them on

*See p. 115 n.

their right hand and on their left. [23] The Egyptians pursued, and went in after them into the midst of the sea, all Pharaoh's horses, his chariots, and his horsemen. [24] *And in the morning watch the* LORD *in the pillar [of fire and] of cloud looked down upon the host of the Egyptians, and discomfited the host of the Egyptians,* [25] *clogging their chariot wheels so that they drove heavily; and the Egyptians said, 'Let us flee from before Israel; for the* LORD *fights for them against the Egyptians.'*

26 Then the LORD said to Moses, 'Stretch out your hand over the sea, that the water may come back upon the Egyptians, upon their chariots, and upon their horsemen.' [27] So Moses stretched forth his hand over the sea, *and the sea returned to its wonted flow when the morning appeared; and the Egyptians fled into it, and the* LORD *routed the Egyptians in the midst of the sea.* [28] The waters returned and covered the chariots and the horsemen and all the host of Pharaoh that had followed them into the sea; not so much as one of them remained. [29] But the people of Israel walked on dry ground through the sea, the waters being a wall to them on their right hand and on their left.

30 *Thus the* LORD *saved Israel that day from the hand of the Egyptians; and Israel saw the Egyptians dead upon the seashore.* [31] *And Israel saw the great work which the* LORD *did against the Egyptians, and the people feared the* LORD; *and they believed in the* LORD *and in his servant Moses.*

After Israel's release from Egypt has been effected through powerful and terrible divine signs and wonders, there unexpectedly comes a further conflict with the Egyptians which is extremely dangerous for Israel. For although Pharaoh consented to the release of Israel, he nevertheless now summons up his powerful battle-strength in order to pursue the Israelites who have journeyed into the wilderness east of the delta and bring them back by force, not because he had already heard or could possibly have heard that they were not going on the pilgrimage into the wilderness which they had purposed (so J), but because afterwards he regretted his release of Israel. In the framework of the present narrative context this event acts as a postlude which in consequence of the miraculous divine help given to the Israelites comes to nothing. Of course in actual fact and within the history of tradition it is something more than just a postlude; in contrast it is the very act which was first and chiefly meant when Israel confessed Yahweh as 'the God who led us up out of Egypt'. In Israel one could speak in hymns of praise of the God who brought about the Exodus from Egypt and in so doing merely make concrete reference to the miracle at the sea (cf. for example Ex. 15.21; Ps. 114.1 ff.). From this point all the previous acts of God against the Egyptians seem like a prelude which culminates in the decisive event at the sea. In this way then the narrative of the deliverance at the sea is to be regarded as the real nucleus of the Exodus theme, and in the present tradition it forms not only the end but also the goal and climax of the whole, although at least in P the catchword 'come out' (Exodus) has already been discontinued earlier (12.41).

The narrative itself is quite short, but is nevertheless not a literary unity. We should not be surprised to find traces in this central section of all the different narrative voices which we have observed up till now. It is however immediately noticeable that there are different concrete presentations of the event itself; it is further striking that the word 'God' occasionally appears alongside the divine name Yahweh, which is used most frequently (13.17–19; 14.19) and that 'the king of Egypt' also occurs alongside the usual 'Pharaoh' (14.5a). The characteristics of the different sources are so clear and numerous that we can complete the literary-critical analysis with relative certainty. The P narrative is by far the most obvious. In 14.1–4 and 14.15–18 we have two pieces that belong together, each with the familiar linguistic characteristics of P. 14.5 cannot have been the original continuation of 14.1–4, as it refers to facts over and above what has already been said in P. On the other hand 14.8 represents the smoothly-fitting, direct continuation of the narrative strand of 14.1–4. 14.9aα is a doublet to what has already been reported in 14.8. The rest of 14.9 is however to be assigned to P in view of the reference to 14.2. 14.10bβ leads up to 14.15 and is therefore—perhaps together with 14.10a—likewise a piece of the P narrative. From 14.15–18 P onwards the continuation of this narrative strand is easy to follow. 14.21aαb–23 refer to the instructions and announcements of 14.15–18. The instructions of 14.16a find their counterpart in 14.26–27a, to which then the continuation 14.28 and the closing statement 14.29 belong. Thus the P material occurs complete and without a gap in 14.1–4, 8, 9aβb, 10abβ, 15–18, 21aαb, 22 f., 26, 27aα, 28 f. Between these P passages stand the elements of older narratives. These begin as early as 13.17–22. In this section the juxtaposition of two originally different descriptions is unmistakable; v. 20 comes too late after v. 18, moreover the word 'God' occurs continually in vv. 17–19, and the divine name 'Yahweh' in vv. 20 f., from which v. 22 is not to be separated. Thus we are to explain the passage 13.17–19 as Elohistic, and are supported in this by the fact that v. 19 refers to Gen. 50.25 E; so it may be established that here the E source again appears after a long interval. Verse 20(–22) joins on directly to 12.37(–39) J and is certainly to be assigned to J. In the pre-Priestly material of 14.5–7 we can again clearly distinguish two sources, indeed as early as v. 5. After it has been said in 14.3 P that Pharaoh seized what seemed to him to be a favourable opportunity to bring the Israelites back again, v. 5 says on the one hand that he received an obviously unexpected report which changed the situation for him (so v. 5a) and on the other hand that he changed his mind by repenting of the release which he had reluctantly granted without any astonishing news being necessary (v. 5b). Add to this the fact that v. 5a speaks in an unusual way of the 'king of Egypt', whereas directly afterwards we have 'Pharaoh' again in v. 5b, and there can be no doubt that v. 5 is composed of two different sources. As the 'king of Egypt' in 1.15 ff. belonged to a piece of the Elohistic source (see p. 23 above), 14.5a must be assigned to E and therefore 14.5b to J. It is next clear that we have a doublet in vv. 6 and 7, even if definite indications are lacking for assigning them to J and E. We cannot assert with certainty any discrepancies in the passage 14.11–14, but it is nevertheless striking that the answer of Moses in vv. 13 f. does not fit the reproach of the people in vv. 11 f. at all. Now as vv. 13 f. (with the divine name 'Yahweh') join smoothly on to v. 10ba ('and they were in great fear'), we can presume that vv. 11 f. come from E, even though there are no positive indications of this. 19a and 19b are again apparent doublets; as the word 'God' is used in v. 19a and the pillar of cloud is mentioned in 19b (cf. 13.20–22 J) the division of sources is here plain. 19b has a continuation in vv. 20 and 24, and in between v. 21 ab (with 'Yahweh') is another J piece in which a different word for 'dry land' is used from that in vv. 16, 22, 29 P ('dry ground'). The two Hebrew words here used for 'to be dry' are distributed between J and P in exactly the same way as they are in the story of the flood. In v. 27abb, where again there is a clear doublet to v. 28 P, we have a piece of J ('Yahweh'), and as this piece is connected with v. 25b this last half verse too (with 'Yahweh') is to be given to J; there are no indications in v. 25a which enable us to assign it to a source. The closing passage, vv. 30 f., is again certainly from J (cf. vv. 13 f. J). Thus we have a J narrative which has been preserved complete and continuous in 13.20–22; 14.5b, 6 (or 7), 9aa, 10bb, 13 f., 19b, 20, 21ab, 24, 25b, 27 abb, 30 f. E on the other hand is preserved only in fragments, in 13.17–19; 14.5a, 6 (or 7) . . . 19a. It is uncertain whether we are to assign 14.11 f. and 14.25a to J or to E.

[**13.17–19**] The E section 13.17–19, introduced by a subordinate clause (v. 17aa) which is presumably only redactional and serves as a connection, answers the obvious question why on their departure from Egypt the Israelites did not choose the most direct route to the cultivated land of Palestine which had been promised to them as their possession, that is, the well trodden trade and military route which from the eastern edge of the Nile delta crossed the wilderness of Sinai near the Mediterranean coast and reached the coastal plain of Palestine at the south-west corner, to lead first of all to Gaza, the first large city in Palestine. In this city of Gaza and in other cities of the same south-west coastal plain of Palestine the Philistines, coming from the Mediterranean world, settled themselves as over-lords after they had conquered it, and so it was possible to call this part of Palestine lying nearest to Egypt 'the land of the Philistines'. In a part of his narrative which is no longer preserved, E must have reported that Israel, hard pressed in Egypt (cf. 3.9 E) had left the land (cf. also below on 14.5a). Israel now began the march into the wilderness of Sinai under the guidance of God, which was exercised in a way of which we are not told. God now does not lead Israel to the land of the Philistines, because there Israel might expect to fight with the inhabitants of the land who would want to deny them access. The mention of the designation 'land of the Philistines', and the idea that certain fighting was to be expected on this particular way of approach, shows that E imagines the south-west coastal plain of Palestine to be inhabited by the Philistines with a warrior power which was justifiably feared by the Israelites for a long time. That is an anachronism, as the Philistines began to settle in this neighbour-hood only at the beginning of the twelfth century BC, by which time the occupation of Palestine by the Israelite tribes was virtually com-plete. Still, even before this the Palestinian coastal plain had been settled particularly densely with strong and powerful cities. If Israel —so argues E—was to recognize the difficulty of entering the Promised Land from this side when it was actually there, the people would in all probability have preferred to return to Egypt, although they had been uncomfortable enough under the oppression (3.9 E). But this was not to happen, for it was not at that time a question of Israel making its own decision about its future, but of the fulfilment of the divine plan of salvation, by which Israel was now to come into the Promised Land. Therefore Israel was led by God round by the 'way of the wilderness to the reed (*not* Red) sea' which was thus in any case not the direct way to Palestine. Unfortunately we can no longer make out where E located the 'reed sea', that is if he had any idea at all about geographical relationships in a neighbourhood far removed from the later habitations of Israel. The name 'reed sea' (*yam sūp*), in which the word 'reed' (*sūp*) is probably borrowed from the Egyptian, is too general to give a certain reference to the place. In I Kings 9.26, as is clear from the context, the gulf of *el-ʿaqaba* on the east side of the Sinai peninsula is described as the 'reed sea'. But this does not demonstrate for certain that in the Exodus tradition the same gulf of *el-ʿaqaba* was understood as the 'reed sea', especially as the north end of it is more than 120 miles as the crow flies from the eastern edge of the Nile delta. The indefinite description 'reed sea' in the Exodus tradition could also refer to the gulf of *es-suwēs* on the west side of the Sinai peninsula or to the stretch of sea north of *es-suwēs*; a 'way of the wilderness' also leads there from the eastern arm of the Nile, viz. from the *wādi ṭumēlāt*, and, moreover, in a south-easterly direction. The uncertainty of what E means by the 'reed sea' also affects the scene of the miracle at the sea; for with the information in 13.18 E doubtless means at the same time to bring Israel to the place at which the decisive rescue of Israel from the power of the Egyptians took place. The reflection by E in 13.17 f. rests on a consideration of the three themes, the Exodus from Egypt, the journey into the wilderness and the entry into the Promised Land. Originally the Exodus theme dealt only with the release of Israel from Egypt and their journey into the wilderness east of the delta. Historically too, it so happened that the Israelites on their departure from Egypt first of all aimed for the regions inhabited by nomads south of the settled land of Palestine, regions from which they had originally come.—The details of 13.19, like the remark which leads up to them in Gen. 50.25 E, derive from the fact that already in Old Testament times (cf. Josh. 24.32), as still today, there was a Palestinian local tradition which knew of a 'tomb of Joseph' at Shechem.

[**13.20–22**] From the neighbourhood of Succoth, where they had eaten the cakes of unleavened bread on the day after the Passover night (12.37–39 J), the Israelites according to J on the next day reach 'Etham, on the edge of the wilderness'. The name 'Etham' presumably represents the Hebraising of an Egyptian place name, but the basic Egyptian form can no longer be discovered and so the situation of this 'Etham' is completely unknown. If, as is probable, in the stereotyped formulations of 12.37a and 13.20 J was thinking of a day's march, he looked for 'Etham' a day's march from Succoth; the explanatory comment 'on the edge of the wilderness' also leads us to think of a place only a short distance from the cultivated land of the Nile delta, the *wadi ṭumēlāt*. This brings us, if the details in J are based on any concrete notion of geographical positions, to the seaboard north of *es-suwēs*. As J provides no more geographical indications before his account of the miracle at the sea, unless a piece of his narrative has been lost in the redactional interweaving of the sources, and has therefore with 13.20 brought Israel to the scene of the great saving act of Yahweh, the 'sea', which he mentions in 14.21a*b*, 27a*bb*, 30 was for him at the same place as 'Etham, on the edge of the wilderness'. He apparently presumes this to be known, as he does not explicitly state it. It is thus probable that J thought of the area mentioned as the scene of the miracle at the sea. The report of the pillars of fire and cloud in 13.21 f. is a retrospective description of the guiding of Israel to 'Etham', but has a significance over and above this, as the iterative imperfect in v. 22 shows, as a preliminary indication of the whole of the divine guidance of Israel in the wilderness. The narrative element of the pillars of cloud and fire in all probability derives from the Sinai tradition. Smoke rising like a cloud and fire are features of the theophany on Sinai (19.18 J), and the phenomenon of the pillars of cloud and fire presumably goes back to observation of an active volcano, to which allusion is without doubt made in the account of the events on Sinai. The pillars of cloud and fire showing the way which is to lead Israel to Sinai are already given to the Israelites as a divine guide, in J, from the Exodus onwards.

[14.1–4] P connects Pharaoh's decision to pursue Israel in 14.1–4 with the route of the departing Israelites. The Israelites do in fact alter their route at a special command from Yahweh. In P's view had they originally intended to take the usual direct route to Palestine? In any case, they are now directed away from the route originally planned to a place which is extremely accurately described in 14.2. Unfortunately we can no longer give the exact locations of all the places which are named there. In particular, the place with the apparently Egyptian name Pi-ha-hiroth is not known elsewhere and therefore can no longer be established; for this reason it is also irrelevant whether the Hebrew expression is to be translated 'in front of Pi-ha-hiroth' (as RSV) or 'east of Pi-ha-hiroth'. The place which we can locate most certainly is 'Baal-Zephon', by which a sanctuary is clearly meant.* This sanctuary of Baal-Zephon, on whose site in

*See O. Eissfeldt, *Baal Zaphon, Zeus Kasios und der Durchzug der Israeliten durchs Meer*, 1932.

the Hellenistic-Roman period a Zeus Kasios was worshipped, lay on a low hill in the now uninhabited place *maḥammadīje* on the western end of the coastal beach belt which separates the lagoon of what in classical times was called the Sirbonian Sea, the present *sebḫat berdawīl*, from the Mediterranean Sea. The region concerned is thus near to the Mediterranean coast east of the mouths of the Nile. If then in the closing clause of 14.2, which is obviously rather surprising but not necessarily secondary because of its address in the second person plural, it is expressly stressed that Israel is to camp 'in front of Baal-Zephon', the scene is meant to be the neighbourhood of the the western shore of the Sirbonian Sea. The further explanation 'between Migdol and the sea' also points to this. Migdol, which occurs as early as the Egyptian sources, lay on the usual route from the delta to Palestine not far north-east of the Egyptian border-fortress *Ṯr* and is probably to be located at the present *tell el-ḥēr*, whereas in this context the 'sea' must almost certainly be understood to be the Mediterranean Sea. The information given in 14.2 therefore in any case leads us to the neighbourhood of the direct route from Egypt to Palestine; but Israel is to leave the route at first proposed, in order to go into the region between this route, which still runs at some distance from the Mediterranean, and the Mediterranean (or the Sirbonian) Sea, there to encamp in front of Baal-Zephon. Now the Sirbonian Sea lay before Israel to the east, and this is certainly what is meant in the following passage by the hindrance which prevented Israel from continuing their journey away from Egypt. It is striking that it is in P, the latest of the sources, that we have such accurate information about the scene of the miracle, information moreover which leads towards an area different from that which is probably indicated by the somewhat indefinite descriptions in the older sources. We must therefore ask whether P here reproduces a very old and perhaps even authentic local tradition unknown to J and E, or whether we have here a secondary localization which locates Israel's deliverance at the sea in what seemed to be an appropriate place near the road connecting Palestine with Egypt which was much travelled at all times. No certain answer can be given to this question, but we must at any rate reckon with the second possibility as well. Pharaoh is now—this is certainly the meaning of P—informed, in some way of which we are not told, of the change in route of the departing Israelites, and concludes that they are now completely 'entangled' in the wilderness which no

longer offers them any track to follow. This seems to him to be a
favourable opportunity for falling upon them with his army and
dragging them back; Yahweh himself has strengthened him in this
resolve and in this sense has 'hardened his heart', because he now
means for the last time to show his glory in sight of Pharaoh and all
his proud host.

[14.5–9] Other reasons are given for Pharaoh's decision in the
older sources. In v. 5a E reports that Pharaoh was 'told' that 'the
people had fled'. This is an extremely surprising statement after everything which we have been told up till now; for hitherto it has not been
said and could not be said that Israel had 'fled' from Egypt, i.e. had
left the land without the knowledge and permission of Pharaoh, as
the climax of both the plague and the Passover narratives is that the
obstinate Pharaoh was finally compelled to consent to the departure
of Israel. Now we can hardly assume that the use of the word 'flee' by
the Elohist was just a *lapsus linguae* and that he—albeit in a clumsy way
—had only meant to say that Israel had departed against Pharaoh's
better judgment; for even the reference to the fact that Pharaoh
was 'told' shows that here some change in the situation for
Pharaoh is indicated. Thus the phraseology of the clause v. 5a, short
though this clause is and isolated though its position may be, must
be taken seriously in that here we have the expression of a tradition
which knew the story of a 'flight' of Israel from Egypt. Then there
only remains the question whether E narrated an eventual 'flight'
from Egypt, although the negotiations with Pharaoh were really
aimed at another outcome, or whether from the beginning he had
separated the events in Egypt from the eventual 'flight' of Israel. We
should at any rate notice that there is no certain indication of the
presence of E in the whole of the plague and Passover narratives. As
far as we are positively able to establish, E has only accounts of the
subjection of the Israelites in Egypt (1.15 ff.), the divine charge to
Moses to lead Israel out of Egypt (3.1, 4b, 6, 9 ff.), the return of
Moses to Egypt with this charge (4.17 f., 20b) and perhaps a fruitless
interview between Moses and Pharaoh about a relaxation of the
harsh forced labour (5.4). The account of a 'flight' from Egypt could
have fitted in well with this, but of course, in view of the now
extremely fragmentary condition of the E material in the combined
Pentateuchal narrative, the force of such an *argumentum e silentio*
should not be overestimated. The fact, however, remains that E
spoke of a 'flight', and in so doing preserved a trace at any rate of

what is doubtless a very old form of the Exodus tradition, whether it be that E consistently followed this form of the tradition and thus, as occasionally elsewhere, has preserved a particularly old stage in the development of the tradition, or whether it be that in this case E combined old traditional material with more recent developments. In any case it is clear that a 'flight' from Egypt by the Israelites provides an especially clear reason for the pursuit by the Egyptian host, and that in fact the story of the deliverance at the sea is very closely connected with the traditional theme of the 'flight'. As a reason for the pursuit, J says that Pharaoh 'changed his mind' (v. 5b) and thus once again picks up an element of the story which he had already used in the plague narrative, though this particular expression did not occur there; under the pressure of the plagues Pharaoh had already made all sorts of concessions which he took back again when the plagues ceased. Now he had consented to the release of Israel; but once the fearful Passover night was over he changed his mind.

In this way, then, the pursuit has been set in motion in all three sources. At the time of the Egyptian New Kingdom the chief feature of the Egyptian host was its chariots; these are now sent out. The language of v. 6b sounds as though Pharaoh himself went out with them in person, but the other remarks do not allow us to draw this conclusion with any certainty. Verse 7b says that there was also an 'officer' (Hebrew 'third man') on each of the chariots, so that all had their full complement; in making this observation the Israelite narrator does not have in mind the peculiarly Egyptian way of manning chariots, where the custom was to have a crew of two, one to drive the chariot and the other to fight from it, but the Hittite-Palestinian way according to which there was also a 'third man' on the chariot to act as aide and shield bearer to the warrior. In v. 8 P uses the particularly solemn phrase 'the Pharaoh, king of Egypt', which occurs occasionally elsewhere in his writings (cf. 6.11). At first the Israelites have no idea of the danger which threatens them; they carry out their Exodus 'with a high hand' (so Hebrew; RSV paraphrases 'defiantly'), i.e. still in confident self-assurance (the same expression also occurs in Num. 15.30 and there means 'deliberately').

As soon as the Israelites become aware of the Egyptian pursuit, they quite understandably become extremely afraid; they 'are in great fear' (v. 10a J), they 'cry to Yahweh' for help (v. 10b*b* P), they reproach Moses (vv. 11 f. E?). The chief thought here is certainly not that Israel is in an inextricable position because of the sea which prevents them from making any further progress; the mere fact that they are being pursued by a swift and powerful Egyptian chariot force is quite sufficient to make their situation appear hopeless. The complaint to Moses (vv. 11 f.) which is frequently repeated in a similar fashion in the later wilderness stories and which perhaps has its origin in the tradition in those stories, is here striking in so far as it refers explicitly to remonstrances made by the Israelites to Moses while they were still in Egypt, remonstrances which, however, have not yet occurred in the previous narrative. If there is an E fragment in vv. 11 f. we could assume that there is here a reference to a passage in the Elohistic narrative which is no longer preserved, but it is also conceivable that a later 'murmuring' of the people in a difficult situation should be expressed in a false reference to a fear which was supposedly expressed earlier. According to J, Moses meets the fear of the people with that cry of 'Fear not' which used to introduce the powerful attack of Yahweh to protect his people.* Yahweh himself will lead the war, and Israel need only stand there and witness the victory of Yahweh over the enemy (vv. 13 f.). This then is what Moses dares to say. Just as in J Moses is only the messenger sent to the Israelites in Egypt to announce to them the acts of Yahweh (3.16 f. J), so also now Yahweh himself will do everything. And it will be a sole occurrence; Israel will never again see the Egyptians defeated and annihilated so miraculously as this time (the *r*'*îtem* must be understood in the sense of a *futurum exactum*, which is quite possible from a linguistic aspect; for if we wanted to refer the 'see' in the subordinate clause to the present pomp of the Egyptian host, still in all its pride, the following expression 'never again' in the main clause would not really make sense).

[**14.15–31**] Now there follows the decisive section about the wonderful act of Yahweh. According to P, Yahweh first answers the 'cries' of the Israelites (v. 10b*b*) with a reproachful question; here Moses is addressed as the spokesman of the 'crying' Israelites (unless perhaps we are to assume that in the original text there stood 'Why do you [pl.] cry to me?') † After this, the Israelites, who had at first 'encamped' at the place which is fully described in v. 2, are instructed to depart (vv. 2, 9a*bb*). But their route as they do so, which is still thought of as being in an easterly direction, was—as we are to infer from what immediately follows—blocked by 'the sea'; and here P

---

*Cf. G. von Rad, *Der Heilige Krieg im alten Israel*, 1951, pp. 9 f.
†[The present Hebrew verb is singular. Tr.]

may have thought of the lagoon of the Sirbonian Sea. Thereupon Moses immediately receives the command to hold up his rod, which had already played a similar role in the plague narrative in P; by this action Moses is to 'divide' the sea so that a passage now appears through its midst. In v. 16a P has chosen a formula which might suggest that the rod had a purely magical effect, but his real meaning was certainly that Yahweh himself intended the 'division' of the sea which he effected to follow directly upon the raising of the rod which he had commanded. Thus the way is made clear for Israel, and it is indicated at least in hints that an overwhelming catastrophe is to come upon the pursuing Egyptians. The further course of events is pictured plainly and simply in P. Moses obeys the command (v. 21a*a*), the promised consequences follow (v. 21b), the Israelites enter the passage (v. 22) and the Egyptian host comes after them (v. 23). After the Israelites have gone through the passage and have again reached dry land proper on the other side, as is said in v. 29 in retrospect, Yahweh once more lets Moses raise his rod (v. 26), and as a consequence of this action (v. 27a*a*) the waters now begin to flow back, covering and completely overwhelming the Egyptian host, which is still in the passage (v. 26). So by a great wonder wrought by Yahweh Israel was finally saved from the danger that threatened them and from all the power of Egypt.

The narrative of the older sources is not so simple. All that is left of E is of course the fragment v. 19a. According to this the E description began in a similar way to that of J; the 'camp' of the Israelites was protected against the pursuing Egyptians by the interposition of a manifestation of the divine presence. In E this is the 'angel of god' who, as we learn here, used after the Exodus to go before the Israelites to lead them on their way. This 'angel' (literally 'messenger') 'of God' represents the divine presence itself; he is an ambassador of God, conceived of as in human form, who above all mediates the action of God which turns towards men and helps them.* He appears when God wishes to be near to earth and acts in the same way as God himself. E especially has spoken of him several times when it has been a question of God having dealings with men, so that excessively human expressions are not used of God himself. If then in E Israel is led in the wilderness by the 'angel of God', this means that God himself leads his people in this form, visible indeed, but nevertheless mysterious. Now according to v. 19a this 'angel of

*Cf. von Rad, *Genesis*, pp. 188 f.

God' appeared before the pursuing Egyptians and behind the Israelite camp so as to prevent the Egyptians falling upon them speedily, so therefore the 'angel of God' was a form which the Egyptians too could see and respect. Whether E went on to describe events in the same way as J is completely beyond our knowledge.

In J too the representation of the divine presence—in this case the pillars of cloud and fire (cf. 13.21 f.)—completely separates the two camps from each other by leaving its place as guide at the head of the Israelites and placing itself behind the camp of Israel and thus between the Israelites and the Egyptians. Thus the Egyptian host had also made camp in the meanwhile, in immediate proximity to the Israelites, who were encamped at 'Etham' (13.20); for it was evening, and the Egyptian attack was apparently planned only for the next day. So as to prevent a possible night attack, the pillar stood between the two camps and made an approach from either side impossible. It would thus have been seen by the Egyptians as well as by the Israelites. Unfortunately we can no longer reconstruct the original wording of the clause v. 20ab with any certainty.* Should its original meaning have been that on this particular night the pillar did not light up as a pillar of fire but remained dark, J may well have imagined that the space between the two camps was shrouded in such a complete and uncanny darkness that no one could, and in view of the miraculous nature of the phenomenon dared, penetrate it. Now in v. 21ab J surprisingly speaks of the 'sea' which must be sought in the immediate vicinity of the two camps, though no more accurate information is given about its exact position. Nor can we make for ourselves any exact picture from the geographical data that are given, as we are unable to say where J located the event. What now happened to this 'sea' was only important as events proceeded; for the time being it is just said that all that night, while the two camps stood opposite one another, Yahweh 'drove back' the sea by means of 'a strong east wind' and 'made the sea dry land'. According to the usual exegesis this is supposed to mean that the water receded from a bight or tongue of the 'sea' so that at this place the sea bed now lay free and waterless. Of course the wording really means that,

---

*The transmitted text is completely incomprehensible at this point and is certainly incomplete. I suggest an original *heḥᵉšik* in place of *wᵉhaḥošek*, and count *wayyāᵉer* as an addition caused by the thought that the pillar must really shine by night. [For RSV 'And there was the cloud and the darkness; and the night passed', Noth would translate 'and the cloud remained dark on this night', making the omission he suggests above. Tr.]

under the effect of the east wind sent by Yahweh, the water completely disappeared from a sea of perhaps quite a moderate size, only later to reappear suddenly in similar fashion (v. 27a*bb*). In any case J is clearly speaking here of a divine miracle; and it is extremely questionable whether it is appropriate to look for a 'natural' parallel for the events he describes and thus seek to explain the whole 'naturally'. Even J can hardly have found any basis in his experience for the fact that a wind, even if it was a 'strong' wind, could 'drive back' a 'sea', even if the sea was only some shallow water, so that the divine action had only consisted in the coming of the strong east wind just at the right time and its being particularly effective. Likewise, the idea that a hot east wind, a sirocco, such as used to appear in spring and autumn in Syria-Palestine, could have dried up a 'sea', despite its well-known drying power, even if its effect was thought to be greatly heightened at the divine command, must be completely unjustified by any possible empirical observation. In that case the words of J in v. 21a*b* could much more easily lead us to think of a mirage, the strange phenomenon which, when the hot (eastern) air comes into the desert, makes 'water' appear and then disappear again before a man's eyes. We could then imagine that J remembered this phenomenon when he was writing the description of the wonderful events at the 'sea'. In no case does the language of J indicate that he is thinking of the movement of the tide, of which he is probably not unaware elsewhere and which scholars have occasionally read out of his words, for a 'strong east wind' would have no connection with this, as J should certainly have known. Even a combination of the pillars of cloud and fire with the 'departure' of the sea in the sense that an earthquake and a disruption of the sea connected with a volcanic eruption resulted in a back-flow of the water at a particular place on the coast is not suggested by J's words; and if it is correct that for J the pillars of cloud and fire are the representation of the divine presence, which derives from the historical tradition of Sinai, he would hardly have envisaged volcanic phenomena at the scene of the miracle at the sea. In short, it must remain uncertain what J meant to express when he said that 'the sea was driven back' and with what phenomenon from what realm of experience he connected it. In view of what has been said, our chief and sole question must be that of the way in which J wished his own words to be understood; the historical question of what really happened is thus outside our scope. Anyway, J provides the first decisive material for his description in v. 24. Towards the end of the night—the 'morning watch' is the last of the three 'watches', i.e. watching periods, into which the night is divided—Yahweh by merely 'looking down' drives the Egyptian host into a panic. According to Job 40.11 f., the fact that God's 'look' is sufficient to throw down the proud is a special proof of his deity. It is repeatedly said in the Old Testament that it is with such a fear of God that Yahweh conquers his enemies and those of his people, by putting them into so great a panic that they are ready to destroy themselves.* In most cases we are not told in any detail how this 'looking' and 'panic' comes about. In the miracle at the sea, it is at least hinted that some part was played by the appearance of the pillar of cloud, in which the Egyptians now in some way recognized the presence of Yahweh. As both the pillar of cloud and the pillar of fire are mentioned in the text of v. 24a we may, if the conjecture about v. 20ab advanced above is correct, think that according to J, after complete darkness had prevailed hitherto during the night, now fire was suddenly to be seen, fire which brought about the fear of God. But if that had been J's meaning he would have said it rather more clearly; and so we ought rather to assume that the word 'fire' in v. 24a has subsequently been inserted in view of the usual connection between the pillar of cloud and the pillar of fire. The fate of the Egyptians is sealed with the panic caused by the 'looking' of Yahweh which is bound up with the pillar of cloud; they can now only run away in headlong flight and therefore pass this cry from mouth to mouth, at the same time expressing the recognition that it is Yahweh himself who is fighting against them (v. 25b). Within this closely knit sequence of events the observation in v. 25a has a disruptive effect, and it also occurs too early, as it already presupposes the flight of the Egyptians, to which they resort only in v. 25b. So in v. 25a we may see an isolated fragment of E which was incorporated into the combined narrative because it contained a motif which does not occur elsewhere in the narrative; alternatively, it may be regarded as a secondary addition. It is supposed that a further inexplicable divine act was the reason why the wheels of the Egyptian chariots were clogged in a miraculous way, so that the Egyptians did not succeed in their attempted flight; the narrator hardly had a 'natural' cause in mind (marshy land or the like). We can imagine how the episode in v. 25a would have continued; the Egyptians, held up in their progress, were completely

*Cf. G. von Rad, *Der Heilige Krieg im alten Israel*, p. 12.

submerged by the returning sea. J describes the events in a different way in v. 27a*b*b; here the Egyptians, flying headlong in the fear of God, rush right into the sea in their confusion and blindness. This was Yahweh's victory over them, and in this way he 'shook off' (see RSV margin) the Egyptians in the midst of the sea (the same language is used of the miracle at the sea in Ps. 136.15). Now according to J it also happened that, when morning broke, the sea, which had been 'driven back' during the night, had 'returned to its wonted flow'. Thus the idea in J's mind must have been that the Egyptians had been confused still more by this, though of course we must ask at this point how the Egyptians could have noticed the sea being 'driven back' in the darkness of the night, so that they were now not reckoning on the 'return' of the sea. It is clear that for J the 'driving back' and the 'return' of the sea is only a subsidiary element of the story which is not absolutely essential for his description of events and which does not fit into it at all smoothly. The essential thing for him is the fear of God which causes the Egyptians to rush into the sea near where they and the Israelites were encamped. From this we must go on to conclude that J incorporated in his description elements of a variant narrative of the miracle at the sea which depended upon the 'driving back' and the 'return' of the sea, and which therefore perhaps told how the Egyptians had encamped at a place from which the sea had gone away and how they were then overwhelmed by the 'returning' sea. According to J, Israel did nothing during the decisive events, just as Moses had announced, according to vv. 13 f. J, that they had only to stand by and see the acts of their God. J does not speak of a passage of Israel through the sea. Israel remained in their camp and according to v. 30 perhaps saw nothing at all of the actual flight and catastrophe of the Egyptians, but merely its consequence—the dead Egyptians which the sea threw up on its shores. In this way the accomplishment of the great saving act of Yahweh was made known, and Israel learnt to fear their God and to 'believe in' him (v. 31). For this God had displayed himself in power, bringing fear upon the Egyptians, and he required of his own people also that they should fear him; moreover he had shown himself true to his promises, at the same time confirming 'his servant Moses' as a real messenger of God. In this way he could claim trust both for himself and for his messenger. Israel had already 'believed' (4.31) the first proclamation of Yahweh's promise which had been brought by Moses; now the promise of the 'Exodus' has been fulfilled, and if J once again speaks of the 'belief' of the people, he in fact means that Israel was convinced that the destruction of the Egyptians, which they themselves had not witnessed, was the work of their God who had spoken to them through Moses.

The different variants of the story of the miracle at the sea wrought by Yahweh which are in part certain, in part only demonstrable with probability, clearly disagree in their representation of the details of the event. But the essential elements of the contents are the same in all forms of the story; and this similarity shows itself all the more clearly against the background of the differences in the individual narratives. All agree in speaking of an act of God in which it was God alone who acted; J expressed this particularly strongly (vv. 13 f. and 30 f.), but P too has expressed himself clearly enough in this respect by making the whole chain of events follow from the hardening of Pharaoh's heart by Yahweh (v. 4), and then, in what follows, having Moses and the Israelites acting exclusively at the command of Yahweh (vv. 15 f., 21a*a*, 26, 27a*a*). All agree in handing down as the nucleus of the story that the fatal danger to the Israelites journeying from the delta to the Sinai peninsula consisted in their being pursued by the Egyptians, and that the Israelites were saved from this danger by the annihilation of the Egyptians in a 'sea'. Now this annihilation is represented in different ways; the most simple, but at the same time the most imposing, is that of P who tells how the sea was 'divided', how first the Israelites passed through and how the Egyptians wanted to follow. J is more mysterious; in his main narrative the Egyptians are driven into the sea through the fear of God, but alongside it he has preserved the traces of what is probably another version, according to which the Egyptians, presumably encamped, were engulfed by the return of a sea which had at first been 'driven back'. Common to all these variants is the thought that the event must be described as a concrete happening, which really took place in space and time. As there was not and could not have been a recorded description of the way in which things happened, this basic thought led to these very differences in the concrete presentations. On the other hand, we are exercised by the historical question of what actually did happen, even if the answer to this historical question cannot be extended beyond the establishing of variant traditions which at an early stage are not clear, and probably not even in agreement, on the location of the event; even J does not, as used to be widely assumed earlier, describe the events in a basically 'natural' way, so that we cannot just make a number of deletions in his account to obtain an essentially 'rational, historical' report. Everywhere we have simply variants of the single theme of the destruction of the Egyptians in 'the sea'. This fact of the saving of Israel through the destruction of an Egyptian chariot force in 'the sea' forms the historical basis of the tradition.

9. THANKSGIVING FOR DELIVERANCE: 15.1–21

15[1] Then Moses and the people of Israel sang this song to the LORD, saying,

'I will sing to the LORD, for he has triumphed gloriously;
　the horse and his rider he has thrown into the sea.
[2] The LORD is my strength and my song,
　and he has become my salvation;
　this is my God, and I will praise him,
　my father's God, and I will exalt him,
[3] The LORD is a man of war;
　the LORD is his name.

[4] 'Pharaoh's chariots and his host he cast into the sea;
　and his picked officers are sunk in the Red Sea.
[5] The floods cover them;
　they went down into the depths like a stone.
[6] Thy right hand, O LORD, glorious in power,
　thy right hand, O LORD, shatters the enemy.
[7] In the greatness of thy majesty thou overthrowest thy adversaries;
　thou sendest forth thy fury, it consumes them like stubble.
[8] At the blast of thy nostrils the waters piled up,
　the floods stood up in a heap;
　the deeps congealed in the heart of the sea.
[9] The enemy said, "I will pursue, I will overtake,
　I will divide the spoil, my desire shall have its fill of them.
　I will draw my sword, my hand shall destroy them."
[10] Thou didst blow with thy wind, the sea covered them;
　they sank as lead in the mighty waters.

[11] 'Who is like thee, O LORD, among the gods?
　Who is like thee, majestic in holiness,
　terrible in glorious deeds, doing wonders?
[12] Thou didst stretch out thy right hand, the earth swallowed them.

[13] 'Thou hast led in thy steadfast love the people whom thou hast redeemed,
　thou hast guided them by thy strength to thy holy abode.

¹⁴ The peoples have heard, they tremble;
    pangs have seized on the inhabitants of Philistia.
¹⁵ Now are the chiefs of Edom dismayed;
    the leaders of Moab, trembling seizes them;
    all the inhabitants of Canaan have melted away.
¹⁶ Terror and dread fall upon them;
    because of the greatness of thy arm, they are as still as a stone,
    till thy people, O LORD, pass by,
    till the people pass by whom thou hast purchased.
¹⁷ Thou wilt bring them in, and plant them on thy own mountain,
    the place, O LORD, which thou hast made for thy abode,
    the sanctuary, O LORD, which thy hands have established.
¹⁸ The LORD will reign for ever and ever.'

19. For when the horses of Pharaoh with his chariots and his horsemen went into the sea, the LORD brought back the waters of the sea upon them; but the people of Israel walked on dry ground in the midst of the sea. ²⁰ Then Miriam, the prophetess, the sister of Aaron, took a timbrel in her hand; and all the women went out after her with timbrels and dancing. ²¹ And Miriam sang to them:

'Sing to the LORD, for he has triumphed gloriously;
    the horse and his rider he has thrown into the sea.'

[20–21] The oldest element in this section is the short passage vv. 20 f. Of course we cannot establish any recognizable connection between it and any of the known sources. Because it is in all probability of relatively great age it is most often assigned to the source J, but there is no conclusive argument in favour of this. Its nucleus is formed by the short hymn v. 21b which is in any case of independent origin from the narrative tradition and which has been handed down within the framework of the cult. Its brevity suggests that it stems from a very early date, and we may reckon with the possibility that we have here the oldest formulation preserved to us in the Old Testament of the account of the divine miracle at the sea, especially as we may also assume that the Exodus theme, like others in the Pentateuch, was first expressed in liturgical praise and was always repeated within the framework of liturgical ceremonies. In v. 21b we have a hymn of solid structure which begins with an invitation, directed to the assembled worshippers, to praise God, and then bases this invitation on a reference to acts of God which have already taken place and been experienced. In the present case this reference is limited to the miracle at the sea, and we may imagine that wherever the Exodus was recalled in the oldest Israelite worship this hymn had a principal place. The language of the hymn, which avoids any individual details and could only fully be understood if the broad outlines of the events of the Exodus were known, in fact stands very close to the J description in Ex. 14, despite other independent means of expression, in that it says that the Egyptian chariots were 'thrown' into the sea and that it was Yahweh who did this. The brevity of this cultic confession makes it easy to understand how, in order to perpetuate the account of the acts of God from generation to generation and at the same time to explain such a confession, someone 'narrated' the story of the miracle at the sea and of the other events of the Exodus in rather more detail, thus making it the subject of a 'narrative' tradition. In vv. 20–21a the hymn has been given an introduction, according to which it was sung for the first time immediately after the event itself. This introduction assumes the custom, not very appropriate to the historical situation at the sea, that the women 'went out' from their homes to meet their victorious husbands on their return, greeting them with song and dance and singing them a song of victory (cf. I Sam. 18.6 f.); in this one of the women was leader of the singers who 'sang to them', i.e. the returning warriors, the song which was then taken up and repeated by the choir formed by the rest of the women. Miriam, whose name is mentioned for the first time, appears as leader of the singers in Ex. 15.20 f. She is also introduced with the explanatory remark that she was Aaron's sister (cf. the connection between Aaron and Miriam in Num. 12). It is thus supposed that Aaron was an already well-known figure. This was probably not the case in the basic material of the J narrative in which Aaron would as yet have made no appearance; he is first introduced by J in secondary material in 4.14 and then repeatedly mentioned alongside Moses. In 15.20, on the other hand, it is not thought that Aaron was the brother of Moses; otherwise Moses would surely have been named there instead of Aaron or at least alongside him. The relationships which are assumed in the late tradition (cf. Ex. 7.1 P; Num. 26.59) are not yet known here. Should Aaron be described in 4.14 as the physical brother of Moses (see pp. 46 f. above) we would have even in this passage (secondary J) a later stage of the tradition than in 15.20. The state of affairs which has been described speaks against any idea that 15.20 f. is to be assigned to the basic material of the J narrative. Aaron and Miriam belong in the tradition to the group of those figures surrounding Moses about whom only remnants of an originally much richer tradition remains, and whose originally independent role we can therefore no longer detect. In time they have been made relations of Moses. In 15.20 Miriam is described as a 'prophetess'; she should thus presumably be characterized as an ecstatic. This corresponds to her appearance at this stage, for ecstasy and (cultic) song belonged closely together in ancient Israel (cf. I Sam. 10.5 f.).

[1–19] The great 'Reed Sea Hymn' in 15.1–19 is a relatively late piece; we cannot give a more accurate indication of the time at which it was composed. In its present form it is no longer a unity. For the most part it is a hymn, and moreover a 'solo hymn' with a single speaker in the first person, but it has also incorporated elements of the thanksgiving form. It was not composed to fill the place it now occupies in the narrative, but is an originally independent hymn which began with the old hymn 15.21, slightly altered, and then sang in praise of the miracle wrought by God at the sea, celebrating in considerable detail one of the most popular subjects of Old Testament hymns. It is therefore probable that the insertion into the present context is secondary. The clause which introduces the hymn, which is loosely attached to the preceding narrative, puts it into the mouth of Moses and the Israelites. The reason for this was the special mention of Moses through the 'I' which appears in the hymn. The form of the hymn is not very strict. It is relatively long, and we cannot certainly discern a series of strophes in it. The rhythm changes; verse lines with a 4 : 4 stress (as in 15.21b) keep recurring from beginning to end, but are frequently replaced by verse lines of another measure. If we are to assume the original to have been a hymn with a regular rhythm, we must postulate a basic form markedly different from the material that has been transmitted. Probably, however, we must reckon with a form which was not very consistent from the beginning.

The old hymn transmitted in v. 21b is placed at the beginning as a theme (1b), but with a change of the hymnic invitation to the assembled crowd. This now becomes the intent of an individual to praise God, a feature which derives from the individual thanksgiving. A formula from the thanksgiving also occurs in v. 2a and is extended still further in v. 2b (cf. Ps. 118.14; Isa. 12.2b) with which the person giving thanks acknowledges the 'help' which has been vouchsafed to him by God. Verse 3 marks a transition to objective hymnic expressions, first of all to the bold expression that Yahweh himself is a 'man of war' and that the mention of his name includes this very thought. This is not meant to designate Yahweh as a 'God of war'; but what it says is that Yahweh is experienced by Israel as the one who acts by fighting for his people himself (cf. 14.14 and the recognition expressed by the Egyptians in 14.25b), who leads the 'war of Yahweh' (Num. 21.14; cf. also I Sam. 18.17; 25.28). The general remark of v. 3 becomes in vv. 4 f. a special allusion to the 'sinking' of the Egyptian chariot force in the sea. Then, with an address to Yahweh which is maintained right up to v. 17, follows a general song in praise of Yahweh's overwhelming power, terrible to his enemies (and those of Israel); here in the customary concrete language of the Old Testament we are told of his right hand and his wrath. The wrath of Yahweh against the enemy is also given as the reason for his wonderful act at the sea, which is now given special mention again in vv. 8–10; for the 'blast of his nostrils' (v. 8) refers to his raging anger. Moreover the expressions 'piled up', 'stood up', 'congealed', of the waters are reminiscent of P's description of the miracle at the sea in 14.15 ff. The haughtiness of the enemy (v. 9) was in a moment laid low by the power of Yahweh (v. 10). It is not absolutely clear what is meant by the word rendered 'wind' of Yahweh in v. 10; it could mean his wrath, as in v. 8, but as the Hebrew word used is *rūaḥ*, which is also the usual word for 'wind', a real wind could be imagined which made the sea come and go. In that case there would be a reference to a part played by the wind in the miracle at the sea similar to that in the element of the J narrative which speaks of the 'strong east wind' (14.21ab). The 'Hymn of the Reed Sea' does not seem to have any concrete picture of what happened in the miracle at the sea, but instead a number of variant narratives are combined together; this is clear from the fact that on the one hand we hear that the Egyptians are 'covered' in the sea (vv. 5a, 10a) and on the other they are directly afterwards said to be 'sunk' in the sea (vv. 5b, 10b). The theme of the miracle at the sea is virtually concluded in v. 11 by the question 'Who is like thee?', a traditional element frequent in the hymn form which exalts the God to be praised as unique among the circle of 'gods'. Thus its ultimate origin is in non-Israelite polytheistic ideas. Perhaps, following the emendation suggested in Kittel's *Biblia Hebraica*, v. 11ba should read 'Who is like thee majestic among the holy ones?'; if this is correct, and it is supported by the parallelism, the mention of the 'holy ones', i.e. the heavenly beings who stand around God, interprets the parallel expression 'gods' in the sense of 'divine' beings and thus completely excludes the originally polytheistic background of the question. With a brief reference to the three themes of the saving act at the sea, the guidance through the wilderness and the conquest, vv. 12 f. make a transition to the second main theme of the 'Hymn of the Reed Sea', the Entry into the Promised Land. Despite the startling nature of the expression, 'the earth swallowed them' surely refers to the overwhelming of the Egyptians in the sea; they thus vanished from the face of the earth and entered the realm of the dead under the earth. Yahweh led Israel along the way through the wilderness to his 'holy abode' (v. 13). This is a general reference to the land promised to Israel. The word *n⁺wēh*, rendered as 'abode', originally described the pasturage, then the resting place in general. The '*n⁺wēh*' of Yahweh in II Sam. 15.25 is meant as a special reference to the Jerusalem sanctuary, but in Jer. 25.30 the expression apparently has a more comprehensive though at the same time indefinite meaning and may most probably refer to the whole land of Israel; this latter application is also likely in the present passage, as the whole of the land of Yahweh is also mentioned in what follows, in the sense that it is the possession of Yahweh, the 'place which he has made for his abode' (v. 17), and so the land of God into which the people of God are now being led. Here, however, the idea of the land as the possession of God in which the Israelites are the 'strangers and sojourners' of Yahweh (Lev. 25.23) conflicts with the concept of the 'Promised Land'.* Yahweh has built Israel a road into this land by letting great fear come over the people who live in the neighbourhood of this road. After the 'people' have been mentioned in completely general terms (v. 14a), we surprisingly hear first of all about the 'inhabitants of Philistia', i.e. the Philistines (v. 14b). This is perhaps because they were settled in that part of Palestine which borders immediately upon Egypt and therefore must have been the first to hear of the Exodus of the Israelites. The mention of Edom and Moab which follows (v. 15) refers to the great detour made by Israel through southern Trans-Jordan (cf. Deut. 2.1 ff.). Canaan refers to the whole of the region in which Israel later settled. This area is characterized as a mountain in v. 17 because Israel settled chiefly in the hilly parts of the land. Here Israel was in Yahweh's 'abode', for in view of the context the expression 'the place which Yahweh has made for his abode' (v. 17ab) must clearly describe the

*See G. von Rad, *Zeitschrift des Deutschen Palaestina-Vereins* 66, 1943, pp. 191–204.

whole of this region. But then we are not to understand the word 'sanctuary' in v. 17b as a single holy place, which would compel us to think of Jerusalem, but we are to see the whole land, because it is the possession of Yahweh and the 'abode of God', as a holy realm. Here the song ends, as v. 19 is a prose addition following 14. 23, 28 f. P. The final verse, v. 18, expresses again in objective hymnic style the eternal kingship of Yahweh which has manifested itself in the great deeds of God to Israel.

IIII

THE BEGINNING OF ISRAEL'S LIFE
IN THE WILDERNESS

15.22 – 18.27

1. THE FIRST STOPPING-PLACES: 15.22–27

22 Then Moses led Israel onward from the Red Sea, *and they went into the wilderness of Shur; they went three days in the wilderness and found no water.* [23] *When they came to Marah, they could not drink the water of Marah because it was bitter; therefore it was named Marah.* [24] *And the people murmured against Moses, saying, 'What shall we drink?'* [25] *And he cried to the* LORD; *and the* LORD *showed him a tree, and he threw it into the water, and the water became sweet.*

[*There the* LORD *made for them a statute and an ordinance and there he proved them,* [26] *saying, 'If you will diligently hearken to the voice of the* LORD *your God, and do that which is right in his eyes, and give heed to his commandments and keep all his statutes, I will put none of the diseases upon you which I put upon the Egyptians; for I am the* LORD, *your healer.'*]

27 Then they came to Elim, where there were twelve springs of water and seventy palm trees; and they encamped there by the water.

At the beginning (v. 22a) and at the end (v. 27) of the section there are sentences with stereotyped phrases which are usual in P and which continue to occur in similar fashion in what follows within the framework of the narratives in P. We must therefore assign these sentences to P, whereas the passage lying in between does not display P's characteristic peculiarities. The story of the water of Marah (v. 22abb–25a) in all probability derives from J. In v. 26 such marked deuteronomistic phrases occur that we must suppose it to be a deuteronomistic supplement to the older Pentateuchal narrative; the only question is whether we are also to assign v. 25b to this supplement or whether to connect it with the preceding J narrative. As in this half verse too only very general expressions are used (for

127

the first clause see Josh. 24.25), we may decide in favour of the first alternative.

[22a*a*, 27] P mentions the departure and arrival, from stopping place to stopping place, after the fashion of an itinerary. The starting place is the 'reed sea' (v. 22a*a*) which has not hitherto been given this name in P, so that we may ask whether P did not use a list of the stopping places which had come to hand to describe the journey through the wilderness. According to P, the first stopping-place in the wilderness is 'Elim' (v. 27), which is described as a small oasis where Israel finds the necessary water. The description surely rests on local knowledge. We have, however, on our part no point of reference for determining the locality of this Elim, and the position is made more uncertain by the fact that we cannot know definitely that the series of stopping-places put forward by P and perhaps drawn from a source really rest on the knowledge of a definite route through the wilderness. Instead they may well be a vague collection of names of some well known places in the wilderness of Sinai. P had no definite tradition of the journeying in the wilderness which could be connected with the stop at the oasis of Elim.

[22a*b*b–26] J first of all brings the Israelites into the 'wilderness (of) Shur' (v. 22a*b*); this may describe a part of the wilderness of Sinai lying close to Egypt. The name Shur is connected with a locality in the wilderness which, according to Gen. 25.18 and I Sam. 15.7 (cf. also I Sam. 27.8), lay 'opposite' or 'before' (RSV 'east of', 'to') Egypt (seen from the Asiatic side). In this part of the desert Israel first had to cross over a long waterless stretch until the water-hole of Marah was reached. Here, however, the water was undrinkable. At this point there occurs for the first time in J the narrative motif which is to occur frequently from now on in the stories set in the wilderness, the 'murmuring' of the people, directed against Moses, who is made responsible for everything, and against God, on whose orders Moses has consistently acted and is still acting. This motif has its roots in the realization of the miserable conditions of life in the wilderness with its constant privations, above all the shortage of food and water; at the same time it brings out the fact that Israel did not follow the way of the Exodus from Egypt by free choice (cf. 14.11 f.) but followed the guidance of their God with which they were not completely happy from the very beginning (cf. 5.20 ff.), so that God's universal plan of salvation might be carried out even against the will of Israel (cf. Gen. 12.1–3). The 'murmuring' of the people of course always leads through the mediation of Moses to the gracious aid of Yahweh. So too it happens in the present instance. Moses is shown a remedy by Yahweh; a 'tree', i.e. a piece of desert vegetation which is available there at that time, when thrown into the water of the spring, makes the water 'sweet' and thus drinkable. The whole rests upon a local tradition. In their later dwelling-places, bordering on the wilderness of Sinai, the Israelites knew of a water-hole whose name 'Marah' indicated that the water of the spring must be 'bitter', just as there were similar 'bitter' springs in the salty ground of the wilderness; this one, however, was sweet, because it had been made sweet at the time of Israel's Exodus from Egypt. Where this water-hole of Marah lay we can no longer discover. The deuteronomistic addition in vv. 25b, 26 is attached only loosely to what goes before. If v. 25b belongs with v. 26, Yahweh must already be meant as the subject in v. 25b. The giving of a 'statute and ordinance' is certainly meant to do no more than create a foundation for the deuteronomistic warning in v. 26. The rather vague observation that Yahweh 'proved' Israel, i.e. put them to the test, is a play on the place-name Massah, which does not come into this story at all (cf. on 17.1–7). The actual connection between the addition and the old 'Marah' story probably lies in the reference to the sending of the 'disease of the Egyptians' which is threatened as a punishment for disobedience (for this cf. with another formula Deut. 7.15; 28. 27,60), which was probably associated in some way with the bitter water. The deuteronomistic addition apparently means that only if Israel observes the 'statute and ordinance', and thus passes the test which he has imposed, will Yahweh help the people in the future as he has done in Marah, and that he alone can help, as only he is the 'healer' for Israel.

2. QUAILS AND MANNA: 16.1–36

16[1] They set out from Elim, and all the congregation of the people of Israel came to the wilderness of Sin, which is between Elim and Sinai, on the fifteenth day of the second month after they had departed from the land of Egypt. [2] And the whole congregation of the people of Israel murmured against Moses and Aaron in the wilderness, [3] and said to them, 'Would that we had died by the hand of the LORD in the land of Egypt, when we sat by the fleshpots and ate bread to the full; for you have brought us out into this wilderness to kill this whole assembly with hunger.'

4 *Then the* Lord *said to Moses, 'Behold, I will rain bread from heaven for you; and the people shall go out and gather a day's portion every day,* [*that I may prove them, whether they will walk in my law or not.*] 5 *On the sixth day, when they prepare what they bring in, it will be twice as much as they gather daily.'* 6 So Moses and Aaron said to all the people of Israel, 'At evening you shall know that it was the Lord who brought you out of the land of Egypt, 7 and in the morning you shall see the glory of the Lord, because he has heard your murmurings against the Lord. For what are we, that you murmur against us?' [8 And Moses said, 'When the Lord gives you in the evening flesh to eat and in the morning bread to the full, because the Lord has heard your murmurings which you murmur against him—what are we? Your murmurings are not against us but against the Lord.']

9 And Moses said to Aaron, 'Say to the whole congregation of the people of Israel, "Come near before the Lord, for he has heard your murmurings." ' 10 And as Aaron spoke to the whole congregation of the people of Israel, they looked toward the wilderness, and behold, the glory of the Lord appeared in the cloud. 11 And the Lord said to Moses, 12 'I have heard the murmurings of the people of Israel; say to them, "At twilight you shall eat flesh, and in the morning you shall be filled with bread; then you shall know that I am the Lord your God." '

13 In the evening quails came up and covered the camp; and in the morning dew lay round about the camp. 14 And when the dew had gone up, there was on the face of the wilderness a fine, flake-like thing, fine as hoarfrost on the ground. 15 When the people of Israel saw it, they said to one another, 'What is it?' For they did not know what it was. And Moses said to them, 'It is the bread which the Lord has given you to eat. 16 This is what the Lord has commanded: "Gather of it, every man of you, as much as he can eat; you shall take an omer apiece, according to the number of the persons whom each of you has in his tent." ' 17 And the people of Israel did so; they gathered, some more, some less. 18 But when they measured it with an omer, he that gathered much had nothing over, and he that gathered little had no lack; each gathered according to what he could eat. 19 And Moses said to them, 'Let no man leave any of it till the morning.' 20 But they did not listen to Moses; some left part of it till the morning, and it bred worms and became foul; and Moses was angry with them. 21 Morning by morning they gathered it, each as much as he could eat; but when the sun grew hot, it melted.

22 On the sixth day they gathered twice as much bread, two omers apiece; and when all the leaders of the congregation came and told Moses, 23 he said to them, 'This is what the Lord has commanded: "Tomorrow is a day of solemn rest, a holy sabbath to the Lord; bake what you will bake and boil what you will boil, and all that is left over lay by to be kept till the morning." ' 24 So they laid it by till the morning, as Moses bade them; and it did not become foul, and there were no worms in it. 25 Moses said, 'Eat it today, for today is a sabbath to the Lord; today you will not find it in the field. 26 Six days you shall gather

it; but on the seventh day, which is a sabbath, there will be none.'
²⁷ On the seventh day some of the people went out to gather, and they
found none. ²⁸ *And the* LORD *said to Moses, 'How long do you refuse
to keep my commandments and my laws?* ²⁹ *See! The* LORD *has given you
the sabbath, therefore on the sixth day he gives you bread for two days; remain
every man of you in his place, let no man go out of his place on the seventh
day.'* ³⁰ *So the people rested on the seventh day.*

31 *Now the house of Israel called its name manna; it was like coriander
seed, white, and the taste of it was like wafers made with honey.* ³² And Moses
said, 'This is what the LORD has commanded: "Let an omer of it be
kept throughout your generations, that they may see the bread with
which I fed you in the wilderness, when I brought you out of the
land of Egypt." ' ³³ And Moses said to Aaron, 'Take a jar, and put
an omer of manna in it, and place it before the LORD, to be kept
throughout your generations.' ³⁴ As the LORD commanded Moses,
so Aaron placed it before the Testimony, to be kept. ³⁵ And the people
of Israel ate the manna forty years, till they came to a habitable land;
they ate the manna, till they came to the border of the land of Canaan.
[³⁶ (An omer is the tenth part of an ephah.)]

The theme of quails and manna appears once more outside the
present chapter, in Num. 11.4 ff. There we are told how the people
had grown tired of the monotonous manna and longed for flesh,
whereupon Yahweh made the quails come. In Ex. 16 we have both
the quails and the manna at the same time, but the quails are mentioned only briefly and the chief interest is in the manna. The
discrepancy between Ex. 16 and Num. 11 may be explained on
literary-critical grounds. In Ex. 16 the language of P predominates,
whereas in Num. 11 there is no indication of P. P thus dealt with
the theme of the feeding of Israel in the wilderness once and for all,
right at the beginning of the story of the journey through the
wilderness—since the departure from the Reed Sea P has previously
only mentioned the stopping-place at Elim, very briefly (15.27). In
so doing P combined all the narrative traditions which he had
received, and simplified the older Pentateuchal material which
first of all only mentioned the manna and then introduced the story
of the quails only at a much later stage. It is clear that the older
material already spoke of the manna at an early stage of the narrative
from the fact that it is also represented in fragments alongside the
predominant P. The lack of literary unity in Ex. 16 is chiefly apparent
from the occurrence of striking repetitions. Verses (28) 29–31 say
once again what has already been mentioned previously; even the
naming of the 'manna' (v. 31a) had already been reported (v. 15a).

On the other side, in vv. 4 f. something is anticipated which is first reported in vv. 21 f. as something new and surprising. The two pieces just mentioned (vv. 4 f. and 28–31) lack the linguistic and stylistic characteristics of P which otherwise appear throughout, and therefore they would seem to derive from the older traditional material and should certainly be regarded as fragments from J. Moreover there are also apparent doublets in v. 35a and 35b which say the same thing; of these one is to be assigned to P and the other to J.

The stories of the quails and the manna are each related to actual phenomena which may be observed on the Sinai peninsula even today. There will be more to be said at Num. 11.4 ff. about how the quails appear in flocks along the Mediterranean coast of the Sinai peninsula on their spring and autumn journeys. The 'manna' is, at least in the old narrative material, so concretely described (cf. especially v. 31b and further Num. 11.7 f., but also v. 14b P) that we get the impression that it was known directly, or at least indirectly, to the narrator. In fact there is still manna today in the inland region of the Sinai peninsula, and it is even called *mann* by the nomadic inhabitants of this region. It is a sort of droplike formation on the leaves of the tree or shrub, native to the wilderness, of the tamarisk, in particular the 'manna-tamarisk' (*tamarix mannifera*) formed of the secretions produced by the sting of a tree louse. It falls from the leaves on to the ground from where it can be picked up after it has grown relatively hard in the cool of the night. As it has a low melting temperature it dissolves in the heat of the day and so is best gathered in the early morning. It has a sweet taste and is still a favourite food of the inhabitants of that particular part of the barren desert-land.* We cannot overlook the fact that the Old Testament story of the manna fits in very accurately with what can now be observed on the Sinai peninsula and what was doubtless also observable as long ago as in the time of the prehistory of Israel. At that time Yahweh fed Israel with the manna of Sinai, which was something new and surprising for the Israelites coming from the agricultural land of Egypt. One peculiarity was that through a miraculous rhythm in the provision of the manna Israel was both shown the keeping of the sabbath rest on each seventh day and was obliged to keep this divine ordinance; this narrative element already

*Cf. most recently A. Kaiser, *Zeitschrift des Deutschen Palaestina-Vereins*, 53, 1930, pp. 69 ff.

occurs in the old Pentateuchal material and is emphatically and purposefully repeated by P.

[1–12] The introduction to the story tells of the 'murmuring' of the people because of the lack of food in the wilderness and of the divine announcement of a remedy. P first of all produces details about the stopping place and an exact dating (v. 1), as he frequently does in the ensuing sections. The wilderness of Sin occurs only in this context (Num. 33.11 f. is literarily dependent on Ex. 16.1; 17.1) and cannot more exactly be defined. P observes that it is to be found 'between Elim and Sinai', but this is no more than a reference to his list of stopping places. We should probably assume that the name of the desert area of 'Sin' is connected with the name 'Sinai', and that P's distinction between the 'wilderness of Sin' and the 'wilderness of Sinai' (19.1 f.) is purely artificial. In allowing one and a half months to have passed between the Exodus from Egypt and the arrival at the 'wilderness of Sin', P has either reckoned on a lengthy stay at Elim and lengthy marches between the stopping places or has assumed further intermediate stopping places which he either was unable or thought it unnecessary to mention in detail. The story of the quails and manna which follows has no special reference to the stopping place mentioned. After the rich oasis of Elim the wilderness of Sin was the first stopping place in which the lack of sustenance in the desert would have made itself felt. Now there follows, for the first time in P, the 'murmuring' of the people (vv. 2 f.) who rebel against the leadership of their God. At this stage the people saw their good life in Egypt in rather too rosy a light. For the slave labour in Egypt would hardly as a rule have eaten boiled 'flesh' by the 'fleshpots'; nevertheless they had never had such pressing hunger as now in the wilderness. The P introduction has forced out a corresponding section of the J narrative; for in the J passage vv. 4 f. report is given of an announcement by Yahweh which was originally in fact a reply to a complaint by the people. Yahweh promises bread which is to come as 'rain' 'from heaven' and which then can be gathered each day by the people from the ground. Such a coming of the manna 'from heaven' is not expressed in P but occurs in Ps. 78.24 f., where in this context we find 'bread from heaven' and 'angels' food'; later Paul made an allusion to the manna in I Cor. 10.3 with the expression *pneumatikon brōma*. J's idea was probably simpler. 'Heaven' in the Old Testament originally means the air space above the earth, and not yet the special domain of God and of divine beings. J has the manna falling upon the earth like rain or dew. Moreover, in the very first announcement J draws attention to the double supply of manna in the sixth day (of each week). This is remarkable, as there can then be no surprise at this provision of manna at a later date because this particular arrangement had already been spoken of now (not so P). In vv. 6 ff. P reports in some detail the answer of God to the murmuring of the people which is handed on to them, of course at the command of God, by Moses and Aaron. God promises powerful aid, by which Israel is to recognize that the Exodus from Egypt is still a work of their God and that his 'glory' accompanies them along their way (vv. 6, 7a). In vv. 7 f. we have some obvious overcrowding. Verse 8 looks to be a secondary variant to v. 7abb; the incomplete sentence 8a in it is a variant of 7ab, and 7b recurs in another form in 8b. In v. 9 the conditions of a future cultic order are anticipated; the future first priest Aaron is to assemble the community at the command of Moses 'before Yahweh', although there is as yet no place in the Israelite camp where God is present or appears, but perhaps just a place of assembly, the place of the future sanctuary. And now Yahweh acts quickly. But the instructions to Aaron are not carried out, as the 'glory' of Yahweh is already seen in 'the wilderness', i.e. somewhere outside the Israelite camp, appearing in the sign of the cloud as is usual in P (v. 10). After the congregation has assembled—P must be understood to mean this, though he does not say it explicitly—and perhaps also the manifestation of the presence of Yahweh has entered the camp, Moses, as the mediator between God and people, receives from the manifestation of the presence of God the announcement of quails and manna for that very evening and the next morning.

[13–21] The promise of God is fulfilled. Quails come up (from the horizon) and, obviously in large quantities, 'cover' the camp, so that Israel now has flesh in abundance. No further mention is made of the quails. There is no indication whether the coming of the quails was a sole occurrence or whether it was repeated each evening. The manna, however, is described in much greater detail. It is there on the next morning and is found after the dispersion of a miraculous cloud of dew which had covered the wilderness round about the camp and had concealed the miracle of the divine gift of manna from human eyes. The Israelites do not know what to make of the 'fine, flakelike' thing which is 'like hoarfrost on the ground', which lies there in great abundance, and by their surprised question 'What is it?' give their name to the phenomenon by using for 'What?' the word man(na), which, while not occurring elsewhere in the Hebrew, was perhaps used in Canaanite dialects. The divine gift thenceforward bears the name 'What?'. This is a popular etymology. We can no longer give a certain etymological explanation of the word man, manna with which men from as early as Israelite times (up till today) have described the phenomenon with which we are concerned. Moses has to explain to the Israelites what this 'What?' is (v. 15b) and he invites the fathers of families to gather an omer apiece for themselves and their relatives. The omer, really a small clay vessel, is a dry measure which occurs only in the present chapter and which according to the gloss in v. 36 represents the tenth part of an ephah, i.e. about six-and-a-half pints. Thus an astonishingly large quantity of manna was collected every day. In the collecting of manna there was now the remarkable fact that however much or however little each man might have gathered he had still collected sufficient for the requirements of his family, as was sometimes found out afterwards if the amount of manna collected in any kind of container was measured at home. God always gives, as Israel is meant to learn, what is requisite for the needs of the moment, the 'daily bread', no less and no more (vv. 17 f.). Nothing is even to be kept for the morrow, perhaps through worry and anxiety (v. 19). 'Tomorrow will take care of itself', i.e. God will provide what is needful day by day. A number of disobedient persons, who still attempted to keep something over, had to learn on the next morning that their supply had gone rotten (v. 20). The whole passage certainly makes sense by itself, but it nevertheless reaches its climax in the story of the following sabbath, and it is there that the tradition has its roots. The pre-Priestly story had already connected the gift of the manna with the ordering of the sabbath rest (vv. 5, 29 f. J), and thus had already introduced the narrative motif of a definitely regulated allocation of manna. P further expanded this narrative motif in the way that has been described.

[22–36] In connection with the gift of manna there now follows the 'revelation' of the divine requirement of the sabbath rest. The word 'sabbath' here occurs for the first time in the Old Testament. According to the J fragment in vv. 29 f., Moses explained the double quantity of manna on the sixth day, which had already been announced (v. 5), by saying that Yahweh had given the sabbath rest to Israel in this way and that they were to remain resting on the seventh day (of each week). J does not of course put this forward as the reason for the sabbath rest, but introduces it as an ordinance which God wills to be valid for Israel both now and even after they have left the wilderness. Here we have presumably the oldest Old Testament passage about the sabbath; and as early as this passage the sabbath is designated as a day of rest and its name *šabbāt* is connected with the Hebrew verb for 'rest' (*šbt* v. 30). This derivation of the word *šabbāt* probably does not represent the origin of the word, but it is extraordinarily close to the Hebrew. The deuteronomistic gloss v. 28, which rebukes the Israelites in conventional phrases, supposes that in the original story in J there had earlier been a remark about the double quantity of manna on the sixth day. P follows the facts of the J narrative as he has already prepared for the sabbath episode. As in P the quantity provided on each of the first days had corresponded to the need, the doubling of this quantity appears all the more striking; it stirs up the 'leaders of the congregation' (for this description cf. Num. 1.16 and pp. 187 f. below on Ex. 22.28) and they obtain from Moses the explanation that they require (vv. 22–23a). The special divine purpose behind this doubling of the quantity is subsequently further confirmed by the fact that on the seventh day the supply of manna kept over from the previous day did not go bad, even if it had not been prepared in some way, either by baking or by cooking (vv. 23b, 24), as it had done on the previous days (v. 20), and that on the seventh day no manna was to be found, as was discovered by those who in spite of Moses' warning had gone out either through unbelief or through curiosity to collect manna (vv. 25–27). Thus even for P it was at that time that God made known to the Israelites his requirements for the sabbath. By 'resting' on the seventh day after the creation (here too we have the verb *šbt* mentioned above) and at the same time 'blessing' and 'hallowing' it (Gen. 2.2–3 P) God had 'completed' this his 'work' of creation by 'rest', and had given to his creation at the same time the ordinance that each six days of 'work' are to be 'completed' by a seventh day of rest;* but at this time this ordinance of creation had not yet been made known to men—at any rate there is no indication of this. It was only with the giving of the manna—as P reports on the basis of the old tradition—that the Israelites learnt that now and on every future seventh day they were to observe the 'holy sabbath to Yahweh' (v. 23). Finally, P has one sample of the wonderful manna

*See von Rad, *Genesis*, pp. 59 ff.

preserved as a tangible sign of the feeding of Israel in the wilderness for all posterity; P does not make the obvious remark that this particular day's ration of an omer of the manna, preserved at the command of God, did not ever rot away. The jar with this manna was placed 'before Yahweh' (v. 33) or 'before the Testimony' (v. 34); here too the future ordering of the cult is anticipated. Such an ordering was certainly not in existence at the time, for it was only later that there was to be a local place where God manifested himself and a place 'of the testimony' ('the law') consisting in the holy ark and the two tables. Nevertheless we are not to assume that P originally had the story of the quails and the manna only after the account of Sinai; for the rather vague formulation 'before Yahweh' (v. 33 and as early as v. 9) shows that P could not yet name here the concrete sanctuary which is rather thought of as in the future. We may ask whether the preservation of the manna is a pure fabrication or whether perhaps in the post-exilic temple which P had in mind a 'jar' with manna was in fact displayed as a remembrance of Israel's journey through the wilderness. In the conclusion of both sources it is expressely said that the manna remained the food of Israel during the whole period of the wanderings in the desert (v. 35). On the 'forty years', which probably belong to the P variant, cf. Num. 14.33–34 P. Josh. 5.12 refers to v. 35b.

3. WATER FROM THE ROCK: 17.1–7

17[1] All the congregation of the people of Israel moved on from the wilderness of Sin by stages, according to the commandment of the LORD, and camped at Rephidim; *but there was no water for the people to drink.* [2] *Therefore the people found fault with Moses, and said, 'Give us water to drink.' And Moses said to them, 'Why do you find fault with me?* [*Why do you put the* LORD *to the proof?*]' [3] *But the people thirsted there for water, and the people murmured against Moses, and said, 'Why did you bring us up out of Egypt, to kill us and our children and our cattle with thirst?'* [4] *So Moses cried to the* LORD, *'What shall I do with this people? They are almost ready to stone me.'* [5] *And the* LORD *said to Moses, 'Pass on before the people, taking with you some of the elders of Israel; and take in your hand the rod with which you struck the Nile, and go.* [6] *Behold, I will stand before you there on the rock at Horeb; and you shall strike the rock, and water shall come out of it, that the people may drink.' And Moses did so, in the sight of the elders of Israel.* [7] *And he called the name of the place* [*Massah and*] *Meribah, because of the faultfinding of the children of Israel,* [*and because they put the* LORD *to the proof by*] *saying, 'Is the* LORD *among us or not?'*

The nucleus of this short piece is formed by the tradition of a spring, of a similar type to the story of Marah in 15.22a*bb*–25a. Despite its brevity it is clearly by no means a literary unity. At the beginning [**1ab***a*] there is a note from P about a stopping-place on the Israelites' route from the 'wilderness of Sin' to Rephidim; the next mention of a stopping place in P, 19.1–2a, is directly connected with this. We have no certain information about the location of this place Rephidim, which is elsewhere attested presumably as a gloss in v. 8 and in the information given at Num. 33.14 f. which has a literary dependence on the present passage. As the derivation of the list of stopping-places in P is completely obscure, and as we cannot with surety assume an internal connection within it, the argument that according to 19.1–2a P seems to have located Rephidim in the neighbourhood of Sinai is not conclusive, quite apart from the fact that we can give no decisive answer to the question of the location of Sinai itself. Against the conjecture made by A. Musil,* that Rephidim should be identified with the mountain ridge now called *er-rafid* on the east coast of the gulf of *el-'aqaba* and thus already on the near side of the traditional Sinai peninsula, a supposition which would suggest some connection with the Sinai tradition, no decisive objection can be made; but of course there is as little positive evidence to recommend it. The detail in P about the stopping-place originally had nothing to do with the following story. True, this story is apparently based on a local tradition, but there are no traces of a P narrative in it and thus it has been attached only at a later stage to the detail of the stopping-place in P. This has happened because it is the last such detail about a stopping-place before the Sinai narrative begins, and all the old Pentateuchal material which stood before the Sinai narrative had to be brought in after it.

[**1b***b*–**7**] The story of the water springing out of the 'rock' in v. 1b*b*–7 is again not in itself a unity. This is principally demonstrated by the fact that there are clear doublets in v. 1b*b*–2 and v. 3; v. 3 is an obvious new beginning connected with geographical details which had come immediately before ('there') and which must have described a definite place at which the Israelites arrived. These geographical details, like the similar ones which should precede v. 1b*b*–2, have been crowded out by the description of the stopping-place which has been prefixed by P. The result is that we now have the old story in its two versions without any details of its location.

* *The Northern Hegaz*, 1926, p. 269.

Apart from this we have no clear criteria for distributing the transmitted material between the two versions which can be detected in v. 1b*b*–2 and v. 3. All that is clear is that v. 1b*b*–2 and v. 7 belong together because of the catchword 'find fault' (*rīb*). It is plausible to suppose that in the combination of two versions E once again appears alongside J, but there are no positive indications of this. For we shall have to assign to J the verse in which the divine name 'Yahweh' appears, so that only v. 3 remains as quite certainly Elohistic; this would have been incorporated into the combined narrative because in it the 'finding fault' with Moses had been framed in definite words. It is further striking that in v. 7 the waterhole receives a double name 'Massah and Meribah'. This is hardly original. As the catchword 'find fault with' (*rīb*) stands in the foreground of v. 2, the story was certainly originally directed towards the name 'Meribah'. Meribah and Massah were two different places, each with its special local tradition from the time of the wandering in the wilderness. In contrast to Meribah, Massah does not occur elsewhere in the Pentateuchal narrative material, but it does (alone, and without Meribah) in the Deuteronomic literature (Deut. 6.16; 9.22). Now as Meribah and Massah are named alongside each other in poetic parallelism in Ps. 95.8 and Deut. 33.8 without being identified the one with the other, a later hand inserted the name Massah into the old story of Meribah in Ex. 17 and made an allusion to this name Massah in v. 2 and v. 7 with the catchword 'put to the proof' (*nissāh*). In the old basic material of the story the Israelites came in their wanderings in the desert to a place where once again they did not find the water which they so needed. Thereupon followed the usual faultfinding, the 'murmuring' against Moses (vv. 1b*b*, 2ab*a*, 3). In v. 3 the juxtaposition of 'I' and 'we' is striking;* presumably the 'we' arose under the influence of v. 2 and originally the first person singular was consistently used in v. 3. When Moses cries for help (v. 4), Yahweh promises his ready help. At the very place there was a 'rock'. Yahweh will stand on this rock, though it is not said whether he will make himself invisible or in some way visible in this place. Moses is now to go to this rock with the rod which had played a part in the plague narrative at the striking of the Nile (7. 17, 20ab J), and to take with him some of the elders as witnesses; it is thus supposed that the rest of the

---

*[This distinction is not brought out in the RSV translation; the speech of the people in the Hebrew reads 'Why did you bring *us* up out of Egypt, to kill *me* and *my* children and *my* cattle . . .' Tr.]

people are not to join in seeing the miracle (this is also implied in the first sentence in v. 5). Then when Moses strikes the rock with his rod Yahweh will make water come out from it. And thus it happens. Thereupon Moses names the place Meribah ('place of faultfinding') because there Israel had 'found fault' with him (v. 7). The story of Meribah is told once again in Num. 20.1–13. It is connected with a definite place in the wilderness which was doubtless still known to the Israelites at a later date. It was the place where there was a spring with the name Meribah; this name originates from the time when nomadic shepherds of the wilderness used to assemble at the spring of Meribah and there determine their 'disputes at law'. The spring of Meribah gushed from a rock in a way which so surprised those who went there that they could only think that at one time the rock had been made to produce water in a miraculous way. According to v. 6 this water-producing rock of Meribah would have been situated 'at Horeb'. But the detail 'at Horeb' is here, as in 3.1, so lame (cf. above pp. 31 f.) that we must regard it as a subsequent addition, especially as it also clashes so much with the preceding word 'there'. In fact the composite name 'Meribah-Kadesh' witnessed in Num. 27.14; Deut. 32.51; Ezek. 47.19; 48.48 shows that the water-hole Meribah is to be sought in the neighbourhood of the Kadesh(-Barnea) region, i.e. in the area of springs which lay about fifty miles south-west of Beersheba in the wilderness of Sinai, which has preserved its old compound name Kadesh(-Barnea) right up to the present day in the name of the spring 'ēn qedēs which flows there. All historical probability suggests that in the time before the conquest of agricultural Palestine the Israelites had stayed in this neighbourhood, characterized by a number of strongly-flowing springs which provided the necessary water both for a large number of men and for their cattle. Within this neighbourhood it is hardly possible to give a more exact location to the spring of Meribah.

4. THE VICTORY OVER THE AMALEKITES: 17.8–16

8 *Then came Amalek and fought with Israel* [*at Rephidim*]. 9 *And Moses said to Joshua, 'Choose for us men, and go out, fight with Amalek; tomorrow I will stand on the top of the hill* [*with the rod of God in my hand*].' 10 *So Joshua did as Moses told him, and fought with Amalek; and Moses, Aaron, and Hur went up to the top of the hill.* 11 *Whenever Moses held up his hand, Israel prevailed; and whenever he lowered his hand, Amalek prevailed.* 12 *But Moses' hands grew weary; so they took a stone and put it under him, and he*

sat upon it, and Aaron and Hur held up his hands, one on one side, and the other on the other side; so his hands were steady until the going down of the sun. ¹³ *And Joshua mowed down Amalek and his people with the edge of the sword.*

14 *And the* LORD *said to Moses, 'Write this as a memorial in a book and recite it in the ears of Joshua, that I will utterly blot out the remembrance of Amalek from under heaven.'* ¹⁵ *And Moses built an altar and called the name of it, The* LORD *is my banner,* ¹⁶ *saying, 'A hand upon the banner of the* LORD*! The* LORD *will have war with Amalek from generation to generation.'*

This piece belongs to the old narrative material and shows no trace of being composed of different narrative strands. It may derive from J. A battle between Israel and the Amalekites in the wilderness forms the background of the narrative which is apparently aimed at the altar built and named by Moses. The Amalekites were a confederacy of nomad tribes in the wilderness of Sinai. In the wilderness it was easy to come into contact with parts of this tribal confederacy, especially at the scanty water holes and cattle pasturages. Even after they had settled in the agricultural land of Palestine the Israelites still had fierce encounters with the inhabitants of the neighbouring wilderness, who threatened the settled land and its inhabitants. We finally hear of them in the account of Saul's victory over the Amalekites (I Sam. 15) and in the reports from the time when David was leader of a band of mercenaries in Ziklag (I Sam. 27.8; 30.1 ff.).

[8–13] According to the present narrative Israel was one day attacked by the Amalekites (v. 8). The description of the place 'at Rephidim' is very probably taken from v. 1ab*b* P. It looks out of place at the end of the verse; had the story of the battle against the Amalekites in its original form had some place-name to describe the scene of the action, we should surely have had an introductory remark that Israel was encamped at such and such a place. Joshua appears quite abruptly and without any introduction in v. 9. He also occurs from time to time elsewhere in the old Pentateuchal narrative material as a companion of Moses (Ex. 24.13; 32.17; 33.11; Num. 11.28), always appearing most unexpectedly. Only in the present story does he appear as leader of the Israelite battle-force in the time of Moses. He is supposed to be a well-known figure. Of course the Joshua of the tradition preserved in the Book of Joshua is meant; it is inferred from this tradition that he was already among the Israelites in Moses' time. On the instructions of Moses, who is the supreme commander, he engages battle with the attacking Amalekites and eventually defeats them (v. 13). The decisive result is of course brought about not by him but through the action of Moses, who on the day of the battle (the 'tomorrow' in v. 9 shows that the preparations had been made on the day before) ascends 'the hill' and there effects Israel's victory by holding up his hands. The mention of 'the hill' gives us to understand that the narrative envisages a quite definite locality which was still known when the story was formulated. From this hill it was possible to look right over the field of battle. The observation about the 'rod of God' at the end of v. 9 is certainly an addition, as this rod has no part at all in what follows. Moses lets Aaron and Hur accompany him up the hill. These two appear as abruptly as did Joshua earlier. In the J narrative Aaron has occurred up till now only in secondary passages, while Hur has not been mentioned at all. Aaron and Hur appear once again alongside each other in 24.14, immediately after Joshua has been named as servant of Moses (v. 13), and moreover apparently as prominent Israelites. This role, which in the tradition as we now have it is very much diminished, was certainly once far clearer in an older tradition which is no longer known to us. On the hill, Moses by raising his hands now exerts an influence on the battle which allows the Israelites to prevail; without this the Amalekites of themselves would have proved superior, as is clear from the fact that as soon as Moses lets his hands fall the Amalekites, who are perhaps thought of as being numerically very strong, begin to prevail (v. 11). In the story the lifting up of the hands appears to have a strikingly impersonal magical effect. Yahweh is not mentioned at all in the whole section vv. 8–13, not even as having given Moses the instructions for his action. A mysterious power seems to come from Moses which is focussed in the direction of the Israelite force, visible from the hill and thus reachable in a straight line by the beam of power. We may compare Joshua stretching out the spear against the city of Ai which he meant to sack in Josh. 8.18, 26. There is no indication that the raising of the hands is to be understood as a gesture of prayer (the customary expression for this in the Old Testament is to 'spread out' the hands) though the action of Moses was perhaps quite early, albeit only secondarily, understood in this way. In spite of the influence emanating from Moses, the battle against the Amalekites was so hard that it lasted a whole day before the Amalekites were defeated; because of this Moses had to have his raised hands supported by Aaron and Hur (v. 12). In doing this he sits upon a stone, and this (stool-like) stone is presumably significant for the story in so far as it was the only permanent visible sign of the war against the Amalekites and could be pointed out as such on 'the hill' even at a later date. [14–16] Further memorials of the war against the Amalekites are mentioned also in the two closing notes, v. 14 and vv. 15 f., both of which speak of a special enmity between Yahweh and the Amalekites. These notes thus derive from a time and a sphere of activity in which the Amalekites appear as particularly evil and particularly dangerous opponents of the people of Yahweh (cf. also Deut. 25.17–19). Such a situation would suit the Israelites living on the southern border of the hill country west of Jordan in the neighbourhood of the wilderness of Sinai and, from what we know of their history, in the early period up to the time of Saul and David. According to v. 14 Moses is to write a report of the victory over the Amalekites (one of the rare occasions on which it is said that Moses is to write an individual piece of the Pentateuchal tradition) and is further to impress the story upon Joshua by talking to him (clearly oral tradition) so that the hostility of the Amalekites, once so dangerous, may still be remembered even when Yahweh, as is here expected, shall one day have destroyed them completely. The second note in vv. 15 f. stands only in a loose connection with what has gone before. Moses is to erect an altar, still at the place of the victory over the Amalekites. This altar was surely still known at a later date. It is quite feasible that this remark may refer to the stone in v. 12, in which case we may suppose that there are here preserved two different explanations of this stone, connected with the memory of the victory over the Amalekites, firstly as the seat of Moses during the slaughter and secondly as the altar erected by Moses after the slaughter. But this is not certain and it may also be a case of two different local occurrences. The question is hard to answer, as the name which Moses gave to the altar he erected is not fully preserved. This name is in fact clearly connected with the saying which Moses utters at the naming of the altar (v. 16). In v. 15 the name runs *yahweh nissī* ('Yahweh is my banner') and the saying in v. 16 says that one is to lay his hand on *kēsyāh*; this is a very obscure expression which even the old translations have understood to mean *kisseyāh*— 'the throne of Yahweh'. Now it is at least clear that originally the 'banner of Yahweh' or the 'throne of Yahweh' were mentioned in each case (in this case the original text of v. 15 must be assumed to have been *Yahweh kis'ī*—'Yahweh is my throne'). Should the latter be right, then the equation of the altar, whose name contains the word 'throne', with the stone seat of Moses in v. 12 would be very probable. But what argues against this possibility is simply the state of the text; for even in v. 16 the word 'throne' does not stand in the text at all, but must be provided by some emendation, albeit slight; and in face of this the alteration of the present *kēsyāh* into a presumably original *nēs yāh* is hardly more extensive, especially as the transmitted text in v. 15 can then remain completely unaltered. There is further the point that the expression 'Yahweh is my throne' is very difficult and hardly explicable as the name of the altar, and the same may be said of the saying 'A hand upon the throne of Yahweh'. The name of the altar was then almost certainly 'Yahweh is my banner'.* Here we must remember that bands of warriors used to assemble around banners and standards which bore pictures or symbols of their gods. There were certainly no images of God in Israel but there may have been some signs of the divine presence. The saying 'Yahweh is my banner' expresses the fact that Israel (for Israel is surely here at least originally the 'I' of the saying) assembles for warlike action in the name of Yahweh, and the altar with this name may in fact have been a point of assembly in the Amalekite wars. There is also evidence elsewhere of an altar being given its own particular name (cf. Gen. 33.20; Judg. 6.24). The saying in v. 16 which requires Israel to assemble at the 'banner of Yahweh' because Amalek is the enemy of Yahweh will have been a rallying cry with which it was customary to give a summons to battle against the Amalekites.

5. THE MEETING WITH THE PRIEST OF MIDIAN:
18.1–27

18 ¹ [*Jethro,*] *the priest of Midian, Moses' father-in-law, heard of all that God had done for Moses and for Israel his people, [how the* LORD *had brought Israel out of Egypt.*] ² *Now* [*Jethro,*] *Moses' father-in-law, had taken Zipporah, Moses' wife, [after he had sent her away]* ³ *and her two sons, of whom the name of the one was Gershom [(for he said, 'I have been a sojourner in a foreign land')],* ⁴ *and the name of the other, Eliezer [(for he said, 'The God of my father was my help, and delivered me from the sword of Pharaoh')].* ⁵ *And* [*Jethro,*] *Moses' father-in-law, came with his sons and*

*[Thus the RSV conjecture is quite plausible. Tr.]

his wife to Moses in the wilderness where he was encamped at the mountain of God. ⁶ *And when one told Moses, 'Lo, your father-in-law [Jethro] is coming to you with your wife and her two sons with her,'* ⁷ *Moses went out to meet his father-in-law, and did obeisance and kissed him; and they asked each other of their welfare, and went into the tent.* ⁸ *Then Moses told his father-in-law [all that the* LORD *had done to Pharaoh and to the Egyptians for Israel's sake,] all the hardship that had come upon them in the way, [and how the* LORD *had delivered them.* ⁹ *And Jethro rejoiced for all the good which the* LORD *had done to Israel, in that he had delivered them out of the hand of the Egyptians.*

10 *And Jethro said, 'Blessed be the* LORD, *who has delivered you out of the hand of the Egyptians and out of the hand of Pharaoh.]* ¹¹ *Now I know that the* LORD *is greater than all gods, because he delivered the people from under the hand of the Egyptians, when they dealt arrogantly with them.'* ¹² *And [Jethro,] Moses' father-in-law, offered a burnt offering and sacrifices to God; and Aaron came with all the elders of Israel, to eat bread with Moses' father-in-law before God.*

13 *On the morrow Moses sat to judge the people, and the people stood about Moses from morning till evening.* ¹⁴ *When Moses' father-in-law saw all that he was doing for the people, he said, 'What is this that you are doing for the people? Why do you sit alone, and all the people stand about you from morning till evening?'* ¹⁵ *And Moses said to his father-in-law, 'Because the people come to me to inquire of God;* ¹⁶ *when they have a dispute, they come to me and I decide between a man and his neighbour, and I make them know the statutes of God and his decisions.'* ¹⁷ *Moses' father-in-law said to him, 'What you are doing is not good.* ¹⁸ *You and the people with you will wear yourselves out, for the thing is too heavy for you; you are not able to perform it alone.* ¹⁹ *Listen now to my voice; I will give you counsel, and God be with you! You shall represent the people before God, and bring their cases to God;* ²⁰ *and you shall teach them the statutes and the decisions, and make them know the way in which they must walk and what they must do.* ²¹ *Moreover choose able men from all the people, such as fear God, men who are trustworthy and who hate a bribe; and place such men over the people as rulers of thousands, of hundreds, of fifties, and of tens.* ²² *And let them judge the people at all times; every great matter they shall bring to you, but any small matter they shall decide themselves; so it will be easier for you, and they will bear the burden with you.* ²³ *If you do this, and God so commands you, then you will be able to endure, and all this people also will go to their place in peace.'*

24 *So Moses gave heed to the voice of his father-in-law and did all that he had said.* ²⁵ *Moses chose able men out of all Israel, and made them heads over the people, rulers of thousands, of hundreds, of fifties, and of tens.* ²⁶ *And they judged the people at all times; hard cases they brought to Moses, but any small matter they decided themselves.* ²⁷ *Then Moses let his father-in-law depart, and he went his way to his own country.*

The occasion of this chapter is the meeting of Moses with his father-in-law in the wilderness. Within the framework of this meeting there are two main events, firstly a cultic act with sacrifice and sacrificial meal (vv. 1–12) and secondly a new arrangement for the administration of justice (vv. 13–27). These two proceedings, which the narrative divides between two consecutive days (v. 13) of course have an extremely close connection in fact in so far as the administration of justice—at least in certain cases—is a sacral act and takes place at some holy spot. The chapter is not a complete literary unity. True, the second part (vv. 13–27) gives us no cause to suppose any literary disunity but offers a smooth, self-contained narrative sequence; the first part (vv. 1–12) however displays striking discrepancies and repetitions. The basis of this first part is in details and language so clearly connected with the second part that we must derive this basis along with the second part from one and the same source. As the word 'God' (and not the divine name Yahweh) is used in particularly important places (especially v. 12) in the first part, and exclusively throughout the second part, the chapter is in essentials to be derived from E. The question now is only whether another source—which could only be J—is recognizable in the repetitions of the first part, especially where the divine name Yahweh appears (vv. 1b, 8 end, 9–11). In fact the repetitions which have been indicated appear to be so little elements of a continuous narrative, even one which is only partially recognizable, that we do better to regard them just as secondary 'J' expansions of the E material. Thus we have here the occasion, rare in the middle of the Pentateuch, of an E passage still preserved complete which was incorporated into the combined Pentateuch narrative as special material from E because it apparently had no counterpart in the other sources.

In the first part the constant periphrastic description of Moses' interlocutor is remarkable. Throughout the second part we hear quite simply of his 'father-in-law'; this is also the case in the first part in vv. 7 f., and where the proper name Jethro appears here it is still explicitly added that he is the father-in-law of Moses (the same thing happens as early as 3.1; 4.18). The proper name Jethro only appears all by itself in vv. 9 and 10, where the appearance of the divine name Yahweh by itself suggests that these are secondary expansions. This position leads us to suppose that the proper name Jethro was first added subsequently, and that probably the father-in-law of Moses was still unnamed in the basic material of E. A traditio-historical investigation in any case reveals that originally no name was known for the father-in-law of Moses and that later different names arose for him (cf. above p. 37 on 2.18; 3.1). On the other hand, the observation that it was the priest of Midian whom Moses had for a father-in-law, made only once in the introduction, is certainly original. True, it had already been mentioned in 2.16 J (cf. also 3.1) and had presumably been narrated previously in E as well, but it was important expressly to recall this fact in this chapter, as family concerns are discussed only here at the beginning; the main section deals with sacral matters, for which it is less important that the man is related to Moses than that he is a priest of Midian. The tradition definitely derives from the fact of a meeting at a definite place in the wilderness between Israel and the priest of Midian; in comparison with this the theme of Moses' kinship is secondary. The local associations belong to the original material. First of all in v. 5 there is a somewhat vague description of a camping place of Israel 'in the wilderness'; this is very indefinite and is perhaps meant to characterize Israel's situation rather than to indicate a concrete locality; it must have been said somewhere previously where Israel was then 'encamped'. This is not the case in the text as we have it now, and, even if we ignore the fact that the preceding narratives derive from other sources, we have to take into consideration the universal principle that each of the 'wilderness' stories is a self-contained entity, and that therefore the local associations of these narratives may not be transferred from one to another. The consequence of this is that the mention of the 'mountain of God' at the end of v. 5, which appears rather lame after the remark about the camping place of Israel 'in the wilderness', and thus seems to be secondary, does not in fact clash with this remark but represents the original details about the location which belong to the present tradition. The tradition presumes that this 'mountain of God' 'in the wilderness' is known, so that there is no need to define the place more accurately. There is now of course the problem of where we are to locate this 'mountain of God'. It would seem most obvious to think of the holy mountain of the Sinai tradition and perhaps this was already the meaning of E. For the portion of E which is still preserved has the account of the great theophany immediately after the present story without giving us any new geographical details (19.2b, 3a; cf. also pp. 31 f. above on 3.1 ff. E). But this does not of course give a conclusive answer to the question whether the pre-literary tradition had already meant by the 'mountain of God' the same mountain which stands at the centre of the special Sinai tradition. We can hardly give a full explanation of this question. Probability argues that in the end it is the same mountain, though at the same time it remains striking that a nameless 'mountain of God' was mentioned outside the Sinai tradition. Now in any case in Ex. 18 this 'mountain of God' does not play the role of the scene of a theophany, but is a place where there was a meeting between Israel and the 'priest of Midian'. Even in this role the 'mountain of God' was a holy mountain, as is shown not only by its name but also by the fact that sacrifices were offered upon it, whether at its foot or at its summit. The tradition of the meeting at the 'mountain of God' probably presupposes that such meetings—at least from time to time—regularly took place in the form of common participation in certain cultic acts. On the 'mountain of God', wherever it is to be located, Israelites and Midianites (for whose dwelling-places and pastures see above p. 31) from time to time assembled. Thus the 'mountain of God' 'in the wilderness' with its holy place was the goal of a pilgrimage and was approached from different sides. The tradition of the encounter between Israel and the priest of Midian during the journey through the wilderness, and of Moses' kinship with the priest, has its root in these Israelite-Midianite meetings on the 'mountain of God'. The role of the priest of Midian indicates that the holy place on the 'mountain of God' was a proper Midianite sanctuary; it is the priest of Midian who according to v. 12 offers sacrifice.

[1–12] The narrative in Ex. 18 is connected with the story of the marriage of Moses to the daughter of the priest of Midian, the story in the E version which is now no longer extant, having been forced out by the J version in 2.16–22; it is however presupposed in 4.18, 20b E. On hearing of the mighty acts of God (v. 1) the father-in-law of Moses seeks Israel out in the wilderness (v. 1b is a badly attached gloss which is striking because of the mere fact of the occurrence of the divine name Yahweh); on this occasion he brings to Moses his wife and his two sons. According to E they had stayed with the priest when Moses had returned to Egypt (cf. above p. 47 on 4.18, 20b.); according to J Moses had at that time taken them with him (4.20a). In view of this remark by J, v. 2b speaks of the 'sending away' of the wife, as though Moses had sent his wife and two sons back home again from Egypt. This is certainly just a redactional addition to smooth out the differences between J and E. According to E Moses had at that time two sons, whereas J knew only of one son (2.22). In vv. 3 f. the names of the two sons are given and explained very wordily. The verbal correspondence with 2.22b J is very striking in the explanation of the first name, so that we can ask whether it was not taken over from J and then a corresponding explanation of the second name was subsequently added. Moses greets his father-in-law on his arrival with all possible courtesy (vv. 6 f.). After this domestic introduction there follows the real substance of the tradition. Moses narrates to the Midianite priest the mighty acts which Yahweh has done for Israel, whereupon the priest makes his recognition of Yahweh. Now this section (vv. 8–11) is obviously overfull, as can be seen from the frequent repetition of the same quite general expressions; and there is above all the question whether the original basis should not be held to be merely a part of v. 8 and perhaps v. 11, as according to v. 1 the father-in-law of Moses had already 'heard of all that God had done'. But in v. 8 the remark about the 'hardship' experienced on the way should be regarded as original, because of its unusual phraseology, especially as the anarthrous juxtaposition of two objects in this clause indicates that the first of these objects is an addition. On vv. 9 f. cf. above p. 146. It is hard to assess v. 11, because the conclusion has been lost. It is possible that in Moses' father-in-law's solemn confession the divine name Yahweh, which is not unknown even in E (cf. 3.13–15), could have been mentioned once again in the Elohistic narrative, especially as the scene is set on the 'mountain of God', and thus at the place of the revelation of the divine name. With respect to the content of this confession the recognition of a 'polytheistic-comparative' exaltation of Yahweh over 'all gods' such as still occurs occasionally in traditional language, especially in the Psalms,* is here put in the mouth of a Midianite whom the divine acts have led to 'enlightenment'. The priest of Midian thereupon prepares a sacrificial feast, which forms the starting point for the whole of the story in the tradition, in which 'Aaron with all the elders of Israel' take part as representatives of Israel. It is not said what role Aaron is thought to play. The special mention of him must stem from special Aaron traditions which were once current but have no longer been preserved (cf. also above pp. 122 f.). At the communal sacrificial meal 'before God', i.e. at the holy place, Moses is of course in the present context thought of as being there; it is, however, striking that he is not explicitly mentioned, as it seems now as though we had a cultic meeting only between the priest of Midian on the one side and Aaron

*Cf. L. Köhler, *Old Testament Theology*, ET 1957, pp. 36 f.

and the elders of Israel on the other, whereas the kinship between Moses and the priest was in fact the reason for this meeting.

[13–27] The new ordering of the administration of justice which is derived from a practical, matter-of-fact counsel by the father-in-law of Moses is certainly meant by this time to be of permanent validity for Israel; indeed it was probably the practice in Israel at one time. It rests on a division between sacral and 'civic' justice, viz. on a separation of 'civic' justice from the sacral sphere. The narrative will certainly be right in supposing that this division was at one time a novelty. To sacral justice, and thus in the present instance to Moses, is reserved 'converse with God' (v. 19) i.e. the proclamation of divine statutes and decisions, the publishing of directives for the right 'way' (vv. 16, 20) and the 'inquiring of God' (vv. 15,19) which was provided for especially in the judging of 'hard cases' (v. 26; of this cf. for example 22.7–10). All the rest is to be handed over to trustworthy men who are to be appointed as the rulers of thousands, of hundreds, of fifties and of tens. The division of the whole which is thus envisaged certainly does not derive from any judicial ideas, but from the organization of the levy. Thus the subordinate commanders of the host will by this have 'civic' justice delegated to them. This points to a time in which there was an organized Israelite levy. Moreover, the formulation at the end of v. 23 seems to presuppose that Israel is firmly settled. In that case we must ask who played at a later date the part here envisaged for Moses. We might think of the 'Judges of Israel' (cf. Judg. 10.1–5; 12.7–15). This would bring us to soon after the settlement. In addition, this quite remarkable derivation of the ordering of Israelite justice from the counsel of a priest of Midian suggests that the present tradition may have arisen at a very early period, in which there were probably still friendly and neighbourly relations between the southern Israelite tribes and the Midianites.

IV

THE MAKING OF THE COVENANT ON
SINAI & THE FIRST DIVINE ORDINANCES

19.1 – 40.38

1. THE THEOPHANY ON SINAI WITH THE
DECALOGUE 19.1–20.21

19[1] On the third new moon after the people of Israel had gone forth out of the land of Egypt, on that day they came into the wilderness of Sinai. [2] And when they set out from Rephidim and came into the wilderness of Sinai, they encamped in the wilderness; *and there Israel encamped before the mountain.* [3] *And Moses went up to God, and the* LORD *called him out of the mountain, saying, 'Thus you shall say to the house of Jacob, and tell the people of Israel:* [4] *You have seen what I did to the Egyptians, and how I bore you on eagles' wings and brought you to myself.* [5] *Now therefore, if you will obey my voice and keep my covenant, you shall be my own possession among all peoples; for all the earth is mine,* [6] *and you shall be to me a kingdom of priests and a holy nation. These are the words which you shall speak to the children of Israel.'*

[7] *So Moses came and called the elders of the people, and set before them all these words which the* LORD *had commanded him.* [8] *And all the people answered together and said, 'All that the* LORD *has spoken we will do.' And Moses reported the words of the people to the* LORD. [9] *And the* LORD *said to Moses, 'Lo, I am coming to you in a thick cloud, that the people may hear when I speak with you, and may also believe you for ever.'*

[*Then Moses told the words of the people to the* LORD.] [10] *And the* LORD *said to Moses, 'Go to the people and consecrate them today and tomorrow, and let them wash their garments,* [11] *and be ready by the third day; [for on the third day the* LORD *will come down upon Mount Sinai in the sight of all the people.]* [12] *And you shall set bounds for the people round about, saying, "Take heed that you do not go up into the mountain or touch the border of it; whoever touches the mountain shall be put to death;* [13] *no hand shall touch him, but he shall be stoned or shot; whether beast or man, he shall not live." When the trumpet sounds a long blast, they shall come up to the mountain.'* [14] *So*

*Moses went down from the mountain to the people, and consecrated the people;
and they washed their garments.* ¹⁵ *And he said to the people, 'Be ready by
the third day; do not go near a woman.'*

16 *On the morning of the third day there were thunders and lightnings,
and a thick cloud upon the mountain, and a very loud trumpet blast, so that all
the people who were in the camp trembled.* ¹⁷ *Then Moses brought the people
out of the camp to meet God; and they took their stand at the foot of the mountain.*
¹⁸ *And Mount Sinai was wrapped in smoke, because the* Lord *descended upon
it in fire; and the smoke of it went up like the smoke of a kiln, and the whole
mountain quaked greatly.* ¹⁹ *And as the sound of the trumpet grew louder and
louder, Moses spoke, and God answered him in thunder.* ²⁰ *And the* Lord *came
down upon Mount Sinai, to the top of the mountain; and the* Lord *called
Moses to the top of the mountain, and Moses went up.* ²¹ *And the* Lord *said
to Moses, 'Go down and warn the people, lest they break through to the* Lord
to gaze and many of them perish. ²² *And also let the priests who come near to
the* Lord *consecrate themselves, lest the* Lord *break out upon them.'* ²³ *And
Moses said to the* Lord, *'The people cannot come up to Mount Sinai; for thou
thyself didst charge us, saying, "Set bounds about the mountain, and consecrate it."'* ²⁴ *And the* Lord *said to him, 'Go down, and come up bringing
Aaron with you; but do not let the priests and the people break through to come
up to the* Lord, *lest he break out against them.'* ²⁵ *So Moses went down
to the people and told them.*

20 ¹ *And God spoke all these words, saying,*

2 *'I am the* Lord *your God, who brought you out of the land of Egypt, out
of the house of bondage.*

3 *'You shall have no other gods before me.*

4 *'You shall not make yourself a graven image, or any likeness of anything
that is in heaven above, or that is in the earth beneath, or that is in the water
under the earth;* ⁵ *you shall not bow down to them or serve them; for I the*
Lord *your God am a jealous God, visiting the iniquity of the fathers upon the
children to the third and the fourth generation of those who hate me,* ⁶ *but
showing steadfast love to thousands of those who love me and keep my commandments.*

7 *'You shall not take the name of the* Lord *your God in vain; for the*
Lord *will not hold him guiltless who takes his name in vain.*

8 *'Remember the sabbath day, to keep it holy.* ⁹ *Six days you shall labour,
and do all your work;* ¹⁰ *but the seventh day is a sabbath to the* Lord *your
God; in it you shall not do any work, you, or your son, or your daughter, your
manservant, or your maidservant, or your cattle, or the sojourner who is within
your gates;* ¹¹ *for in six days the* Lord *made heaven and earth, the sea, and
all that is in them, and rested the seventh day; therefore the* Lord *blessed the
sabbath day and hallowed it.*

12 *'Honour your father and your mother, that your days may be long in
the land which the* Lord *your God gives you.*

13 *'You shall not kill.*

14 *'You shall not commit adultery.*

15 '*You shall not steal.*
16 '*You shall not bear false witness against your neighbour.*

17 '*You shall not covet your neighbour's house; you shall not covet your neighbour's wife, or his manservant, or his maidservant, or his ox, or his ass, or anything that is your neighbour's.*'

18 *Now when all the people perceived the thunderings and the lightnings and the sound of the trumpet and the mountain smoking, the people were afraid and trembled; and they stood afar off,* [19] *and said to Moses, 'You speak to us, and we will hear; but let not God speak to us, lest we die.'* [20] *And Moses said to the people, 'Do not fear; for God has come to prove you, and that the fear of him may be before your eyes, that you may not sin.'*

21 *And the people stood afar off, while Moses drew near to the thick cloud where God was.*

The account of the theophany on Sinai, which belongs to the basic stratum of the special history of Israel, is divided into a number of sub-sections. Remarks about the arrival of the Israelites at Sinai (19.1 f.) are followed first by a general divine address about the purpose of God, delivered to Israel by Moses, and then by an answer from the people (19.3–9). Moses next receives instructions about the preparations for the theophany (19.10–15) which now takes place (19.16–20). After a number of warnings against coming up on the holy mountain (19.21–25) God makes known the 'Decalogue' (20.1–17); thereupon the people, terrified by the theophany, ask Moses to act as mediator for them (20.18–21). Even this preliminary sketch, though on the whole consistent, contains some inconsistencies. It is striking that, after the need to observe the holiness of the mountain has already been strongly stressed in the section describing the preparations for the theophany, the subject is taken up once again after the following theophany. It is even more striking that the people's request for Moses to act as mediator only comes after God has already delivered the whole Decalogue. Many other peculiar details reveal themselves at a closer inspection. The ascent and descent of Moses is repeated remarkably often and, moreover, in a way which is not always consistently connected with the position of Moses which is from time to time presupposed in the course of the narrative (cf. 19.3a with 19.3b and 19.8b with 19.9b). There is also the repeated change of the divine name for no apparent reason (cf. 19.3a with 19.3b; 19.17, 19 with 19.18, 20) and the appearance of conspicuous doublets (cf. 19.2a*b* with 19.2b). We can therefore recognize the juxtaposition of different, originally independent strands of narrative which have subsequently been interwoven. The language of the introductory notes in 19.1–2a clearly demonstrates that they belong to P, which then makes no further appearance in what follows, first appearing again in ch. 24. In 19.2b–20.21 we have primarily to deal with the sources J and E and must employ their usage of different names of God to separate them. The word 'God' occurs in 19.3a, 17, 19; 20.1, 19–21. In these verses, to which a number of connected passages (in which no name for God appears) belong (19.16b; 20.18) the source E may be present. It is in any case clear that only fragments of it have been incorporated in the later combined narrative. It appears to be peculiar to the E narrative that the mighty signs of the divine presence appear immediately after the Israelites arrive at the holy mountain (19.16b, 17, 19) whereupon the people in terror keep their distance and ask Moses to act as mediator (20.18–21), whereas in the other variant the people have to be warned emphatically before the theophany against coming too near to the mountain (19.12 f.). In this other variant we must see the essentials of the J narrative (with the divine name Yahweh). Of course it is no longer possible to make a smooth and satisfactory division of the whole between the two older sources. This is not surprising, as it is easily understandable that the important central section of the tradition of the theophany on Sinai should frequently have been worked over and provided with expansions. Thus the section 19.3b–9a (9b) in particular looks like a later addition, because it anticipates the theophany and, as early as v. 5, speaks of the keeping of the covenant which has not as yet been concluded. We also certainly have a number of additions in 19.21–25, which add a number of supplementary details to the theme of the approach to the holy mountain. Perhaps the hardest question to answer is that of whether the Decalogue has its original literary setting in the narrative context which it now occupies. Although itself using the divine name Yahweh, it is framed by 'Elohistic' passages (20.1, 18–21). But the introductory remark 20.1 is of quite general content, and vv. 18–21 do not connect immediately with the Decalogue but with the description of the theophany in 19.16b, 17, 19. The Decalogue is thus so loosely inserted into the narrative that we are led to the conclusion that from a literary aspect it is a secondary passage in the account of the theophany on Sinai. This implies nothing about its age and provenance, especially as it represents in any case a self-contained and independent entity which originally certainly had its own tradition-history. We can no longer answer the question of the stage of the literary development of Ex. 19–20 at which it might have been incorporated. Its position between 'Elohistic' pieces—at times people have been inclined to call it the 'Elohistic Decalogue' to distinguish it from the 'Yahwistic Decalogue' in Ex. 34—implies very little, especially in view of the fragmentary character of 19.21–20.1. We can thus only come to the negative conclusion that the Decalogue did not originally stand in any of the old narratives of the theophany on Sinai, but was only inserted into them during the course of time.

[19.1–2] The P introduction in 19.1–2a names first of all, as apparently the most important information, the circumstances of the arrival at Sinai; P immediately follows this in ch. 24 with the appearance of the 'glory of Yahweh' and the ascent of Moses up the mountain to receive the divine instructions. As Israel had come out of Egypt at Passover and the feast of unleavened bread in the first month (cf. p. 95 above on 12.3), they therefore arrived at Sinai in the third month (reckoning the new year in the spring), and moreover on the day of the new moon, i.e. the first day of this month; the reference in v. 1b to a definite day shows that the first word in v. 1a does not have the general meaning 'month', but is meant in the special sense of the 'day of the new moon'. These details may rest on tradition and may show that the Sinai event was fixed and celebrated on this very day. They were apparently so essential for P that he puts the note about the itinerary (v. 2a), which connects with 17.1 ab*a*, as an addition after them, although these notes about the itinerary usually stand at the beginning and even belong there. The 'wilderness of Sinai' takes its name from the mountain and is a general description of the desert region in the neighbourhood of the mountain. It is no longer possible to ascertain the location of Sinai with certainty. From the Byzantine period one of the very high mountains in the southern part of what is today called the Sinai peninsula has been recognized as the scene of the Old Testament theophany, either the 'Mountain of Moses' (*jebel mūsa*, 7,647 ft) or 'Mount St Catherine' (*jebel qāterīn*, 8,649 ft) at whose foot stands the Greek Orthodox monastery of St Catherine. It is evident, from the numerous inscriptions by Nabataean pilgrims on the approaches to this mountain chain, that this neighbourhood was the goal of pagan pilgrimages even in the pre-Byzantine period, and it is possible that the holiness of this region and the pilgrimages to it go back to a still earlier time, although concrete evidence for this is completely lacking. We can no longer decide whether the Byzantine choice of Sinai could have been connected with an old and genuine tradition which may perhaps have existed in Israel and then in Judaism, or whether it merely represents a secondary localization of the Old Testament Sinai tradition on an imposing mountain of traditional holiness. The Old Testament reports of Sinai are mostly too indefinite to be of help in the question of identifying the holy mountain. The notes in the Priestly itinerary (Ex. 15.22a*a*, 27a*a*; 16.1a; 17.1ab*a*; 19.2a; Num. 12.10 etc.) give details of places, but these do not help us much as the places mentioned are unknown to us. Moreover, they are a relatively late element of the tradition and may well belong to a late attempt to fix a definite route for the journey of the Israelites (cf. also p. 110 above on the P localization of the miracle at the sea). As the theophany on Sinai is the subject of a special element of the tradition we must be careful in any attempt to determine its location on the basis of geographical details given in other elements of the tradition. The pilgrimage to Sinai was in any case a special event, and its goal may have been far removed from the places of the Exodus and the rest of Israel's journey through the wilderness. Men have never been afraid of long and difficult journeys to find a holy place, and the journey to Sinai was indeed for Israel just such a pilgrimage to a famous holy mountain, even if Israel did not know beforehand what decisive event was to confront them on this holy mountain. It is therefore not completely irrelevant to adduce the only concrete information in the Old Testament about the character of the holy mountain, the fact that volcanic eruptions were to be seen on it (cf. 19.18, 20, and also p. 109 above on 13.21 f.), to answer the question of its location. In that case of course we should no longer look for it on the present 'Sinai peninsula', for there have never been any active volcanoes upon it in historical times. Instead we must go quite a long way from the normal routes between Egypt and Palestine, right over to the other side of the gulf of *el-ʿaqaba* in the north-west part of what is now Saudi Arabia, where in the neighbourhood of the place *tebūk* which lies on the great road to Medina and Mecca—in roughly the same latitude as the southern part of the Sinai peninsula—there are volcanoes which are still active today. These might have a bearing on the question if the description of volcanic phenomena in Ex. 19 does not merely represent the acceptance of traditional elements of a theophany description but has preserved some character of the experience of Israel at Sinai. As we can give no certain answer to this latter question (see p. 160 below) there is even here no completely reliable clue for the localizing of Sinai and the 'wilderness of Sinai' in which the Israelites 'encamped'. The repetition in v. 2b of the remark about this encamping in v. 2ab indicates a fragment from the introductory phrases of one of the older sources which has in other respects fallen out in favour of P.

[19.3–9] After an Elohistic note about the ascent of Moses 'to God' (v. 3a) which has no direct continuation in the extant passages of the E narrative strand and was perhaps originally followed by a first announcement of the theophany to Moses, there comes an initial command from Yahweh, for Moses to pass on a message from him to the people (vv. 3b–6). This message, formulated in ceremonial language (cf. the *parallelismus membrorum* as early as the formula of command), is from the point of view of its style alone remarkable in the brief narrative style of the older sources; it contains deuteronomistic phrases, particularly in v. 5, and with the surrounding material represents a later addition, especially as it anticipates the report of the concluding of the covenant and the imparting of the law. It recalls to the people of Israel the deeds of their God in bringing them out of Egypt and guiding them through the wilderness and makes the obedience of Israel the condition of the special place among the nations which is marked out for her. The image of the eagle (or vulture) who can safely carry its young on its mighty wings (v. 4) also occurs in Deut. 32.11; so safely has Yahweh brought Israel 'to himself', to his (dwelling) place, i.e. in the present context to Sinai. Israel is to be the special possession of Yahweh (v. 5), to whom the whole earth and so all nations belong; she is therefore a 'holy' people, i.e. set apart from the rest of the nations (v. 6). The singular expression 'kingdom of priests' (v. 6) obviously also refers to this. There is no particular emphasis on the word 'kingdom' in this expression; it may be understood to mean 'state' in just the same way as the nations on the earth are usually organized into states. Israel is to have the role of the priestly member in the number of earthly states. Israel is to have the special privilege of priests, to be allowed to 'draw near' God, and is to do 'service' for all the world (cf. also Isa. 61.5 f.); this is the purpose for which Israel has been chosen, as has been demonstrated by the earlier acts of God towards the people. Thereupon the people pledge themselves to obedience (vv. 7 f.), and then Yahweh announces to Moses his impending appearance and converse with him, with the purpose of authenticating him before the people and confirming his full power of mediator by the message which he brings; for 'belief' in Moses cf. 14.31 J. There is an addition in v. 9b which does not fit the context very well and which is meant merely to adjust the transition to the new speech of Yahweh in vv. 10 ff.

[19.10–15] In 19.10–15 we have the account of the preparations for the theophany according to the J variant. Moses, who is here presumed to be on the mountain (cf. v. 14a)—a previous remark about this in J has been lost—receives instructions about the necessary precautions and hands them on to the people. These are first to be consecrated for the theophany which is announced for the third day, i.e. to observe the ritual purificatory actions which are customary in the cult, among which special mention is made of washing their garments and also presumably the observance of certain regulations concerned with continence (cf. v. 15b where sexual restraint is enjoined, albeit in a remarkably lame way which perhaps suggests an addition). Then they are strictly to observe the dangerous holiness of the mountain as the place of the impending theophany. An inadvertent or a wilful violation of this holiness would result in death. The formulation of v. 12b suggests that here the punishment of the transgression with death is required, whereas in v. 13a, which looks like a variant to 12b, it is imagined that the holiness of the mountain is in itself fatal in its effect on any living being who comes too near. The occurrence of Yahweh in the third person in the middle of a speech of Yahweh in v. 11b is striking; perhaps it is an explanatory gloss. Verse 13b is barely comprehensible. The blast of the ram's horn, which has given its name to the year of 'jubilee' (Lev. 25.8 ff.), customarily introduced a feast day in the cult and the cultic ceremonies which took place on it; here it is apparently to serve to announce the appearing of God. The emphatic 'they' in v. 13b is the most remarkable of all; it appears to designate a definite group of people who do not, however, occur in the text in its present state. These are to ascend the mountain at the given sign. We therefore have in this passage a fragment from a narrative sequence no longer extant, which appears to have some factual connection with Ex. 24.1 f., 9–11, where a clearly defined group of people are said to ascend the mountain.

[19.16–20] In 19.16–20 we have the report of the theophany on

Sinai in very compressed narrative form, and moreover in two variants which may be very clearly distinguished by the difference in their designation of God and the difference in their ideas of the natural phenomena which accompany the theophany. In this section, v. 16a*a* might belong to the J version (vv. 18, 20) as it refers to the three-day period of preparation which had already been mentioned by J in v. 11a. In that case vv. 16a*bb*, 17, 19 are left over for E. In the original Hebrew text of the passage vv. 16 a*a*, 18, 20 we have a single sentence construction which contains in v. 16a*a* a preliminary introduction giving an indication of the time; v. 18 pictures the circumstances with a clear descriptive clause which is then fully developed, and v. 20 contains the most important of the statements. The description of the circumstances speaks of three manifestations, the smoke on the whole mountain, the fire which is connected with the descent of Yahweh and the great quaking of the whole mountain. To illustrate the first manifestation we have the special simile of the smelting oven, which used to consist of a space walled up with stones or tiles tapering into a cone at the top. In this the smelting fire was kindled, whose smoke, occasionally with ascending flame, escaped through a funnel-like opening made in the top. The manifestations mentioned point quite clearly to a volcanic eruption. This natural occurrence was the sign for the 'descent' of Yahweh on the summit of the mountain—so v. 20. Thus according to this idea the mountain was not the divine abode but the place of his appearance to which he descended from his heavenly dwelling (cf. Gen. 11.5 J), and Moses is immediately ordered to the summit of the mountain to meet Yahweh.

The E variant first of all speaks of thunder and lightning and a thick cloud, which lay on the mountain; it thus apparently imagines a tremendous storm-appearance (v. 16a*b*). For E then the trumpet blast, which grows louder and louder all the time, is particularly important; it is evidently to be understood as a sign of the divine presence. The trumpet blast (again a ram's horn, but a different word is used from that in v. 13b) served chiefly to sound the alarm, but was also used as a summons to a cultic assembly and ceremony (cf. e.g. Josh. 2.15; Ps. 81.4 and also Isa 27.13). It is this last usage which is here intended. The trumpet blast makes the people in the camp tremble before the presence of the God who now proclaims himself. Nevertheless Moses leads the people from their camp to the foot of the mountain 'to meet God'. Here God seems to be thought to be living on the mountain (cf. also v. 3a). Immediately a conversation between Moses and God begins; we are told nothing at all about its content but it leads to a direct meeting between God and Israel. The fact that the two variant narratives describe the natural phenomena accompanying the theophany in different ways raises the question of what really happened at Sinai. Now the reference to a volcanic eruption is surely more unusual and original in comparison with that to a storm. We may therefore be inclined to think the tradition of the volcano to have its original roots in the Sinai tradition and to see the storm tradition as a subsequent weakening of it, especially as the tradition of the pillar of cloud and the pillar of fire (13.21 f.) can hardly be explained except as resting on the observance of an active volcano. Nevertheless we cannot be completely sure that the other variant narrative ever existed; we must always reckon with the possibility that both the volcanic and the storm traditions are derivative ways of describing a theophany. Therefore we cannot obtain any completely reliable reference to the situation of Sinai even from the existence of the volcano-tradition.

[**19.21–25**] The passage 19.21–25, already recognized to be secondary, brings a number of additions to the theme of the dangerous holiness of the mountain which is to be respected, a theme already treated in vv. 12, 13a. The preparatory 'consecration' and the reverent keeping of a distance from the mountain is expressly enjoined upon the priests also (vv. 22, 24b). The instruction that Aaron also is to accompany Moses on the mountain (v. 24a) is completely isolated and without sequel. Verse 25 is a fragment.

[**20.1–17**] The Decalogue in 20.2–17, which is loosely joined to the narrative of the theophany on Sinai by the quite general introductory sentence v. 1, consists of a short and therefore easily memorable series of clauses of the so-called apodeictic law, i.e. a law which advances requirements written in the form 'You shall (not)', requirements which are unconditional and valid without any 'if' or 'but'. The fact that there are ten of these commandments, from which has arisen the description 'Decalogue', which has been customary since the time of the early Christian Church (cf. also 34.28), will belong to the original design of this collection, although in the form in which it has been transmitted the enumeration of the commandments is not completely clear. Similar brief ten- or twelve-membered series of legal clauses also occur elsewhere in the Old Testament (cf. especially Ex. 34.14–26 and—with different language—

Deut. 27.15–26). There are some noticeable discrepancies in Ex. 20.2–17. The alternation between commandments formulated positively (vv. 8, 12) and prohibitions formulated in the negative (all the rest) is not among them; such an alternation also occurs elsewhere (cf. e.g. Ex. 34.14–26) and is sometimes rooted in the matter expressed. But the disproportion between the commandments formulated with the utmost brevity in vv. 13–17a and the commandments which have been more or less extensively expanded by explanations, reasons and recommendations in vv. 3–12 (also v. 17b) is remarkable. If we add to this the fact that the quotation of the Decalogue in the secondary introduction to the Deuteronomic Law (Deut. 5.6–21) at least in essentials corresponds almost verbally with Ex. 20.2–17, but goes its own way in giving reasons for the sabbath commandment (cf. Deut. 5.14b*b*–15 with Ex.20.11), we are driven to the conclusion that the expansions of the commandments which stand at the beginning represent a secondary and variable element, added here and there from time to time. We have to look for the original material only in the brief legal clauses themselves. In any case the expansions must have been added at quite an early date, as apart from the one instance mentioned they also occur in Deut. 5 in essentially the same scope and wording as in Ex. 20. A further discrepancy consists in the change between divine speech and human speech, i.e. between the 'I' of God and the mention of God in the third person, both in the brief legal clauses (cf. v. 3 with v. 7a) and in the expansions which are attached in some places (cf. vv. 5 f. with vv. 7b, 10–12). This discrepancy is hard to explain; it arouses the suspicion that the beginning of the Decalogue is no longer in its original form but has subsequently been altered in connection with the preliminary remark of v. 2, which is also written with the 'I' of God. When a piece which, like the Decalogue, represents a catechism-like collection of the fundamental requirements of God, has been handed down over a long period and has often been repeated, the secondary appearance of expansions and alterations is not to be wondered at.

[20.2] In referring to the acts of God at the Exodus from Egypt the prologue to the Decalogue in v. 2 advances an 'introductory formula' which was native to the proclamation of divine law in Israel, divine law which is to be thought of in a cultic setting. This formula, especially with the completely pertinent expansion, recalls that the action of God towards Israel, which is already indicated by the divine name

Yahweh, precedes the commandments and is the justification for them. **[20.3]** The prohibition of 'other gods' (v. 3) is the basic demand made of Israel, who is addressed here, as in what follows, in the collective second person.* The unconditional exclusiveness of the recognition and worship of the God of Israel stands rightly as *the* most important point at the beginning of the series of divine commandments. The expression which is rendered in the RSV 'before me' probably points to the cultic sphere, in so far as it contains the concept of the 'face' of God ('before' in Hebrew is literally 'before my face'), which frequently describes the presence of God which is encountered in the worship of him. Where this presence of God appears, i.e. in all the cult of Israel, there may not be other gods; and as the Decalogue certainly does not reckon with the possibility of a non-cultic worship of God, this means that no other gods may exist for Israel at all. Apart from the 'I' formulation mentioned above, the expression 'other gods', which is current in the Deuteronomic-deuteronomistic language, is noteworthy; we may think of a later paraphrase of a prohibition originally expressed rather differently. Nevertheless, it is certainly to be assumed that the series right from the beginning commenced with a prohibition of any conceivable worship of foreign deities (on the possibility of another formulation cf. 34.14a*a*).

[20.4] The prohibition of images (v. 4a*a*) uses here an expression for any plastic representation, and as we have not to reckon with any painted pictures this means an expression for any representation at all. The word is to be understood quite generally. As the possibility of a merely ornamental art is surely not envisaged this means a cultic image, be it of the god to be worshipped, of a being which serves him, or a power which is subordinate to him. As the strict prohibition of other gods has already been expressed previously, the prohibition of images is hardly concerned with the images of strange gods but with any images which might possibly be made for the legitimate worship of Israel. We should hardly look for the reason for the prohibition of images in a 'spiritual' conception of God which forbade the introduction of any creaturely being from the sphere of the 'world', as is delineated in the additional explanation in v. 4a*b*b, to portray God or the divine realm. The basis for it rather lies in the idea, widespread in the ancient world, that an image had a firm connection with the

*[Modern English usage does not allow this distinction to be made, so it is not perceptible in the RSV. Tr.]

being it portrayed, and that with the help of an image a man might gain power over the being represented in the image. Israel is forbidden any image so that the people cannot even make the attempt to gain power over God or that which is of God.

[20.5–6] The explanations in vv. 5 f., in which again God appears in the first person, probably belong to the later expansions of the Decalogue. In form and content they belong rather to v. 3 than to v. 4a*a* and in the way they are formulated they again recall the Deuteronomic-deuteronomistic style. The 'jealousy' of the God of Israel is mentioned as the reason for the demand of strict exclusiveness in divine worship; God is spoken of in a human way which is not unusual in other places in the Old Testament. In praise of the power of God it is said that his punishments and his rewards reach far beyond the single individual. It is evidently not realized here that this gives rise to the problem of a 'just' individual divine retribution. The Hebrew participial phrases in vv. 5b*b* and 6 certainly correspond in form but not in content. Verse 5b*b* speaks of the extension of the punishment of God over several generations of those who 'hate' him, i.e. do not love him and therefore do not keep his commandments; in v. 6 the steadfast love of God is generally promised to 'thousands', i.e. an inconceivable number; here however no reference is made to the sequence of generations. For the thought that love towards God is shown in the keeping of his commandments (v. 6b), cf. Deut. 6.5 ff. and I John 5.3.

[20.7] In the original form of the Decalogue the prohibition of images is followed appropriately enough by the prohibition of speaking the divine name 'in vain' (v. 7); here the term 'in vain' is synonymous with the term 'evil'. Behind it lies the idea that the name is a part of the being who bears it, and that the bearer of the name is therefore present in some mysterious way in the name. Anyone who knows a divine name can make use of the divine power present in the name to effect blessings and curses, adjurations and bewitchings and all kinds of magical undertakings. To this extent the divine name is comparable with the divine image. The divine image was forbidden to Israel (v. 4a*a*); the divine name was revealed for the praise of God and for calling upon him, but it must be protected from possible misuse. This is done in the apodeictic commandment v. 7a, which is formulated in a very general way and is therefore comprehensive. The word of warning in v. 7b emphasizes this, but in view of what has been said above this may be a secondary addition.

[20.8] The sabbath commandment (v. 8) is hard to understand because we are so much in the dark about the pre-history and early history of the sabbath, which are perhaps quite complicated. Even the form of the commandment itself in Deut. 5.12a differs slightly from Ex. 20.8 in so far as in the former the 'observance' of the sabbath day and in the latter the 'remembrance' of the sabbath day is required. There is hardly any difference in content, as 'remember' means that the sabbath day is not to be overlooked, not to remain unnoticed, and this comes to the same thing as 'observe', 'keep'. In both cases the mode of expression indicates that the sabbath day was not marked out by definite exterior characteristics, such as cultic actions, so that Israel had expressly to be commanded that it was not to pass unobserved. The explanatory definition means that this day is to be 'kept holy', that it is to be distinguished from the series of 'profane' days for which there are no distinguishing or prohibitory ordinances. **[20.9–10]** The following explanation, which was certainly added later, says in words which correspond in essentials in Ex. 20.9–10 and Deut. 5.13–14aba that the sabbath is a 'sabbath of Yahweh' and thus a day which is in some way specially devoted to Yahweh, and that this is to be every seventh day, on which there is to be rest from everyday work. This last is also presupposed in two of the other relatively early Old Testament passages in which the sabbath occurs (Amos 8.5; II Kings 4.23; at both places, as elsewhere in the older tradition of the Old Testament, the sabbath is mentioned alongside the new moon). It is not expressly said in the demonstrably early passages of the Old Testament that the sabbath was every seventh day (cf. however 16.29; 23.12), but perhaps this is generally presupposed throughout, so that we can reckon that the additional explanation given to the sabbath in the Decalogue is in fact concerned with the significance of the day which is at all times binding upon Israel. **[20.11]** The reason given for the sabbath commandment in Ex. 20.11—in contrast to the 'social' reason given in Deut. 5.14bb–15—is based on a reference to the Priestly account of the creation (Gen. 1.1–2.3) which for its part, by a division of the work of creation into six days of work and a seventh day of rest, seeks to provide a reason for the already existing institution of the sabbath rest on each seventh day. The explanation in our passage may have been added at quite a late stage. We must, however, regard the 'keeping holy of the sabbath day' itself, a phrase whose meaning can no longer certainly be ascertained with the help available from accounts both within and without the Old Testament, as a custom which was probably already very ancient in Israel. The frequent juxtaposition of 'new moon and sabbath' in the Old Testament might suggest that it was connected with the phases of the moon, but this is questionable, as the continuous seven-day week, which determines the sabbath in the Old Testament wherever it is mentioned in rather more detail, does not correspond accurately with the interval in the phases of the moon. We must therefore assume that a former association with the phases of the moon has subsequently for reasons unknown to us been dissolved and that to replace it the smooth seven-day week has been introduced.*

Up to the sabbath commandment the requirements of the Decalogue are concerned directly with Israel's worship of God. Commandments follow which deal with the life of the human community in Israel. [20.12] The commandment about parents (v. 12a) which again has been expanded by a promise and a warning (v. 12b) does not apply to children who stand under the *patria potestas* but to adults who themselves exert the *patria potestas* and are to show due honour to their aging parents. [20.13] The prohibition against killing (v. 13) uses one of the two words current in Hebrew for 'doing to death'. These verbs apparently express no distinction between premeditated murder and unpremeditated killing, but both evidently include the concept of the arbitrary. It was customary in Hebrew for other expressions to be used both for the execution of the death penalty imposed by legitimate trial and for the killing of an enemy in war (in the former case one says 'put to death' [so for example Ex. 19.12b] and in the latter 'smite'). [20.14] The prohibition of adultery (v. 14) is clear. The verb there corresponds in fact closely enough to our 'commit adultery', so that we are only left to realize that for the Old Testament the very fact of betrothal is a ground of marriage in law and that therefore the betrothed comes under the scope of this commandment just as much as the wife. [20.15] In the commandment against stealing (v. 15) the unnamed object is not so clear as in the two preceding commandments. The position of this commandment among a group of commandments which are concerned with the person of the 'neighbour' (see below), and the difference in content which is to be assumed between this commandment and the last in the Decalogue suggests that, as elsewhere when this particular verb occurs, a human object is imagined (cf. e.g.

*On other aspects see p. 190 below on 23.12.

Gen. 40.15). It probably therefore has in mind the loss of freedom, particularly of free Israelites; it is forbidden to enslave free Israelites by force whether it be for one's own use or to sell to another.*

[20.16] In its present wording, the following commandment is concerned with bearing false witness in legal trials; in the period of settled life in an agricultural community these took place in the setting of the local legal assembly which used to meet 'at the gate', the relatively spacious meeting place, and to which all free Israelites belonged. The term 'neighbour' appears in this commandment; without expressing a definite legal relationship it means the man with whom one lives and comes into contact in the conditions of life.

[20.17] The commandment in v. 17 is formulated with a verb which is rendered 'covet'. But it describes not merely the emotion of coveting but also includes the attempt to attach something to oneself illegally. The commandment therefore deals with all possible undertakings which involve gaining power over the goods and possessions of a 'neighbour', whether through theft or through all kinds of dishonest machinations. The first object to be named is the neighbour's house. The term 'house' can in a narrow and special sense describe the dwelling-place, primarily the built house but also in every case the tent-'house' of the nomad; it can, however, also be used in a more or less wide or transferred sense to mean, for instance, the family, or to sum up everything which is included in the house. The last-named possibility deserves primary consideration in the present passage, especially if we see v. 17b as a subsequent interpretation of the commandment. And we must do this, because in view of the surely intended number ten v. 17b cannot be counted as an independent commandment (the parallelism with v. 17a also militates against this), while on the other hand the brevity of the commandments, which must be regarded as original, prohibits the whole of v. 17 from being counted as the original material of the last commandment. Verse 17b paraphrases the whole inclusive term 'house', as meaning 'possession', beginning with the wife, who according to the Old Testament law of marriage was the possession of the husband, and ending with a quite general formulation which saves other individual enumerations. By the addition of v. 17b the word 'house' in v. 17a of course becomes superfluous, but it is appropriately given a more precise definition.

The Decalogue contains a brief collection of the basic demands

*Cf. A.Alt, *Kleine Schriften zur Geschichte des Volkes Israel* I, 1953, pp. 333–440.

made by God on Israel in respect of worship and the life of the human community. In form and content it does not stand quite alone in the Old Testament, but is nevertheless unique in its concentration on what is fundamental and essential; this leaves open the possibility of a far deeper interpretation (cf. the exegesis by Luther in the *Kleine Katechismus*). The lack of special cultic requirements is noteworthy. This corresponds to the fact that in the Old Testament cultic action is indeed generally presupposed as a possible, even a requisite way of worship, but that the special and unique element in the relationship between God and Israel is not evident in the cultic sphere but in the obedience to the one God and his demands which pertain to human relationships. Even the sabbath commandment is no exception here, for whatever may have been the significance of the sabbath in the view of the Decalogue it was at all events not thought of as a cultic feast. There are no reliable criteria for answering the question of the age and derivation of the Decalogue. As the literary inclusion of the Decalogue in the narrative of Ex. 19–20 cannot contribute to solving the problem of the date (see pp. 154 f. above), there remains only the content of the Decalogue itself as a basis for argument. But this content is so little bound by time and so directly rooted in the special permanent relationship between God and Israel that it offers only a little information towards a definite date. It is probable that the Decalogue—and by this is meant the basic material before it has been expanded by additions—derives from the time before classical prophecy. This is supported first by the fact that the Decalogue does not yet contain social requirements in the narrower sense, that element which was so important even for the earliest prophets, and secondly by the further fact that the prophets appear to presuppose the knowledge of the Decalogue in Israel (cf. especially Hos. 4.2). But for the pre-prophetic period all possibilities of dating remain open. We cannot even answer the question whether the Decalogue derives from a time before or after Israel took possession of Canaan. It has already been said that the occurrence of the word 'house' in v. 17a is not conclusive in this respect, nor does the sabbath commandment give us any further help in view of the obscurity of the origin and original significance of the sabbath. The Decalogue is the only legal entity in the Old Testament which indicates no certain reference to the conditions of life in an agricultural community, but we cannot of course conclude from this negative statement that the basic material of the Decalogue came into being in the time before the conquest.

Even the inclusion—whenever it took place—of the Decalogue in the Sinai narrative may not be advanced as an argument, as almost all the Old Testament laws have been drawn into this narrative, even those which demonstrably only derive from the period after the settlement. This is because of the quite appropriate idea that the whole of Old Testament 'Law' has its basis in the relationship between God and people which has its foundation in the covenant on Sinai, even if some happens to be later re-formulations of this law. In fact the question of the dating of the Decalogue is less important than that of its nature and its significance. God has of course always been regarded as the 'author' of the Decalogue, even if the Decalogue, which in its original form was probably consistent (see p. 161 above), mentions Yahweh in the third person. Therefore the question of its human author (thus even the question of its 'Mosaic' origin) is not of fundamental importance. It is Israel that is addressed, even if the individual requirements (especially vv. 12–17) with the address in the second person singular in fact are meant for the individual Israelite, who as a member of the whole is for his part responsible for the obedience of all Israel.

[20.18–21] The section 20.18–21 goes back beyond the Decalogue to Ex. 19 and moreover, as we evidently have here an Elohistic piece, to its E element. Verse 18 with the zeugmatic connection of the verb 'see' with some inappropriate objects* and with the mixture of elements of the J and E narratives ('the mountain smoking') is a secondary derivation which was necessary after the insertion of the Decalogue. Verse 18b has the people of their own accord standing far off from the terrifying phenomena of the theophany; according to this version there was evidently no need to warn the people as in 19.12–13a J. 20.18b could originally have been attached directly to 19.19 E if the statement at the beginning of 20.18b was meant to read 'the people were afraid' (instead of 'the people saw it'), which is quite possible with the Hebrew consonantal text as it has been transmitted.† Moses takes over the role of mediator (v. 21) as has been requested by the people (v. 19) after he has approved the attitude of the people (v. 20) with the remark that they have withstood the 'proving' which God has laid upon them; the people have shown the right 'fear' of God and have not attempted to go too near the theophany.

*[The RSV rendering 'perceive' obscures this discrepancy. Tr.]
†[This reading is in fact accepted in the RSV text. Tr.]

2. THE BOOK OF THE COVENANT: 20.22–23.33

22 And the LORD said to Moses, 'Thus you shall say to the people of Israel: "You have seen for yourselves that I have talked with you from heaven. ²³ You shall not make gods of silver to be with me, nor shall you make for yourselves gods of gold. ²⁴ An altar of earth you shall make for me and sacrifice on it your burnt offerings and your peace offerings, your sheep and your oxen; in every place where I cause my name to be remembered I will come to you and bless you. ²⁵ And if you make me an altar of stone, you shall not build it of hewn stones; for if you wield your tool upon it you profane it. ²⁶ And you shall not go up by steps to my altar, that your nakedness be not exposed on it."

21¹ 'Now these are the ordinances which you shall set before them. ² When you buy a Hebrew slave, he shall serve six years, and in the seventh he shall go out free, for nothing. ³ If he comes in single, he shall go out single; if he comes in married, then his wife shall go out with him. ⁴ If his master gives him a wife and she bears him sons or daughters, the wife and her children shall be her master's and he shall go out alone. ⁵ But if the slave plainly says, "I love my master, my wife, and my children; I will not go out free," ⁶ then his master shall bring him to God, and he shall bring him to the door or the doorpost; and his master shall bore his ear through with an awl; and he shall serve him for life.

7 'When a man sells his daughter as a slave, she shall not go out as the male slaves do. ⁸ If she does not please her master, who has designated her for himself, then he shall let her be redeemed; he shall have no right to sell her to a foreign people, since he has dealt faithlessly with her. ⁹ If he designates her for his son, he shall deal with her as with a daughter. ¹⁰ If he takes another wife to himself, he shall not diminish her food, her clothing, or her marital rights. ¹¹ And if he does not do these three things for her, she shall go out for nothing, without payment of money.

12 'Whoever strikes a man so that he dies shall be put to death. ¹³ But if he did not lie in wait for him, but God let him fall into his hand, then I will appoint for you a place to which he may flee. ¹⁴ But if a man wilfully attacks another to kill him treacherously, you shall take him from my altar, that he may die.

15 'Whoever strikes his father or his mother shall be put to death.

16 'Whoever steals a man, whether he sells him or is found in possession of him, shall be put to death.

17 'Whoever curses his father or his mother shall be put to death.

18 'When men quarrel and one strikes the other with a stone or with his fist and the man does not die but keeps his bed, ¹⁹ then if the man rises again and walks abroad with his staff, he that struck him shall be clear; only he shall pay for the loss of his time, and shall have him thoroughly healed.

20 'When a man strikes his slave, male or female, with a rod and the slave dies under his hand, he shall be punished. [21] But if the slave survives a day or two, he is not to be punished; for the slave is his money.

22 'When men strive together, and hurt a woman with child, so that there is a miscarriage, and yet no harm follows, the one who hurt her shall be fined, according as the woman's husband shall lay upon him; and he shall pay as the judges determine. [23] If any harm follows, then you shall give life for life, [24] eye for eye, tooth for tooth, hand for hand, foot for foot, [25] burn for burn, wound for wound, stripe for stripe.

26 'When a man strikes the eye of his slave, male or female, and destroys it, he shall let the slave go free for the eye's sake. [27] If he knocks out the tooth of his slave, male or female, he shall let the slave go free for the tooth's sake.

28 'When an ox gores a man or a woman to death, the ox shall be stoned, and its flesh shall not be eaten; but the owner of the ox shall be clear. [29] But if the ox has been accustomed to gore in the past, and its owner has been warned but has not kept it in, and it kills a man or a woman, the ox shall be stoned, and its owner also shall be put to death. [30] If a ransom is laid on him, then he shall give for the redemption of his life whatever is laid upon him. [31] If it gores a man's son or daughter, he shall be dealt with according to this same rule. [32] If the ox gores a slave, male or female, the owner shall give to their master thirty shekels of silver, and the ox shall be stoned.

33 'When a man leaves a pit open, or when a man digs a pit and does not cover it, and an ox or an ass falls into it, [34] the owner of the pit shall make it good; he shall give money to its owner, and the dead beast shall be his.

35 'When one man's ox hurts another's, so that it dies, then they shall sell the live ox and divide the price of it; and the dead beast also they shall divide. [36] Or if it is known that the ox has been accustomed to gore in the past, and its owner has not kept it in, he shall pay ox for ox, and the dead beast shall be his.

22[1] If a man steals an ox or a sheep, and kills it or sells it, he shall pay five oxen for an ox, and four sheep for a sheep. He shall make restitution; if he has nothing, then he shall be sold for his theft. [4] If the stolen beast is found alive in his possession, whether it is an ox or an ass or a sheep, he shall pay double.

2 'If a thief is found breaking in, and is struck so that he dies, there shall be no bloodguilt for him; [3] but if the sun has risen upon him, there shall be bloodguilt for him.

5 'When a man causes a field or vineyard to be grazed over, or lets his beast loose and it feeds in another man's field, he shall make restitution from the best in his own field and in his own vineyard.

6 'When fire breaks out and catches in thorns so that the stacked grain or the standing grain or the field is consumed, he that kindled the fire shall make full restitution.

7 'If a man delivers to his neighbour money or goods to keep, and it is stolen out of the man's house, then, if the thief is found, he shall pay

double. ⁸ If the thief is not found, the owner of the house shall come near to God, to show whether or not he has put his hand to his neighbour's goods.

9 'For every breach of trust, whether it is for ox, for ass, for sheep, for clothing, or for any kind of lost thing, of which one says, "This is it," the case of both parties shall come before God; he whom God shall condemn shall pay double to his neighbour.

10 'If a man delivers to his neighbour an ass or an ox or a sheep or any beast to keep, and it dies or is hurt or is driven away, without any one seeing it, ¹¹ an oath by the LORD shall be between them both to see whether he has not put his hand to his neighbour's property; and the owner shall accept the oath, and he shall not make restitution. ¹² But if it is stolen from him, he shall make restitution to its owner. ¹³ If it is torn by beasts, let him bring it as evidence; he shall not make restitution for what has been torn.

14 'If a man borrows anything of his neighbour, and it is hurt or dies, the owner not being with it, he shall make full restitution. ¹⁵ If the owner was with it, he shall not make restitution; if it was hired, it came for its hire.

16 'If a man seduces a virgin who is not betrothed, and lies with her, he shall give the marriage present for her, and make her his wife. ¹⁷ If her father utterly refuses to give her to him, he shall pay money equivalent to the marriage present for virgins.

18 'You shall not permit a sorceress to live.

19 'Whoever lies with a beast shall be put to death.

20 'Whoever sacrifices to any god, save to the LORD only, shall be utterly destroyed.

21 'You shall not wrong a stranger or oppress him, for you were strangers in the land of Egypt. ²² You shall not afflict any widow or orphan. ²³ If you do afflict them, and they cry out to me, I will surely hear their cry; ²⁴ and my wrath will burn, and I will kill you with the sword, and your wives shall become widows and your children fatherless.

25 'If you lend money to any of my people with you who is poor, you shall not be to him as a creditor, and you shall not exact interest from him. ²⁶ If ever you take your neighbour's garment in pledge, you shall restore it to him before the sun goes down; ²⁷ for that is his only covering, it is his mantle for his body; in what else shall he sleep? And if he cries to me, I will hear, for I am compassionate.

28 'You shall not revile God, nor curse a ruler of your people.

29 'You shall not delay to offer from the fulness of your harvest and from the outflow of your presses.

'The first-born of your sons you shall give to me. ³⁰ You shall do likewise with your oxen and with your sheep: seven days it shall be with its dam; on the eighth day you shall give it to me.

31 'You shall be men consecrated to me; therefore you shall not eat any flesh that is torn by beasts in the field; you shall cast it to the dogs.

23¹ 'You shall not utter a false report. You shall not join hands with a wicked man, to be a malicious witness. ² You shall not follow a multi-tude to do evil; nor shall you bear witness in a suit, turning aside after a multitude, so as to pervert justice; ³ nor shall you be partial to a poor man in his suit.

4 'If you meet your enemy's ox or his ass going astray, you shall bring it back to him. ⁵ If you see the ass of one who hates you lying under its burden, you shall refrain from leaving him with it, you shall help him to lift it up.

6 'You shall not pervert the justice due to your poor in his suit. ⁷ Keep far from a false charge, and do not slay the innocent and righteous, for I will not acquit the wicked. ⁸ And you shall take no bribe, for a bribe blinds the officials, and subverts the cause of those who are in the right.

9 'You shall not oppress a stranger; you know the heart of a stranger, for you were strangers in the land of Egypt.

10 'For six years you shall sow your land and gather in its yield; ¹¹ but the seventh year you shall let it rest and lie fallow, that the poor of your people may eat; and what they leave the wild beasts may eat. You shall do likewise with your vineyard, and with your olive orchard.

12 'Six days you shall do your work, but on the seventh day you shall rest; that your ox and your ass may have rest, and the son of your bond-maid, and the alien, may be refreshed. ¹³ Take heed to all that I have said to you; and make no mention of the names of other gods, nor let such be heard out of your mouth.

14 'Three times in the year you shall keep a feast to me. ¹⁵ You shall keep the feast of unleavened bread; as I commanded you, you shall eat unleavened bread for seven days at the appointed time in the month of Abib, for in it you came out of Egypt. None shall appear before me empty-handed. ¹⁶ You shall keep the feast of harvest, of the first fruits of your labour, of what you sow in the field. You shall keep the feast of ingathering at the end of the year, when you gather in from the field the fruit of your labour. ¹⁷ Three times in the year shall all your males appear before the LORD God.

18 'You shall not offer the blood of my sacrifice with leavened bread, or let the fat of my feast remain until the morning.

19 'The first of the first fruits of your ground you shall bring into the house of the LORD your God.

'You shall not boil a kid in its mother's milk.

20 'Behold, I send an angel before you, to guard you on the way and to bring you to the place which I have prepared. ²¹ Give heed to him and hearken to his voice, do not rebel against him, for he will not pardon your transgression; for my name is in him.

22 'But if you hearken attentively to his voice and do all that I say, then I will be an enemy to your enemies and an adversary to your adversaries.

23 'When my angel goes before you, and brings you in to the Amorites, and the Hittites, and the Perizzites, and the Canaanites, the Hivites, and the Jebusites, and I blot them out, ²⁴ you shall not bow

down to their gods, nor serve them, nor do according to their work, but you shall utterly overthrow them and break their pillars in pieces. [25] You shall serve the LORD your God, and I will bless your bread and your water; and I will take sickness away from the midst of you. [26] None shall cast her young or be barren in your land; I will fulfil the number of your days. [27] I will send my terror before you, and will throw into confusion all the people against whom you shall come, and I will make all your enemies turn their backs to you. [28] And I will send hornets before you, which shall drive out Hivite, Canaanite, and Hittite from before you. [29] I will not drive them out from before you in one year, lest the land become desolate and the wild beasts multiply against you. [30] Little by little I will drive them out from before you, until you are increased and possess the land. [31] And I will set your bounds from the Red Sea to the sea of the Philistines, and from the wilderness to the Euphrates; for I will deliver the inhabitants of the land into your hand, and you shall drive them out before you. [32] You shall make no covenant with them or with their gods.[33] They shall not dwell in your land, lest they make you sin against me; for if you serve their gods, it will surely be a snare to you.'

Apart from the addition in 23.20–33, we have in Ex. 20.22–23.33 a collection of judgments of differing form and differing content which in view of 24.7 are customarily described as the 'Book of the Covenant'. It is probable that this collection once formed an independent book of law which has been inserted into the Pentateuchal narrative as an already self-contained entity. We can no longer say with certainty at what stage of the literary growth of the Pentateuch this insertion was made; no clear relationship to any one of the Pentateuchal narrative 'sources' is recognizable. The beginning of the section in 20.22 is indeed connected without a break to the narrative which precedes it, but right in the introductory verse 20.22 the divine name Yahweh is used, and thus we can hardly assume an original connection with 20.18–21 E. Instead we must consider a connection with the narrative passage 24.3–8 which speaks of the 'words of Yahweh' brought down by Moses to the people and then written down to produce the very 'Book of the Covenant' mentioned in 24.7. But it is questionable to which source this narrative passage itself should be assigned (cf. pp. 198 f. below). All that we may say then is that at some time which can no longer be discovered with any accuracy the 'Book of the Covenant' has been inserted into the Sinai section at the place between the narratives of the theophany (19.1–20.21) and of the making of the covenant (24.1–11). It must therefore be interpreted as a self-contained unity. The addition 23.20–33, which is evidently secondary to the law-book proper (20.22–23.19), may already have been in existence at the time of the insertion, as this is the only explanation of the discussion of the question of the presence and activity of God in the impending conquest at so early a stage. In the following narratives this question is in fact only dealt with later in Ex. 33. Now as this addition is formulated in deuteronomistic style we certainly cannot imagine the incorporation of the Book of the Covenant into the Pentateuchal narrative in the period before Deuteronomy.

The addition refers the Book of the Covenant to the impending conquest. It is right in this in so far as the majority of elements of the Book of the Covenant in fact presuppose the circumstances of an agricultural land. We must draw the conclusion from this that the groups of judgments which are united in the Book of the Covenant have for the most part been formulated only after Israel became a settled nation. The Book of the Covenant as a whole therefore derives from this period, even though some groups of judgments which have been incorporated in it may be still older. This is not, however, demonstrable with certainty. A date during the time after the settlement is also supported by the fact that certain parts of the Book of the Covenant display very close relationships in form and content with the tradition of law in the ancient East. Now this tradition of law was doubtless the custom in the agricultural lands of the ancient East and surely only became known to Israel on the soil of the agricultural land of Palestine. A connection with the ancient oriental tradition of law is chiefly evident in the sphere of 'casuistically' formulated judgments which stand alongside those which are formulated 'apodeictically' in the Old Testament 'Law' and are represented in considerable number in the Book of the Covenant. If the apodeictic clauses with their 'You shall (not) . . .' put forward unconditional demands (cf. for instance the Decalogue, Ex. 20.2–17), the casuistic sentences in their protases introduced by 'if' envisage definite cases at law whose treatment is regulated by the following apodosis. As a definite case can be treated differently if there are special circumstances, further special conditions, introduced by the words 'in case', 'but if', 'then if' etc., are frequently added to such a sentence introduced by 'if'. This follows because casuistic law is essentially complicated and requires far more detailed formulations than apodeictic law. The 'casuistic' judgments are generally concerned with civil affairs. They represent an apparently codified common law and serve for use at trials held by the legal assembly 'at the gate' by setting out the legal consequences of cases which may occur or at least offering the basis for an appropriate application of the law. In the Old Testament the casuistic judgments also are valid as the divine requirements for Israel, even if in them the divine purpose of law is not expressed so clearly as in the apodeictic clauses. For, clearly though the difference between apodeictic and casuistic law meets the eye, there is nevertheless no difference between the two in the Old Testament; apodeictic and casuistic sentences stand side by side in immediate proximity. Only research into the history of law has taught us how to differentiate between the two.* We have in the Book of the Covenant a collection of apodeictic and casuistic law whose judgments were at one time regarded as important and binding upon Israel.

On the basis of the idea that all the divine legal requirements made of Israel have their root in the covenant relationship between God and people (cf. p. 160 above), the Book of the Covenant has been incorporated into the Sinai narrative although it was only compiled at the time of the settlement in an agricultural land. As far as the dating of the book is concerned we can only say with certainty —and this is quite apart from the question, which is barely answerable, of the prehistory of the individual elements of which the whole is composed—that it is pre-Deuteronomic, as in several respects the Deuteronomic law shows a more progressive stage in the development of the law. As there is no reference in the Book of the Covenant to institutions of state we may assume that it was compiled before Israel became a state; there is, however, no proof of this.

[20.22–26] The very brief *introduction* (v. 22a) is followed by the remark that Yahweh is speaking 'from heaven' (v. 22b), which on its part gives the reason for the prohibition of (images of) gods of gold and silver (v. 23). Verse 23 is also connected with v. 22b in form by virtue of a plural address, which is then followed directly in vv. 24–26 by an address in the singular.† The speech of Yahweh from heaven which supposes heaven to be the divine realm is surprising after the previous narrative both according to the J version, which has Yahweh descending on Sinai (19.18, 20), and still more according to the E version in which God is present on the mountain itself in the

---

*See especially A. Alt, *Die Ursprünge des israelitischen Rechts*, 1934 = *Kleine Schriften zur Geschichte des Volkes Israel* I, pp. 278–332.

†[Once again this cannot be reproduced in modern English idiom. Tr.]

thick cloud (19.17; 20.21b). We evidently have here an idea which is independent of these narratives. The prohibition of 'gods of silver and gods of gold' is a general prohibition of all images of gods, as such a prohibition would be all the more valid for images of less value. Images of gods, whether images of Yahweh or images of strange gods, are not compatible with the God who rules in heaven. The *law of the altar* (20.24–26), which immediately follows, stands, remarkably, before the superscription 21.1 which, as no further superscriptions follow in the Book of the Covenant, may once have introduced the whole law book, even if it originally belonged perhaps only to one subsection of the book. The law of the altar may therefore have been put at the beginning of the book at a later date. In fact it would best fit in with the cultic regulations of the Book of the Covenant in 23.10–19. But as there is no clear reason why it should subsequently have changed its place we must suppose that in it we have a subsequent literary addition which appeared so important that it was placed at the high point of the book. The law itself is of course old, as it presupposes very simple conditions. An altar of piled-up earth is normally used for all sacrifices (v. 24a); alongside it an altar erected of stones is permitted, but the stones must remain unworked, as working with human tools would do away with their original condition and integrity and hence their requisite holiness (v. 25). These ordinances seem to presuppose a country without hills, as in such a country natural blocks of stone would form the principal altars (cf. Judg. 6.20f.; 13.19). Of course they do not have in mind a region of wilderness or steppe, as the word 'earth' (v. 24) describes the cultivated soil of an agricultural land. On the other hand, they do not mean sanctuaries in places with fixed settlements, but altars erected in free land. We must therefore suppose this ordinance to originate perhaps from communities of nomadic herdsmen who during the summer pastured their animals on the plains of the cultivated land, animals which consisted chiefly of sheep, though occasionally including a number of oxen (v. 24a). The ordinances thus presuppose the conditions of the early life of Israel, which of course had not completely died out. Verse 24b contemplates a number of holy places. In fact holy places with altars could not be founded at whatever place men wished, but only where God 'caused his name to be remembered', i.e. to be called upon in the cult; this could perhaps happen through theophanies in visions or dreams. But then God will 'come' again to cultic actions at these places, and pour out his blessing, which is the aim of the cultic act. The prohibition of altar steps (v. 26) which would form part of the altar rests on the idea that the sexual sphere is part of a dark, mysterious realm, a realm which played an elevated role in many cults in the ancient East. For this very reason, however, it was impossible for it to be associated with the sphere of the holy in Israel (there is a later regulation of a different kind on the same subject in 28.42 f.).

[21.1–11] The *law for slaves* in 21.1–11 is an example of a detailed casuistic judgment. Two main cases are provided for, each introduced by 'when' (Hebrew *kî*), first that of a male slave (v. 2) and secondly that of a female slave (v. 7). In both sections regulations are then made for special circumstances, each beginning with 'if' (Hebrew *'im*). It is said of the male slave that he must be released after six years (v. 2); of the female slave, on the other hand, that she shall not be released (v. 7). This distinction, later abolished by the Deuteronomic law (Deut. 15.12 ff.), may rest on the view that only the man is a person, while the woman on the other hand is a possession. In fact the latter of these two basic vases appears already to be contradicted in the special regulations of the Book of the Covenant (vv. 8–11). In the main judgment about male slaves (v. 2) two technical terms appear which derive from the ancient legal language of Asia Minor and are frequently in evidence especially in Mesopotamia and in Syria-Palestine; their exact meaning, however, is hard to discover. First of all we have the term *'ibrî* ('Hebrew', 'Hebraic'; cf. pp. 21 f. above). It is certain that this term does not describe membership of a particular people, but a legal and social status within the framework of 'class' ordering of ancient oriental community life in the second millennium BC. The 'Hebrews' were people of different nationality who belonged to the under-privileged or even unprivileged classes and who undertook, indeed had to undertake, subordinate service, though this was not, as far as we can see, actual slavery. The description 'Hebrew slave' is certainly meant proleptically in so far as a 'Hebrew' became a slave by being 'bought' by an Israelite. The basis of this 'purchase' may primarily have been that such a 'Hebrew' was compelled to 'sell' himself through financial necessity. In any case this does not concern prisoners of war, who were customarily sold into permanent slavery, and whose descendants then were the 'house-born' slaves (e.g. Gen. 14.14) who remained the permanent possession of their lord. The other problematical term is *ḥopšî* ('freed'). This likewise describes a legal and social status which cannot be defined with certainty; in the Old Testament it is used for one who has been freed from an obligation but in this has apparently still not reached the full rights of the free man. Now according to Old Testament law the 'Hebrew' slave is only to a limited extent treated as a thing, in so far as his time of slavery has bounds set to it without any redemption being necessary (v. 2). The seventh year here appears as the time for his 'restitution' (cf. pp. 189 f. below on 23.10 f.). The special regulations in vv. 3–6 stipulate that if the 'Hebrew' on his entry into slavery was the 'possessor' of a wife he also remains the possessor of this wife at his release, but if the master gives a wife to the slave during the period of slavery—this may primarily be the case of a female slave 'born in the house'—the wife, along with the children born to them in the meanwhile, remains the possession of the master at the release of the slave. It is in this case striking that the children follow the mother and not the father; in this regulation the interest of the owner—without reference to the marriage law which is valid in the case of the free Israelite—is carried through at the expense of the slave. Verses 5 f. provide for the case when the slave does not wish to make any use of his claim to release; perhaps he 'loves his master' because his master has treated him well, and because he has fared better in this way than he could possibly expect to fare after his release with no means of subsistence (the Deuteronomic law attempts to solve the latter problem through a special regulation, Deut. 15.14); perhaps too he loves his wife and children who, according to v. 4, belong to his master. In this case his right of release is lost once and for all and he occupies the position of a slave for life. This is confirmed by boring through an ear (this may mean the lobe of the ear, presumably the right); the pierced ear is the sign of slavery, perhaps because the ear is the organ of hearing and the piercing of it was understood as a removal of its integrity and thus the original freedom of hearing. The ear is bored through after the slave has been 'brought to God', 'to the door' of the house. These two formulae look like variants and in any case mean the same thing, for 'God' in this evidently very old regulation means a domestic deity who had his place at the door. Thus permanent slavery is given a cultic seal, and the permanent slave is also drawn into the cult community of the house.

The section about the female slave (vv. 7–11) has in mind a girl 'sold' by her father. Such a transaction would as a rule be for business reasons. Evidently conditions within Israel are envisaged and in any case not the enslaving of women and girls from areas sacked in war. In normal cases no release is provided for female slaves (v. 7). Verses 8–11 contain special regulations if the girl in question is to be given in marriage, for in that case she may no longer be treated simply as a female slave, i.e. as a 'thing', but acquires—at least to a certain extent—the rights of a wife. This is the case whether the master himself takes the female slave to wife or whether he gives her as a wife to one of his sons (v. 9; the former instance is not explicitly mentioned). If the master should then grow weary of her he cannot just simply reduce her to her former slavery, nor may he sell her to a foreigner but must give her up for redemption (by her family or clan, v. 8). If he takes yet another wife he may not lessen the claims which his former wife has on him; if he does he must set her free without recompense (vv. 10 f.).

The Old Testament law, as that of the whole ancient and oriental world, supposes the presence of the institution of slavery even within Israel. This basic view may only have arisen with the transition to a settled life in an agricultural setting. The treatment of male and female slaves as 'things' possessed is already limited in some aspects in the slave law of the Book of the Covenant.

[**21.12–17**] 21.12–17 contains a list of *offences punishable by death* in a stereotyped form which also occurs elsewhere in Old Testament law. Sometimes a sentence occurs in which the predicate standing at the end runs *mōt yūmāt* ('shall be put to death'). The participial subject, to which a number of closer definitions may be added if necessary, describes the way in which the law is broken. The result is a compromise between apodeictic and casuistic formulation. The brevity and absolute nature of these sentences stands close to the apodeictic formulation; the explicit and emphatic description of the legal consequences (the condemnation to death) is reminiscent of the casuistic formulation. In contrast to the casuistic law, however, in the present instance we evidently have here not a codified common law but a collection of a series of pregnant judgments which on certain cultic occasions were proclaimed as the will of God. In content, they deal with fundamental attacks on the common life of family and people as ordered according to the will of God. The offences carrying the death penalty in the present section are the striking of a 'man' (v. 12; cf. 20.13—it is here assumed that in practice acts of this kind only occur among men; the murder of a woman would not go unpunished), the 'striking' (v. 15) and cursing (v. 17) of parents (by which is meant even a 'striking' which does not result in death—a different expression is used in v. 12—and a curse as being potentially of harmful effect), and finally the 'stealing' of a man (v. 16; cf. 20.15). The last-named regulation further contains a special clause which appears superfluous for the actual case and represents an exposition in the 'casuistic' manner. It is not certain how we are to interpret it. The RSV translation reproduces the probable meaning, according to which the case is to be treated in the same way whether the 'stolen' man has already been sold as a slave or whether he is still in the possession of the offender. According to another possible interpretation, the clause may mean that the proceeds of the sale of the 'stolen' man in the hands of the offender count as evidence. The excursuses to the 'offences punishable by death' in the case of killing (vv. 13 f.) are clearly secondary additions which were perhaps inserted only after the compilation of the Book of the Covenant. They make the distinction, not envisaged in the main clause v. 12, between unintentional killing and premeditated murder. The additions, though not consistent, are formulated in a casuistic way. This is in any case so with the protases (vv. 13a, 14a). Unpremeditated killing is first defined negatively in v. 13a as the lack of evil intent and then described positively as an inexplicable act of providence which must be seen where the actions of men are no longer rational. The apodoses (vv. 13b, 14b) with God in the first person and an address directed to Israel again diverge from the casuistic style. They provide places of refuge for the killer in which the blood vengeance may not reach him. The altars of Yahweh (v. 14b) are such places of refuge (cf. I Kings 1.51; 2.28) in which Yahweh himself protects the killer. Of course the murderer is to be denied the protection of the altar (v. 14b). Now for this regulation to be put in practice it is supposed that the question of the intent or otherwise of the killing has already been determined, but in what way this question is to be decided is not discussed here (cf. on this the later but still brief Deuteronomic explanations in Deut. 19.4 ff., 11 ff., and especially the still later explicit discussions in Num. 35.9–34).

[21.18–36] This section examines cases of *bodily injury* which do or do not result in death. Most of it is written in the casuistic style. By and large the chief point in the treatment of cases of bodily injury is the assessment of compensation for the damage that has been inflicted. This is immediately clear in the case which is provided for in v. 18 of a hand-to-hand fight between two men in which one of

them is seriously injured. It is not at all obvious whether the action of
the offender in using 'a stone or his fist' is relevant to the judgment
in appearing to prove the presence of an evil intent. If death were to
follow it would be a case of murder; if the injured party remains alive
no punishment is inflicted, as is expressly remarked. Only the damage
that has arisen is to be assessed; this damage consists in the time
during which the injured man is unfit for work and the cost of having
him healed. How defective the casuistic law must necessarily be, as it
cannot envisage all possibilities, is clear from the fact that the possibility of a permanent illness is not taken into consideration. The
regulation given in vv. 20 f. in the case of a man 'striking' a male or
female slave with his rod, especially if this 'striking' leads to death, is
quite remarkable. Should death follow immediately, 'punishment' is
to be inflicted; if on the other hand death follows only after a day or
two, no punishment is provided for on the ground that the man has
destroyed his own possession and thus has injured himself. The
distinction between intentional and unintentional killing probably
underlies this very different treatment. In the former case the slave is
treated not as a possession, but as a man. The formulation of the
clause 20b is very striking, as it does not lay down a definite punishment as is usual in casuistic law but appears to lay down a quite
general requirement of 'punishment'. The word used for 'punishment' however means blood-vengeance and thus the death of the
killer. It is not said who is to carry out this blood vengeance in the
case of a slave, vengeance which is the duty of the clan of the man
who has been killed. Perhaps blood vengeance, which begins automatically and is therefore not demanded by law, is here required
because it is to be executed for the slave by the legal assembly. The
case provided for in v. 22, which presupposes the not unusual
occurrence of a fight with fists with a circle of people standing round,
is again ruled as a punishment by reparation. The fixing of the
amount of the recompense for the child lost is left to the husband of
the woman concerned. The wording and meaning of the final clause
of v. 22 is most obscure. The translation of the transmitted text runs
'and he shall pay (it) before the arbitrators', but there is doubt
whether this text is original. It may perhaps mean that the 'arbitrators' are to superintend the payment of the recompense to the amount
required by the husband of the injured woman.* To the word

*[As can be seen by Noth's comments above, the RSV translation is somewhat
free, perhaps resting on the emendation of the initial *b* of the last word to a *k*. Tr.]

'harm', which occurs in v. 22, the *lex talionis* is loosely attached in vv. 23–25. This evidently does not specially belong to the case at law under discussion, but, according to the introduction in v. 23a, is to be of general validity in cases of 'harm', particularly bodily harm. In form it perhaps derives ultimately from cultic language and there served to describe the appropriateness of cultic penalties of reparation.* In the Book of the Covenant it is used to formulate the basis of the appropriate 'recompense' for the decision of the judges. This basis is thus in no way valid for the personal relationship of man to man but solely for the judgment of the legal assembly in cases of bodily harm. Of course in the *lex talionis* we have a basic law which has been handed down from extreme antiquity. For its wording must originally have meant that that the offender should be punished in exactly the same way as he had caused bodily harm to another. In that case the punishment is considered not from the view-point of reparation, i.e. making good, but of retribution. This is not generally the case in the casuistic law in the Book of the Covenant, and we must therefore ask whether this basis for retribution which has been incorporated into the Book of the Covenant has, in the legal practice generally presupposed in the Book of the Covenant, been still applied in its proper sense, or whether the bodily punishment incurred could not be replaced by some sort of reparation. Reparation is in any case provided for in the case of bodily harm to a male or female slave discussed in vv. 26 f., as the demand for release in practice represents a payment of the purchase price of a slave. Verses 28–32 deal with the killing of a man by an *ox who gores*. In this event the ox must in any case be stoned. The stoning represents the execution of the death penalty by the community and the solemn exclusion from the community of one who has ranged himself against it. By killing a man the ox in effect commits an offence against the community and is appropriately punished without the question of responsibility being raised, as by his action he has become taboo and therefore may not be used for food. The question of responsibility is raised only in respect of the owner of the ox. He is punished as a deliberate murderer only if he is responsible through his knowledge of the dangerous character of the ox (v. 29; cf. on the other hand v. 28); though in this case it is left possible for the legal assembly to decide that he must pay a ransom for the life which he has forfeited (v. 30). In this section slaves are only valued as property possessed, so that only the usual

*Cf. A. Alt, *Kleine Schriften zur Geschichte des Volkes Israel* I, pp. 341 ff.

purchase price of a slave is to be paid to his owner (v. 32); in this verse the responsibility of the owner of the ox is still presupposed according to v. 29. Under the catchword 'ox' there is loosely attached in vv. 33 f. the case of an ox or an ass falling into a pit which has carelessly been left open. In this event the owner of the pit must pay for any damage that may arise, as he has incurred guilt through his own carelessness. If an ox is killed by another ox who gores it, the responsibility is again decided as in vv. 28 f. (vv. 35 f.). In this way it is determined in what way the damage which has been caused is to be repaired.

[22.1–17] This section deals with cases of *damage to property*; not exhaustively, but by means of instances which probably arose frequently. This would certainly be the case with cattle stealing, which is discussed in 22.1–4. As there is always an evil intent in stealing not only must the reparation for what has been stolen be considered, but also a punishment, which consists in the repayment of a number of times the value of the stolen property. From the amount of the fine imposed in 22.1b it is evident that the theft of an ox was considered to be more serious than the theft of a sheep. It is regarded as particularly incriminating if the thief slaughters or sells the stolen animal as quickly as possible, as this betrays a systematic evil intent. If this does not happen, and the stolen object is still in the possession of the thief when it is found (22.4), the punishment is milder. The list of animals in 22.4 in which the ass is inserted alongside the ox and the sheep is perhaps an addition which commended itself once the special regulation in 22.2–3a had been added. This now separates the clauses 22.1 and 4 which in fact belong together* and refer to any kind of theft, not merely the theft of cattle. The killing of a thief surprised in the darkness by night does not bring with it bloodguilt which could give rise to blood vengeance, because not only can no intent to kill be established in those circumstances, but the person involved may be deemed to have acted in justifiable necessity, as he could not be sure of the intention of the thief (22.2). This does not, however, apply in broad daylight as even the life of a thief is protected by blood vengeance (22.3a). 22.3b may also be an addition to 22.1 or 22.4; if the thief is unable to pay the fine imposed upon him he must be sold as a slave and thus meet the sum required with his own person. The ruling in v. 5 is not easy to interpret, as the verb translated in RSV 'to graze over' (*b'r*) has several meanings and

*[The RSV prints vv. 1, 4, 2, 3 in that order. Tr.]

mostly means to 'consume by fire'; indeed it occurs with this meaning in the verse immediately following. The wording which has been handed down supports the idea that here it means to 'graze over', to 'graze off'. It is not said in what way anyone can have his own field or his vineyard grazed upon by his beasts (oxen or sheep). In any case he must be responsible for the damage which arises if he does not supervise his beasts properly and they therefore stray and graze on the field of a neighbour. The same is the case, according to v. 6, if anyone causes damage by fire, as for example when a fire lit for baking bread or for any other usual purpose catches hold of heaps of thorns and from there spreads to a neighbour's field. 22.7–13 is concerned with goods which have been delivered for safe-keeping and are then lost or stolen. If valuables given for safe-keeping are stolen, then the thief, if he is found, is punished (v. 7). If, however, he is not found, the owner of the house cannot prove beyond all objection that he has not misappropriated the deposited goods and that they have been stolen from him (this last is not expressly said but is pre-supposed) and must therefore confirm his attestation through an oath (v. 8). This oath is to be made 'before God', i.e. in the (local) sanctuary, and affirms that the self-cursing in which the oath consists will take effect if the person who makes it is guilty. Thus what can no longer be determined by human means is handed over to God for a decision, as the work of the curse which follows from the oath is in his hands. The same thing is said once again quite generally in v. 9, in a statement which is not formulated as a legal judgment but as an axiom and which refers not merely to entrusted goods but to property disputes in general. It occurs in a very old formulation which is evidently taken over from pre-Israelite times, as is clear from the fact that 'gods' are mentioned in the plural.* It is supposed that someone finds in the possession of another something which he assumes to be his own property, but that the other disputes this. In contrast to v. 8, the punishment is not left to the working of an oath, but the question of guilt is determined by a 'divine judgment' so that in the appropriate case the fine provided for in the last words of the verse may be inflicted by the legal assembly. It is not said in what way the 'divine judgment' is to be obtained. Verses 9–12 deal with the keeping of beasts delivered for safety. If for any reason such a

---

*[In the Hebrew of the phrase rendered in the RSV as 'he whom God shall condemn', the word for 'God' ('ᵉlohīm), which of course always has a plural form, also takes a plural verb. Hence 'gods' is the accurate rendering. Tr.]

beast should be lost without the person who has had it in his care being able to prove his innocence, the matter is once again as in v. 8 left to an oath. At this point the Old Testament divine name is mentioned ('an oath by Yahweh'), so we may suppose that this section about beasts delivered for safe keeping is a special Israelite extension of the law of deposit which was important for the Israelites, strongly interested in domestic animals even in an agricultural setting. The oath renders unnecessary any further action on the part of the legal assembly, as is expressly stated in v. 11b. In vv. 12 f. it is presumed that, the loss explained, there is no need for an oath. If the beast entrusted for safe keeping has demonstrably been stolen, there is nevertheless negligence on the part of its keeper, who, while not being punished, must make restitution (v. 12). If it has been torn by a wild beast no guilt is incurred so long as the keeper can produce the savaged beast as evidence (v. 13). Verses 14 f. discuss the hiring of beasts which must be primarily thought of as working beasts (ox or ass). If the hired beast is lost or comes to grief, a replacement must be provided so long as the owner of the beast was not himself present at the mishap; in that case he could and should have ensured the safety of his beast (vv. 14, 15a). If a hired man is lent a beast by his employer (for his work) and then loses it, the necessary recompense must be set against his wages.* Among damage to property there is finally included the ravishing of a virgin who is not yet betrothed and is still in the possession of her father (vv. 16 f.). The offender must in any case pay the usual bride price to her father, whether the latter is prepared to give the girl to him as his wife (v. 16) or whether he refuses (v. 17), as is his right in this case, as no betrothal ceremony has yet taken place.

[22.18–31] 22.18 marks the beginning of quite a long sequence of apodeictic law which is often interrupted by explanations made in another form. The very first of the sentences (v. 18) has a characteristic form, which then recurs frequently, with the object placed first and the formulation of the commandment following. For the belief of the Old Testament, sorcery means trafficking with strange divine powers or those hostile to God. The prohibition supposes that it is a feminine practice (cf. I Sam. 28.7 ff.; Ezek. 13.18 ff.). The negative formulation as a prohibition is characteristic, and is

*[Noth translates a somewhat laconic Hebrew text in a different way from the RSV, referring the 'hiring' to a man and not to the beast. He would translate: 'If (the man) is a hired man (the damage) is charged to his hire.' Tr.]

preferred even when as in the present instance a positive formulation would have been more appropriate. In v. 19 follows an isolated *mōt yūmāt* clause (cf. p. 179 above on 21.12) which deals with bestiality. Verse 20 is similar to it in form and indeed may be based on an original *mōt yūmāt* clause which was subsequently distorted: 'Whoever sacrifices to other gods shall be put to death (the word for 'other', *'ḥrm*, could easily have been wrongly written as *yḥrm* 'he shall be utterly destroyed'). The 'utter destruction' of the present text (lit. 'put to the ban') represents exclusion from the community and thus in practice results in death; 'to any god' means strange gods as is expressly stated in the gloss which follows—the phrase would originally have been self-explanatory. From v. 21 onwards, apodeictic clauses follow which aim to protect those who are underprivileged in law, work and society (*personae miserabiles*). The 'stranger' (*gēr*) is one who lives outside his family and his tribe and entrusts himself to the protection of an individual or a community. As he is in this situation without his own portion of land and his own legal representation, it is directed that he should be shown the customary laws of hospitality and not be 'wronged', a phrase which refers principally to exploitation in work. The second verb in v. 21a is already presumably a secondary addition; this is all the more so in the case of the reason given in v. 21b, which goes over to a plural address.* According to v. 22, even widow and orphan enjoy the protection of apodeictic law, as they lack the legal protection of husband and father and are therefore liable to 'affliction', as for example the brutal exploitation of their capacity for work. The plural address in v. 22 may not be original; it may perhaps have been occasioned by the presence of v. 21b. The statements in vv. 23 f., which again represent subsequent expansions, emphatically promise divine assistance to widows and orphans; God will hear the cry of widow and orphan, i.e. the cry for help of those who are unjustly oppressed, and will relentlessly punish the evil-doer in accordance with the maxim of the *lex talionis* (v. 23a is a protasis formulated in the singular, to which the relevant apodosis has been lost; the sentence construction of vv. 23b, 24 is again striking because of its plural address). In vv. 25–27 there are apodeictic clauses expanded by being preceded by a conditional clause and thus secondarily being made into the form of casuistic law. Verse 25 deals with lending money. Usury is forbidden; this is probably what is meant by being

*[This is again indistinguishable in English. Tr.]

'a creditor' as the gloss v. 25b written in the plural explains in detail. The practice of charging interest which was usual in trading and commerce throughout the ancient East is not allowed in dealing with anyone who is 'poor'(cf. Lev. 25.36–38; Deut. 23.20 f.); he borrows money for pressing needs, not to finance himself in commercial undertakings (Deut. 23.21 allows the charging of interest to foreigners). So a rule of life is put forward and affirmed for Israel, who is and is to remain separate from the urban character of the settled lands of the ancient East with their life of business and trade. Limits are also set to the taking of a pledge against a neighbour (vv. 26 f.). Once again a poor man is considered who can only give his 'garment', i.e. his long overcoat, as pledge for a loan; this he needs urgently, at least at night, because he has nothing else to serve him as an underlay and a covering when he goes to sleep. His coat is therefore to be restored to him before the sun goes down, in which case of course the use of the coat as a pledge is completely illusory. The explanatory, emphatic remarks in v. 27 may be later expansions.

In v. 28 the juxtaposition of 'God' and *nāsî'* is noteworthy. No difference in content can be established between the two words which are translated 'revile' and 'curse' (cf. Gen. 12.3); we may have here merely a change of expression. The outrage of cursing God (cf. Lev. 24.15 and Job 2.9 [with a euphemistic alteration of 'curse' into 'bless']) has beside it the cursing of a *nāsî'*. The word *nāsî'*, which here as elsewhere is translated 'ruler', is used later in the Old Testament, particularly in Ezekiel, as a term for one who bears rule. But this is evidently a secondary usage, for which there are special reasons. True, we read in I Kings 21.10; 'You have cursed (lit. blessed) God and the king.' But in the passage with which we are concerned the word for king does not occur, and there is certainly no thought of the king here. The word *nāsî'* will therefore have a special meaning of its own and appears with this meaning among other places in Num. 1.16 (as in countless other P passages, e.g. Ex. 16.22). Although we are in this way dealing with a relatively late tradition, the word *nāsî'* nevertheless appears in a particular concrete significance, as is evidently presupposed in Ex. 22.28. We may therefore apply the late tradition to explain this already old term. According to this the *nāsî'* is the representative of the twelve tribes on the occasions when all Israel is gathered together (in 16.22 above the word has been translated 'leader'—the word 'spokesman' might be

clearer). The apodeictic clause 22.28 may therefore have its foundation in the existence of the old Israelite association of twelve tribes in
the time before the monarchy. The importance of its institutions,
among which the office of *nāsī'* belongs, in the setting of the Old
Testament relationship between Israel and God, is clear from the fact
that God and the *nāsī'* stand parallel alongside each other.

In vv. 29 f. the usual cultic offerings are required; v. 29a apparently covers the offering of the produce of the land; in view of
Num. 18.27; Deut. 22.9, the word 'fulness' refers specially to wine,
while the word 'outflow', which occurs only here, perhaps refers to
oil. Only the general demand is made, no exact details about the
amount of the offerings are given (cf. in contrast Deut. 14.22; 26.12
etc.). Even the demand for the offering of all first-born is only
formulated as an axiom in vv. 29b, 30a, without a word as to whether
the offering, i.e. the sacrifice, of human first-born is really to be
practised or whether it is not rather to be replaced by a vicarious
offering (cf. pp. 101 f. above on 13.1 f., 11 ff.). Verse 31 contains a
plural address and is therefore certainly secondary; it forbids, in view
of the 'holiness' of Israel, the eating of the flesh of animals which
might in themselves be eaten but which have been torn by wild
beasts (the mere idea of 'holiness', put forward as a reason for the
requirement, suggests a later style of law). The reason for this
requirement, with which Lev. 7.24 and 17.15 (with a divergent
special regulation) are to be compared, is that a savaged beast has
not been slaughtered in the requisite sacral manner, which is the
necessary basis for all permitted eating of flesh.

[23.1–9] Here there are apodeictic regulations for the conduct of
cases at law. They do not represent a 'model for judges' in the sense
that they apply to a professional judge, as there was no such person in
ancient Israel (the 'judges' of Judg. 10.1–5; 12.7–15 were hardly
concerned with practical justice); they are rather directed towards
all free Israelites who had to discuss and decide together in the local
legal assembly. The principal aim of these requirements is to protect
the poor and the weak against a partial judgment in favour of the
rich and the powerful; thus they already presuppose the presence of
such distinctions in business and society. Verse 1 first of all makes a
general prohibition of flippant and partisan statements in the legal
assembly, and similarly v. 7 contains a warning against a 'false
charge' or a 'false action' and forbids unjust judgments; here the
terms *ṣaddīq* (the one who is in the right) and *rāšā'* (the one who is in

the wrong) are contrasted, the one with the other. This contrast would be still clearer if the last clause in v. 7 had originally read 'and do not acquit the wicked', which would require the assumption of only a very small error in the transmitted text. Moreover, it is emphatically forbidden to exert influence in dishonest ways on statements and judgments made in the legal assembly, whether through bribery (v. 8), through a man's power and prestige (v. 3),* in which case few men of power and reputation would not succeed in their suits (v. 6), or through the opinion of the 'multitude' in the legal assembly, who because of error or malicious intent could 'do evil' (v. 2). Finally in v. 9 also in this context the 'stranger' (*gēr*) is given express consideration; he must not be 'oppressed', i.e. deprived of his rights, even if he himself plays no part in the legal assembly (the fact that the emphatic clause v. 9b which is added to this requirement is written in the plural shows that it is an obvious addition). The requirements of vv. 3 and 6, which correspond with each other in content, are now separated by the regulations of vv. 4 f., which are introduced by an 'if' clause (cf. p. 186 above on 22.25 f.) and which deal not with conduct in the legal assembly but with extra-legal conduct towards an 'enemy' or 'one who hates you'. This 'enemy' 'who hates you' apparently means a man with whom one is having or has had a dispute at law or with whom perhaps a dispute at law is now for the first time imminent, and for this reason these clauses have been inserted in the present context. It is axiomatic that a man should not act towards such an adversary in everyday life in any other way than he would normally act towards his 'neighbour', to whom it is supposed that he would usually accord the assistance which is mentioned in vv. 4. f. (what is here only presumed is expressly required in Deut. 22.1–4).

[**23.10–13**] The regulations about the *sabbath year* and the *sabbath day* (vv. 10–13) bring the Book of the Covenant into the sacral sphere, for even if the reasons for these ordinances as given in the Book of the Covenant appear to be of a predominantly social nature, there doubtless stands behind them the thought of a 'return to the original state', a *restitutio in integrum* which is to be effected at certain intervals, as is clearly recognizable in the year of jubilee (the sabbath year of the sabbath year) of Lev. 25. It is expressly enjoined that in the sabbath year the produce of the earth is not to be gathered (vv. 10 f.),

---

*[Reading 'powerful' for 'poor', in accordance with the emendation suggested in Kittel's *Biblia Hebraica*. Tr.]

and this means at the same time that the cultivation of the land is to lapse during this year. What grows of its own accord is to be allowed to the 'poor', i.e. in this context particularly those who have no land of their own; what is left by them is to be left for the 'beasts of the field', i.e. those animals which are not domesticated (cf. RSV 'wild'). Thus its original 'rest' is to be given back to the land, undisturbed by the hand of man (cf. Lev. 25.4). To let the land lie fallow from time to time is hardly thought of as having the practical use of preserving or increasing the productivity. Nothing is said as to whether the sabbath year is to be observed simultaneously throughout the land or whether it is to be observed for each piece of land in rotation. We only hear briefly of the practical enforcement of the sabbath year in the Old Testament in Neh. 10.31 (but cf. also I Macc. 6.49, 53). The association of sabbath day and sabbath year which occurs in this way only here in the Old Testament suggests that there was also a similar basis to the former. True, in v. 12b the reason for refraining from work on every seventh day is said to be consideration for the beasts of burden and all dependent working men, among whom in a surprising way 'the alien' as well as the slave is included. But there is still the question whether this exhausts all the reasons for the injunction, or whether the essential point here is not rather of rest in general in the sense of a return to something original. Hence we could also understand that express concern is taken for animals on the sabbath day and in the sabbath year, not because they were the object of a love which we can hardly presuppose in the ancient world, but because they are an integral part of the creation which from time to time is to return to its 'rest'. Verse 13 with its plural address (apart from the last clause) and with its general warning to observe the divine ordinances and its general prohibition of 'other gods' is a later addition.

[23.14–19] Special *cultic regulations* follow in vv. 14–19, formulated in the apodeictic style, like the regulations about the sabbath year and the sabbath day. First of all a thrice yearly 'pilgrimage', i.e. an assembly of all males (cf. v. 17) at the local sanctuaries of the land, is enjoined for the three feasts which are enumerated in what follows. These feasts are to Yahweh, as is explicitly said. The three feasts derive from the tradition of the cultivated land and are extremely closely connected with the life of an agricultural community and the cycle of nature. This emerges clearly from the description of them. They were thus only taken over by Israel after the settlement and were now to be celebrated 'to Yahweh', who for Israel is the sole Lord of the land and of its blessing. In the Book of the Covenant the three feasts are described with their original, or at least with what are to us the oldest still extant, names as the feast of unleavened bread, the feast of harvest and the feast of ingathering. The feast of unleavened bread (v. 15), alongside which there is still no mention of the Passover sacrifice which was later associated with it, is the feast of the beginning of the corn harvest in the spring. At this feast, for seven days, i.e. for a period which is governed by the recurrence of the sabbath day (see above), bread made from the first produce of the new crop is to be eaten in its original state, untouched by leaven. The subordinate clauses in v. 15, which make the regulations about the feast of unleavened bread far longer than the brief regulations about the two other feasts, are certainly later additions. The second of these subordinate clauses gives the feast of unleavened bread a 'historical' reference and reason; it is in accordance with the 'historicization' of the agricultural feasts which was in time carried out in Israel, but was probably still lacking in the original form of the Book of the Covenant. Perhaps all that is original is the detail about the fixed time, the 'month of gleaning' (March/April). The final clause of v. 15, which requires that no one is to come to the sanctuary without an offering, has a disruptive effect on the enumeration of the feasts, and is either an addition (perhaps after 34.20b*b*) or has subsequently been put in the wrong place by mistake (it would be in place after v. 17). The feast of harvest (v. 16a) would certainly take place at the end of the corn harvest. 'The first fruits of your labour' means either the whole of the corn harvest as the first gift which the cultivated land provides in the year or alternatively an offering of the first-fruits of the grain which is preserved and brought to the sanctuary at the end of the harvest. The feast of ingathering (v. 16b) refers to the gathering of fruits from the plants (especially olives and grapes); it takes place in the autumn and therefore at the turn of the year according to the old system of the autumn new year. Verse 17 once again requires that all males shall appear three times a year at the sanctuary; it makes no reference to the three feasts mentioned above. It is however quite possible that these feasts are meant as the chief occasions of a general visit to the sanctuary, and it is here merely added that at those times 'all males' shall appear at the sanctuary. Of course the wording only prescribes a yearly minimum of visits to the sanctuary for each man, whether at feast times or on other occasions. For the visit to the sanctuary the evidently derived, stereotyped expression 'see the face of God (Yahweh)'* is used (cf. also v. 15b). It was at one time originally meant literally with reference to an image of the god in the sanctuary. In Israel it has been taken over without prejudice and with no respect to its original meaning (cf. also 20.4); the Massoretic text has in fact subsequently altered it slightly because the wording was objectionable to Israel. A number of individual cultic instructions follow in vv. 18 f. (in essentials identical with 34.25 f.). The formulation of v. 18a is striking and not fully comprehensible; in its forced brevity it perhaps means that leavened bread may not be eaten at a sacrificial meal because the leaven destroys the original character of the dough (in other kinds of sacrifices leavened bread is not merely allowed but enjoined according to Lev. 7.13; 23.17; cf. also Amos 4.5). According to v. 18b the fat of the 'festal sacrifice' is to be offered complete (for burning) on the feast day itself; if it were left over until the next day, which is evidently no longer counted as a feast day, it would become deconsecrated. The requirement to offer the best of the produce of the land at the sanctuaries (v. 19a)—the singular 'house of Yahweh' means the sanctuary belonging to the settlement in question—refers to the arable ground; cf. 22.28a, where especially wine and oil appear to be meant. Verse 19b presumably forbids a practice usual in foreign cults. In the section 23.14–19 the unmotivated change between the appearance of Yahweh in the first person (vv. 14, 15, 18) and in the third person (vv. 17, 19a) is striking; we evidently have a collection of individual groups of cultic regulations, already shaped, whose special derivation remains unknown to us.

The addition 23.20–33, which is hardly all one piece, but appears gradually to have grown to the form in which it has been transmitted, bears a generally deuteronomistic stamp in style and content. It refers the Book of the Covenant to the impending conquest and thus has it given to Israel at Sinai. It deals with guidance for Israel on the way which now lies before them into the Promised Land and with the future behaviour of Israel towards the previous inhabitants of the land. No less than three times is it said that Yahweh will send someone before Israel; a 'messenger' ('angel', v. 20) to protect Israel on the way and to lead them to their goal, his 'terror', which will throw the inhabitants of the promised land into a confused panic and

---

*[The RSV translates the Hebrew expression as 'appear before'; this follows the Massoretic pointing of *niphal* for *qal*, cf. below; cf. also Isa. 12.1. Tr.]

put them to flight (v. 27), and 'hornets', which will drive out the inhabitants of the land (v. 28). The 'angel' is the ambassador of Yahweh (cf. 'my angel', v. 23) who represents Yahweh himself and in whom Yahweh himself is present; the latter is expressed in v. 21 by saying that the 'name' of Yahweh is present in the 'angel' as the name represents the one who bears it. Therefore Israel must behave towards the angel as though he were Yahweh himself (v. 21; the first clause in v. 21b is noteworthy because of its plural address). If Israel behaves in this way Yahweh himself (in the person of his angel) will fight for Israel (v. 22) and bring them into the land whose mixture of inhabitants are described with the usual series of peoples' names (v. 23). According to vv. 27 f. the 'terror' and the 'hornet' (the meaning of this last word is not quite certain) are given by Yahweh to his people as a means of overcoming the inhabitants of the land. In contrast to the 'angel' who accompanies Israel, this is an idea which is rooted in the concept of the Holy War, according to which Yahweh smites his enemies and those of his people by a panic which is caused in a mysterious way. Once in the land, the conduct of Israel towards the inhabitants of the land who still remain will be decisive. Only if Israel keeps well away from the foreign cults of the inhabitants of the land and destroys their cultic apparatus (v. 24) will it participate in or remain in possession of the divine blessing which is the basis of its natural life and gives 'the number of his days' to each individual (vv. 25 f.; this passage is not completely smooth; we find plural addresses alongside singular and Yahweh both in the third person and in the first person). Finally in vv. 29–33 the problem of the groups of old inhabitants still left in the land is raised; this stemmed from the fact that while the whole of the land was promised to Israel, in fact these older inhabitants remained in possession of the land or at least in some parts of it. This problem (on which cf. also Judg. 3.1–6) is here solved by the thought that Yahweh did not want the land, which at that time Israel could not inhabit fully, to go to waste, and therefore only allowed the older inhabitants to be driven out gradually until Israel had so increased that it was able to occupy the whole land. This of course never happened in history even in Palestine itself, much less in the substantial part of Syria and the surrounding territory which is promised to Israel in v.31; the borders of the territory in v. 31 have in mind the extent of David's sovereignty; the 'reed sea' (cf. p. 11 n. above), may here as elsewhere (e.g. I Kings 9.26) mean the gulf of *el-ʿaqaba*, while the word 'river', which occurs alone in the Hebrew, usually describes the Euphrates in the Old Testament, as is made clear by the RSV rendering. A further warning against associating with the earlier inhabitants of the land and their cults marks the close of the book in vv. 32 f.

3. THE MAKING OF THE COVENANT: 24.1–11

24 [1] *And he said to Moses, 'Come up to the* LORD, *you and Aaron, Nadab, and Abihu, and seventy of the elders of Israel, and worship afar off.* [2] *Moses alone shall come near to the* LORD; *but the others shall not come near, and the people shall not come up with him.'*

3 *Moses came and told the people all the words of the* LORD *and all the ordinances; and all the people answered with one voice, and said, 'All the words which the* LORD *has spoken we will do.'* [4] *And Moses wrote all the words of the* LORD. *And he rose early in the morning, and built an altar at the foot of the mountain, and twelve pillars, according to the twelve tribes of Israel.* [5] *And he sent young men of the people of Israel, who offered burnt offerings and sacrificed peace offerings [of oxen] to the* LORD. [6] *And Moses took half of the blood and put it in basins, and half of the blood he threw against the altar.* [7] *Then he took the book of the covenant, and read it in the hearing of the people; and they said, 'All that the* LORD *has spoken we will do, and we will be obedient.'* [8] *And Moses took the blood and threw it upon the people, and said, 'Behold the blood of the covenant which the* LORD *has made with you in accordance with all these words.'*

9 *Then Moses and Aaron, Nadab, and Abihu, and seventy of the elders of Israel went up,* [10] *and they saw the God of Israel; and there was under his feet as it were a pavement of sapphire stone, like the very heaven for clearness.* [11] *And he did not lay his hand on the chief men of the people of Israel; they beheld God, and ate and drank.*

The theophany on Sinai ends with the solemn making of a covenant between God and the people, which is described in 24.1–11. In this section two different literary strata may easily be distinguished. In vv. 1 f. and 9–11 the covenant is made on the mountain, in vv. 3–8 on the other hand at the foot of the mountain. Verses 1 f. contain the introduction to the passage 9–11; these passages, which obviously belong together, are separated by the narrative vv. 3–8. We are thus given in this chapter two versions of the account of the making of the covenant which, while dealing with the same subject, are widely different in their individual details.

[9–11] According to vv. 9–11 a deputation from Israel ascends the hill. Apart from Moses, the group consists of Aaron, whose relationship to Moses is not given here (on the question of this relationship in the old tradition cf. p. 122 above on 15.20), and Nadab and Abihu, who appear abruptly here without either an introduction or any details about their relationship with Aaron or Moses. In the late source P Nadab and Abihu appear as sons of Aaron (cf. Lev. 10.1 and the different genealogies, e.g. Ex. 6.23). This late genealogical arrangement in all probability rests on the juxtaposition of names in this chapter and not on any old tradition. The abrupt and isolated appearance in the narrative of Ex. 24, which is in any case old, suggests that at one time the tradition had more to tell about them but in the course of the handing down of the tradition their figures gradually faded. The fact that they appear only in Ex. 24 and in only one version can hardly be understood otherwise than to mean that they belonged to an ancient tradition about the making of the covenant probably along with the seventy elders, whose role as the representatives of Israel is immediately obvious. If we make a traditio-historical analysis of the list in v. 9, we may even come to the conclusion that only the group of seventy unnamed elders belonged to the first stage (cf. also pp. 54 f. above on 5.3–19) but that, among the individuals who are named, Nadab and Abihu, who now appear superfluous alongside Moses and Aaron, in any case represent very old traditional material which was not completely forced out of this narrative of the making of the covenant even after Moses and Aaron had come so much to the forefront in the Sinai narrative, as in the other narratives of this early period. In v. 10 it is now astonishingly reported of the deputation of Israelites that they 'saw the God of Israel'. True, in what follows only the appearance 'under his feet' is described and it is thus intimated that the deputation did not dare to raise their eyes to the 'God of Israel' himself. But the first expression in v. 10 is nevertheless there (cf. on the other hand 33.20). The description of what was 'under his feet' certainly indicates the heavens. Sapphire (if this is a correct rendering of the word *sappîr*) is a sky-blue semi-precious stone, and a 'pavement of sapphire stone' can hardly refer to anything but a pavement painted and perhaps glazed in a sapphire colour, the kind of pavement which was known particularly in Mesopotamia, and the object so described would at least in respect of its 'clearness' (literally 'purity') have been comparable with the 'very heaven'. It is thus thought that the summit of the mountain is 'in heaven' and that here 'in heaven' the 'God of Israel' is present. Verse 11a hints that this meeting was something quite out of the ordinary by observing that the 'God of Israel' did not do any harm to the men who appeared on the mountain, as might have been expected. It was a unique occurrence that the God who was present on the mountain allowed the representatives of Israel to come so near. These latter are here described with a singular and probably old expression as the 'chief men of the Israelites'; as the application of this description to Moses and Aaron is most remarkable, we may ask whether in an older stage of the tradition it did not perhaps refer specially to Nadab and Abihu (including the seventy elders). The main clause stands at the end in v. 11b. Once again the men are said to 'behold God' and then in a mysterious way to 'eat' and 'drink'. In this context this can only refer to a covenant meal which takes place, just as among men too a common meal can form an effective and valid seal on the making of a covenant (cf. Gen. 31.46, 54). It is not said and cannot be said here of course that both partners in the covenant share in the covenant meal. The fact that God lets the representatives of Israel hold a meal in his presence on the mountain indicates the making of the covenant between God and people. The content of this covenant is now binding on both sides without the need for formulated clauses which regulate the relationship which is so formed, just as there is no mention of any such conditions in the present context. As the word 'God' is used in the conclusive clause v. 11b (in v. 10 the 'God of Israel') we must assign this narrative version of the making of the covenant to the E version. In view of the fragmentary remains of this source it is hard to say just how it is to be fitted into the sequence of events in E. [1–2] Even the introduction which belongs to it is of no real help in this, as it obviously no longer presents its original wording. An explicit command from God must certainly have preceded the narrative in vv. 9–11, for without such a command the deputation from Israel would not have dared to ascend the mountain. This command is preserved in vv. 1 f., but hardly in its original form. The 'to Moses' which precedes it in v. 1 is evidently attached to a speech of God directed towards another audience which may now be lost from the E context. But it is also possible that this formula refers to the Book of the Covenant which has been inserted in the meantime, which was regarded as a speech of God designated for the people even if according to 20.22 it was primarily a divine address to Moses. But the chief surprise of vv. 1 f. is the occurrence of Yahweh in the third person, as though some third person was giving the instructions to go up the mountain 'to Yahweh'. Who can this third person be? We might posit an alteration to the text and assume for 'Yahweh' an original 'I', which in view of the Hebrew text would not be completely inexplicable. But we might just as well suppose that the whole passage vv. 1 f. is secondary and has not been appropriately formulated. This is also supported by the content of vv. 1b, 2, which does not fit very well with vv. 9–11; for according to this latter passage the whole deputation without any distinction participates in the meeting with God on the mountain. In that case the unusual and startling nature of this meeting would only have been diminished at a later date by the 'command to ascend' in vv. 1b, 2, so that only Moses was to go up really near to God while the other members of the deputation were merely to throw themselves down in worship 'from afar'. We thus have in vv. 1 f. a passage which has largely been worked over in a redactional way, and in which the original command of God for the ascent of the mountain by the deputation is missing. The incomplete E account of the events on the holy mountain may be reconstructed hypothetically in approximately the following way: after his arrival Moses ascends 'to God' (19.3a), probably to receive the announcement of the impending theophany. The theophany, which leads to a 'conversation' between God and Moses whose content is not recorded (19.16b, 17, 19) causes the people who have been led by Moses to the foot of the mountain (19.17) to request that they may keep their distance and that Moses alone may act as mediator (20.18, 19–21*); Moses now presumably receives instructions for the ascent of the mountain by the deputation (24.1 f.*) which is eventually followed by the solemn making of the covenant on the mountain (24.9–11). It remains questionable whether perhaps the isolated clause 19.13b (see p. 158 above) is a displaced piece of the E narrative; it could belong to the instructions for ascending the mountain which in that case would perhaps have been more detailed than the remains in 24.1 f. leads us to suppose.

[3–8] According to the version 24.3–8, the act of making the covenant is completed by a sacrifice at the foot of the mountain—the one possible form of making a covenant among men. This sacrifice is now associated with the reading, writing and learning of the words of Yahweh which Israel is to 'do'. This refers to definite regulations and requirements laid down by Yahweh. Now the report of the sacrifice is an independent entity and could form a proper account of the making of the covenant even without any reference to the 'words of Yahweh'. There is in any case no decisive reason for explaining the

*These verses contain other elements besides E.

clauses about the 'words of Yahweh' as being a secondary literary addition, and thus we may assume that the obligation to the 'words of Yahweh' was a part of this covenant narrative from the beginning. The act thus begins with Moses 'coming' into the assembly of the people and handing on to the people the 'words of Yahweh' (the observation that these were 'ordinances' is superfluous in this context and is in fact a completely secondary element of interpretation); he receives from the people a preliminary agreement to these words, whereupon he writes them down (vv. 3, 4a*a*). Then an altar is built and twelve stones (*maṣṣēboth*) are erected in the neighbourhood of the altar or round about it to represent the twelve tribes. At the command of Moses sacrifices are offered by 'young men' (vv. 4a*b*b, 5). Hereupon follows the blood rite essential for the concluding of the covenant; the blood of the communal sacrifice applied to the partners in the covenant joins them together. The altar here represents the divine partner in the covenant (v. 6b). The people are only included in the covenant after a now final obligation to the 'words of Yahweh', which have in the meantime been written down as law and are read out as the basis of the covenant ('Book of the Covenant'; vv. 7, 8a). Then the 'blood of the covenant' is sprinkled on the people, not on the twelve representative pillars, which no longer have a part to play. This forms a valid conclusion to the covenant, as Moses finally declares in a detailed formulation which is characterized by the use of the so-called declarative perfect tense (v. 8b). The question of the larger literary context to which this narrative version of the making of the covenant belongs is not easy to answer. The source J, which suggests itself because of the use of the divine name Yahweh, cannot be involved, as in it the making of the covenant only follows in the context of what is narrated in ch. 34 (see p. 260 below). The reference to the 'words of Yahweh' in 24.3–8 presupposes the delivery of such words. But then the most obvious thing is to think of the words of Yahweh which have been reported immediately beforehand, i.e. of the book of the covenant which is in fact proved to be the 'Book of the Covenant' by 24.7. In that case 24.3–8 may be given a literary connection with the Book of the Covenant, as a covenant narrative which would once have been attached to the originally independent 'Book of the Covenant' to anchor this law book expressly in the covenant at Sinai. This must already have happened at a relatively early period, as the narrative is evidently quite old, in any case older than the addition to the Book of the Covenant in 23.30–33, as is clear in particular from the role of the (non-priestly) 'young men' in the offering of the sacrifice (v. 5). A brief narrative introduction corresponding to this closing narrative would at the same time have formed a part of the Book of the Covenant; when the Book of the Covenant was later incorporated into the Pentateuchal narrative it would have been sacrificed, whereas the closing narrative in Ex. 24 was preserved as a bridge between vv. 1 f. and vv. 9–11.

4. THE INSTRUCTIONS GIVEN ON THE MOUNTAIN FOR THE ESTABLISHMENT OF THE CULT: 24.12–31.17

(a) INTRODUCTION: 24.12–25.9

12 The LORD said to Moses, 'Come up to me on the mountain, and wait there; and I will give you the tables of stone, [with the law and the commandment,] which I have written for their instruction.' 13 So Moses rose with his servant Joshua, and Moses went up into the mountain of God. 14 And he said to the elders, 'Tarry here for us, until we come to you again; and, behold, Aaron and Hur are with you; whoever has a cause, let him go to them.'

15 Then Moses went up on the mountain, and the cloud covered the mountain. 16 The glory of the LORD settled on Mount Sinai, and the cloud covered it six days; and on the seventh day he called to Moses out of the midst of the cloud. 17 Now the appearance of the glory of the LORD was like a devouring fire on the top of the mountain in the sight of the people of Israel. 18 And Moses entered the cloud, and went up on the mountain. And Moses was on the mountain forty days and forty nights.

25¹ The LORD said to Moses, ² 'Speak to the people of Israel, that they take for me an offering; from every man whose heart makes him willing you shall receive the offering for me. ³ And this is the offering which you shall receive from them: gold, silver, and bronze, ⁴ blue and purple and scarlet stuff and fine twined linen, goats' hair, ⁵ tanned rams' skins, goatskins, acacia wood, [⁶ oil for the lamps, spices for the anointing oil and for the fragrant incense, ⁷ onyx stones, and stones for setting, for the ephod and for the breastpiece.] ⁸ And let them make me a sanctuary, that I may dwell in their midst. ⁹ According to all that I show you concerning the pattern of the tabernacle, and of all its furniture, so you shall make it.'

[24.12–15a] This section introduces the detailed instructions which Moses now receives from Yahweh on the mountain. It consists of two parts, each of which speaks of Moses' ascent of the mountain (24.15a and 24.18). The first part (24.12–15a) prepares for the narrative of ch. 32; Moses is summoned for a (lengthy) stay on the mountain (24.12a, cf. 32.1) and is there to receive the tables of stone inscribed by Yahweh. Originally no details were given about the inscriptions on these tables, so a glossator felt compelled to insert in rather a clumsy way at the end of v. 12 the still quite general terms 'law and commandment' (24.12b; cf. 32.15 f., 19b). Moses takes his 'servant' Joshua to accompany him (24.13a; cf. 32.17) and in case disputes should arise entrusts the people, represented by their elders (24.14a), to the care of the two men Aaron and Hur, of whose position or function we are told nothing even here (24.14b; cf. 17.10, 12, and on Aaron 32.1 ff.). The clause 24.13b has a disruptive effect as it inappropriately anticipates the statement in 24.15a and has Moses ascending the mountain before he has given the instructions of v. 14. This indicates that the passage 24.12–15a is not a complete unity (see further about this on chs. 32 and 34). But in any case this passage belongs to the older source which is present in chs. 32 and 34.

[24.15b–18] 24.15b marks the beginning of a long continuous section of the P narrative (24.15b–31.18) in which a full description is given of how Moses receives from Yahweh on the mountain the detailed instructions for the making of the sanctuary and all the apparatus that is necessary for cultic worship. This section connects directly with the last of the preceding P passages 19.1–2a. Thus in P as soon as the Israelites have arrived in the 'wilderness of Sinai' the 'glory of the Lord', which represents the divine presence (24.16a), descends upon the mountain, now covered with cloud (24.15b), and, after a six-day period of waiting and preparation as a proper interval before the impending great event, during which only the cloud is visible, appears in such a way that the Israelites now perceive a 'devouring fire' on the summit of the mountain (24.17). Moses is summoned (24.16b), whereupon he goes into the cloud and climbs the mountain, to remain there for forty days during which time he is to receive the words of Yahweh. For P the whole significance of the events at Sinai is that Moses receives these words and that the instructions for the establishment of the cult which they contain are subsequently carried out. P no longer speaks of the making of a covenant at Sinai; after the covenant between God and Abraham (Gen. 17) there is no longer room for one. For P the encounter with God at Sinai represents the beginning of legitimate cultic worship, which is of course in P's view of fundamental importance for the continuance of the relationship between God and people; only in this does God's promise that he will 'be the God of' the descendants of Abraham

(Gen. 17.8b) find permanent confirmation. God himself regulates cultic worship down to the smallest detail of its preparation and performance. Without such ordering cultic worship was not legitimate in P's eyes. Thus in contrast to the older sources P has no knowledge of cultic acts before Sinai.

The sanctuary, erected and equipped by divine ordinance, built first on Sinai and then carried about on the journey through the wilderness, is in P quite clearly orientated on the picture of the later temple at Jerusalem. The only question is whether the model is the temple of Solomon (which may have been elaborated further during the period of the monarchy in Judah) or the temple of Zerubbabel, of whose details we know but little. Whichever it may be, in any case for P the Jerusalem temple is the only legitimate sanctuary. This sanctuary is directly derived from the divine instructions given at Sinai. There was evidently no decisive break in the tradition of the legitimate sanctuary, as is seen from the fact that the tent-sanctuary erected in accordance with the 'pattern' (25.9) shown to Moses on the mountain, and used at Sinai and during the wanderings, was eventually replaced after the conquest by a stone sanctuary built in Jerusalem roughly in accord with the design that had been given.

[25.1–9] First of all, in 25.2–7, Moses is given instructions to have the material necessary for the building of the sanctuary brought by a free-will 'offering' on the part of the Israelites. In the detailed instructions which then follow, this material and the use to which it is put are mentioned over and over again. Apart from unrefined metal (25.3b), the chief concern is primarily for raw materials for more or less costly fabrics (25.4). In ancient times purple-dyed wool was chiefly manufactured on the Phoenician coast by using dye extracted from the glands of certain shellfish. The bluish-purple dye (RSV 'blue') is described by the word *tᵉkēlet*, which is also known in Accadian, but whose origin cannot be ascertained with certainty. The word *'argāmān*, which likewise also occurs in Accadian and perhaps derives from Asia Minor, means reddish-purple dye. The scarlet dye (and the wool coloured with it) is named after the insect from which it is produced; the special name for this insect is once again a word which cannot certainly be derived from the Hebrew. An Egyptian word is used for 'fine twined linen', which suggests that it derives from a special kind of Egyptian linen-weaving. Goats' hair has been used at all times to make tent coverings. For making leather not only rams' skins but also the skins of *tᵉḥāšîm*, probably a certain kind of dolphin,* are mentioned. The valuable acacia wood is to be used for the woodwork. The fact that the purpose of the (olive) oil and the aromatic resin of the balsam shrub is mentioned when they occur (25.6) shows that they are secondary in this context; their cultic use is already envisaged. The incomplete and disproportionate mention of the costly stones for parts of the priest's clothing in 25.7 is evidently also secondary.

P apparently gave no thought to where the Israelites were to get all these precious materials on Sinai. They were, as their names partly of certain foreign derivation show, expressly the products of a civilized society and were used in not inconsiderable quantities, as the following individual details make plain.

(b) INSTRUCTIONS FOR MAKING THE ARK: 25.10–22

10 'They shall make an ark of acacia wood; two cubits and a half shall be its length, a cubit and a half its breadth, and a cubit and a half its height. 11 And you shall overlay it with pure gold, within and without shall you overlay it, and you shall make upon it a moulding of gold round about. 12 And you shall cast four rings of gold for it and put them on its four feet, two rings on the one side of it, and two rings on the other side of it. 13 You shall make poles of acacia wood, and overlay them with gold. 14 And you shall put the poles into the rings on the sides of the ark, to carry the ark by them. 15 The poles shall remain in the rings of the ark; they shall not be taken from it. 16 And you shall put into the ark the testimony which I shall give you. 17 Then you shall make a mercy seat of pure gold; two cubits and a half shall be its length, and a cubit and a half its breadth. 18 And you shall make two cherubim of gold; of hammered work shall you make them, on the two ends of the mercy seat. 19 Make one cherub on the one end, and one cherub on the other end; of one piece with the mercy seat shall you make the cherubim on its two ends. 20 The cherubim shall spread out their wings above, overshadowing the mercy seat with their wings, their faces one to another; toward the mercy seat shall the faces of the cherubim be. 21 And you shall put the mercy seat on the top of the ark; and in the ark you shall put the testimony that I shall give you. 22 There I will meet with you, and from above the mercy seat, from between the two cherubim that are upon the ark of the testimony, I will speak with you of all that I will give you in commandment for the people of Israel.'

The detailed instructions from God to Moses begin with the ark, which is the central sanctuary proper of the place where the cult is to be established. It stands first because of this position of importance,

* [The RSV 'goatskins' appears to be a conjecture. Tr.]

whereas, when the instructions are carried out, the tabernacle for the ark is made first before the ark itself (36.8 ff.). The command to make the ark, as all the following commands for the sanctuary as a whole, is given to Moses in person as the leader responsible for everything, even if the practical work is carried out by people expressly detailed for it. There are no solid reasons for doubting that the section on the ark and those which follow are essentially a literary unity. Only v. 19, which has a divergent formulation at the beginning of the verse, gives the impression of being an addition and moreover only mentions in broad detail what has already been said quite plainly immediately beforehand. In addition, v. 16 makes a secondary anticipation of what is reported in v. 21b, evidently in the original context.

The description of the ark in P derives from the actual presence of the ark in the Jerusalem sanctuary during the monarchy, after it had been brought into Jerusalem by David (II Sam. 6) and placed by Solomon in his temple, in the Holy of Holies (I Kings 8.6 ff.). We may expect from P neither historical information about the origin of the ark, which is for us so obscure, nor details of its original form. P probably knew no more than that the ark had stood in the innermost part of the pre-exilic temple, and from this made up a picture of the ark. We are hardly to assume that the ancient shrine of the pre-monarchical Israelite amphictyony as it had been brought by David into his new royal city of Jerusalem should have been so richly adorned with an overlay of beaten gold; and even Solomon would have incorporated the old traditional shrine into his temple essentially untouched and unaltered—at any rate there is nowhere any report of Solomon having decked the venerable ark in a new splendour. We must imagine the historical ark, about whose appearance we are given no concrete information in the old tradition, as having been quite simple. Its name alone implies that it was in the form of a chest, and this underlies the P description (cf. II Kings 12.10 f., also Gen. 50.26).

The description of the ark, as of the other parts of the sanctuary, contains numerous technical terms which in many cases cannot be interpreted exactly, as they occur only in this or in similar contexts. The rendering of the text therefore includes more elements of interpretation here than elsewhere. For measuring length the unit chiefly used is the 'cubit' i.e., the length of the forearm from the tip of the elbow—about nineteen inches. No exact definition is possible as different 'cubits' were known in the ancient East and even within the Old Testament (cf. II Chron. 3.3). The customary 'cubit' appears to have measured eighteen inches; it was further subdivided into the 'span' (half a cubit) and the 'handbreadth' (one sixth of a cubit).

[10–16] Brief particulars of the body of the ark (vv. 10 f.)—the 'moulding' (v. 11b) served only for decoration—are followed by more detailed specifications for making the ark portable (vv. 12–15). P has taken great care that all the parts of the sanctuary should be capable of being moved during the wanderings in the wilderness. Perhaps we are to imagine the 'feet', to which the rings for the carrying poles are to be attached, not as real feet, but merely as the lower ends of the moulding at the corner. [17–22] The 'cover' (RSV margin) presents a special problem. The body of the text follows the traditional English translation and renders the word *kapporet* standing in the Hebrew text as 'mercy seat' because of the Greek and Latin translation (*hilasterion, propitiatorium*; cf. also Heb. 9.5). This translation is based on the assumption that the root of the Hebrew word, whose original meaning is 'to cover', is chiefly used in the Old Testament in a transferred sense, 'to absolve'. But it can hardly be doubted that the simple, original meaning of the root lies behind the word *kapporet*. Probably only the box 'lid' of the ark is meant (in vv. 10, 11a it remains open whether a lid to the ark is already to be included at this stage of the description) and this lid is only mentioned particularly briefly because the two cherubim are to be attached to it and they will be described in more detail in vv. 18 (19) and 20. The joining of the cherubim to the ark once again has the model of the temple of Solomon in mind. Originally the cherubim did not belong to the ark, as it is said in I Kings 8.6 that Solomon had the ark brought into the innermost part of the Jerusalem temple 'underneath the wings of the cherubim'. Thus the cherubim first belonged to the furnishings of this inner sanctuary (I Kings 6.23–28) and here the ark was placed 'under their wings'. P then attached these cherubim firmly to the ark and in particular to its 'lid'. We cannot form any exact picture of these cherubim from either Ex. 25.18–20 or I Kings 6.23–28. In any case they are mixed beings who were known especially in Mesopotamia as tutelary deities at the entrances of temples and palaces; P too (v. 20) still speaks of 'overshadowing' (cf. also I Kings 8.7 and Ezek. 28.14, 16). Of their appearance we only hear that they had wings and faces, which certainly means human faces, but we are told nothing about their bodies, so we are not certain whether to imagine human bodies; perhaps the lack of specific information should be understood in this latter sense. According to v. 21b the 'testimony' is to be put in the ark. This means the law, evidently the law inscribed on the two tables of stone. Here P is linked with the Deuteronomic tradition according to which the two tables of stone on which the Decalogue was written (Deut. 5.22; but cf. pp. 266 f. below on Ex. 34.1 ff.) were put by Moses in the ark (Deut. 10.1–5). True, P has hitherto neither reported the Decalogue (on Ex. 31.18 cf. p. 247 below) nor spoken of the tables of stone, but as a matter of course tacitly assumes that the Deuteronomic tradition is known. According to v. 22, the place from which Yahweh will in future 'meet with' Moses and give him his instructions is to be above the cover of the ark containing the 'testimony' and between the wings of the cherubim. Two different ideas meet in this expression, first the conception that Yahweh is present 'above' the ark, stemming from the probably original idea of the ark as the throne of the invisibly present deity (cf. especially Num. 10.35 f.) and secondly the conception of the God who 'meets with' Moses and the Israelites, which originally belongs to the 'tent of meeting' (the 'tabernacle') but has here been transferred to the ark (in v. 22 the same Hebrew root is used for 'to meet with' as is contained in the phrase 'tent of meeting').

(c) INSTRUCTIONS FOR MAKING THE TABLE: 25.23–30

23 'And you shall make a table of acacia wood; two cubits shall be its length, a cubit its breadth, and a cubit and a half its height. 24 You shall overlay it with pure gold, and make a moulding of gold around it. 25 And you shall make around it a frame a hand breadth wide, and a moulding of gold around the frame. 26 And you shall make for it four rings of gold, and fasten the rings to the four corners at its four legs. 27 Close to the frame the rings shall lie, as holders for the poles to carry the table. 28 You shall make the poles of acacia wood, and overlay them with gold, and the table shall be carried with these. 29 And you shall make its plates and dishes for incense, and its flagons and bowls with which to pour libations; of pure gold you shall make them. 30 And you shall set the bread of the Presence on the table before me always.'

[23–30] The ark is followed by the contents of the sanctuary which have their place within the tent-'tabernacle'. The table is imagined quite simply as a level surface with four legs (cf. v. 26b*b*); the height of it then refers to the height of the legs. The frame (v. 25) is to be imagined as put up around the edges of the table top. Once again (cf. 11b) the table top and the frame are given a moulding all round as decoration. The table is made portable by an arrangement of poles which is again described in quite considerable detail (vv. 26–28). As the 'rings' for the poles are to lie 'close' to the frame, the 'corners' of the legs (v. 26b*b*) must mean their upper ends. The table is chiefly for the 'bread of the Presence' (v. 30), i.e. for the cakes of bread which are to be set down—and renewed daily—as gifts before the 'Presence' of Yahweh (the traditional rendering of the AV, 'Shrewbread', is not quite accurate). This custom of setting bread before the 'Presence' of the deity, maintained in the Old Testament simply as a tradition, originally represents the feeding of the deity. It was known at old Israelite sanctuaries (cf. I Sam. 21.5) and the temple of Solomon had a golden table for the 'bread of the Presence' (I Kings 7.48, perhaps also 6.20). The representation on the arch of Titus* shows that such a table was still among the contents of the temple of Herod. It is remarkable that according to v. 29 all sorts of golden vessels also belonged to this table, for libations (drink-offerings) which, as is expressly enjoined, are not merely to be placed there but are to be 'poured', obviously on the ground by the table before the 'Presence' of Yahweh. Thus the table serves for all the non-animal offerings to be brought to Yahweh in his sanctuary.

(d) INSTRUCTIONS FOR MAKING THE LAMPSTAND: 25.31–40

31 ' And you shall make a lampstand of pure gold. The base and the shaft of the lampstand shall be made of hammered work; its cups, its capitals, and its flowers shall be of one piece with it; [32] and there shall be six branches going out of its sides, three branches of the lampstand out of one side of it and three branches of the lampstand out of the other side of it; [33] three cups made like almonds, each with capital and flower, on one branch, and three cups made like almonds, each with capital and flower, on the other branch—so for the six branches going out of the lampstand; [34] and on the lampstand itself four cups made like almonds, with their capitals and flowers, [35] and a capital of one piece with it under each pair of the six branches going out from the lampstand. [36] Their capitals and their branches shall be of one piece with it, the whole of it one piece of hammered work of pure gold. [37] And you shall make the seven lamps for it; and the lamps shall be set up so as to give light upon the space in front of it. [38] Its snuffers and their

---

*Cf. H. Gressmann, *Altorientalische Bilder zum Alten Testament*,[2] 1927, plate 205, fig. 509; L. H. Grollenberg, *Atlas of the Bible*, 1956, p. 138, fig. 407.

trays shall be of pure gold. [39] Of a talent of pure gold shall it be made, with all these utensils. [40] And see that you make them after the pattern for them, which is being shown you on the mountain.

The description of the ingenious seven-branched candlestick is extraordinarily complicated, first because the author obviously lacks the means of expression to put everything clearly (the marked paucity of the verbal element in the description is particularly noticeable and results in a style which is nothing but the catchwords strung together) and secondly because numerous words occur in a derived meaning as technical terms, so that their exact meaning cannot be determined. Despite a fulness of detail which is in part circumstantial (cf. especially v. 35), the description is still not complete enough to give us a really clear picture of the lampstand. Now it is in fact clear that the lampstand described here was a predecessor of the lampstand in the temple of Herod which is portrayed on the Arch of Titus (cf. previous note). Therefore despite a number of different characteristics which were evidently peculiar to the Herodian lampstand, this portrayal can help to elucidate the description given here.

The lampstand of Ex. 25 evidently represents an innovation which was presumably introduced into the temple of Zerubbabel. The temple of Solomon had ten lampstands, each presumably with one lamp (I Kings 7.49; it cannot be established with any certainty whether the lampstand with seven lamps set on the rim of a bowl, described briefly in the setting of the account of a vision in Zech. 4.2, is described along the lines of a lampstand set up in the later preexilic temple or whether it is to be understood as a free representation of a lampstand burning with seven lamps). It goes without saying that the interior of the Jerusalem temple needed one or more lampstands just to provide light.

The section 25.31–40 can be regarded as essentially a literary unity, even though the word for 'lampstand' is used differently, first to describe the whole apparatus (so v. 31) and secondly in a simplified way to describe the central piece (so vv. 33b, 34 f.). These different usages do not cause any confusion. It is surprising to find in vv. 37, 39 verbs in the third person whose subject must be the craftsman who makes the lampstand, and it is noticeable that in v. 40 the reference to the pattern shown to Moses deviates from the setting in which it is put elsewhere (v. 40 has moreover a formal connection with v. 39).

As it is hardly permissible to smooth out the language and make it more simple by emending the text, vv. 37b–40 (including v. 38, which stands in isolation) should be regarded as a secondary addition.

The lampstand, to be made out of beaten gold, has first of all a central shaft whose ornamentation is not to be attached but is to be built up out of it (v. 31). What is meant by 'base' is questionable; ought this word perhaps to be read as a plural (this is possible without changing the consonants) and is the 'base' meant to be a form of three- or four-legged stand, which is needed but not mentioned elsewhere? The ornamentation of the shaft (cf. vv. 34 f.) is to consist of hammered (calyx) cups. The term 'cup' is from time to time explained by 'capital and flower' (vv. 31, 33 f.). Now the peculiarity of the lampstand consists in the fact that three arms ('branches') are to go out from the shaft on each of the two sides (v. 32), running obliquely upwards and arranged one above the other, as is shown by the representation of the Herodian lampstand (as no other remarks are made, the description in Ex. 25 suggests straight arms, so that the curving of the arms is perhaps to be regarded as a characteristic peculiar to the Herodian lampstand). The 'branches' are further so arranged that their upper ends form a straight line with the top of the central shaft. Hammered 'cups' serve to decorate both the branches and the shaft and usually consist of a 'capital', i.e. a swelling with a 'flower' which is evidently placed upon it (v. 33–35). These cups are described with a technical term which is usually rendered 'made like almonds', but this translation is extremely dubious. The cups are to be arranged along the arms, one above the other at intervals. In any case this is so on the shaft (v. 35); here the cups are placed each under the branching of a pair of arms. In these cases sometimes only the 'capital' is mentioned, so that it must be assumed that the branching pair of arms takes the place of the 'flowers' or that the flowers are attached directly above the branching of the pairs of arms. The fourth cup on the shaft (cf. v. 34) is to be imagined below, or better above, the branching pairs of arms. Verse 36a is not fully comprehensible as there is no reference which is suitable for the plural possessive pronoun 'their'; if we are not to give up all hope of an explanation, we cannot reach any solution without assuming some distortion of the text. The 'simplest' solution would be to assume that the text originally ran 'its (viz. of the lampstand, i.e. of the shaft) capitals and its branches.' It is impossible to determine whether the seven lamps (v. 37a), i.e. the usual containers, pinched in at the side to make a place for the wick,* are to consist of gold, or whether, as this is not expressly mentioned, ordinary clay lamps are intended. In any case, these seven lamp-containers belong at the upper end of the shaft and of the six arms. The addition (see above) vv. 37b–40 speaks of the 'space in front' of the lampstand upon which the lamps are to shed light; this means that the lamp containers with their openings for wicks are all to be arranged broadside so that they are towards the 'space in front'. Snuffers and trays (v. 38), the latter for preparing the oil, form the necessary accessories for the lampstand. According to v. 39 a talent of gold is to be used for the lampstand; the customary talent (distinctions were made between different scales of value; cf. II Sam. 14.26) probably weighed something over seventy-five pounds. It looks as though the addition vv. 37b–40 had forced out the original conclusion to the section.

(e) INSTRUCTIONS FOR MAKING THE 'TABERNACLE': 26.1–37

26[1] 'Moreover you shall make the tabernacle with ten curtains of fine twined linen and blue and purple and scarlet stuff; with cherubim skilfully worked shall you make them. [2] The length of each curtain shall be twenty-eight cubits, and the breadth of each curtain four cubits; all the curtains shall have one measure. [3] Five curtains shall be coupled to one another; and the other five curtains shall be coupled to one another. [4] And you shall make loops of blue on the edge of the outmost curtain in the first set; and likewise you shall make loops on the edge of the outmost curtain in the second set. [5] Fifty loops you shall make on the one curtain, and fifty loops you shall make on the edge of the curtain that is in the second set; the loops shall be opposite one another. [6] And you shall make fifty clasps of gold, and couple the curtains one to the other with the clasps, that the tabernacle may be one whole.

[7] 'You shall also make curtains of goats' hair for a tent over the tabernacle; eleven curtains shall you make. [8] The length of each curtain shall be thirty cubits, and the breadth of each curtain four cubits; the eleven curtains shall have the same measure. [9] And you shall couple five curtains by themselves, and six curtains by themselves, and the sixth curtain you shall double over at the front of the tent. [10] And you shall make fifty loops on the edge of the curtain that is outmost in one set, and fifty loops on the edge of the curtain which is outmost in the second set.

[11] 'And you shall make fifty clasps of bronze, and put the clasps into

---

*Cf. K. Galling, *Biblisches Reallexikon*, 1937, cols. 347 f., figs. 1–4; E. W. Heaton, *Everyday Life in Old Testament Times*, 1956, p. 73, fig. 23.

the loops, and couple the tent together that it may be one whole.
[12] And the part that remains of the curtains of the tent, the half curtain that remains, shall hang over the back of the tabernacle. [13] And the cubit on the one side, and the cubit on the other side, of what remains in the length of the curtains of the tent shall hang over the sides of the tabernacle, on this side and that side, to cover it. [14] And you shall make for the tent a covering of tanned rams' skins and goatskins.

15 'And you shall make upright frames for the tabernacle of acacia wood. [16] Ten cubits shall be the length of a frame, and a cubit and a half the breadth of each frame. [17] There shall be two tenons in each frame, for fitting together; so shall you do for all the frames of the tabernacle. [18] You shall make the frames for the tabernacle: twenty frames for the south side; [19] and forty bases of silver you shall make under the twenty frames, two bases under one frame for its two tenons, and two bases under another frame for its two tenons; [20] and for the second side of the tabernacle, on the north side twenty frames, [21] and their forty bases of silver, two bases under one frame, and two bases under another frame; [22] and for the rear of the tabernacle westward you shall make six frames. [23] And you shall make two frames for corners of the tabernacle in the rear; [24] they shall be separate beneath, but joined at the top, at the first ring; thus shall it be with both of them; they shall form the two corners. [25] And there shall be eight frames, with their bases of silver, sixteen bases; two bases under one frame, and two bases under another frame.

26 'And you shall make bars of acacia wood, [27] five for the frames of the one side of the tabernacle, and five bars for the frames of the other side of the tabernacle, and five bars for the frames of the side of the tabernacle at the rear westward. [28] The middle bar, halfway up the frames, shall pass through from end to end. [29] You shall overlay the frames with gold, and shall make their rings of gold for holders for the bars; and you shall overlay the bars with gold. [30] And you shall erect the tabernacle according to the plan for it which has been shown you on the mountain.

31 'And you shall make a veil of blue and purple and scarlet stuff and fine twined linen; in skilled work shall it be made, with cherubim; [32] and you shall hang it upon four pillars of acacia overlaid with gold, with hooks of gold, upon four bases of silver. [33] And you shall hang the veil from the clasps, and bring the ark of the testimony in thither within the veil; and the veil shall separate for you the holy place from the most holy. [34] You shall put the mercy seat upon the ark of the testimony in the most holy place. [35] And you shall set the table outside the veil, and the lampstand on the south side of the tabernacle opposite the table; and you shall put the table on the north side.

36 'And you shall make a screen for the door of the tent, of blue and purple and scarlet stuff and fine twined linen, embroidered with needle-work. [37] And you shall make for the screen five pillars of acacia, and overlay them with gold; their hooks shall be of gold, and you shall cast five bases of bronze for them.'

The 'tabernacle' is constructed to house the shrine of the ark and to provide for cultic worship before it. Yahweh is thought of as the one who 'tabernacles', in the same way as the Jerusalem temple was built by Solomon as a place where 'Yahweh had said that he would dwell in thick darkness' (I Kings 8.12), a place where, according to a frequent Deuteronomic-deuteronomistic phrase, Yahweh wished 'to make his name dwell there' (Deut. 12.11 f. etc.). According to P this 'tabernacle' is a remarkable composite building consisting on the one hand of a tent and on the other of a solid building which is however to be made of wooden frames in such a way that it remains portable. There is no analogy to this astonishing construction anywhere in cultic history. We have a design by P which fuses together two disparate elements, first a tent sanctuary such as has always existed and still exists among nomadic tribes and peoples, and which was commensurate with the situation of the Israelites at Sinai as it also knows the Old Testament tradition, certainly already ancient, of the 'Tent (of meeting)' (Ex. 33.7 ff.; Num. 11.16, 24, 26; 12.4, 10), and secondly the pattern of the Jerusalem temple, which must here be transformed into a wooden structure capable of being dismantled. Attempts have been made to make a literary distinction between these two contradictory elements, and to argue that an original literary stratum knew only of a real tent sanctuary, while the wooden construction and the complicated nature of the whole were only introduced in a secondary literary stratum. But the transmitted wording offers no plausible scope for such a literary distinction and, if this distinction is to be carried right through, substantial omissions from the original material of the older stratum must be posited. These conditions argue against the hypothesis of two literary strata, and for this reason difficulties in the content of the description of the 'tabernacle' are to be explained not as literary, but as inherent in the history of the tradition as it has been described.

[15–30] The woodwork, which forms the basis of the whole construction (vv. 15–30), consists of long individual frames which are set up vertically next to each other. Two tenons let into the lower narrow side of each of the frames serve to fit them together (we cannot properly understand the remark about the 'fitting together' of these two tenons in v. 17ab, as the technical term rendered 'fit together' occurs only in this context and so really remains obscure). The tenons are to be set each in a 'base of silver', which is not very accurately described, so that the frames can stand upright. When the frames are placed alongside each other a larger wall of frames is constructed; this surrounds a rectangle open on one side (the east). The narrow western side is joined to the two longer sides by two corner frames (vv. 23 f.) whose measurements are not given. We have no exact idea of what they looked like, as the special meaning of the technical term 'twins' (v. 24)* is not known and the significance of the 'one' ring in this context is not explained. These corner frames, which are to be imagined 'in the rear' of the narrow side (v. 23), are evidently meant to serve to clamp this narrow side to the two longer sides. Bars (the word used elsewhere for 'bolt' occurs, just as the 'bolt' of a gate or a door is in fact a bar) are made to join the frames firmly together on the three sides when they have been put next to each other; they are to be put through rings which are attached to the frames—presumably on the outside (v. 29). The transmitted wording in vv. 26–29 can only be understood to mean that bars are imagined arranged parallel, one above another; each of these reaches the whole length of one side though in that case bars of an extra-ordinary length must be planned for the two long sides. It is not very obvious why in v. 28 particular emphasis is laid on the 'middle bar', which is to be attached to the centre of the upright frame. According to the numbers and measurements given, the space enclosed by the wall of frames is 30 cubits long and 10 cubits high; the breadth should also be 10 cubits (the frames on the narrow side measure 9 cubits, but we must add to this the corner frames which also belong to the narrow side—their measurements are left undefined). These represent about half the measurements of the temple of Solomon (cf. I Kings 6.2,20), the only difference being that for simplification the difference in height between the 'house' and the 'inner sanctuary' is omitted and the 'forecourt' of the temple is left out. Thus we are to suppose that the installation of the veil, which in vv. 31 f. is not given a concrete description, divides off a 'Holy of Holies' measuring 10 × 10 × 10 cubits.

[1–14] This wall of frames, which can be dismantled and is there-fore portable, is given a large awning which is put together from individual tent curtains. It forms the only roof covering and at the

* [Noth here gives a translation so different from the RSV that the whole verse must be reproduced here to make his comments intelligible; v. 24 reads 'and there shall be "twins" (*Zwillinge*) beneath and in like manner there shall be "twins" (a slight emendation is made here following Kittel's *Biblia Hebraica*) at the top for the one ring; thus shall it be. . . .' For further details of the Hebrew text and its relationship to these two renderings the reader is referred to Kittel. Tr.]

same time clothes the two long sides and the rear end (vv. 1–6). Here we have a tent curtain made from very costly material and embroidered with cherubim who are not given any further description (v. 1); this main curtain consists of two composite pieces, each made up of five long tent curtains sewn together (v. 3). These are coupled together by costly 'clasps' with the help of loops attached to the inner edges, but can be taken apart to make transport easier (vv. 4–6). According to the numbers and measurements given in v. 2, this whole tent curtain is 40 cubits long and 28 cubits wide. No detailed description is given of how the tent curtain is to be fitted over the woodwork. We must understand the measurement of 28 cubits to signify that when the costly fabric is spread over the woodwork on the two long sides it ends one cubit above the ground and does not touch it. We must then, however, ask whether the tent curtain which overhangs the rear side is meant to touch the ground there (as the measurement of 40 cubits would suggest) or whether one cubit is not to be left spare here also and the then supernumerary cubits are to hang over on the front side. Perhaps P was not concerned, or had not thought, that at the two corners of the rear side the fabric would necessarily have to fall down on the ground. In the same way, it is remarkable that the costly tent curtain, with its embroidered cherubim, who are evidently modelled on the carved cherubim on the panelling of the inner rooms of the temple of Solomon (I Kings 6.29, 32, 35), could only be seen on the ceiling of the inner room, as it was covered on the outside by the over-curtain which is to be mentioned immediately. The single over-curtain (vv. 7 ff.) is made of goats' hair, the usual material for tent curtains. Like the costly tent curtain it is to consist of two pieces made of long tent curtains sewn together and to be coupled to each other; the only difference is that in this case the material is less valuable in every respect. It serves to protect the precious first curtain and is therefore also somewhat larger in its measurements. Its width, 30 cubits, shows that on the two long sides this over-curtain is to exceed the first, precious curtain by about a cubit and thus is to fall right down to the ground. This may also be the intention at the rear side. Now the length measures the width of eleven tent curtains, i.e. 4 cubits more than in the case of the first curtain. The chief thought thus appears to be that the over-curtain should exceed the other curtain by about a cubit on each side. But if it is made in this way on the three other sides, there remains a surplus of 3 cubits on the front side. Therefore according to v. 9b the sixth tent curtain on the front side is to be 'doubled over', so that its breadth only measures 2 cubits. Great care has been taken so that the uniformity of the tent sections is preserved and it is not necessary to have a tent-curtain of half-width. Now in vv. 12 f. another arrangement seems to have been provided for, so that the surplus of a half tent curtain will 'hang over the back', i.e. in fact lie on the ground so that the 'doubling over' of one tent curtain (on the front side) becomes unnecessary. We must therefore regard vv. 12 f. as an addition which intends the goats' hair tent curtains to be arranged in a rather different way from that in v. 9b. In v. 14 two further covers are enjoined; their measurements are not given, but they are nevertheless to be spread over the whole. First there is a large, solid cover made of rams' skins, which is to be dyed red for decoration in some unspecified way, and finally a last over-covering of precious $t^{e}h\bar{a}\check{s}im$ skins.*

[31–37] In conclusion another feature of the 'tabernacle' is the veil, which is to be attached by golden nails† to four acacia pillars which are set upright on stands (vv. 31–33a); it represents the dividing wall between the 'house' and the 'inner sanctuary' in the temple of Solomon. A further veil, described as a 'screen', shuts off the front side (vv. 36 f.). It is to be made out of the same costly material as the inner veil and to be hung on five wooden pillars, but, as it is only to protect the entrance, it does not need any embroidered cherubim (cf. in contrast v. 31b), and bronze is sufficient for the stands of the pillars. The position of the ark in the 'most holy place' (v. 33abb) corresponds to that in the temple of Solomon (I Kings 8.6), but that of the table and the lampstand (v. 35) does not, as P knows only one seven-branched lampstand instead of the ten lampstands of the temple of Solomon (I Kings 7.49) and now places the table and lampstand to one side of the 'house', whereas in the temple of Solomon the table stood right in the middle.

(f) INSTRUCTIONS FOR MAKING THE ALTAR AND THE COURT: 27.1–21

27[1] 'You shall make the altar of acacia wood, five cubits long and five cubits broad; the altar shall be square, and its height shall be three cubits. [2] And you shall make horns for it on its four corners; its horns shall be of one piece with it, and you shall overlay it with bronze. [3] You

---

*[For these two last items see above pp. 201 f.; the RSV rendering 'tanned' of the rams' skins is misleading. Tr.]

†[The RSV rendering differs slightly here. Tr.]

shall make pots for it to receive its ashes, and shovels and basins and forks and fire pans; all its utensils you shall make of bronze. ⁴ You shall also make for it a grating, a network of bronze; and upon the net you shall make four bronze rings at its four corners. ⁵ And you shall set it under the ledge of the altar so that the net shall extend half way down the altar. ⁶ And you shall make poles for the altar, poles of acacia wood, and overlay them with bronze; ⁷ and the poles shall be put through the rings, so that the poles shall be upon the two sides of the altar, when it is carried. ⁸ You shall make it hollow, with boards; as it has been shown you on the mountain, so shall it be made.

9 'You shall make the court of the tabernacle. On the south side the court shall have hangings of fine twined linen a hundred cubits long for one side; ¹⁰ their pillars shall be twenty and their bases twenty, of bronze, but the hooks of the pillars and their fillets shall be of silver. ¹¹ And likewise for its length on the north side there shall be hangings a hundred cubits long, their pillars twenty and their bases twenty, of bronze, but the hooks of the pillars and their fillets shall be of silver. ¹² And for the breadth of the court on the west side there shall be hangings for fifty cubits, with ten pillars and ten bases. ¹³ The breadth of the court on the front to the east shall be fifty cubits. ¹⁴ The hangings for the one side of the gate shall be fifteen cubits, with three pillars and three bases. ¹⁵ On the other side the hangings shall be fifteen cubits, with three pillars and three bases. ¹⁶ For the gate of the court there shall be a screen twenty cubits long, of blue and purple and scarlet stuff and fine twined linen, embroidered with needlework; it shall have four pillars and with them four bases. ¹⁷ All the pillars around the court shall be filleted with silver; their hooks shall be of silver, and their bases of bronze. ¹⁸ The length of the court shall be a hundred cubits, the breadth fifty, and the height five cubits, with hangings of fine twined linen and bases of bronze. ¹⁹ All the utensils of the tabernacle for every use, and all its pegs and all the pegs of the court, shall be of bronze.

20 'And you shall command the people of Israel that they bring to you pure beaten olive oil for the light, that a lamp may be set up to burn continually. ²¹ In the tent of meeting, outside the veil which is before the testimony, Aaron and his sons shall tend it from evening to morning before the LORD. It shall be a statute for ever to be observed throughout their generations by the people of Israel.'

[1–8] The altar—the lack of any closer definition shows that here only a single altar is intended (the 'table' of 25.23–30 is not regarded as an altar)—goes along with the court because it has its place in the court of the sanctuary, a fact of which nothing is said in the present context, for the pattern is the altar of burnt offering in the temple of Solomon. This latter altar was made of stone; here, because the altar must be portable, it is made of a wooden framework encased in sheet bronze. No question is asked as to whether such a construction could

withstand the heat when animal sacrifices were being burnt. The wooden framework is clearly visualized as an open chest. The measurements given (v. 1) are remarkably small (cf. in contrast Ezek. 43.13 ff.). According to v. 2 it is to be an altar with 'horns'.*
We can easily understand that in the case of a stone altar the 'horns' situated at the four upper corners should be of one piece with the altar, but it is hard to visualize this with a wooden structure encased in sheet bronze. The note about the utensils necessary for the functioning of the altar (v. 3) interrupts the description of the altar and may be an addition. The arrangements for making the altar portable (vv. 4–7) appear to have been devised so that a 'ledge', to be understood as a kind of ridge, is made half way down the altar which rests on the bronze grating which goes round the lower half of the four sides; to this again the rings for the carrying poles are attached at an unspecified height. Verse 8 once again goes back to the body of the altar proper, which is described as being 'hollow, with boards', as was already to be inferred from the previous description; this verse, with its reference to the pattern shown to Moses (cf. on 25.40) may be an addition.

[9–19] The court (vv. 9–19) is to be a large rectangle measuring 100 by 50 cubits, and the 'tabernacle' is clearly to have its place in the rear half (though nothing is said about this). The stone enclosing wall of the holy precinct of the Jerusalem temple appears in the wilderness sanctuary in the form of a system of hangings which are suspended on pillars. It is noteworthy that P knows only one court (unlike Ezek. 40.5 ff. and the later temple of Herod). For 'hanging' in this context a word is used whose basic meaning is probably 'sail' (another word is used for the 'curtain' in 26.31 ff.). These linen hangings are evidently meant on occasion to hang between two pillars, so that their size is given by the distance between the pillars (every 5 cubits) and the indication of their height (5 cubits; v. 18) while the number of pillars and the total length and breadth measurements reveals how many of these hangings there were (vv. 9, 11 f., 18). The number of the pillars is the same as that of the hangings and in this it is not supposed that one pillar is lacking (at one of the corners). An opening is left in the middle of the front side, to the east (in v. 16 it is described as a 'gate', a term really only applicable to stone buildings) as an entrance 20 cubits wide. This is closed with a 'screen' (the same word as in 26.36 f.) of costly material

*Cf. K. Galling, *Biblisches Reallexicon*, cols. 17 ff.

which is likewise hung on pillars. The two side pieces of the system of hangings to the right and left of the opening on the front side are described in vv. 14 f. as 'shoulders' (RSV 'side'). Four pillars are provided for the opening of the entrance, again one pillar too few, as the distance between pillars should surely measure 5 cubits here also (or, if the corner pillars of the two 'shoulders' at the sides are also to serve for the entrance 'screen', one pillar too many). Insufficient description is given about the way in which the hangings are suspended. In any case the hooks on the pillars are meant for them, but it remains uncertain what is meant by the 'fillets' (vv. 10 f.) and the 'filleting' of the pillars (v. 17) (if this is in fact the right translation); does the term refer to the cross-poles between the pillars to which the hangings are to be attached, or to some arrangement on the pillars themselves, as is suggested by the appearance of this technical term alongside the hooks in the description of the individual pillars (vv. 10 f.)? Despite extensive repetitions the description is on the whole poorly and feebly expressed, and is therefore not really sufficient for an accurate reconstruction of the arrangement described. There are further a number of additions at the end of the section. The last words of v. 18 are an inadvertent repetition of the last words of v. 17, and v. 19 represents an addition which is apparently not a self-contained entity. In content it does not correspond with what has gone before and in secondary fashion speaks of 'pegs', which were not mentioned earlier—rightly so, as we are not to regard the 'tabernacle', much less the 'court', as a proper tent which needs to be pegged down. **[20–21]** The passage about the oil, vv. 20 f., and the lamp on the 'light' (the word 'lampstand' of 25.31–40 is not used) which is to be filled with it, is clearly also an addition. According to v. 21 the lamp is evidently only to burn at night.

(g) INSTRUCTIONS FOR MAKING THE PRIESTLY GARMENTS: 28.1–43

28[1] 'Then bring near to you Aaron your brother, and his sons with him, from among the people of Israel, to serve me as priests—Aaron and Aaron's sons, Nadab and Abihu, Eleazar and Ithamar. [2] And you shall make holy garments for Aaron your brother, for glory and for beauty. [3] And you shall speak to all who have ability, whom I have endowed with an able mind, that they make Aaron's garments to consecrate him for my priesthood. [4] These are the garments which they shall make: a breastpiece, an ephod, a robe, a coat of chequer work, a turban, and a girdle; they shall make holy garments for Aaron your brother and his sons to serve me as priests.

5 'They shall receive gold, blue and purple and scarlet stuff, and fine twined linen. ⁶ And they shall make the ephod of gold, of blue and purple and scarlet stuff, and of fine twined linen, skilfully worked. ⁷ It shall have two shoulder-pieces attached to its two edges, that it may be joined together. ⁸ And the skilfully woven band upon it, to gird it on, shall be of the same workmanship and materials, of gold, blue and purple and a scarlet stuff, and fine twined linen. ⁹ And you shall take two onyx stones, and engrave on them the names of the sons of Israel, ¹⁰ six of their names on the one stone, and the names of the remaining six on the other stone, in the order of their birth. ¹¹ As a jeweller engraves signets, so shall you engrave the two stones with the names of the sons of Israel; you shall enclose them in settings of gold filigree. ¹² And you shall set the two stones upon the shoulder-pieces of the ephod, as stones of remembrance for the sons of Israel; and Aaron shall bear their names before the LORD upon his two shoulders for remembrance. ¹³ And you shall make settings of gold filigree, ¹⁴ and two chains of pure gold, twisted like cords; and you shall attach the corded chains to the settings.

15 'And you shall make a breastpiece of judgment, in skilled work; like the work of the ephod you shall make it; of gold, blue and purple and scarlet stuff, and fine twined linen shall you make it. ¹⁶ It shall be square and double, a span its length and a span its breadth. ¹⁷ And you shall set in it four rows of stones. A row of sardius, topaz, and carbuncle shall be the first row; ¹⁸ and the second row an emerald, a sapphire, and a diamond; ¹⁹ and the third row a jacinth, an agate, and an amethyst; ²⁰ and the fourth row a beryl, an onyx, and a jasper; they shall be set in gold filigree. ²¹ There shall be twelve stones with their names according to the names of the sons of Israel; they shall be like signets, each engraved with its name, for the twelve tribes. ²² And you shall make for the breastpiece twisted chains like cords, of pure gold; ²³ and you shall make for the breastpiece two rings of gold, and put the two rings on the two edges of the breastpiece. ²⁴ And you shall put the two cords of gold in the two rings at the edges of the breastpiece; ²⁵ the two ends of the two cords you shall attach to the two settings of filigree, and so attach it in front to the shoulder-pieces of the ephod. ²⁶ And you shall make two rings of gold, and put them at the two ends of the breastpiece, on its inside edge next to the ephod. ²⁷ And you shall make two rings of gold, and attach them in front to the lower part of the two shoulder-pieces of the ephod, at its joining above the skilfully woven band of the ephod. ²⁸ And they shall bind the breastpiece by its rings to the rings of the ephod with a lace of blue, that it may lie upon the skilfully woven band of the ephod, and that the breastpiece shall not come loose from the ephod. ²⁹ So Aaron shall bear the names of the sons of Israel in the breastpiece of judgment upon his heart, when he goes into the holy place, to bring them to continual remembrance before the LORD. ³⁰ And in the breastpiece of judgment you shall put the Urim and the Thummim, and they shall be upon Aaron's heart, when he goes in

before the LORD; thus Aaron shall bear the judgment of the people of Israel upon his heart before the LORD continually.

31 'And you shall make the robe of the ephod all of blue. 32 It shall have in it an opening for the head, with a woven binding around the opening, like the opening in a garment, that it may not be torn. 33 On its skirts you shall make pomegranates of blue and purple and scarlet stuff, around its skirts, with bells of gold between them, 34 a golden bell and a pomegranate, a golden bell and a pomegranate, round about on the skirts of the robe. 35 And it shall be upon Aaron when be ministers, and its sound shall be heard when he goes into the holy place before the LORD, and when he comes out, lest he die.

36 'And you shall make a plate of pure gold, and engrave on it, like the engraving of a signet, "Holy to the LORD." 37 And you shall fasten it on the turban by a lace of blue; it shall be on the front of the turban. 38 It shall be upon Aaron's forehead, and Aaron shall take upon himself any guilt incurred in the holy offering which the people of Israel hallow as their holy gifts; it shall always be upon his forehead, that they may be accepted before the LORD.

39 'And you shall weave the coat in chequer work of fine linen, and you shall make a turban of fine linen, and you shall make a girdle embroidered with needlework.

40 'And for Aaron's sons you shall make coats and girdles and caps; you shall make them for glory and beauty. 41 And you shall put them upon Aaron your brother, and upon his sons with him, and shall anoint them and ordain them and consecrate them, that they may serve me as priests. 42 And you shall make for them linen breeches to cover their naked flesh; from the loins to the thighs they shall reach; 43 and they shall be upon Aaron, and upon his sons, when they go into the tent of meeting, or when they come near the altar to minister in the holy place; lest they bring guilt upon themselves and die. This shall be a perpetual statute for him and for his descendants after him.'

It is hard to understand the individual details in the description of the ceremonial dress of the High Priest—for the section is chiefly concerned with him, the ceremonial dress of the other priests being dealt with quite briefly in v. 40—not only because of the constant recurrence of technical terms whose meaning is uncertain or obscure (from time to time the translation is bound to posit a particular explanation which frequently represents only one possible interpretation), but also because the general appearance of the main items of this dress are presumed to be known and are therefore inadequately described. Instead, the description loses itself in explanations of all sorts of less important details for whose exact understanding a knowledge of the main items is a prerequisite. The essentials are however moderately clear.

The large number of articles of clothing and decoration which make up the dress of the High Priest is remarkable, most of all because these pieces do not fit together into a convincing overall picture, but to some extent stand in the way of each other. This difficulty can hardly be obviated on literary-critical grounds by positing several different literary strata, each with a different presentation of the High Priest's dress. True, the chapter is not a complete literary unity. [1–5] The introductory passage (vv. 1–5) has apparently been given secondary expansions and originally—corresponding with the preceding sections—gave brief instructions for making the priestly garments (v. 2); the two closing verses (vv. 42 f.) clearly represent an addition, as their position after the closing sentence v. 41 indicates. But otherwise there is no reason for a literary-critical division of the chapter into various literary strands. The abundance of the individual pieces belonging to the dress of the High Priest should instead be given a historical explanation; i.e. in this dress pieces from different times and from different backgrounds have become amalgamated, as can still be demonstrated in part from individual items. The question then arises whether a High Priest was ever dressed in the way here described, or whether the description merely represents an 'ideal' pattern in which all possible elements of priestly and (see below) kingly adornment have been combined. Probability speaks for the former alternative, because no clear reason can be found why in this case P should have created a fantasy, with the possible exception of several individual details; in any case it is to be assumed that after the reception of P the priestly dress was in some points along the lines of P. So in fact the post-exilic High Priest bore in his ceremonial dress the signs of a long history of priesthood.

[6–14] The 'ephod', which is first given a name and then described with some detail, was a loincloth worn with the aid of a girdle encircling the body above. It is to be skilfully worked from the most precious material like the other parts of the High Priest's ornaments. Of course this luxury is not in the nature of the object, for it is to be regarded as an archaic item of clothing. Old and supposedly original elements are often preserved for a very long time in the cultic sphere. There is evidence from the ancient East for the cultic nakedness of the priest in very early times, but even at this period the custom was for men to clothe themselves. The loin-cloth of the priest certainly derives from a time when men were usually clothed in just this way and it kept its place in the priest's dress even after a more complete set of clothing had in other respects become the norm. Thus it is to be assumed that the ephod had once been the only item of the ceremonial priestly dress, whereas later, as in the case of the post-exilic High Priest, it appears merely as a traditional part of the general ceremonial dress. The older position is still fairly clear in those passages in which the priests are described as 'bearing the ephod' (I Sam. 2.28; 14.3; 22.18). The 'shoulder-pieces' of the ephod may be understood as band-like straps running over the shoulders whose under ends came together ('were joined together') at the front and at the back, to which the ephod was fastened by its front and rear upper 'edge' (perhaps the extremely obscure second clause in v. 7 is to be understood in this sense). A picture of dancing men from the Egyptian Old Kingdom shows loin-cloths with straps of this kind.* The two signet stones set in gold, engraved with the names of the twelve tribes of Israel, which are to be attached to the two 'shoulder-pieces' and which are described in very great detail, were evidently of extreme importance for P. We may here ask whether they are a traditional article of the priestly adornment or just an 'idea' of P's. True, signets of precious stones set in gold and inscribed with engraved names were certainly known throughout the Israelite monarchy, while in the cult of the 'amphictyony' the priest had to act 'in the name' of the twelve tribes of Israel and so in a way—in a metaphorical sense—to use the signet of the tribes. But to carry the twelve names inscribed on an official dress seems a very artificial objectifying of a situation, old though it may be. The attachment of the signet stones to the shoulder-pieces has an equally artificial look; not once is an accurate indication given of where they are to be placed (up on the shoulders or more preferably on the front sides); for to be attached in this way contradicts the usual purpose of a signet and its availability for use. According to v. 12 the High Priest is to bear all Israel 'in remembrance' with these signets so that Yahweh 'will remember Israel for good' (Neh. 5.19; 13.31) whenever the High Priest comes before him in his ceremonial dress. The arrangement for hanging the 'breast-piece' which is not described until the next section, is given as early as vv. 13 f., as it still belongs to the shoulder-pieces of the ephod; the arrangement consists of (two) gold rings in the form of signet settings, on which gold chains hang. Reference is then made to this arrangement in v. 26.

*J. B. Pritchard, *The Ancient Near East in Pictures Relating to the Old Testament*, 1954, p. 66, fig. 210.

[**15–16, 30**] The literal meaning of the word *ḥōšen*, translated 'breastpiece', which occurs only in P, is obscure to us; the rendering here rests on the form of this article of equipment, which is still to some extent recognizable. A piece of fabric, once again made of the most costly material, which is to be 'double' and evidently sewn together along the sides, forms a 'bag' of about 9 × 9 inches (a 'span'), into which something can be put (v. 30). The contents are in fact to be the 'Urim and Thummim', lots with which an oracle could be produced in answer to a question put in the form of two alternatives (I Sam. 14.41 LXX). The words 'Urim and Thummim' (RV marg. 'lights and perfections') are unexplained, and the form of the lots which were 'cast' (I Sam. 14.42) is also unknown to us. But in any case the 'casting' of the Urim and Thummim was an old piece of priestly activity (Deut. 33.8 and also Ezra 2.63 = Neh. 7.65) and in this way a divine judgment could be obtained (so I Sam. 14). For this reason the 'bag' for these lots is described in Ex. 28.15, 19, 30 as a 'breastpiece of judgment'. It is of course quite obvious from v. 30 that P no longer envisages a practical use of this ancient oracle-by-lot. The Urim and Thummim are merely to rest on the breast ('upon the heart') of the High Priest as a symbol of the power of Yahweh, the righteous judge, over the Israelites. Thus for the post-exilic High Priest this bag with the lots was merely a traditional inheritance from the early history of the priesthood. We may perhaps assume that even in the early period the priest used to carry the lots in a purse on the breast, which hung from a cord placed round the neck.

[**17–21, 29**] This does not of course explain the adorning of the bag with twelve precious stones (vv. 17–21) which gives it the appearance of a costly breastplate and at the same time supposes that the bag lay smooth and flat upon the breast (the emphasis on its square shape in v. 16 is a further indication of this). If this is in fact to be the case the bag must be stiffened in some way, and this leads the bag at the same time to take over the function of a breastpiece. But a breastpiece of this kind in all probability derives not from the priestly but from the kingly tradition. A royal breastpiece, very reminiscent of the *ḥōšen* of Ex. 28, which despite its Egyptian style seems to rest on native tradition, has been found in the tomb of a king of Byblos of the Middle Bronze Age. It consists of an approximately rectangular gold plate set with precious stones and hangs from a gold chain which is directly reminiscent of the 'twisted chains' of v. 14; true, the precious stones make up an Egyptian pattern on the

plate, but they are also arranged in rows at the edges.* Ezek. 28.13 is
perhaps also to be understood in the light of this ancient Phoenician
royal pectoral; there it is said of the king of Tyre that his 'covering'
consisted of all kinds of precious stones, whereupon nine stones are
enumerated which all occur in Ex. 28.17–20 (though in a different
order). This number nine would fit the square shape better than the
number twelve, which is occasioned by the reference to the twelve
tribes of Israel. The *ḥōšen* thus represents a composite article—
perhaps first created in this way by P—in which the old priestly bag
for giving oracles-by-lot has been combined with the royal pectoral.
There is finally added the thought which we already know from
vv. 9–12, that the High Priest bears the signet with the names of the
tribes of Israel to 'bring them to continual remembrance before
Yahweh' (v. 29). So the name of a tribe of Israel is to stand on each
of the precious stones, now twelve in number (the interpretation of
the individual names of the stones given in vv. 17–20 is uncertain
throughout). Now in this the precious stones of the *ḥōšen* clash with
the two signet stones on the shoulder-pieces of the ephod and give
rise to the question which of the two arrangements is to be regarded
as primary and which secondary. True, individual details of the
ḥōšen go back to a very old tradition, but the whole object as described here cannot be claimed as old. The incorporation of royal
insignia into the ceremonial dress of the High Priest certainly presupposes the downfall of the monarchy in Israel and the transference
of once royal cultic functions to the chief priest of the once royal
sanctuary in Jerusalem in the setting of a reorganization of the cult
which only resulted after this downfall; only then did the opportunity
arise of reinterpreting the costly stones of the royal pectoral as stones
to bring the tribes of Israel 'to remembrance before Yahweh'. In any
case, we could imagine that P gave a similar new interpretation both
to the two stones on the shoulder-pieces, which were perhaps purely
ornamental and already extremely old, and to the costly stones on the
royal-priestly pectoral.

[22–28] The description in Ex. 28 takes a great deal of trouble
over the question of the suspension of the *ḥōšen*. The instructions in
vv. 22–28 are probably to be understood in the following way: gold
rings are to be attached to the two upper corners of the *ḥōšen*, from
which the twisted gold chains are to run to the 'settings' on the front
side of the shoulder-pieces of the ephod; these chains occur twice,

*See P. Montet, *Byblos et l'Egypte*, 1928–29, pp. 162 ff., plates 93 f.

both in v. 14 and in vv. 22, 24 f., because they can be counted with the
ephod as much as with the *ḥōšen*.* Two other gold rings are to be set
at the lower corners of the *ḥōšen*, at the back, just as the rings for
suspending the above-mentioned pectoral of the king of Byblos are
also attached on the back; a further two rings are to be put on the
shoulder-pieces of the ephod right underneath, close to the band of
the ephod. A cord is to be drawn through these last four rings so that
the *ḥōšen* is made fast both above and below and cannot slip; this last
is evidently very important to the author of the description.

[**31–35**] The robe (Hebrew *mᵉ'îl*) is represented as a long and
probably armless wrap made out of one piece, as is indicated by the
reference to an opening for the head 'in the middle'.† In contrast to
the ephod it is to be of one colour. It is noteworthy that in v. 31 it is
said to be 'of the ephod', although it represents a completely different kind of clothing. Elsewhere it was customarily worn by
prosperous and reputable people. We find it worn by kings, Saul in
I Sam. 24.5, 12, 'the princes of the sea' in Ezek. 26.16 (cf. also I Sam.
18.4, Jonathan, and I Chron. 15.27, David); it was not, however,
particularly a feature of royal dress, though on the other hand it was
hardly characteristic of the priest (cf. further Job 1.20; 2.12, Job and
his friends; Ezra 9.3, 5, Ezra). The High Priest has it because he is a
prominent man. The chief interest in Ex. 28—apart from the opening
for the head, the careful fashioning of which is specially enjoined—is
the border of 'pomegranates' and 'bells' at the lower edge of the
skirts. The former are perhaps to be understood merely as decoration
and to be imagined in embroidery along the edge. The golden bells
attached at intervals between these pomegranates are of apotropaic
significance (v. 35), as the terrifying effect produced on demons by
bells and gongs is an idea widespread in the history of religion. In
Ex. 28 this effect is still borne well in mind; the ringing of the bells
will protect the High Priest from the deadly powers of darkness,
especially when he enters and leaves the sanctuary, as thresholds and
doors are particularly threatened by such powers (cf. I Sam. 5.5).
The robe goes badly with the ephod and breastpiece, as we cannot

---

*One cannot help suspecting that vv. 13 f. form a secondary addition which
intends that two special 'settings' (which in fact have nothing to 'set') should be
attached to the shoulder-pieces, whereas originally v. 25 was meant to refer to the
'settings' of each of the two signet stones on the shoulder-pieces mentioned in
v. 11. These would thus at the same time fulfil the practical purpose of suspending
the *ḥōšen*.

†[The RSV 'in it' is an insufficiently detailed rendering of the Hebrew. Tr.]

imagine it being worn in any other way than over the ephod and breastpiece which means that these are then no longer visible. If need be, v. 35 might be understood to mean that the High Priest wore the robe only when entering and leaving the sanctuary, leaving it aside in the sanctuary itself; but this is not said clearly. Whereas the ephod and bag for the lots were traditional items, whose actual presence in the ceremonial dress of the High Priest is all that matters, the chief importance of the pectoral was that it should be seen, and this is prevented by the robe. The piling up of the different items of the High Priest's adornment inevitably leads to inconsistency of this nature.

[36–38] The 'flower'* of gold, which is to be attached to the front of the High Priest's turban by a lace of blue (purple wool), is also to serve an apotropaic purpose. Here the turban, which has not been mentioned previously and whose manufacture is quite briefly enjoined only in v. 39, is presupposed. The inscription 'Holy to Yahweh' to be engraved on this 'flower' is certainly to strengthen its apotropaic effect; the mention of the divine name serves to ward off hostile powers both from this piece of attire and from its wearer. The flower is of course already in itself a prophylactic, as it is an element of life and life-giving power. When hung at the front of the turban by the 'lace' mentioned above, it is in a clearly visible place 'upon the forehead' of the High Priest and thus protects him from the dangers associated with the cultic act, as is explained in the somewhat turgid language of v. 38. The sacrifice which the High Priest offers for the whole of Israel is—as is said with a cultic technical term— 'to be well pleasing before Yahweh'; to this end the 'flower' is to be worn. Should the sacrifice for any reason at all not be 'well-pleasing', perilous 'guilt' would result, which the High Priest would have to take upon himself; the flower is in this case to protect him from the consequences of this 'guilt'. Now of course in this special way of putting the significance of the 'flower' we have a secondary transference to the peculiar functions of the High Priest. For originally the 'flower' was a royal badge; the king wears a *nēzer* (II Sam. 1.10; II Kings 11.12; Ps. 89.39) on his head as a material sign of his kingly rank. This word is usually translated 'crown', but it means only 'consecrated', 'consecration' and is in fact a 'flower'. This is particularly clear in Ps. 132.18, where it is promised that the *nēzer* worn by

*[RSV 'plate' Tr.]

the Davidic king will 'blossom';* cf. also Ex. 29.6, where the word
nēzer stands in the place of *ṣîṣ* ('flower'), as also in Ex. 39.30, and
Lev. 8.9 where the two words are joined together. Just as the
Egyptian pharaohs used to wear on their foreheads the prophylactic
primitive serpent, the kings of Israel wore a 'flower' as 'consecration',
and eventually the royal insignia of the 'flower', like the pectoral
discussed above, passed over to the post-exilic High Priest and
acquired a special significance with reference to him.

[39] Three further items of the ceremonial dress of the High Priest
are mentioned with remarkable brevity in v. 39. First of all the linen
coat is mentioned in a formula differing from what has been usual;
the coat was a customary piece of clothing and was normally worn by
everyone. In the case of the High Priest, however, the question of its
relationship to the ephod arises. We are not told whether it is
supposed to be worn above or below the loin-cloth of the ephod (and
at the same time as the *ḥōšen*). The subsequent mention of the turban,
however, is hardly superfluous in this context, as its place in the
attire of the High Priest has already been presupposed in the description of the 'flower'. Unfortunately, its appearance is imagined
to be familiar and is therefore not described apart from the information that it is to be of 'fine linen'. This is all the more regrettable as
once again this turban is a most remarkable piece. It is evidently a
head-dress of a special kind and is described in Hebrew as *miṣnepet*.
Now apart from the description of the ceremonial dress of the High
Priest this word occurs only once more in the Old Testament, in
Ezek. 21.26, in a description of the 'prince of Israel', i.e. the king of
Judah, and once the turban is taken off the deposition of the ruler is
complete. So in the *miṣnepet* the post-exilic High Priest wears yet
another piece of royal attire. Finally, the girdle characterizes the
High Priest as a person in office. In any case, the word *'abnēṭ* (perhaps
deriving from the Egyptian) used to describe it occurs outside the
description of the priestly dress only in Isa. 22.21 to describe an item
which characterizes a royal official. It is an ornamental girdle, as
distinct from the girdle belonging to the armour of a warrior, which
is described by another Hebrew word.

[40] In contrast with that of the High Priest the dress of the rest of
the priests is very simple and unrelated to royal adornment (v. 40).
It consists just of the usual coat, the decorative girdle pertaining to
their rank and a head-covering which was wound round like a

*[This point is missed in the RSV rendering. Tr.]

turban (RSV 'cap'; cf. Ex. 29.9; Lev. 8.13). This last was distinct from the *miṣnepet*, as is clear from the use of another word which does not occur elsewhere and whose specific meaning is obscure.

[41–43] In its present context the closing sentence of v. 41 anticipates by drawing attention to the anointing and ordination of the priests as well as to their clothing. For this reason it is perhaps to be regarded as a first addition. In a further addition (vv. 42 f.) all priests are required to wear breeches, as is also the case in Ezek. 44.18, not on the grounds of general decency, but in view of the danger to the priests which could emanate from the peculiar holiness of the altar to that part of the body which is surrounded by uncanny powers. It was not the custom elsewhere in Israel to wear breeches, and in Ex. 20.26 this usage is not yet presupposed even in the cultic sphere; instead, an attempt is made to prevent the same danger by instructions of a different kind. The wearing of breeches is evidently only a secondary development, even in the post-exilic priestly dress, as is shown by the subsidiary character of the passage Ex. 28.42 f.

(*h*) INSTRUCTIONS FOR THE INSTALLATION OF THE PRIESTS:
29.1–46

29[1] 'Now this is what you shall do to them to consecrate them, that they may serve me as priests. Take one young bull and two rams without blemish, [2] and unleavened bread, unleavened cakes mixed with oil, and unleavened wafers spread with oil. You shall make them of fine wheat flour. [3] And you shall put them in one basket and bring them in the basket, and bring the bull and the two rams. [4] You shall bring Aaron and his sons to the door of the tent of meeting, and wash them with water. [5] And you shall take the garments, and put on Aaron the coat and the robe of the ephod, and the ephod, and the breastpiece, and gird him with the skilfully woven band of the ephod; [6] and you shall set the turban on his head, and put the holy crown upon the turban. [7] And you shall take the anointing oil, and pour it on his head and anoint him. [8] Then you shall bring his sons, and put coats on them, [9] and you shall gird them with girdles and bind caps on them; and the priesthood shall be theirs by a perpetual statute. Thus you shall ordain Aaron and his sons.

10 'Then you shall bring the bull before the tent of meeting. Aaron and his sons shall lay their hands upon the head of the bull, [11] and you shall kill the bull before the LORD, at the door of the tent of meeting, [12] and shall take part of the blood of the bull and put it upon the horns of the altar with your finger, and the rest of the blood you shall pour out at the base of the altar. [13] And you shall take all the fat that covers

the entrails, and the appendage of the liver, and the two kidneys with the fat that is on them, and burn them upon the altar. [14] But the flesh of the bull, and its skin, and its dung, you shall burn with fire outside the camp; it is a sin offering.

15 'Then you shall take one of the rams, and Aaron and his sons shall lay their hands upon the head of the ram, [16] and you shall slaughter the ram, and shall take its blood and throw it against the altar round about. [17] Then you shall cut the ram into pieces, and wash its entrails and its legs, and put them with its pieces and its head, [18] and burn the whole ram upon the altar; it is a burnt offering to the LORD; it is a pleasing odour, an offering by fire to the LORD.

19 'You shall take the other ram; and Aaron and his sons shall lay their hands upon the head of the ram, [20] and you shall kill the ram, and take part of its blood and put it upon the tip of the right ear of Aaron and upon the tips of the right ears of his sons, and upon the thumbs of their right hands, and upon the great toes of their right feet, and throw the rest of the blood against the altar round about. [21] Then you shall take part of the blood that is on the altar, and of the anointing oil, and sprinkle it upon Aaron and his garments, and upon his sons and his sons' garments with him; and he and his garments shall be holy, and his sons and his sons' garments with him.

22 'You shall also take the fat of the ram, and the fat tail, and the fat that covers the entrails, and the appendage of the liver, and the two kidneys with the fat that is on them, and the right thigh (for it is a ram of ordination), [23] and one loaf of bread, and one cake of bread with oil, and one wafer, out of the basket of unleavened bread that is before the LORD; [24] and you shall put all these in the hands of Aaron and in the hands of his sons, and wave them for a wave offering before the LORD. [25] Then you shall take them from their hands, and burn them on the altar in addition to the burnt offering, as a pleasing odour before the LORD; it is an offering by fire to the LORD.

26 'And you shall take the breast of the ram of Aaron's ordination and wave it for a wave offering before the LORD; and it shall be your portion. [27] And you shall consecrate the breast of the wave offering, and the thigh of the priests' portion, which is waved, and which is offered from the ram of ordination, since it is for Aaron and for his sons. [28] It shall be for Aaron and his sons as a perpetual due from the people of Israel, for it is the priests' portion to be offered by the people of Israel from their peace offerings; it is their offering to the LORD.

29 'The holy garments of Aaron shall be for his sons after him, to be anointed in them and ordained in them. [30] The son who is priest in his place shall wear them seven days, when he comes into the tent of meeting to minister in the holy place.

31 'You shall take the ram of ordination, and boil its flesh in a holy place; [32] and Aaron and his sons shall eat the flesh of the ram and the bread that is in the basket, at the door of the tent of meeting. [33] They shall eat those things with which atonement was made, to ordain and

consecrate them, but an outsider shall not eat of them, because they are holy. [34] And if any of the flesh for the ordination, or of the bread, remain until the morning, then you shall burn the remainder with fire; it shall not be eaten, because it is holy.

35 'Thus you shall do to Aaron and to his sons, according to all that I have commanded you; through seven days shall you ordain them, [36] and every day you shall offer a bull as a sin offering for atonement. Also you shall offer a sin offering for the altar, when you make atonement for it, and shall anoint it, to consecrate it. [37] Seven days you shall make atonement for the altar, and consecrate it, and the altar shall be most holy; whatever touches the altar shall become holy.

38 'Now this is what you shall offer upon the altar: two lambs a year old day by day continually. [39] One lamb you shall offer in the morning, and the other lamb you shall offer in the evening; [40] and with the first lamb a tenth measure of fine flour mingled with a fourth of a hin of beaten oil, and a fourth of a hin of wine for a libation. [41] And the other lamb you shall offer in the evening, and shall offer with it a cereal offering and its libation, as in the morning, for a pleasing odour, an offering by fire to the LORD. [42] It shall be a continual burnt offering through your generations at the door of the tent of meeting before the LORD, where I will meet with you, to speak there to you. [43] There I will meet with the people of Israel, and it shall be sanctified by my glory; [44] I will consecrate the tent of meeting and the altar; Aaron also and his sons I will consecrate, to serve me as priests. [45] And I will dwell among the people of Israel, and will be their God. [46] And they shall know that I am the LORD their God, who brought them forth out of the land of Egypt that I might dwell among them; I am the LORD their God.'

Whereas the instructions in chs. 25–28 bear upon the sanctuary and its contents and include the requisite dress for the priests, ch. 29 deals no longer with the preparation of the furnishings for the life of the cult soon to be inaugurated, but with the planning of the cultic celebration of the ordination of Aaron and his sons as priests. Moreover, as the chapter contains a number of divergencies, albeit insignificant, in the details of the priests' dress from those given in the previous chapter, Ex. 29 is to be regarded as a supplement to P. In addition, this chapter is not a literary unity. A connection, smooth in essentials, runs only as far as v. 25. Then follow individual sections in a rather confusing order, which only have a partial bearing on the proper theme of the chapter. In this part of the chapter we have to reckon with numerous secondary expansions without being able to establish in detail the sequence in which these additions were made.

[1–3] According to the superscription (v. 1a), the following instructions deal with the 'consecration' of the priests previously named ('Aaron and his sons'), i.e. the priestly ordination through which the priests are transferred from the sphere of the profane into that of the 'holy'. To this end there is need of definite sacrificial actions for which the materials must be made ready (vv. 1b–3).

[4–9] There then follows the washing, enrobing, and—in the case of the High Priest—the anointing of the persons chosen for the office of priest. These acts take place at the entrance to the sanctuary (v. 4a), as the priests still may not enter the sanctuary before their consecration. Bodily purity obtained through washing with water (v. 4b) is at the same time a part of cultic purity and stands in a mysterious relationship with it. The items enumerated for the dress of the High Priest are those described in ch. 28; only the girdle is missing, and also the breeches, which are mentioned in ch. 28 only in a supplement. The question arises whether the order in which the items are listed in v. 5 is the order in which they are put on. In that case it would mean here that the High Priest is to wear the coat and the robe under the ephod and the ḥōšen. But it is hard to imagine this happening in practice, nor can it be inferred with any certainty from v. 5. In v. 6 the insignia on the turban of the High Priest is described as a 'crown' (nēzer), differing from 28.36 where a 'flower' (ṣîṣ; RSV 'plate') is mentioned (see pp. 225 f. above). According to v. 7 it is only the High Priest, and not the rest of the priests, who is anointed with oil; the oil is poured over his head. That only he should be anointed is the original custom; it is only later that anointing was extended to all priests. Even in the case of the High Priest, however, anointing is a relatively late custom and the only evidence for it is from the post-exilic period. The Old Testament knows nothing of the anointing of priests for an earlier period. From the earliest times, however, the Old Testament witnesses to the anointing of kings. From this it may be concluded that after the end of the monarchy the act of anointing as a consecration to an office, along with a number of royal insignia (see pp. 222 ff. above) was transferred to the post-exilic High Priest, as he had also to take over the cultic functions of the king. This could not be the case with the other priests, and these are clothed only with items described in 28.40 (v. 9a). The 'Aaron and his sons' in v. 9a, has obviously been added by someone who felt the lack of the girdle in the description of the clothing of Aaron. At the conclusion in 9b it is said that the hands of Aaron and his sons are to be filled.* To

*[RSV renders the Hebrew phrase here as 'to be ordained'.]

'fill the hand' is an ancient technical term meaning to install a priest. It already occurs in what is probably the oldest literary passage to describe the installation of a priest,* and remains a stereotyped formula right up to the latest of the Old Testament writings. The expression 'fill the hand', which outside the Old Testament is in evidence in so early a source as the cuneiform texts of Mari, originally referred to the payment of certain fees for the performance of certain offices. In the Old Testament the expression is applied specially to priests and has the formal meaning of instituting a priest in his office, perhaps with the passage of time losing its reference to its original etymological significance.

[10–14] The cultic act in the narrower sense which now follows begins with a sin offering (v. 14b) which in essentials is to be offered in accordance with the directions given in the setting of the 'Law of Sacrifice' in Lev. 4. The essential details of the sacrificial act are the application of part of the blood of the animal to the horns of the altar and the pouring out of the rest of the blood at the foot of the altar, along with the burning of certain pieces of fat on the altar, and finally the burning of the remaining parts of the sacrificial victim which are not used for the sacrifice outside the sanctuary. An expiatory effect is ascribed to this sacrifice. Those for whom the sacrifice is offered, in this case Aaron and his sons, have to lay their hands upon the beast before it is slaughtered, a process through which in some indefinable way the sacrifice is identified as their own. According to Lev. 4 the sin offering is provided for past sins. Here it is intended as a prophylactic. Moses officiates in it as a priest; as mediator of the divine instructions he evidently enjoys the status of a priest without further ado. He may thus approach the altar on his own authority.

[15–18] The first ram is then offered as a burnt offering (v. 18) in accordance with the instructions for the burnt offering given in Lev. 1. The throwing of blood on the altar and the burning of the whole beast on the altar are parts of the usual rite. The burnt offering, which once again Aaron and his sons make their own by laying their hands on it, is to be regarded as a gift to find divine favour and thus prepares for the act of ordination proper. [19–25] The second ram plays a special part in this act, and is therefore expressly described as the 'ram of ordination' (v. 22). In this it has the character of a peace offering or a community offering, though with a number of

*[Judg. 17.5, 12, where RSV renders 'install'. Tr.]

peculiarities to fit the special circumstances of an ordination to the priesthood. A sacrifice of this kind is meant to achieve a connection between God and those who offer it, and one feature of it is a cultic meal (cf. the directions in Lev. 3 and the expansions made to them in Lev. 7.11 ff., 28 ff.). In the ordination of priests the acts of laying the hands on the animal and killing it (vv. 19, 20a*a*) are first followed by a special blood rite, in which some of the blood of the victim is applied to some parts of the bodies of those to be ordained which are important in the performance of priestly actions; the rest of the blood is thrown against the altar round about (v. 20). This establishes a mysterious relationship between the altar and those who are to be ordained priests. In the sprinkling of some of the blood thrown on the altar and the anointing oil, which here once again makes a surprising appearance, on the priests and upon their ceremonial dress (v. 21a), the holiness of the altar is transferred to the priests and to their robes of office (v. 21b). The prosaic reflection that this would 'spoil' the costly priests' garments should hardly lead us to the conclusion that we have here a purely theoretical set of directions which were never carried out in practice. Indeed we need only imagine a few drops of blood (and oil) and these were a part of the 'consecration' of the priests and their garments. The meal forms the main part of the sacrifice proper; part of the meal is burnt on the altar and is thereby given to God, while the other part is eaten by those who offer the sacrifice; bread accompanies the flesh of the sacrificial victim. In the same way certain delicacies from the 'ram of ordination' (v. 22), along with some of the bread prepared according to the instructions in vv. 2, 3a (v. 23), are burnt on the altar in addition to the burnt offering already offered as a gift to Yahweh (v. 25), after this gift has been offered ceremonially through the ceremony of 'waving' before Yahweh by those making sacrifice (here Aaron and his sons). This 'waving', which has become a stereotyped cultic technical term, is effected by moving the offered gift to and fro in the hands; this indicates the distributing of the food. Now those who are offering the sacrifice must go on to participate in the cultic meal. **[31–32]** For this reason vv. 31 f. surely belong in the present context. The fleshy parts of the 'ram of ordination' still remaining are boiled (v. 31) and eaten by Aaron and his sons, again together with the bread (v. 32). Thus the sacrifice with the 'ram of ordination' is concluded and the ordination of the priests complete.

[26–30] Between v. 25 and v. 31 there are some evidently secondary additions. Verse 26 lays the greatest claim to belong to the original context. At the ordination Moses acts as a priest, and the priest customarily received a special portion at the sacrificial meal; he is therefore to receive the breast of the beast after it too has been 'waved' in its turn, as the priest's portion is basically a part of the divine side of the sacrificial meal. Verses 27 f. with their extremely turgid writing are, however, surely secondary; they do not fit with v. 26 and recall the ruling for the priest's part in the sacrifice which is customary in general elsewhere. Verses 29 f. likewise interrupt the sequence. It is here prescribed that at his ordination, which is to last seven days (cf. v. 35), each of the followers of Aaron is to wear once again the ceremonial dress made for Aaron at his ordination and—as is tacitly assumed—to continue to wear it generally during his course of office in the sanctuary.

[33-46] The rest of the chapter (vv. 33-46) also essentially consists of secondary additions. Verse 33 adds the term 'atonement' which has not occurred hitherto in this chapter, and, as would go without saying, prohibits any 'outsider' from participating in the sacrificial meal. Verse 34 adds a regulation which derives from the nocturnal Passover sacrifice, that any of the sacrificial food remaining over until the morning must be consumed with fire. Verse 35 is most likely to be the closing formula of the original narrative. It is here specially prescribed that the 'ordination' is to last for seven days; in other words, we are to understand that the whole sacrificial complex which has just been described is to be repeated on each of the seven days. All that follows this hardly has any real connection with the theme of the chapter. This applies both to the 'atonement' and consecration of the 'most holy' altar (vv. 36 f.), an act of purification which is apparently conceived as running concurrently with the seven-day ordination of the priests (according to the present wording the altar appears most unusually as the object of an 'anointing'; cf. on this 30.26 ff.), and more so with the continual daily morning and evening burnt offerings (vv. 38-42a), which are here regarded as having been enjoined for the first time on the occasion of the priestly ordination (on the earlier history of this 'continual offering', *tāmīd*, cf. II Kings 16.15; Neh. 10.33; Ezra 9.4; Ezek. 46.13 f.). The closing passage, vv. 42b-46, is somewhat unskilfully composed of familiar expressions of P language; in it Yahweh once again appears in the first person, a manner of speaking which has sunk into the background in previous instructions (cf. the constantly repeated formula 'before Yahweh').

(*i*) INSTRUCTIONS FOR MAKING THE ALTAR OF INCENSE: 30.1–10

30[1] 'You shall make an altar to burn incense upon; of acacia wood shall you make it. [2] A cubit shall be its length, and a cubit its breadth; it shall be square, and two cubits shall be its height; its horns shall be of one piece with it. [3] And you shall overlay it with pure gold, its top and its sides round about and its horns; and you shall make for it a moulding of gold round about. [4] And two golden rings shall you make for it; under its moulding on two opposite sides of it shall you make them, and they shall be holders for poles with which to carry it. [5] You shall make the poles of acacia wood, and overlay them with gold. [6] And you shall put it before the veil that is by the ark of the testimony, before the mercy seat that is over the testimony, where I will meet with you. [7] And Aaron shall burn fragrant incense on it; every morning when he dresses the lamps he shall burn it, [8] and when Aaron sets up the lamps in the evening, he shall burn it, a perpetual incense before the LORD throughoug your generations. [9] You shall offer no unholy incense thereon, nor burnt offering, nor cereal offering; and you shall pour no libation thereon. [10] Aaron shall make atonement upon its horns once a year; with the blood of the sin offering of atonement he shall make atonement for it once in the year throughout your generations; it is most holy to the LORD.'

If even ch. 29 had to be regarded as a supplement to the P narrative (see p. 229 f. above), this is all the more the case—as is generally agreed—with the various passages of mixed content which stand in chs. 30 and 31. With special regard to 30.1–10 it should be pointed out that the instructions here given for the making of an altar of incense are out of sequence. The proper place for them would have been in the setting of the instructions of chs. 25–27. It may thus be established that P made no provision for an altar of incense in the sanctuary which he himself envisaged. This is remarkable, as cultic 'incense', to which a primarily exorcistic significance may have been attached, is a widespread usage which is also attested in the ancient East. Of course a special altar of incense would not necessarily have been needed for this; one would only need suitable utensils such as incense pans, which archaeological discoveries show to have been known even in pre-Israelite Palestine. The 'incense' in the pre-exilic sanctuary at Jerusalem which is probably presupposed in Isa. 6.4b could have been produced by means of such apparatus. Now a golden altar (of incense) is in fact mentioned in I Kings 7.48 as being part of the temple of Solomon, and in any case there is archaeological evidence of stone altars of incense as early as the pre-exilic Israelite period in Palestine. We must therefore suppose that P deliberately excluded an altar of incense from his design for the sanctuary, perhaps envisaging a possible illegitimate attitude to and use of incense, but that the post-exilic Jerusalem temple (as perhaps even the pre-exilic sanctuary) had an altar of incense (cf. I Macc. 1.21) and that in view of this the section 30.1–10 was added.

[1–10] The instructions envisage an altar in the form of a base about three feet high, square in shape, with a moulding running round the top and with (four) 'horns' on the upper corners; in form and size this roughly corresponds to the stone altars which have been found in Palestine.* In respect of materials and the arrangements for transportation the altar of incense matches the corresponding furnishings mentioned in chs. 25 and 27. The position before the entrance to the Holy of Holies, covered with a curtain, may have been usual in the post-exilic temple. The same goes for the requirement of a twice daily 'perpetual' (*tāmīd*; see p. 233 above) incense which is to be burnt by the High Priest ('Aaron'); we are also told that the lamps (25.37) are to be 'dressed' i.e. to be cleaned and supplied with new oil, in the morning and 'set up', i.e. put on the lampstand (cf. 25.31 ff.) and lit, in the evening of each day. These details about the use of the altar of incense go beyond the framework given in chs. 25–28, which is purely descriptive of the cultic apparatus, and thus by themselves reveal the passage to be an addition. It is now impossible to discover why a warning against the misuse of the altar of incense should have seemed necessary. The atonement for the altar of incense which is to be made once a year in fact belongs in the context of the atonement for the whole of the sanctuary (cf. Lev. 16.15–19) and here appears as a single anticipated regulation on the theme of general atonement.

(*k*) INSTRUCTIONS FOR LEVYING A POLL-TAX: 30.11–16

11 The LORD said to Moses, 12 'When you take the census of the people of Israel, then each shall give a ransom for himself to the LORD when you number them, that there be no plague among them when you number them. 13 Each who is numbered in the census shall give this: half a shekel according to the shekel of the sanctuary (the shekel is twenty gerahs), half a shekel as an offering to the LORD. 14 Every one who is numbered in the census, from twenty years old and upward, shall give the LORD's offering. 15 The rich shall not give more, and the poor

*Cf. K. Galling, *Biblisches Reallexikon*, col. 19, figs. 7 and 8; J. B. Pritchard, *The Ancient Near East in Pictures*, p. 192, fig. 575; E. W. Heaton, *Everyday Life in Old Testament Times*, p. 124, fig. 63.

shall not give less, than the half shekel, when you give the LORD's offering to make atonement for yourselves. [16] And you shall take the atonement money from the people of Israel, and shall appoint it for the
service of the tent of meeting; that it may bring the people of Israel
to remembrance before the LORD, so as to make atonement for yourselves.'

[11–16] This section, like those that follow, is introduced by a
stereotyped formula which is not necessary in the context and points
to the secondary character of the passage. The content of the section
presupposes a numbering ('census') of the adult male members of the
cult community which is only enjoined and carried out in Num. 1. A
levy of half a shekel per head is to be levied as 'atonement money' so
that no plague (lit. 'blow') breaks out among them. The thought
behind this reasoning is that a census is something dangerous, as it
could bring down the wrath of God to threaten the lives of those who
were counted (on this cf. II Sam. 24), but that the danger can be
averted by the payment of an 'atonement for the life'. In Num. 1 of
course the census is in accord with the explicit command of God and
thus is not dangerous to human life. The present section evidently
deals with a secondary justification of a general poll-tax customary
in the post-exilic community which, remarkably enough, goes back
to primitive ideas. The payment of this tax is to supply the needs of
the cult (so expressly v. 16a) but at the same time is meant 'to bring
the people of Israel to (a beneficent) remembrance before Yahweh'
(v. 16b). The wording seems to envisage just a single levy; in reality
it may deal with a poll-tax which was currently levied in the post-
exilic community and is described with a cultic technical term as a
'levy', i.e. as a sacral gift offered by 'elevating' it. As cultic rights are
and are meant to be the same for all, the contribution must also be
the same for all (v. 15) so that the rich, for example, do not lay claim
to more cultic rights and the poor are not displaced. A number of
passages which obtrude themselves either by being repetitive or by
having a second person plural address are later additions.

(*l*) INSTRUCTIONS FOR MAKING A LAVER: 30.17–21

17 The LORD said to Moses, [18] 'You shall also make a laver of
bronze, with its base of bronze, for washing. And you shall put it between the tent of meeting and the altar, and you shall put water in it,
[19] with which Aaron and his sons shall wash their hands and their feet.
[20] When they go into the tent of meeting, or when they come near the
altar to minister, to burn an offering by fire to the LORD, they shall

wash with water, lest they die. ²¹ They shall wash their hands and their feet, lest they die: it shall be a statute for ever to them, even to him and to his descendants throughout their generations.'

[17–21] At this point orders have been added for the making of a bronze laver for cultic ablutions and the placing of it in the sanctuary. It is remarkable that in the inventory of the sanctuary in chs. 25–27 P made no provision for an object so necessary for the ancient conception of cultic purity. It certainly existed at the time of the post-exilic temple; it was for this reason that a short descriptive section was inserted here, giving neither measurements nor a detailed account. The laver has its place in the court of the sanctuary just in front of the centre of the 'tent of meeting' (the altar of 27.1–8 is meant by the term 'altar' in v. 18). For cultic ablutions the temple of Solomon had the 'molten sea' and the 'ten stands', which had been set on the sides of the temple building (I Kings 7.23–29); the post-exilic temple contented itself with a more simple apparatus. The order for the High Priest and priests to wash themselves is made more emphatic by the observation that death will follow any performance of the priestly functions without cultic purity, as the 'holy' works destruction on the 'unholy'. Here external, bodily purity is thought to have a mysterious connection with cultic purity and is most probably a part of it.

(m) INSTRUCTIONS FOR MAKING THE HOLY ANOINTING OIL: 30.22–33

22 Moreover, the LORD said to Moses, ²³ 'Take the finest spices: of liquid myrrh five hundred shekels, and of sweet-smelling cinnamon half as much, that is, two hundred and fifty, and of aromatic cane two hundred and fifty, ²⁴ and of cassia five hundred, according to the shekel of the sanctuary, and of olive oil a hin; ²⁵ and you shall make of these a sacred anointing oil blended as by the perfumer; a holy anointing oil it shall be. ²⁶ And you shall anoint with it the tent of meeting and the ark of the testimony, ²⁷ and the table and all its utensils, and the lampstand and its utensils, and the altar of incense, ²⁸ and the altar of burnt offering with all its utensils and the laver and its base; ²⁹ you shall consecrate them, that they may be most holy; whatever touches them will become holy. ³⁰ And you shall anoint Aaron and his sons, and consecrate them, that they may serve me as priests. ³¹ And you shall say to the people of Israel, "This shall be my holy anointing oil throughout your generations. ³² It shall not be poured upon the bodies of ordinary men, and you shall make no other like it in composition; it is holy, and it shall be holy to you. ³³ Whoever compounds any like it or whoever puts any of it on an outsider shall be cut off from his people"'.'

[22–33] The recipe given here for making anointing oil for sacral anointings may rest upon a tradition of undefinable antiquity, but in the present form it doubtless corresponds to post-exilic usage. The materials listed in vv. 23, 24a produced sweet-smelling juices, which were mixed with the olive oil. The quantity to be made cannot be established with any accuracy, as the size of the 'hin', a dry measure, has not been determined when it is used for liquids (about $11\frac{1}{2}$ pints, or perhaps about 7 pints). Even in the older Old Testament tradition (cf. Gen. 28.18b; 31.13a) not only human beings but also sacral objects were anointed with oil, an act which was originally understood as the supplying of new life-power mediated through the oil. According to vv. 26–28 the sanctuary and all that it contains is to be anointed and thus consecrated, 'made holy'; also included in the list are the laver and the altar of incense, objects which only appear in the additions to ch. 30. Physical contact with the objects 'consecrated' in this way makes that which touches them 'holy' (v. 29b; cf. 39.37b); a man who becomes 'holy' in this way cannot return into the sphere of the profane, except by taking special precautions whose character, however, is not mentioned. After the concluding sentence v. 29, v. 30 looks like an addition; the anointing of the High Priest has already been mentioned elsewhere, in 29.7 (on this cf. p. 230). It is understandable that firm prohibitions are placed on the use of the holy consecrating oil for the purpose of everyday hygiene and against the compounding of any oil prepared in a similar way for such a use or even for sale to an 'outsider', i.e. an unauthorized person or even a foreigner. The punishment for such a betrayal of the 'most holy' must be the uprooting of the offender from the company of his fellow men (by force). This is said in a presumably ancient expression which is still directed to the earlier community of the twelve tribes and not as yet to the post-exilic cult community.

(*n*) INSTRUCTIONS FOR MAKING THE INCENSE: 30.34–38

34 And the LORD said to Moses, 'Take sweet spices, stacte, and onycha, and galbanum, sweet spices with pure frankincense (of each shall there be an equal part), [35] and make an incense blended as by the perfumer, seasoned with salt, pure and holy; [36] and you shall beat some of it very small, and put part of it before the testimony in the tent of meeting where I shall meet with you; it shall be for you most holy. [37] And the incense which you shall make according to its composition, you shall not make for yourselves; it shall be for you holy to the LORD. [38] Whoever makes any like it to use as perfume shall be cut off from his people.'

[34–38] The recipe for making the material for the 'incense' also may be supposed to come from the post-exilic period, though it may well have been taken over from an older usage. The wording of v. 36 is probably to be understood in the following way: of the present supply of substances a part is from time to time to be beaten very small and of this a further part is to be burnt as incense once a day (perhaps twice a day according to 30.7 f.). It is remarkable that the altar of incense of vv. 1–10 is not mentioned in v. 36, so that we get the impression that here only censing by means of a censer is intended 'before the testimony', i.e. before the Holy of Holies and the 'Ark of the testimony' that is contained within. It remains striking that in v. 36 no express mention of 'burning' or 'censing' is made, just that the incense is to be brought in front of the Holy of Holies; we cannot however understand this to mean anything but 'censing'. The prohibition of vv. 37 f. corresponds roughly to that of vv. 32 f.

(*o*) THE APPOINTMENT OF THE CRAFTSMEN: 31.1–11

31[1] The LORD said to Moses, [2] 'See, I have called by name Bezalel the son of Uri, son of Hur, of the tribe of Judah: [3] and I have filled him with the Spirit of God, with ability and intelligence, with knowledge and all craftsmanship, [4] to devise artistic designs, to work in gold, silver, and bronze, [5] in cutting stones for setting, and in carving wood, for work in every craft. [6] And behold, I have appointed with him Oholiab, the son of Ahisamach, of the tribe of Dan; and I have given to all able men ability, that they may make all that I have commanded you: [7] the tent of meeting, and the ark of the testimony, and the mercy seat that is thereon, and all the furnishings of the tent, [8] the table and its utensils, and the pure lampstand with all its utensils, and the altar of incense, [9] and the altar of burnt offering with all its utensils, and the laver and its base, [10] and the finely worked garments, the holy garments for Aaron the priest and the garments of his sons, for their service as priests, [11] and the anointing oil and the fragrant incense for the holy place. According to all that I have commanded you shall do.'

[1–11] The position of this passage and its introduction by the stereotyped introductory formula (v. 1) indicates that here too we have a literary addition to the P narrative. In any case the list in vv. 7–11 is secondary as it includes—in the same way as the list in 30.26–28—the items which are only introduced as an addition in ch. 30 (altar of incense and laver, oil of anointing and incense). Of course this list could itself be secondary in comparison to the passage vv. 2–6, as it is quite superfluous after the clause v. 6b which sums the passage and rounds it off. But in view of what has already been said the passage vv. 2–6 is already to be regarded as a later addition. We can unfortunately no longer ascertain the derivation of the tradition of the two craftsmen under whose direction and supervision the 'able men' are to carry out the manifold tasks involved in the making of the sanctuary and all that it contains. The names of Bezalel and his father Uri are attested as personal names from the post-exilic period (Ezra 10.30 and 24 respectively) and the name Hur occurs in I Chron. 2.50; 4.1, 4 (cf. also Neh. 3.9) in the genealogy of Judah. This could suggest a post-exilic origin for the tradition. The names Oholiab and Ahisamach do not occur elsewhere in the Old Testament, but the latter belongs to a frequent and old type of personal-name construction, and while the former is unusual it is not necessarily an artificial construction, as there is also evidence of its elements in West Semitic nomenclature. We must therefore accept the possibility that behind these names and even behind their assignation to certain Israelite tribes, there stand the historical figures of craftsmen who were at one time involved in the furnishing of the sanctuary. But all clues which might accord them some concrete date or description are lacking.

(p) INSTRUCTIONS FOR KEEPING THE SABBATH: 31.12–17

12 And the LORD said to Moses, 13 'Say to the people of Israel, "You shall keep my sabbaths, for this is a sign between me and you throughout your generations, that you may know that I, the LORD, sanctify you. 14 You shall keep the sabbath, because it is holy for you; every one who profanes it shall be put to death; whoever does any work on it, that soul shall be cut off from among his people. 15 Six days shall work be done, but the seventh day is a sabbath of solemn rest, holy to the LORD; whoever does any work on the sabbath day shall be put to death. 16 Wherefore the people of Israel shall keep the sabbath, observing the sabbath throughout their generations, as a perpetual covenant. 17 It is a sign for ever between me and the people of Israel that in six days the LORD made heaven and earth, and on the seventh day he rested, and was refreshed." '

[12–17] The emphasis on the sabbath commandment (cf. 16.22–27 P, and on that passage pp. 135 f. above) is evidently here to be understood in connection with what has immediately gone before. Apart from the position of this section this is principally clear from the formulation of the opening words of the command in v. 13ab, where particular reference is made to what has just been said. It therefore means that rest on the sabbath day is to be observed strictly even during the work of erecting the sanctuary which has been enjoined by God; the death penalty will be carried out on any transgressor. For the sabbath is the 'sign' of the peculiar relationship between God and people by which the whole world is to recognize the existence of this relationship (v. 13b) which makes Israel 'holy', i.e. which marks Israel off from the other nations. Verse 14 gives the impression of clumsiness, as v. 14a in effect only repeats something which has already been said and v. 14b threatens the death penalty in two different formulations (on the formulation of v. 14b*a* cf. p. 179 above on 21.12 ff.; on that of v. 14b*b* cf. p. 238 above on 30.33). Nevertheless, perhaps these repetitions may be explained by the emphasis which the author wishes to make in his stressing of the sabbath commandment. In vv. 15–17, however, we certainly have a secondary addition, as is evident from the carelessness of the phrasing alone. In vv. 15 and 17b Yahweh is named in the third person without any reference to the context, but in between v. 17a has him speaking again in the first person. This addition is substantially composed of repetitions of previous verses, variants on the sabbath commandment of 20.8–11 and a reference to Gen. 2.2 f.; it concludes with the striking statement that Yahweh 'was refreshed' after the six days of creation.

5. APOSTASY AND ANOTHER COVENANT: 31.18–34.35

(a) THE APOSTASY OF THE GOLDEN CALF: 31.18–32.35

18 And he gave to Moses, when he had made an end of speaking with him upon Mount Sinai, the two tables of the testimony, tables of stone, written with the finger of God.

32¹ When the people saw that Moses delayed to come down from the mountain, the people gathered themselves together to Aaron, and said to him, 'Up, make us gods, who shall go before us; as for this Moses, the man who brought us up out of the land of Egypt, we do not know what has become of him.' ² And Aaron said to them, 'Take off the rings of gold which are in the ears of your wives, your sons, and your daughters, and bring them to me.' ³ So all the people took off the rings of gold which were in their ears, and brought them to Aaron. ⁴ And he received the gold at their hand, and fashioned it with a graving tool, and made a molten calf; and they said, 'These are your gods, O Israel, who brought you up out of the land of Egypt!' ⁵ When Aaron saw this, he built an altar before it; and Aaron made proclamation and said, 'Tomorrow shall be a feast to the LORD.' ⁶ And they rose up early on the morrow, and offered burnt offerings and brought peace offerings; and the people sat down to eat and drink, and rose up to play.

7 And the LORD said to Moses, 'Go down; for your people, whom you brought up out of the land of Egypt, have corrupted themselves; ⁸ they have turned aside quickly out of the way which I commanded them; they have made for themselves a molten calf, and have worshipped it and sacrificed to it, and said, "These are your gods, O Israel, who brought you up out of the land of Egypt!" ' ⁹ *And the* LORD *said to Moses, 'I have seen this people, and behold, it is a stiff-necked people;* ¹⁰ *now therefore let me alone, that my wrath may burn hot against them and I may consume them; but of you I will make a great nation.'*

11 *But Moses besought the* LORD *his God, and said, 'O* LORD, *why does thy wrath burn hot against thy people, whom thou hast brought forth out of the land of Egypt with great power and with a mighty hand?* ¹² *Why should the Egyptians say, "With evil intent did he bring them forth, to slay them in the mountains, and to consume them from the face of the earth?" Turn from thy fierce wrath, and repent of this evil against thy people.* ¹³ *Remember Abraham, Isaac, and Israel, thy servants, to whom thou didst swear by thine own self, and didst say to them, "I will multiply your descendants as the stars of heaven, and all this land that I have promised I will give to your descendants, and they shall inherit it for ever." '* ¹⁴ *And the* LORD *repented of the evil which he thought to do to his people.*

15 And Moses turned, and went down from the mountain with the two tables [of the testimony] in his hands, tables that were written on both sides; on the one side and on the other were they written. ¹⁶ And the tables were the work of God, and the writing was the writing of God, graven upon the tables. ¹⁷ When Joshua heard the noise of the people as they shouted, he said to Moses 'There is a noise of war in the camp.' ¹⁸ But he said, 'It is not the sound of shouting for victory, or the sound of the cry of defeat, but the sound of singing that I hear.' ¹⁹ And as soon as he came near the camp and saw the calf and the dancing, Moses' anger burned hot, and he threw the tables out of his hands and broke them at the foot of the mountain. ²⁰ And he took the calf which they had made, and burnt it with fire, and ground it to powder, and scattered it upon the water, and made the people of Israel drink it.

21 And Moses said to Aaron, 'What did this people do to you that you have brought a great sin upon them?' ²² And Aaron said, 'Let not the anger of my lord burn hot; you know the people, that they are set on evil. ²³ For they said to me, "Make us gods, who shall go before us; as for this Moses, the man who brought us up out of the land of Egypt, we do not know what has become of him." ²⁴ And I said to them, "Let any who have gold take it off"; so they gave it to me, and I threw it into the fire, and there came out this calf.'

25 And when Moses saw that the people had broken loose [(for Aaron had let them break loose, to their shame among their enemies)], ²⁶ then Moses stood in the gate of the camp, and said, 'Who is on the LORD's side? Come to me.' And all the sons of Levi gathered themselves together to him. ²⁷ And he said to them, 'Thus says the LORD God of Israel, "Put every man his sword on his side, and go to and fro from gate

to gate throughout the camp, and slay every man his brother, and every man his companion, and every man his neighbour".' [28] And the sons of Levi did according to the word of Moses; and there fell of the people that day about three thousand men. [29] And Moses said, 'Today you have ordained yourselves for the service of the Lord, each one at the cost of his son and of his brother, that he may bestow a blessing upon you this day.'

30 On the morrow Moses said to the people, 'You have sinned a great sin. And now I will go up to the Lord; perhaps I can make atonement for your sin.' [31] So Moses returned to the Lord and said, 'Alas this people have sinned a great sin; they have made for themselves gods of gold. [32] But now, if thou wilt forgive their sin—and if not, blot me, I pray thee, out of thy book which thou hast written.' [33] But the Lord said to Moses, 'Whoever has sinned against me, him will I blot out of my book. [34] But now go, lead the people to the place of which I have spoken to you; behold, my angel shall go before you. Nevertheless, in the day when I visit, I will visit their sin upon them.'

35 And the Lord sent a plague upon the people, because they made the calf which Aaron made.

In its present form, ch. 32 must be examined in the context of the whole complex of chs. 32–34. The theme of the tables, broken (ch. 32) and then renewed (ch. 34), holds the whole together, whereas ch. 33 is a further independent development of the subordinate theme of the departure from Sinai which appears at the end of ch. 32. Apart from small additions in the style of the P narrative, in chs. 32–34 we are once again dealing with old Pentateuchal narrative material. Thus the threads of the narrative which were let slip in ch. 24 are here taken up once more; indeed we were already prepared for chs. 32–34 by the mention in 24.12–15a that Moses went up into the mountain to receive 'tables of stone' and to stay there for some time. Thus in any case we must suppose that J is continued in chs. 32–34; and it is quite generally agreed that at least the major portion of ch. 34 is to be assigned to the J narrative, while most would also add parts of ch. 32 and even of ch. 33. This may be correct. The state of the sources is certainly extremely confused in this complex and something further should be said about individual details. The nucleus of the whole historical tradition is to be found in ch. 34, the narrative of the making of the covenant based on the 'words of the covenant' (34.27 f.) communicated to Moses on the mountain and then written on the tables. Here—and only here—we are told what was written on the tables which Moses was summoned up the mountain to receive. On the other hand, the narrative of the broken tables (ch. 32), about whose inscription the old

Pentateuchal material has as yet told us absolutely nothing, appears to be a secondary tradition. The main narrative about the tables, their contents and their significance stands only in ch. 34. Now if all that we have here is a renewal of some tables about whose contents we have been told nothing and which were at one time broken, we can hardly hold the account to be original. The story of the broken tables must therefore be regarded as an addition to the historical tradition, which may go back to the pre-literary period.

To answer the latter question it is necessary to make a literary-critical and traditio-historical analysis of ch. 32. It is generally recognized that this section is not a literary unity. First, it is certain that because of their style vv. 9–14 must be regarded as a deuteronomistic addition which explains the sparing of Israel—represented as historical—after their apostasy from cult worship by Yahweh's concern for his reputation among the Egyptians (and thus among the peoples of the world) and also by the oath which he had given to the Patriarchs, but goes on to anticipate the question of the punishment of Israel in an inappropriate way.

It is further striking that Aaron's role is not very deeply rooted in the narrative. It is quite clear that the subordinate clauses which refer to Aaron in v. 35 and similarly in v. 25 are secondary additions. But even the conversation between Moses and Aaron in vv. 21–24 is evidently an addition; it is out of sequence after the actions of Moses reported in vv. 19 f., as Moses would surely have interrogated Aaron before taking definite steps. Moreover, it is remarkable that Aaron's confession had no further consequences for his own person. Now in this confession Aaron refers to what is reported about him in vv. 1b–4, but not completely accurately; the difference between Aaron's words in v. 24b and the language of the narrative in v. 4a is surely to be understood as an attempt on the part of the narrator to provide a rather lame and hollow-sounding exculpation of Aaron. But in that case we must use vv. 21–24 to question whether the occurrence of Aaron in vv. 1b–4 is original and consider whether this passage was not originally written with the people as the subject of the action (cf. also vv. 7 f., where the people are likewise mentioned in this role). This is also supported by v. 5, as the beginning of this verse reads as though Aaron had hitherto had nothing to do with the matter and now wished to give a fairly tolerable turn to the proceedings by guiding them along the lines of a regulated Yahweh cult. Now Aaron himself of course occurs in v. 5, so that we are driven to assume that the Aaron additions occur in two different strata. As v. 5 presupposes a more original text than 1b–4 it is to be assumed that Aaron was first introduced into the story as one who tolerated the *fait accompli* of the people and took part in the proceedings willy-nilly (so v. 5; v. 25b could also belong to this) and that Aaron's activity was emphasized more strongly at a later date—even if the initiative did come from the people (so the transmitted wording of vv. 1b–4 and also vv. 21–24 and 35b*b*). Unfortunately we can no longer ascertain the time or the circumstances of the addition of these passages. They must derive from circles in which the (priestly) sons of Aaron were accused of participating in illegitimate cults and must in any case have come into being before Aaron had become the ancestor of the sole legitimate priesthood of Yahweh (thus P).

Even after these secondary elements have been taken away all is not yet smooth. There are a number of variants, especially with respect to the reprimanding of the people. According to v. 20, Moses gave the people a 'water of cursing' to drink, while according to vv. 25–29 the Levites punished the apostasy with the sword, and v. 34 says that Yahweh postponed the visitation of the sinners to an unspecified time which he reserves for himself. Now in any case it is clear that the Levite-passage is to be judged a later addition; its real aim is not to describe the punishment of Israel but to narrate and give reasons for the entrusting of the priestly office to the Levites, and in so doing it presupposes the occasion of this punishment. As the single mention of Aaron has evidently been added later to the introduction to this section, v. 25b, the section will be older than the insertion of Aaron into the narrative of the golden calf. But apart from vv. 25–29 there remains the juxtaposition of the narrative theme of the 'water of cursing' (v. 20b) which would have culminated in a description of the consequences, now missing, and at best might have its continuation and conclusion in the extremely vague remark about the 'sending of a plague' by Yahweh in v. 35 ab*a*, and on the other hand of the reference to a postponement of the punishment in vv. 30–34. In the explanation of individual details which now follows it will be necessary to investigate this present difficulty. It can, however, be said at this stage that this juxtaposition is not sufficient to justify the assumption that there are two continuous narrative threads in this chapter, for which there are no clear indications elsewhere. The situation rather favours the presence of a basic narrative which has been expanded into several strata by secondary additions, none of which prove themselves to be the fragmentary remains of a second, originally complete, variant narrative. The basic narrative is certainly—if only in view of its connection with the main part of ch. 34—to be related in some way to J.

The history of the tradition of the narrative of the golden calf cannot be separated from the setting up of two 'golden calves' in the sanctuaries of Bethel and Dan by King Jeroboam of Israel, reported in I Kings 12.28f. This is supported not only by the general correspondence of the main features but also by the explanatory formula in Ex. 32.(4b) 8b*b* which is verbally identical with I Kings 12.28b*b*. As the reason for the plural phrasing of this formula is that there are two 'golden calves' in I Kings 12 ('. . . your gods, who brought you up . . .') and this would not be appropriate in Ex. 32, it is to be assumed that the basic narrative of Ex. 32 on its part presupposes the prophetic narrative of I Kings 12.(13) 14 in at least an already stereotyped oral form if not fixed in writing. Its purpose is therefore to condemn Jeroboam's measures as apostasy and a breach of the covenant which finds special expression in the breaking of the tables on which 'the words of the covenant' (34.28) were written. It connects the setting up of the 'golden calves' by Jeroboam and the worship accorded by Israel to these calves with a tendency to disloyalty which was native to Israel from the beginning. We can ask whether perhaps Ex. 32 contains an older tradition of a cultic apostasy of Israel even on Sinai which was only later transformed into a polemic against the 'golden calves' of Jeroboam. It is, however, impossible to find any concrete clues for such an assumption, and so we must therefore reckon with the possibility that the narrative of Ex. 32 was originally composed with reference to Jeroboam's cult-politics. We might then assume that Jeroboam introduced no innovations, but that there had already been 'golden calves' at cultic places in Israel before his time, though of course we know nothing of them. Should the connection with Jeroboam in Ex. 32 be original, there would be difficulties in assigning the basic matter of the chapter to J if J, as seems probable, belongs to the time of David and Solomon. In that case either J must be brought down to the post-Solomonic period in respect of Ex. 32 or—and this I hold to be the most probable solution—Ex. 32 must be regarded as a subsequent literary addition to the J narrative which was inserted to accommodate the condemnation of the cult introduced by Jeroboam within the great comprehensive description of the prehistory and early history of Israel provided by J.

[31.18] This verse provides the link between the preceding P narrative and Ex. 32. As, however, the mere position of the temporal indications in the Hebrew text, which refer specially to what has gone before, proves them to be an addition, the basic matter of the verse will belong to the older narrative material (in that case the P expression 'tables of the testimony' is also to be regarded as an addition) and will originally have been joined to 24.12–15a. In view of what follows, it is expressly remarked that Moses received the tables. The statements about the tables are, where they occur, noticeably different. The most original is surely the tradition that Moses himself hewed out two tables of stone on the mountain at the command of God and then also himself wrote upon them (so 34.1, 28). On the other hand, according to 31.18 they were 'given' to him by God, and a similar statement is made at 24.12b; at the same time it follows from this that 24.12b (to which in that case 24.13a, 14, 15a also belong) is to be regarded as an introduction to the special tradition of ch. 32, whereas in 24.12a, 13b we have to find the literary connection with ch. 34. Deut. 9.10 says, in exactly the same words as 31.18, that the tables were written 'with the finger of God', and may have been transferred from there to its present position, as in 32.15–16 the tables are inscribed in a different way.

[32.1–6] According to the hypothesis advanced above, the description of the preparation and cultic use of the 'golden calf' (32.1–6) was originally written with the people as the subject of the action. To bring in Aaron (in two different strata) only a little recasting and expansion was necessary (perhaps v. 1b originally ran 'We will make us gods'). Here as in I Kings 12.28 the 'calf' is explained as a representation of God, indeed as an image of the God who had brought Israel up out of Egypt. This explanation contains a pejorative exaggeration of the original circumstances which has purposely been introduced with polemical intent. As the ancient Near East (in contrast to Egypt) knows no theriomorphic deities but only the association of beasts with deities pictured in human form whose companions and bearers they are, the 'golden calves' of the royal sanctuaries of Jeroboam are also surely meant merely as pedestals for the God who is imagined to be standing invisibly upon them. As Moses, who has hitherto been mediator between God and people and the representative of God, appears to be missing, Israel will no longer trust the God who is appearing to him on Sinai, but desire a visible God to lead them on their way. The attitude of the people is shown to be rough and coarse. They speak of Moses, to whom (instead of to God) they ascribe their deliverance from Egypt, in a contemptuous tone (v. 1). Then they 'take off' (v. 3a) their golden earrings and make out of them a molten calf (v. 4a). The term 'calf' here (as in I Kings 12) is a derogatory description given by the writer; the image of the bull was quite small, indeed only a 'calf' in relation to the God imagined, if not depicted, in human form. Nevertheless the people of Israel meant it to represent the God who had led Israel out of Egypt (v. 4b) and who bore the name Yahweh (v. 5, if a basic element of this verse may be said to have belonged to the original narrative without Aaron). Special emphasis is laid on the extravagant celebrations at the cult feast which inaugurates the new divine worship (v. 6). True, eating (and drinking) form part of the rite of the communal sacrifice. Here, however, they are expressly mentioned with a purpose; 'and rose up to play' doubtless refers to sexual orgies (see Gen. 26.8) such as played a part in the Canaanite fertility cults. The description of the one golden calf in the plural as 'gods' (vv. 4b, 5b, 8b) is striking. According to the hypothesis advanced above, it derives from I Kings 12.28, but there too it already has a polemic twist in that it represents Jeroboam's two golden calves (doubtless contrary to the king's real intention) as a plurality of gods and thus as a piece of idolatrous Canaanite cultic practice. In Ex. 32 the one golden calf is condemned with this phrase as an element of polytheistic worship whose character should not escape us just because the cult, which begins with a feast, is nominally one of Yahweh.

[32.7–16] At this point (vv. 7 f.) Moses upon the mountain is briefly informed of what has happened and is reminded of his responsibility for the people whom he has brought up out of Egypt (here too, as in v. 1, he is made the chief actor in the Exodus). Thereupon (on the addition vv. 9–14 see p. 244 above) he descends from the mountain with the two 'tables' which have been given to him (31.18). In this context, in vv. 15 f., something more is said about the tables so as to elucidate the significance of the breaking of the tables which soon follows. To that extent the description of the tables at this point makes good sense. But of course we must also reckon with the possibility that this description of the tables is a subsequent addition which was inserted in the course of a further development of the tradition of the tables—perhaps even in several strata—and that originally only 'the two tables' in the hand of Moses were mentioned (the expression 'tables of the testimony' is elsewhere found only in P). The mere fact that the tables are inscribed on both sides shows that they are something out of the ordinary, as it was the custom for inscribed stones (*stēlai*) to bear the inscription on one side only. It is all the more extraordinary that the tables were 'the work of God' and the inscription 'the writing of God' (in these contexts the word 'God' is meant generally and could have been used in this way even by J). The terms 'work of God' and 'writing of God' do not necessarily imply that the tables had been made and inscribed by God; the words could also mean that the tables were of a wonderful kind, with a sacral form of writing, without the formula, framed so strikingly in an impersonal way, giving any further information about their origin. But perhaps the formula is meant to be understood as a mysterious reference to the divine origin of the tables and the writing.

[**32.17–20**] The uproar in the Israelite camp is misunderstood by Joshua, who was introduced in 24.13a as a companion of Moses and here appears once again as a subordinate companion, to give greater prominence to the superior knowledge of Moses, who has already been informed (vv. 7 f.). In Moses' words of v. 18, which have poetical form and appear to represent a stereotyped remark, but whose original *Sitz im Leben* is nevertheless obscure, the decisive word is missing in the transmitted text, whether it has fallen out by mistake or whether it has been suppressed because of its inappropriateness (perhaps referring to v. 6 b*b*). Moses' breaking of the tables at the foot of the mountain, i.e. before he has entered the camp, means that he now declares the covenant between God and people to be broken and therefore null and void. If he then burns and grinds the calf, this presupposes two different kinds of material. The burning can only apply to wood. The assumption that the calf was made of a wooden centre overlaid with plate gold does not harmonize with the expression 'molten calf' (vv. 4, 8). On the other hand, however, it is also difficult to see in v. 20 an element of a variant tradition of which there is no evidence elsewhere. Is it perhaps tacitly to be presupposed that the calf had been set up on a wooden pedestal? Moses grinds the gold of the calf in the same way as a man grinds corn between two stones. The narrator evidently has taken no thought as to how this was technically possible. For him the main thing is that the gold dust is strewn on the water so that this water becomes a 'water of cursing'. For this must be the sense of v. 20b. Elsewhere (cf. Num. 5.11–28) such a 'water of cursing' serves to introduce a judgment from God;

the 'water of cursing' produces effects on the guilty which demonstrate their guilt. In the present case of course it was not necessary to discover the guilty ones, as all Israel is presumed to be guilty. It is evidently meant here that Moses with the 'water of cursing' hands over to God the punishment of Israel. Certainly the old 'water of cursing' narrative theme is not continued in the narrative as it has been handed down to us (cf. p. 251 below on v. 35).

[21–29] According to the secondary section vv. 25–29 (on vv. 21–24 see pp. 244 f. above), Moses himself arranged the punishment by calling together those who had wanted to stand by Yahweh, i.e. the 'real' Yahweh, who had had nothing to do with the bull image, and with prophetic authority (cf. the introduction of his speech in v. 27a*a*) commanded them in the name of 'Yahweh, the God of Israel' to pay no attention to bonds of kinship or humanitarian feeling, but to cause a great massacre with the sword throughout the Israelite camp. 'The sons of Levi' followed his outcry and his command. Many questions remain unanswered in this context. Had these 'sons of Levi', the 'Levites', previously looked on at the erection of the golden calf and the worship of it without opposition, perhaps even themselves being concerned in it, and did they only realize later what was happening? And what had been their status up to now? As they are to kill even relations and neighbours, it does not seem as though they were thought of as a 'tribe' in the usual sense of a great community connected at least fictitiously by blood. The question of what happened earlier is of no interest to the writer. Even the sequel itself is described only fragmentarily. How great a part of the whole the three thousand 'fallen' (v. 28b) represents, and why only a part were attacked (as is also stated in the formulation of v. 28b), and on what grounds this particular three thousand were killed all remains unsaid. The interest in this section is in the appointment of the Levites to be priests, as is reported at the close where it is described by the technical term 'ordination' (on this see pp. 230 f.). Evidently the passage derives from a time when the right of the Levites to be the priests or even their right to be sole priests was still disputed (cf. Deut. 33. 8–11, especially v. 11b) and a historical justification was deemed necessary. The insertion of the section into the narrative of the golden calf may indicate that the claim of the Levites to priestly privileges etc. had to be carried through against the priesthood of the royal sanctuaries of the state of Israel (cf. Jeroboam's appointment of non-Levitical priests in I Kings 12.31b). Unfortunately the reasons in v. 29 for the right of the Levites to the priesthood are no longer preserved intact; the clause giving the reasons has apparently been transmitted in a defective form, and there is little possibility of filling the gaps by conjectures. All that is clear is that the Levites were entrusted with the priestly office because they paid no attention to sons and brothers (on this cf. Deut. 33.9a) and—so we must expand the meaning of the narrative—will have nothing to do with them in the future. Thus it seems to have been a characteristic of the Levites that they were loosed from all family ties.

[30–35] In the closing section vv. 30–35 we have an unbalanced juxtaposition of, on the one side, a brief remark about the 'plague' (lit. 'blow') of Yahweh with which he punishes the apostasy of the people (v. 35) and, on the other, the description of the postponement of the punishment (vv. 30–34). We must see in v. 35 the still extant continuation and conclusion of the narrative theme of the 'water of cursing' (v. 20). According to this the effect of this water was no longer thought to be magical but was handed over to the divine power; Yahweh made it result in a plague for Israel, a term which we must understand to mean something like a deadly sickness. We are, however, given no details about the character and extent of this sickness. In comparison with this information vv. 30–34 must be regarded as a literary addition. This passage too joins on to v. 20 by way of an addition, as the temporal details in v. 30 can only refer to the proceedings described in vv. 19 f. The 'water of cursing' has not yet made its effect felt, for 'on the morrow' Moses resolves to make an attempt at atoning for the 'great sin' by offering himself as a vicarious sacrifice (v. 32). The way in which Moses speaks in v. 32b presupposes that God has a register of the living, and that from time to time he strikes out from this register those who are to die (cf. 'the book of the living' or 'of life' in Ps. 69.28). This offer is rejected with a reference to the principle that the guilty shall be personally punished, but this is reserved for the time being; meanwhile Moses is to lead the people away from Sinai (the indication of the accompanying divine 'angel' in v. 34 a*b* is an addition). Thus the punishment is postponed to an unspecified time and an indeterminate place. This is most remarkable, but can, however, probably be explained by the reference of the story of the golden calf to the cultic measures of Jeroboam I; this cultic apostasy must still—so the writer gives us to understand—be expiated even if this is not apparent at the time. God has still marked it out for some time. Thus the passage vv. 30–34 may come from the time before the end of the state of Israel and its royal sanctuaries. From vv. 30–34, v. 35ab*a* has acquired the subsidiary meaning that Yahweh still 'smote' Israel sometime and somewhere, although v. 35ab*a* certainly meant originally that the punishment followed immediately upon the apostasy.

(*b*) THE PRESENCE OF YAHWEH WITH HIS PEOPLE: 33.1–23

33[1] The LORD said to Moses, 'Depart, go up hence, you and the people whom you have brought up out of the land of Egypt, to the land of which I swore to Abraham, Isaac, and Jacob, saying, "To your descendants I will give it." [2] And I will send an angel before you, and I will drive out the Canaanites, the Amorites, the Hittites, the Perizzites, the Hivites, and the Jebusites. [3] Go up to a land flowing with milk and honey; but I will not go up among you, lest I consume you in the way, for you are a stiff-necked people.'

4 When the people heard these evil tidings, they mourned; and no man put on his ornaments. [5] For the LORD had said to Moses, 'Say to the people of Israel, "You are a stiff-necked people; if for a single moment I should go up among you, I would consume you. So now put off your ornaments from you, that I may know what to do with you".' [6] Therefore the people of Israel stripped themselves of their ornaments, from Mount Horeb onward.

7 Now Moses used to take the tent and pitch it outside the camp, far off from the camp; and he called it the tent of meeting. And every one who sought the LORD would go out to the tent of meeting, which was outside the camp. [8] Whenever Moses went out to the tent, all the people rose up, and every man stood at his tent door, and looked after Moses, until he had gone into the tent. [9] When Moses entered the tent, the pillar of cloud would descend and stand at the door of the tent, and the LORD would speak with Moses. [10] And when all the people saw the pillar of cloud standing at the door of the tent, all the people would rise up and worship, every man at his tent door. [11] Thus the LORD used to speak to Moses face to face, as a man speaks to his friend. When Moses turned again into the camp, his servant Joshua the son of Nun, a young man, did not depart from the tent.

12 Moses said to the LORD, 'See, thou sayest to me, "Bring up this people," but thou hast not let me know whom thou wilt send with me. Yet thou hast said, "I know you by name, and you have also found favour in my sight." [13] Now therefore, I pray thee, if I have found favour in thy sight, show me now thy ways, that I may know thee and find favour in thy sight. Consider too that this nation is thy people.' [14] And he said, 'My presence will go with you, and I will give you rest.' [15] And he said to him, 'If thy presence will not go with me, do not carry us up from here. [16] For how shall it be known that I have found favour in thy sight, I and thy people? Is it not in thy going with us, so that we are distinct, I and thy people, from all other people that are upon the face of the earth?'

17 And the LORD said to Moses, 'This very thing that you have spoken I will do; for you have found favour in my sight, and I know you by name.' 18 Moses said, 'I pray thee, show me thy glory.' 19 And he said, 'I will make all my goodness pass before you, and will proclaim before you my name "The LORD"; and I will be gracious to whom I will be gracious, and will show mercy on whom I will show mercy. 20 But,' he said, 'you cannot see my face; for man shall not see me and live.' 21 And the LORD said, 'Behold, there is a place by me where you shall stand upon the rock; 22 and while my glory passes by I will put you in a cleft of the rock, and I will cover you with my hand until I have passed by; 23 then I will take away my hand, and you shall see my back; but my face shall not be seen.'

The very varied pieces of Ex. 33 are held together by the theme of the presence of God in the midst of his people, which plays some part in all of them. This common theme was evidently also the reason for the collection of all the passages. The whole joins up with 32.34a, where Moses receives the command to lead the people away from Sinai. This command raises the question of how the people can preserve the presence of God experienced on the mountain of the theophany once this place has been left behind. As the command 32.34a stands in the context of a section which is probably already secondary in comparison with the basic material of ch. 32, we must all the more hold the sections in ch. 33 to be literary additions. It will be necessary to make a detailed examination to see whether we can learn any more about the literary and traditional derivation of these passages.

[1–6] The first section, vv. 1–6, is interspersed with Deuteronomic phrases and is thus most probably to be accounted of Deuteronomic origin throughout. It is further not a literary unity. To the instructions, given in the form of a command directed to Moses, to set off for the land already promised to the Patriarchs (v. 1) are added words in which the people are addressed directly (v. 3b), and these words form the continuation of v. 2a (the intermediary section vv. 2b, 3a consists of familiar clauses and phrases inserted later), where the special reference of the 'you' in the address remains doubtful. As in 23.20, Yahweh promises that an 'angel' (cf. on 23.20) will accompany them to guide them (v. 2a) and here gives the reason that he himself will not go with them as his presence would consume the 'stiff-necked' people (v. 3b). This allusion to 'stiff-neckedness' refers to the wilfulness of the people in their apostasy towards the golden calf (cf. the same expression in the deuteronomistic insertion in 32.9). The leaving off of ornaments is part of the mourning with which the people bewail Yahweh's announcement that he will not go with them (v. 4). Only the immediate sequel explains why this is expressly mentioned. Verses 5 f. are only an apparent variant of v. 4; in fact the command of Yahweh reported in v. 5 is to the effect that the ornaments are not merely to be laid aside but to be thrown away completely. And so the Israelites 'put off their ornaments', 'stripped themselves' actually on Horeb (so we are to understand the somewhat unclear formula at the end of v. 6 in which at the same time the deuteronomistic name for the mountain—Horeb instead of Sinai—is noteworthy). This is to be understood as a sincere and lasting repentance on the part of the Israelites, so that Yahweh can now 'do something with them' (v. 5bb). What he can do is of course not immediately said. According to the transmitted state of the chapter this allusion refers to the tent discussed in the following section as the place of 'meeting' between God and Moses (viz. the people) and thus as an occasion of the divine presence, something more than that of the 'angel', which is now vouchsafed to the penitent people. It is probable that this connection between vv. 5 f. and vv. 7–11 was originally meant by the text, i.e. that the Deuteronomic excerpt vv. 1–6 has vv. 7–11 in view from the beginning and forms the Deuteronomic transition to the section about the 'tent of meeting'. Of course it has often been assumed that something has fallen out after 33.6, namely a description of the making of the ark from the (golden) ornaments put off by the people, and that the tent described after it was intended just for this ark. It can, however, be said against this assumption that there is no positive place in the present text into which it might fit, though it may at the same time be conceded that an old narrative about the making of the ark, which is later at Num. 10.35 f. surprisingly supposed to be extant even in the old Pentateuchal narrative material, could have been suppressed by a redactor in view of 25.10–22 P. The principal argument against this, however, is that according to the wording of vv. 4b, 5b, 6 the Israelites did not hand over their (golden) ornaments for them to be made into something, but 'stripped them off'. Finally, the presence of an ark in the tent is evidently not envisaged in the section vv. 7–11. Thus the allusion in vv. 5bb of the Deuteronomic section from the beginning referred to the section on the tent (vv. 7–11) and therefore presupposed this to be already at hand.

[**7–11**] In fact we have in vv. 7–11 an old pre-Priestly, pre-deuteronomistic tradition, traces of which also meet us elsewhere;

in the old narrative of Num. 11.24 ff. (cf. also Num. 12.4 f., 10) we likewise find the 'tent (of meeting)', the descending cloud as the manifestation of the divine presence, and Joshua as the 'servant' of Moses. The tent of meeting also occurs as early as I Sam. 2.22. Of course the section vv. 7–11 speaks only of the setting up and use of the tent without anything having been said earlier about the making of this tent; in this case it is a probable hypothesis that in view of 26.1 ff. P the beginning of the section was subsequently omitted, especially as the formula at the beginning of v. 7 suggests that originally mention of the tent had already been made before this point. The tenses in vv. 7–11 are all imperfects, so we are not concerned here with a single occurrence, but with something which 'used' to happen. The question of the derivation of the tradition of vv. 7–11 is very hard to answer. From a literary aspect the section could be derived from the J narrative (the divine name Yahweh is used throughout) but in its present position it can have stood neither in the basic material of J, which runs from 24.12a, 13b directly to ch. 34, nor in the secondary stratum, in which the restoration of the tables in ch. 34 certainly followed directly upon their being broken in ch. 32.* Now if this is the case, then the whole of the derivation from J is questionable, and it is more plausible to assume that a special tradition was subsequently taken up into the J narrative, even in the pre-Deuteronomic period, so that the writer of vv. 1–6 already found it in this position. The question of the history of the tradition is also hard to answer. By its very nature a tent sanctuary belongs in the *milieu* of men who are not firmly settled and themselves live in tents; thus everything is in favour of the tradition of a tent-sanctuary going back to the time before Israel became settled in a cultivated land. But it is hardly possible to say more than this, for it is only said in much later literature (II Chron. 1.3, 13; cf. I Chron. 16.39; 21.29) that the 'tent of meeting' of the time of Moses still existed after the conquest and was erected in some place. We would thus be dealing with a tradition handed down from the time of the wanderings of Israel without any concrete point of attachment.

In a different way from P (25.8) the tent is represented as being pitched at some distance outside the camp (v. 7a). It was thus separated from the profane sphere of living, just as in the cultivated land it was usual for the sanctuaries to lie apart from the settlement's dwellings. The tent was thought of as a place of 'meeting', thus not

*This chapter contains other elements beside J.

as a place where God 'dwelt' permanently, but where he appeared from time to time. In this respect the concept of the tent is quite substantially different from the concepts associated with the ark, according to which the latter was a place for the constant (invisible) presence of God (cf. Num. 10.35). The divine presence proclaimed its approach in a descending 'pillar of cloud' (vv. 9 f.; cf. p. 109 above on 13.21 f.). Whether the pillar of cloud also used to descend if an individual Israelite inquired at the tent of meeting (v. 7b) is not said. The whole stress of the narrative lies on the great meetings between God and Moses which all Israelites witnessed at a distance from their tents with great awe (vv. 8, 10). At that time Moses used to enter the tent to await the appearance of Yahweh, who thereupon revealed himself in the pillar of cloud at the tent entrance (v. 9). Here in the tent, which is presumably to be imagined as a pointed tent,* Moses was vouchsafed a unique means of conversing with God which was not accorded to anyone elsewhere (that is the meaning of v. 11a, with which in particular Num. 12.6–8 and Deut. 34.10 should be compared). At the end, Joshua appears once again as Moses' closest companion (cf. 24.13a; 32.17) in his cultic function as keeper of the tent.

[12–17] The rest of the chapter introduces reflections, in the form of a conversation between Yahweh and Moses, about the means and possibility of the divine presence in Israel and especially before Moses. It is loosely joined to the command for departure in 32.34a (33.1a). Once again it seems as though Moses is imagined as present on the mountain. The 'tent of meeting' of vv. 7–11 is apparently not taken into consideration, so it must be assumed that the section vv. 12 ff. was in its present literary context earlier than vv. 7–11 (and vv. 1–6). But even the connection with ch. 32 is not completely smooth. Not only does the command to depart run differently in v. 12a*a* from that in vv. 32, 34a; also the repeated and emphasized reference to the fact that Moses has 'found favour in the sight of Yahweh' (vv. 12b, 13, 16 f.) has no special reference to ch. 32 or to any single Moses story which has anywhere gone before, but is certainly based just on the frequent dealings which God has hitherto had with Moses. We may therefore have here a subsequent literary addition to ch. 32 about whose period and derivation nothing definite can now be said. The demanding and forceful tone in which Moses speaks to Yahweh is striking. Faced with the command to depart, Moses asks to know whom (or what) Yahweh means to send

*Cf. A. Alt, *Kleine Schriften* III, pp. 233 ff.

with him as a sign or guarantee of his presence and his guidance (v. 12a) and what is his general intention (the 'ways of God' in v. 13 are certainly meant in this wider sense). Here the presupposition is that Sinai is the real place of the divine presence, and that with the departure from Sinai the further presence of God becomes questionable for Moses (and for Israel) and in any case needs to be mediated. In his request Moses appeals to the personal converse which has hitherto been vouchsafed to him by Yahweh (this is to be understood from the phrase 'know by name', vv. 12b, 17b) and the good will which has hitherto been shown towards him ('find favour', *ibid.*). Yahweh explains that his presence is to go with Moses (v. 14). This verse is often regarded as a question which is not indicated externally and is expressed only by the tone of voice, because this is the only way in which the continuation of the conversation is comprehensible. The present wording does not however favour this conception. The text rather means that the first, brief promise of Yahweh, which is to 'give Moses rest' (v. 14b should be understood in this simple way) is still not a sufficient reply to Moses' urgent request and that he requires an explicit confirmation over and above this. It is not said how the 'presence', the side of the divine being presented to men which gives a particularly direct representation of this being,* is to manifest itself in such a way that men may 'know' (v. 16a) it to be there and know that because it is there Israel has been marked out above all the other peoples upon earth (v. 16b). Perhaps the thought here is of the worship of Yahweh in the cult at the sanctuaries of Israel, to which men go to 'see' the divine 'face' (cf. p. 192 above on 23.17). In this way Yahweh's 'face' reveals its presence in the cult.

[18–23] Moses' request that he may catch sight of Yahweh's 'glory', i.e. the appearance of the divine majesty, joins on very abruptly to the closing promise, v. 17. We evidently have here a supplement which, moreover, is not itself a literary unity, as is shown by the threefold beginning to the divine speech in vv. 19–21. As the word 'glory' occurs only once again, in v. 22, the primary continuation of v. 18 may be in vv. 21–23. According to this Yahweh grants the fulfilment of the request, but only with qualifications. Near to Yahweh's abode—so concretely is the event here imagined—there is a place (perhaps even a 'holy place' is meant); there on a rock Moses is to await the passing of Yahweh's 'glory' (v. 21). But while his

*Cf. Isa. 63.9, also Deut. 4.37 and as a summary W. Eichrodt, *Theologie des Alten Testaments* II, ch. 12.3.

glory passes by, Yahweh will show Moses a place in the cleft of a rock
and at the same time—with a view to the dangerousness of this
moment—will cover him protectively with his hand (v. 22) so that
eventually Moses can only look at the back of the glory when it has
passed by (v. 23a). It must be enough for him to know that the glory
of Yahweh has passed by him. He may not see it 'from the front'
(v. 23b); in this last sentence the word 'face' is to be understood in its
context as meaning 'front side', but at the same time the word 'face'
is nevertheless there. With regard to this a later writer has inserted
the sentence v. 20, as no mortal man may see the face of Yahweh. The
reason why Moses is nevertheless granted the request which he
makes in v. 18, at least to the extent that is possible for him as a
mere man, is given in the supplementary v. 19, which says that God
can bestow his grace and mercy upon whom he will, even to the
extent of making his 'goodness' (the application of this term to God
is here strange) pass before a man favoured in this way, while at the
same time proclaiming his real name. Although the language is
completely different, the passage vv. 18, 21–23 recalls I Kings 19.9a,
11–13a. It gives the impression that some definite local knowledge,
perhaps even a local Sinai tradition, underlies it.

(c) ANOTHER COVENANT: 34.1–35

34 [1] The LORD said to Moses, 'Cut two tables of stone like the first;
and I will write upon the tables the words that were on the first tables,
which you broke. [2] Be ready in the morning, and come up in the morning to Mount Sinai, and present yourself there to me on the top of the
mountain. [3] No man shall come up with you, and let no man be seen
throughout all the mountain; let no flocks or herds feed before that
mountain.' [4] So Moses cut two tables of stone like the first; and he rose
early in the morning and went up on Mount Sinai, as the LORD had
commanded him, and took in his hand two tables of stone. [5] And the
LORD descended in the cloud and stood with him there, and proclaimed
the name of the LORD. [6] The LORD passed before him, and proclaimed,
'The LORD, the LORD, a God merciful and gracious, slow to anger, and
abounding in steadfast love and faithfulness, [7] keeping steadfast love
for thousands, forgiving iniquity and transgression and sin, but who will
by no means clear the guilty, visiting the iniquity of the fathers upon
the children and the children's children, to the third and fourth
generation.' [8] And Moses made haste to bow his head toward the earth,
and worshipped. [9] And he said, 'If now I have found favour in thy
sight, O LORD, let the LORD, I pray thee, go in the midst of us, although
it is a stiff-necked people; and pardon our iniquity and our sin, and
take us for thy inheritance.'

10 And he said, 'Behold, I make a covenant. Before all your people I will do marvels, such as have not been wrought in all the earth or in any nation; and all the people among whom you are shall see the work of the LORD; for it is a terrible thing that I will do with you.

11 'Observe what I command you this day. Behold, I will drive out before you the Amorites, the Canaanites, the Hittites, the Perizzites, the Hivites, and the Jebusites. 12 Take heed to yourself, lest you make a covenant with the inhabitants of the land whither you go, lest it become a snare in the midst of you. 13 You shall tear down their altars, and break their pillars, and cut down their Asherim 14 (for you shall worship no other god, for the LORD, whose name is Jealous, is a jealous God), 15 lest you make a covenant with the inhabitants of the land, and when they play the harlot after their gods and sacrifice to their gods and one invites you, you eat of his sacrifice, 16 and you take of their daughters for your sons, and their daughters play the harlot after their gods and make your sons play the harlot after their gods.

17 'You shall make for yourself no molten gods.

18 'The feast of unleavened bread you shall keep. Seven days you shall eat unleavened bread, as I commanded you, at the time appointed in the month Abib; for in the month Abib you came out from Egypt. 19 All that opens the womb is mine, all your male cattle, the firstlings of cow and sheep. 20 The firstling of an ass you shall redeem with a lamb, or if you will not redeem it you shall break its neck. All the first-born of your sons you shall redeem. And none shall appear before me empty.

21 'Six days you shall work, but on the seventh day you shall rest; in ploughing time and in harvest you shall rest. 22 And you shall observe the feast of weeks, the first fruits of wheat harvest, and the feast of ingathering at the year's end. 23 Three times in the year shall all your males appear before the LORD God, the God of Israel. 24 For I will cast out nations before you, and enlarge your borders; neither shall any man desire your land, when you go up to appear before the LORD your God three times in the year.

25 'You shall not offer the blood of my sacrifice with leaven; neither shall the sacrifice of the feast of the passover be left until the morning. 26 The first of the first fruits of your ground you shall bring to the house of the LORD your God. You shall not boil a kid in its mother's milk.'

27 And the LORD said to Moses, 'Write these words; in accordance with these words I have made a covenant with you and with Israel.' 28 And he was there with the LORD forty days and forty nights; he neither ate bread nor drank water. And he wrote upon the tables the words of the covenant, the ten commandments.

29 When Moses came down from Mount Sinai, with the two tables of the testimony in his hand as he came down from the mountain, Moses did not know that the skin of his face shone because he had been talking with God. 30 And when Aaron and all the people of Israel saw Moses, behold, the skin of his face shone, and they were afraid to come near him. 31 But Moses called to them; and Aaron and all the leaders of the congregation returned to him, and Moses talked with them.

[32] And afterward all the people of Israel came near, and he gave them in commandment all that the LORD had spoken with him in Mount Sinai. [33] And when Moses had finished speaking with them, he put a veil on his face; [34] but whenever Moses went in before the LORD to speak with him, he took the veil off, until he came out; and when he came out, and told the people of Israel what he was commanded, [35] the people of Israel saw the face of Moses, that the skin of Moses' face shone; and Moses would put the veil upon his face again, until he went in to speak with him.

It is generally recognized that the basic material of this chapter is the J narrative of the covenant on Sinai, and that at the same time it provides the most explicit details we have in the Old Testament about the way in which this covenant is made. Yahweh's announcement in v. 10 that he now intends to make a covenant, and his closing words in v. 27 that he has now made a covenant, leave no doubt that it is here that we have the fundamental action of the covenant. In the Book of Exodus as it has been transmitted these circumstances are somewhat obscured, as in the present context it seems as though we have merely the renewal of the broken tables and as according to other sources there has already been mention of a covenant in 24.1–11. But no part of 24.1–11 belongs to J, and the story of the golden calf and of the breaking of the tables is manifestly a later addition to the J narrative (see pp. 243 f. above). In J as it was originally written, the preparations for the theophany on mount Sinai and the theophany itself were first reported in ch. 19, and then the original J probably had some part of 24.12–15a according to which Moses was summoned up the mountain. Ch. 34 was at first attached directly to this point. The references to the first, broken tables at the beginning of ch. 34 are inserted only loosely into the basic material of the text and can easily be separated as secondary references to ch. 32. Ch. 34 also seems to have acquired all sorts of secondary additions elsewhere; they betray themselves through their interruption of the smooth sequence of events and so can easily be recognized and excised. It is understandable that a great deal more which seemed as though it should have appeared in this important passage has been added to the report of the central act of the covenant by later hands. This is particularly true of the closing section, vv. 29–35 (on this see p. 267 below).

[1–9] Moses receives the command that he shall 'cut' two tables of stone out of the rock of the sacred mountain, i.e. he is to prepare stone to make smooth tables with some sort of regular shape. Their purpose is not at first indicated (only secondarily in v. 1b) but Moses is presumed to know it. 'Be ready' (v. 2a) probably means a cultic or ritual preparation for the forthcoming encounter with God (cf. 19.11a) for which Moses is to present himself the following morning 'on the top of the mountain' (v. 2b*b*). As according to the original J text of 24.12–15a Moses has already climbed the mountain, the meaning must be that he is to go up from his immediate position somewhere on the massif of the mountain and climb to the summit, as the express mention of 'the top' makes clear. In that case we are to regard v. 2b*a* as an addition which has Moses descending from the mountain again perhaps at the end of ch. 32 (otherwise it would have to be assumed that the original J had no part at all of 24.12–15a); then the prohibition in v. 3 is also to be explained as secondary; as in view of the imminent theophany (cf. 19.12–13a), so now too in view of the imminent covenant, it is intended so that the *tabu* of the holy mountain may be strictly preserved. The description of the carrying out of the command in v. 4 in that case means the ascent of Moses to the summit. Now too Yahweh 'descends' on the mountain just as in the theophany narrated by J (19.18, 20; cf. p. 159 above). It is hard to decide whether the subject of the clause 5a*b* is meant to be Moses or Yahweh. In any case Moses pays Yahweh the cultic honour of calling upon his name when he appears (v. 5b). According to v. 6a*a*, whose authenticity in J is in fact questionable, Yahweh only passes before Moses when he appears and then speaks to him from some distant place shrouded in mystery. In any case, v. 8 describes the reaction of Moses to the appearance, or passing by, of Yahweh. A more lengthy address by Yahweh to Moses, which now stands in vv. 6 ab*b*, 7, is out of place in front of it; we have here an addition which is made up of customary, stereotyped phrases (on v. 6ab*b* see Ps. 103.8 etc. and on v. 7 cf. Ex. 20.5 f. etc.). Verse 9 is surely also secondary, as it broaches the subject of the departure from Sinai, which does not belong here.

[10–13] With lapidary brevity there now follows in the original text the proclamation of the covenant (v. 10a*a*) and the introduction to a set of 'commandments' (v. 11a). This brevity is now obscured by some obviously later additions. The rest of v. 10 introduces a promise of awesome 'marvels' which God will 'do with Moses', which will be seen by all the people. This promise interrupts the train of thought in the divine speech, and its purpose remains obscure; perhaps it has in mind the marvels narrated in the continuation of the theme of the desert wanderings (Num. 11 ff.), though in this passage there is no real occasion for a reference to them. There are additions in vv. 11b–13 in deuteronomistic language, in which the people are addressed partly in the singular and partly in the plural; they introduce the warning, frequent in Deuteronomy and the deuteronomistic writings, against the inhabitants of the land which is to be taken in possession and against their cultic institutions. [14–26] Then with v. 14a the series of 'commandments' announced in v. 11 begins. They are once again interrupted at the beginning in vv. 14b–16 by a lengthy addition. Now these commandments are, as in 20.2–17, formulated with apodeictic brevity. Accordingly, this brevity might also be expected in the first commandment, and the statements which give reasons for and expand the commandment are here, as in 20.4 ff., to be regarded as secondary. Moreover, once again in vv. 14b–16 we find a deuteronomistic style, and especially the deuteronomistic warning against the dwellers in the land and their cults, thus giving the general prohibition of v. 14a a definite application. The series of commandments in vv. 14a, 17 ff. is formed by the collecting together of apodeictic sentences of mixed style and is in this respect comparable with 20.2–17;* here, however, the mixture of styles is still more marked, as among the requirements formulated both negatively and positively we have the general statement of v. 19a. It has of necessity to be asked whether the collection is still in its original form. According to v. 28b*b* Yahweh spoke 'ten commandments'. The mere position of this remark, at the end, shows that it is an addition. But whoever made this addition must have found 'ten commandments' in vv. 14–26,* and in view of 20.2–17 the original number of ten is most probable. The present passage offers more than 'ten commandments'. Now the separation of the instructions for the three feasts (vv. 18, 22) which in content belong together is in itself particularly striking. It can lead us to two different conclusions. These particular instructions might subsequently have been added in the margin and then have been brought into the text at different places, particularly in view of 23.14–19, a passage which is extremely closely connected with 34.10–26. The requirement to appear three times a year before the face of Yahweh (v. 23) would thus be interpreted in a suitable way. But alternatively the central passage between v. 18 and v. 22 could be a secondary addition which was unfortunately introduced into the text between v. 18 and v. 22, which belong together, at a

*This section is derived from more than one source.

later date. This intermediary section also consists of clauses familiar from elsewhere which could subsequently have been added here. In either case the result would be an original number of ten commandments. It is hardly possible to come to a firm conclusion in choosing between these two possibilities, especially as the content of the whole collection does not show any marked signs of arrangement elsewhere.

[**14a**] At the beginning stand the sentences whose content is without doubt the most important. First of all comes the prohibition of any foreign cult (14a). As 'worship' is a feature of the cult of all deities, the formula of v. 14a is to be understood as a general prohibition against the worship of all other gods. It thus says the same thing as 20.3, but in a different way. The expression 'no other god' presupposes the existence of a definite relationship with God. The foundation of a lasting relationship between God and the people here addressed is primary; it is only on this basis that the sentences have any validity and it is in this context that the first fundamental sentence has its setting. [**17**] After this requirement the 'molten gods' of v. 17 cannot possibly refer to foreign deities, which are already excluded by v. 14a, but only to images in the framework of the Yahweh cult (just as in 20.4). We cannot say definitely why the commandment particularly mentions molten images here, for images of gods made by another technique would hardly be permissible. Does this commandment in practice only contemplate the danger of the manufacture of molten images, so that other possibilities can be ignored? The reason for the commandment is certainly the same as in 20.4 (see pp. 162 f. above). [**18**] The clause about the feast of unleavened bread (v. 18) is almost identical verbally with 23.15a and may here as there originally have lacked the subordinate clauses which provide an introduction and justification for it. [**19–20**] The wording of the regulations about the first-born of man and beast (vv. 19, 20ab*a*) recurs almost completely in 13.1 f., 12 f. (for an explanation of the content see pp. 101 f. above). Only the catchword-like remarks of v. 19b, which do not fit the context well and were probably added later, have no close counterpart in ch. 13. The shorter composition of ch. 34 is surely original in comparison with the wider presentation of ch. 13, which refers to the slaughter of the first-born and the Exodus from Egypt. If vv. 19, 20ab*a* belong to the basic material of ch. 34, it follows on literary grounds that 13.1 f., 11–16 is of secondary character; even if we have here a supplement

to ch. 34 this would still be more original than the parallel piece in ch. 13. The short regulation v. 20b*b* is verbally identical with 23.15b. [21] The formulation of the sabbath commandment (v. 21) corresponds in the first half with 23.12a (another way of expressing this which still means the same thing occurs in 20.8 and 9–11). The regulation in v. 21b is unique; it enjoins the sabbath rest in ploughing time and in harvest also, i.e. in the chief working seasons of the agricultural year; this is evidently its meaning and not, as can also be understood from the wording, that the sabbath is only to be kept at the time specified. With this additional regulation the sabbath commandment, wherever its origin is to be sought, is in a remarkable way expressly introduced into the life of people firmly settled as inhabitants of an agricultural land. [22] The double sentence v. 22 corresponds with 23.16 except that here instead of the description 'Feast of harvest', the new expression 'Feast of weeks', which is certainly more recent and which became current usage at a later period, makes an appearance (for an explanation cf. Deut. 16.9), and the feast is referred especially to the wheat harvest as being the most important part of the whole of the grain harvest. Moreover, the term 'turn of the year' is used instead of 'beginning of the year' to define the time of the autumn festival, although both mean the same thing. [23–24] Verse 23 is again almost verbally identical with 23.17. In ch. 34, however, what is certainly a secondary addition has been made, which is meant to dispel any anxiety among the male Israelites, a number of whom must be imagined to live a good way from the centres of population, that the thrice yearly pilgrimages could endanger the safety of their land tenure (v. 24). Yahweh promises to see that no one (who that could be is not said; the formula does not allow us to think of external enemies) attempts to take over Israelite possessions; the phraseology at the beginning of this verse is deuteronomistic and so the whole verse may well be a deuteronomistic addition which understands the definition of v. 23 along the lines of the well-known deuteronomistic requirement of one central sanctuary, whereas the older time envisaged numerous sanctuaries throughout the land and therefore would have obviated the anxiety presupposed in v. 24. [25–26] The four clauses of vv. 25 f. also occur in 23.18–19 (for an explanation of their content see p. 192 above) in almost exactly the same words. In v. 25a, however, the formulation is rather more harsh than in 23.18, in so far as here we have the concrete word for 'slaughter' which can hardly have blood as its object* (the slaying of the victim and the offering of the blood are here combined in one sentence), and v. 25b makes special mention of the Passover, which in view of its nocturnal celebration fits very well with the content here and is presumably original (cf. 12.10); 23.18b on the other hand speaks quite generally of the 'feast' (the word 'feast' has almost certainly found its way into the text of 34.25b from 23.18b, for there is quite rightly no mention elsewhere of a 'Passover feast' as the Passover was not a feast but a special sacrificial usage).

The series of sentences in 34.10–26 has, as has been shown, a very close relationship with the collection of cultic regulations in 23. 14–19, within the framework of the Book of the Covenant, but at the beginning it also has unmistakable affinities of content with 20.2–17 (cf. also the original number ten which moreover occurs in similar fashion in 23.14–19). Nevertheless we can hardly speak of a mutual literary dependence of these pieces one upon another (apart from secondary individual additions). We rather have two different series of clauses of apodeictic law in Israel, each arranged into an easily understandable, easily memorable group of ten. For this reason we cannot with certainty define the temporal relationship between the two passages; they could have stood together and have been handed down together as early as in the stage of oral tradition. One thing alone is clear, that in 34.10–26 Israel is presumed to live in an agricultural land with its cultic festivals (the same also applies to 23.14–19, whereas nothing certain can be established in this respect for 20.2–17). It is customary to distinguish between 34.10–26 as 'a Cultic Decalogue' and 20.2–17 as an 'Ethical Decalogue'. This distinction expresses quite pertinently, though in somewhat unhappy terminology, a difference in the predominant interest, but we cannot speak of a fundamental opposition. J certainly did not for his part collect together the sentences of ch. 34, but took over the whole from the tradition which he knew as a collection of the basic divine commands laid upon Israel and understood it as the foundation of the Sinai covenant. [27–28] Then 'in accordance with these words' the covenant was made, according to J, with Yahweh (v. 27) and remarkably enough with Moses. True, 'with Israel' still stands at the end of the verse, but the remarkably lame position of these words hardly allows us to take them to be original, but requires us to see in them an interpretation which—naturally enough in fact—lets Moses

*[This harshness is toned down in the RSV rendering. Tr.]

stand vicariously for Israel as a partner in the covenant. According to J the covenant is made by Yahweh through a solemn declaration of his will; the verb in v. 27b is in the so-called declarative perfect, which is usually employed to express a statement which becomes binding the moment it is spoken. In this way J has expressed the one-sidedness of the act of making the covenant in a more unequivocal way than the narratives in 24.9–11 and 24.3–8, which still give the human partner a share in the making of the covenant by his participation in a covenant meal and his association in a sacrificial act. In J, Moses, as representative of Israel, has only to receive the explanation of the divine will; over and above that there remains only the task of writing on the prepared tables (v. 28) the 'words of the covenant' which he has been given and which from now on are to regulate the relationship between Israel and its God. In doing this J has at the same time firmly kept from the act of making the covenant on Sinai all thoughts of its being an action which is effective in itself, and has rooted it exclusively in the word of Yahweh. This word of Yahweh bases the Law of the Old Testament on the covenant relationship made by Yahweh, for the 'words of the covenant' are the sentences of apodeictic justice of vv. 10–26 which have just been given to Moses and which are now binding upon Israel as a partner in the covenant (cf. 24.8b, where it is Moses who explains 'all these words' as the basis of the covenant relationship). Human law also knew the making of a one-sided covenant in which someone in a high position took another person into a covenant relationship which gave this other the benefit of his protection, advocacy and the like.* The content of the term 'covenant' could thus without any alteration to its meaning be transferred to the relationship between God and people which was not a natural one, but which had been brought about by a one-sided, sovereign declaration of intent and had made Israel 'the people of Yahweh'. It is hard to explain the traditional element of the tables containing the 'words of the covenant', as nothing more is said in the old traditional material of the later fate of these tables, and only the deuteronomistic and Priestly writings have them transferred into the ark. Even the old tradition must surely have started from the fact that Israel took the tables along and that at a later date they were still preserved somewhere. Could a historic tradition stand behind the deuteronomistic reports of the 'great

*Cf. J. Begrich, *Zeitschrift für die alttestamentliche Wissenschaft*, NF 19, 1944, p. 1–11.

stones' with 'all the words of the law' (Deut. 27.2 ff.) which were to be set up on Mount 'Gerizim', and should this in fact be connected with the tradition of the Sinai tables?

[29–35] Also hard to assess is the story of Moses' 'shining face' (vv. 29–35). Despite some elements of P language which can, however, easily be cut out as additions ('Aaron', 'all the leaders of the congregation', 'the tables of the testimony') the passage as a whole does not give the impression of coming from P. But a place cannot be found for it in J either. In J the presuppositions for 'going in' and 'coming out' and 'speaking' with Yahweh (vv. 34 f.) are lacking; they were, however, given through the tent-tradition of 33.7–11. It is therefore probable that we have a special tradition comparable with 33.7–11 which was perhaps associated with a few observations by J about the descent of Moses and his report to the people (v. 29a*a*, 32b). The story is meant to explain the 'veil' (the Hebrew word occurs only here and etymologically perhaps means the 'covering') which Moses was accustomed to put on his face when he 'came out' from speaking with Yahweh to speak in the name of Yahweh to the people. Priests' masks are well evidenced in the history of religion; in the Old Testament world they occur in Egypt. With them the priest assumes the 'face' of his deity and identifies himself with him. This usage is unknown elsewhere in the Old Testament, though it may be that the so-called *tᵉrāpîm* originally used to be a mask for the face. But the present passage, which says nothing at all about the appearance of this mask, shows that the priest's mask (for Moses here appears in a priestly function) was not totally lacking in Israel even though we can discover no more about the time and place at which it was used. The Old Testament belief in God could not of course accept the original significance of the mask. It is therefore derived from Moses and explained by saying that because of Moses' unique meeting with God the skin of his face shone, so that the Israelites dared not look upon it and Moses had to cover up the divine glow on his face. The word used here for 'become shining' is rare in this significance; its meaning has to be deduced from the context. The word has a root similar in sound to the word 'horn'; for this reason old translations, among them the Latin Vulgate, speak here of a 'horned' Moses, and this rendering has had well-known influence in the pictorial arts. This idea cannot, however, be fitted in with the original sense, as one cannot say that the skin of the face is 'horned'.

6. THE INSTRUCTIONS ARE CARRIED OUT: 35.1 – 39.43

35[1] Moses assembled all the congregation of the people of Israel, and said to them, 'These are the things which the LORD has commanded you to do. [2] Six days shall work be done, but on the seventh day you shall have a holy sabbath of solemn rest to the LORD; whoever does any work on it shall be put to death; [3] you shall kindle no fire in all your habitations on the sabbath day.'

4 Moses said to all the congregation of the people of Israel, 'This is the thing which the LORD has commanded. [5] Take from among you an offering to the LORD; whoever is of a generous heart, let him bring the LORD's offering: gold, silver, and bronze; [6] blue and purple and scarlet stuff and fine twined linen; goats' hair, [7] tanned rams' skins, and goatskins; acacia wood, [8] oil for the light, spices for the anointing oil and for the fragrant incense, [9] and onyx stones and stones for setting, for the ephod and for the breastpiece.

10 'And let every able man among you come and make all that the LORD has commanded: the tabernacle, [11] its tent and its covering, its hooks and its frames, its bars, its pillars, and its bases; [12] the ark with its poles, the mercy seat, and the veil of the screen; [13] the table with its poles and all its utensils, and the bread of the Presence; [14] the lampstand also for the light, with its utensils and its lamps, and the oil for the light; [15] and the altar of incense, with its poles, and the anointing oil and the fragrant incense, and the screen for the door, at the door of the tabernacle; [16] the altar of burnt offering, with its grating of bronze, its poles, and all its utensils, the laver and its base; [17] the hangings of the court, its pillars and its bases, and the screen for the gate of the court; [18] the pegs of the tabernacle and the pegs of the court, and their cords; [19] the finely wrought garments for ministering in the holy place, the holy garments for Aaron the priest, and the garments of his sons, for their service as priests.'

20 Then all the congregation of the people of Israel departed from the presence of Moses. [21] And they came, every one whose heart stirred him, and every one whose spirit moved him, and brought the LORD's offering to be used for the tent of meeting, and for all its service, and for the holy garments. [22] So they came, both men and women; all who were of a willing heart brought brooches and earrings and signet rings and armlets, all sorts of gold objects, every man dedicating an offering of gold to the LORD. [23] And every man with whom was found blue or purple or scarlet stuff or fine linen or goats' hair or tanned rams' skins or goatskins, brought them. [24] Every one who could make an offering of silver or bronze brought it as the LORD's offering; and every man with whom was found acacia wood of any use in the work, brought it. [25] And all women who had ability spun with their hands, and brought what they had spun in blue and purple and scarlet stuff and fine twined linen; [26] all the women whose hearts were moved with ability spun the goats' hair. [27] And the leaders brought onyx stones and stones to be set, for the ephod and for the breastpiece, [28] and spices and

oil for the light, and for the anointing oil, and for the fragrant incense.
[29] All the men and women, the people of Israel, whose heart moved
them to bring anything for the work which the LORD had commanded
by Moses to be done, brought it as their freewill offering to the LORD.

[30] And Moses said to the people of Israel, 'See, the LORD has called by
name Bezalel the son of Uri, son of Hur, of the tribe of Judah; [31] and
he has filled him with the Spirit of God, with ability, with intelligence,
with knowledge, and with all craftsmanship, [32] to devise artistic designs, to work in gold and silver and bronze, [33] in cutting stones for
setting, and in carving wood, for work in every skilled craft. [34] And he
has inspired him to teach, both him and Oholiab the son of Ahisamach
of the tribe of Dan. [35] He has filled them with ability to do every sort
of work done by a craftsman or by a designer or by an embroiderer in
blue and purple and scarlet stuff and fine twined linen, or by a weaver
—by any sort of workman or skilled designer. **36**[1] Bezalel and Oholiab
and every able man in whom the LORD has put ability and intelligence
to know how to do any work in the construction of the sanctuary shall
work in accordance with all that the LORD has commanded.'

2 And Moses called Bezalel and Oholiab and every able man in
whose mind the LORD had put ability, every one whose heart stirred
him up to come to do the work; [3] and they received from Moses all the
freewill offering which the people of Israel had brought for doing the
work on the sanctuary. They still kept bringing him freewill offerings
every morning, [4] so that all the able men who were doing every sort of
task on the sanctuary came, each from the task that he was doing, [5] and
said to Moses, 'The people bring much more than enough for doing the
work which the LORD has commanded us to do.' [6] So Moses gave
command, and word was proclaimed throughout the camp, 'Let
neither man nor woman do anything more for the offering for the
sanctuary.' So the people were restrained from bringing; [7] for the stuff
they had was sufficient to do all the work, and more.

8 And all the able men among the workmen made the tabernacle
with ten curtains; they were made of fine twined linen and blue and
purple and scarlet stuff, with cherubim skilfully worked. [9] The length
of each curtain was twenty-eight cubits, and the breadth of each curtain four cubits; all the curtains had the same measure.

10 And he coupled five curtains to one another, and the other five
curtains he coupled to one another. [11] And he made loops of blue on
the edge of the outmost curtain of the first set; likewise he made them
on the edge of the outmost curtain of the second set; [12] he made fifty
loops on the one curtain, and he made fifty loops on the edge of the
curtain that was in the second set; the loops were opposite one another.
[13] And he made fifty clasps of gold, and coupled the curtains one to the
other with clasps; so the tabernacle was one whole.

14 He also made curtains of goats' hair for a tent over the tabernacle;
he made eleven curtains. [15] The length of each curtain was thirty
cubits, and the breadth of each curtain four cubits; the eleven curtains
had the same measure. [16] He coupled five curtains by themselves, and

six curtains by themselves. [17] And he made fifty loops on the edge of the outmost curtain of the one set, and fifty loops on the edge of the other connecting curtain. [18] And he made fifty clasps of bronze to couple the tent together that it might be one whole. [19] And he made for the tent a covering of tanned rams' skins and goatskins.

20 Then he made the upright frames for the tabernacle of acacia wood. [21] Ten cubits was the length of a frame, and a cubit and a half the breadth of each frame. [22] Each frame had two tenons, for fitting together; he did this for all the frames of the tabernacle. [23] The frames for the tabernacle he made thus: twenty frames for the south side; [24] and he made forty bases of silver under the twenty frames, two bases under one frame for its two tenons, and two bases under another frame for its two tenons. [25] And for the second side of the tabernacle, on the north side, he made twenty frames [26] and their forty bases of silver, two bases under one frame and two bases under another frame. [27] And for the rear of the tabernacle westward he made six frames. [28] And he made two frames for corners of the tabernacle in the rear. [29] And they were separate beneath, but joined at the top, at the first ring; he made two of them thus, for the two corners. [30] There were eight frames with their bases of silver: sixteen bases, under every frame two bases.

31 And he made bars of acacia wood, five for the frames of the one side of the tabernacle, [32] and five bars for the frames of the other side of the tabernacle, and five bars for the frames of the tabernacle at the rear westward. [33] And he made the middle bar to pass through from end to end halfway up the frames. [34] And he overlaid the frames with gold, and made their rings of gold for holders for the bars, and overlaid the bars with gold.

35 And he made the veil of blue and purple and scarlet stuff and fine twined linen; with cherubim skilfully worked he made it. [36] And for it he made four pillars of acacia, and overlaid them with gold; their hooks were of gold, and he cast for them four bases of silver. [37] He also made a screen for the door of the tent, of blue and purple and scarlet stuff and fine twined linen, embroidered with needlework; [38] and its five pillars with their hooks. He overlaid their capitals, and their fillets were of gold, but their five bases were of bronze.

37[1] Bezalel made the ark of acacia wood; two cubits and a half was its length, a cubit and a half its breadth, and a cubit and a half its height. [2] And he overlaid it with pure gold within and without, and made a moulding of gold around it. [3] And he cast for it four rings of gold for its four corners, two rings on its one side and two rings on its other side. [4] And he made poles of acacia wood, and overlaid them with gold, [5] and put the poles into the rings on the sides of the ark, to carry the ark. [6] And he made a mercy seat of pure gold; two cubits and a half was its length, and a cubit and a half its breadth. [7] And he made two cherubim of hammered gold; on the two ends of the mercy seat he made them, [8] one cherub on the one end, and one cherub on the other end; of one piece with the mercy seat he made the cherubim on its two ends. [9] The cherubim spread out their wings above, overshadowing the mercy seat with their wings, with their faces one to another; toward the mercy seat were the faces of the cherubim.

10 He also made the table of acacia wood; two cubits was its length, a cubit its breadth, and a cubit and a half its height; [11] and he overlaid it with pure gold, and made a moulding of gold around it. [12] And he made around it a frame a handbreadth wide, and made a moulding of gold around the frame. [13] He cast for it four rings of gold, and fastened the rings to the four corners at its four legs. [14] Close to the frame were the rings, as holders for the poles to carry the table. [15] He made the poles of acacia wood to carry the table, and overlaid them with gold. [16] And he made the vessels of pure gold which were to be upon the table, its plates and dishes for incense, and its bowls and flagons with which to pour libations.

17 He also made the lampstand of pure gold. The base and the shaft of the lampstand were made of hammered work; its cups, its capitals, and its flowers were of one piece with it. [18] And there were six branches going out of its sides, three branches of the lampstand out of one side of it and three branches of the lampstand out of the other side of it; [19] three cups made like almonds, each with capital and flower, on one branch, and three cups made like almonds, each with capital and flower, on the other branch—so for the six branches going out of the lampstand. [20] And on the lampstand itself were four cups made like almonds, with their capitals and flowers, [21] and a capital of one piece with it under each pair of the six branches going out of it. [22] Their capitals and their branches were of one piece with it; the whole of it was one piece of hammered work of pure gold. [23] And he made its seven lamps and its snuffers and its trays of pure gold. [24] He made it and all its utensils of a talent of pure gold.

25 He made the altar of incense of acacia wood; its length was a cubit, and its breadth was a cubit; it was square, and two cubits was its height; its horns were of one piece with it. [26] He overlaid it with pure gold, its top, and its sides round about, and its horns; and he made a moulding of gold round about it, [27] and made two rings of gold on it under its moulding, on two opposite sides of it, as holders for the poles with which to carry it. [28] And he made the poles of acacia wood, and overlaid them with gold.

29 He made the holy anointing oil also, and the pure fragrant incense, blended as by the perfumer.

38[1] He made the altar of burnt offering also of acacia wood; five cubits was its length, and five cubits its breadth; it was square, and three cubits was its height. [2] He made horns for it on its four corners; its horns were of one piece with it, and he overlaid it with bronze. [3] And he made all the utensils of the altar, the pots, the shovels, the basins, the forks, and the fire pans: all its utensils he made of bronze. [4] And he made for the altar a grating, a network of bronze, under its ledge, extending halfway down. [5] He cast four rings on the four corners of the bronze grating as holders for the poles; [6] he made the poles of acacia wood, and overlaid them with bronze. [7] And he put the poles through the rings on the sides of the altar, to carry it with them; he made it hollow, with boards.

8 And he made the laver of bronze and its base of bronze, from the mirrors of the ministering women who ministered at the door of the tent of meeting.

9 And he made the court; for the south side the hangings of the court were of fine twined linen, a hundred cubits; 10 their pillars were twenty and their bases twenty, of bronze, but the hooks of the pillars and their fillets were of silver. 11 And for the north side a hundred cubits, their pillars twenty, their bases twenty, of bronze, but the hooks of the pillars and their fillets of silver. 12 And for the west side were hangings of fifty cubits, their pillars ten, and their sockets ten; the hooks of the pillars and their fillets were of silver. 13 And for the front to the east, fifty cubits. 14 The hangings for one side of the gate were fifteen cubits, with three pillars and three bases. 15 And so for the other side; on this hand and that hand by the gate of the court were hangings of fifteen cubits, with three pillars and three bases. 16 All the hangings round about the court were of fine twined linen. 17 And the bases for the pillars were of bronze, but the hooks of the pillars and their fillets were of silver; the overlaying of their capitals were also of silver, and all the pillars of the court were filleted with silver. 18 And the screen for the gate of the court was embroidered with needlework in blue and purple and scarlet stuff and fine twined linen; it was twenty cubits long and five cubits high in its breadth, corresponding to the hangings of the court. 19 And their pillars were four; their four bases were of bronze, their hooks of silver, and the overlaying of their capitals and their fillets of silver. 20 And all the pegs for the tabernacle and for the court round about were of bronze.

21 This is the sum of the things for the tabernacle, the tabernacle of the testimony, as they were counted at the commandment of Moses, for the work of the Levites under the direction of Ithamar the son of Aaron the priest. 22 Bezalel the son of Uri, son of Hur, of the tribe of Judah, made all that the LORD commanded Moses; 23 and with him was Oholiab the son of Ahisamach, of the tribe of Dan, a craftsman and designer and embroiderer in blue and purple and scarlet stuff and fine twined linen.

24 All the gold that was used for the work, in all the construction of the sanctuary, the gold from the offering, was twenty-nine talents and seven hundred and thirty shekels, by the shekel of the sanctuary. 25 And the silver from those of the congregation who were numbered was a hundred talents and a thousand seven hundred and seventy-five shekels, by the shekel of the sanctuary: 26 a beka a head (that is, half a shekel, by the shekel of the sanctuary), for every one who was numbered in the census, from twenty years old and upward, for six hundred and three thousand, five hundred and fifty men. 27 The hundred talents of silver were for casting the bases of the sanctuary, and the bases of the veil; a hundred bases for the hundred talents, a talent for a base. 28 And of the thousand seven hundred and seventy-five shekels he made hooks

for the pillars, and overlaid their capitals and made fillets for them. [29] And the bronze that was contributed was seventy talents, and two thousand and four hundred shekels; [30] with it he made the bases for the door of the tent of meeting, the bronze altar and the bronze grating for it and all the utensils of the altar, [31] the bases round about the court, and the bases of the gate of the court, all the pegs of the tabernacle, and all the pegs round about the court.

39[1] And of the blue and purple and scarlet stuff they made finely wrought garments, for ministering in the holy place; they made the holy garments for Aaron; as the Lord had commanded Moses.

2 And he made the ephod of gold, blue and purple and scarlet stuff, and fine twined linen. [3] And gold leaf was hammered out and cut into threads to work into the blue and purple and the scarlet stuff, and into the fine twined linen, in skilled design. [4] They made for the ephod shoulder-pieces, joined to it at its two edges. [5] And the skilfully woven band upon it, to gird it on, was of the same materials and workmanship, of gold, blue and purple and scarlet stuff, and fine twined linen; as the Lord had commanded Moses.

6 The onyx stones were prepared, enclosed in settings of gold filigree and engraved like the engravings of a signet, according to the names of the sons of Israel. [7] And he set them on the shoulder-pieces of the ephod, to be stones of remembrance for the sons of Israel; as the Lord had commanded Moses.

8 He made the breastpiece, in skilled work, like the work of the ephod, of gold, blue and purple and scarlet stuff, and fine twined linen. [9] It was square; the breastpiece was made double, a span its length and a span its breadth when doubled. [10] And they set in it four rows of stones. A row of sardius, topaz, and carbuncle was the first row; [11] and the second row, an emerald, a sapphire, and a diamond; [12] and the third row, a jacinth, an agate, and an amethyst; [13] and the fourth row, a beryl, an onyx, and a jasper; they were enclosed in settings of gold filigree. [14] There were twelve stones with their names according to the names of the sons of Israel; they were like signets, each engraved with its name, for the twelve tribes. [15] And they made on the breastpiece twisted chains like cords, of pure gold; [16] and they made two settings of gold filigree and two gold rings, and put the two rings on the two edges of the breastpiece; [17] and they put the two cords of gold in the two rings at the edges of the breastpiece. [18] Two ends of the two cords they had attached to the two settings of filigree; thus they attached it in front to the shoulder-pieces of the ephod. [19] Then they made two rings of gold, and put them at the two ends of the breastpiece, on its inside edge next to the ephod. [20] And they made two rings of gold, and attached them in front to the lower part of the two shoulder-pieces of the ephod, at its joining above the skilfully woven band of the ephod. [21] And they bound the breastpiece by its rings to the rings of the ephod with a lace of blue, so that it should lie upon the skilfully woven band of the ephod, and that the breastpice should not come loose from the ephod; as the Lord had commanded Moses.

22 He also made the robe of the ephod woven all of blue; [23] and the opening of the robe in it was like the opening in a garment, with a binding around the opening, that it might not be torn. [24] On the skirts of the robe they made pomegranates of blue and purple and scarlet stuff and fine twined linen. [25] They also made bells of pure gold, and put the bells between the pomegranates upon the skirts of the robe round about, between the pomegranates; [26] a bell and a pomegranate, a bell and a pomegranate round about upon the skirts of the robe for ministering; as the LORD had commanded Moses.

27 They also made the coats, woven of fine linen, for Aaron and his sons, [28] and the turban of fine linen, and the caps of fine linen, and the linen breeches of fine twined linen, [29] and the girdle of fine twined linen and of blue and purple and scarlet stuff, embroidered with needlework; as the LORD had commanded Moses.

30 And they made the plate of the holy crown of pure gold, and wrote upon it an inscription, like the engraving of a signet, 'Holy to the LORD'. [31] And they tied to it a lace of blue, to fasten it on the turban above; as the LORD had commanded Moses.

32 Thus all the work of the tabernacle of the tent of meeting was finished; and the people of Israel had done according to all that the LORD had commanded Moses; so had they done. [33] And they brought the tabernacle to Moses, the tent and all its utensils, its hooks, its frames, its bars, its pillars, and its bases; [34] the covering of tanned rams' skins and goatskins, and the veil of the screen; [35] the ark of the testimony with its poles and the mercy seat; [36] the table with all its utensils, and the bread of the Presence; [37] the lampstand of pure gold and its lamps with the lamps set and all its utensils, and the oil for the light; [38] the golden altar, the anointing oil and the fragrant incense, and the screen for the door of the tent; [39] the bronze altar, and its grating of bronze, its poles, and all its utensils; the laver and its base; [40] the hangings of the court, its pillars, and its bases, and the screen for the gate of the court, its cords, and its pegs; and all the utensils for the service of the tabernacle, for the tent of meeting; [41] the finely worked garments for ministering in the holy place, the holy garments for Aaron the priest, and the garments of his sons to serve as priests. [42] According to all that the LORD had commanded Moses, so the people of Israel had done all the work. [43] And Moses saw all the work, and behold, they had done it; as the LORD had commanded, so had they done it. And Moses blessed them.

Chs. 35–39 report in detail, and for the most part in parallel wording, how the divine instructions of chs. 25–31, given to Moses on the mountain, are carried out. We thus meet the P tradition here once again. Of course this long report of the work does not belong to the original basic P narrative. The pedantic repetition of the whole of chs. 25–31, given there in the form of a command and now in the form of a report on the execution of the work, would not in itself be a valid reason for holding the section to be secondary, for in view of the character of P as it can be observed elsewhere, such a long repetition in his work might be deemed quite possible. But it is quite clear that the secondary literary elements in chs. 25–31, which by their very position prove to be additions (cf. especially chs. 30–31), have in chs. 35–39 been worked into the whole and have been incorporated into a quite probable systematic order. Thus chs. 35–39 presuppose both the basic material and the additions of chs. 25–31. In some points the narrative in chs. 35–39 has been extended even beyond that of chs. 25–31. But even here it is not so much a case of the communication of further independent traditions as of making obvious narrative constructions on the basis of chs. 25–31. Besides this there are still in chs. 35–39 a number of secondary literary passages which have subsequently been added.

[35.1–3] Both these two last features are immediately true of the beginning of ch. 35. Before a detailed description, developed in narrative form beyond the relatively brief instructions of 25.1–7, of the offerings required of the Israelites in ch. 25, the sabbath commandment is stressed in 35.1–3, a passage which by its position before the introductory formula v. 4 is shown to be an addition with its own introductory formula (v. 1). Remarkable in this addition is the special prohibition against kindling fire in the Israelite dwellings on the sabbath (v. 3). Whether this note, as a literary product very late, can in fact be regarded, in view of its concrete nature, as being a primitive sabbath regulation in whose place the general commandment for rest from work, elsewhere customary, was only later introduced, unfortunately can no longer be decided because of the lack of parallels to the passage.

[35.4–36.7] Once the divine command of 25.2–7 has in vv. 4–9 been handed on almost literally to the Israelites, there follows first of all in vv. 10–19, before it has been said that the command was carried out, a long list of all the items to be provided, which interrupts the sequence and is probably to be regarded as secondary. In a description which has been given quite extensive narrative form, vv. 20–29 report how the Israelites carried out the orders of vv. 4–9; these verses are intended to show the zeal of the Israelites in providing the materials necessary for the building of the entire sanctuary. Men and women together gave up their pieces of golden jewellery, among which brooches (or nose-rings), earrings, signet rings and armlets are mentioned (v. 22; v. 22b*b* is an addition of quite general content).

All the men together looked for whatever material they had to bring, whether it was costly fabric or the hides of beasts or silver or bronze or acacia wood (vv. 23 f.), while the women, who were skilful in this, busied themselves in spinning for the costly fabric and goats' hair (for the sides of the tent) (vv. 26 f.). Finally, the leaders, as the most prominent among the Israelites, brought the necessary precious stones and the costly spices (vv. 27 f.). General eagerness was so great that it did not even cease once the skilled craftsmen had gone off to the work for which they had been detailed, so that these felt themselves compelled to go to Moses to bring a stop to the surplus of contributions, as there was already more material than was necessary (36.3b–7). Meanwhile Moses had handed on to the Israelites the divine choice of Bezalel as the leader of all works of handicraft (35.30–33 following 31.2–5). According to the divine command he, together with Oholiab (cf. 31.6a), who is introduced in a noticeably lame way in 35.34, and also the other men who are skilled in a craft, are to carry out all the necessary work (36.1), and therefore once Moses has expressly summoned them to this work (36.2) they receive the contributions of material made by the Israelites (36.3a). There are a number of difficulties in 35.34 f. At the beginning, Moses reveals that Yahweh has given the gift of teaching to Bezalel and also to Oholiab, who was introduced later. This apparently means that these two are to instruct the great host of manual workers who are engaged on the work in their special tasks. But this is not said in what follows, so that one may assume that in v. 35 the transmitted text is no longer fully intact and perhaps no longer quite complete.

[36.8–39.43] Once the necessary preparations had been made, the great work could begin. From 36.8 onwards it is reported how the minute instructions of chs. 25–31 were in fact carried out. Here in 36.8 the whole of the body of able men appears as a subject, whereas in what follows (for the first time in 36.14) a singular subject appears which according to 37.1 (cf. also 38.22) is meant to be Bezalel. This discrepancy, which is only of a formal nature and has been taken over automatically from the transmitted text of 25.10, obviously escaped the notice of the author. There is a difference in the sequence of work between chs. 25–31 and chs. 36–39. Whereas in the setting of the instructions the ark and the remaining contents of the inner sanctuary stand at the beginning as being the most important, when the instructions are carried out the making of the tabernacle comes first and, as the real sanctuary would require, progress is made from the outside inwards, as evidently seemed appropriate to the author of chs. 35–39.

[36.8–38] Chs. 36.8–38 describes the making of the whole of the complicated tent construction, generally following 26.1–37 word for word in the form of a report of the construction. Only in a few places has the formulation been slightly altered, though without in fact making any difference. 26.30 and 26.33–35 have consistently been omitted, as they already anticipate the theme of the equipping and ordering of the sanctuary; this theme is only mentioned in the report of the construction in ch. 40. In a more remarkable way, the writer of the report has omitted 26.9b, 12, 13 also, taking this simple way of obviating the difficulty of the somewhat conflicting detail in these verses (see pp. 213 f. above). From this it also appears that he already found ch. 26 in the form in which it has been transmitted. In other respects, however, he is completely faithful to his model in ch. 26.

[37.1–24] The position of the report in the section which now follows of the making of the ark with its covering, the table and the lampstand (37.1–24) in relationship to the corresponding pattern in 25.10–40, is similar. Apart from a few alterations in the formulation which have little bearing on the content, there is once again the omission of all details of the positioning and use of the different cult-items; this is the case with 25. 15 f., 21 f., 30, 37b and 40, in all of which instances, including 37b–40, the present form of ch. 25 may already be presupposed.

[37.25–29] There now follows in 37.25–28 the report of the making of the altar of incense in accordance with 30.1 ff. This is consistent, as the altar of incense belongs with the ark, the table and the lampstand to the equipment of the inner sanctuary. In 30.1–10 the altar of incense only appeared among the supplements to the basic P narrative about the sanctuary. In the report on the making of the items the basic material and the additions have been worked up into a whole and the altar of incense has been given appropriate place in this whole. The wording of 37.25–28 corresponds with that of 30.1–5; as always, the orders for positioning and use which follow in 30.6–10 are omitted. By way of addition, however, a short note about the making of the anointing oil and the incense is introduced in 37.29 in which the instructions of 30.22–33 and 30.34–38 appear quite summarily in the form of brief extracts from 30.25 and 30.34–35. Thus apparently the transmitted state of 30.22–38 is once again presupposed as the pattern; all, however, is cut down to the minimum. The making of the incense has been given quite an appropriate place in connection with the section about the altar of incense. Furthermore, in view of the proximity and affinity of the passages 30.22–33 and 30.34–38 the notice about the oil of anointing has been inserted at the same time, as there is no really appropriate place elsewhere in the report about the making of the items.

[38.1–20] The sanctuary proper is followed in 38.1–20 by the fore-court with the items which it contains (corresponding to ch. 27). The altar of burnt offering which belongs in the forecourt is described first of all in 38.1–7. This was named simply 'the altar' in ch. 27, as the basic P material knew only this altar. Once the altar of incense had been taken out of the supplements of ch. 30 and had been incorporated in chs. 35–39, it was necessary to give the altar in the forecourt a closer, distinctive description, and therefore in 38.1 it is appropriately named the 'altar of burnt offering'. In other respects, the detailed description of 38.1–7 once again follows the wording of 27.1–8 with a few discrepancies in language. In 38.8 the bronze laver and its bronze base make an appearance from the supplements (30.18–21) because they belong to the forecourt along with the altar of burnt offering. Once again the instructions for positioning and use of 30.18b–21 are omitted, but a most remarkable note about the material for the laver and base is added; it is made from 'the mirrors of the ministering women who ministered at the door of the tent of meeting' (these women also appear with the same description in I Sam. 2.22). The reason for this note remains obscure, all the more so as at the point of time here imagined there was still no ministering at the entrance to the tent of meeting. The description of the tent-entrance to the forecourt in 38.9–20 once again corresponds with the parallel section 27.9–19. The alterations to the language are here rather more marked than usual, in so far as in vv. 17–20 the order of the pattern has been altered and in fact improved. There are no differences of content, and for the most part the wording of the original is also preserved here.

[38.21–31] The report of the making of the items is interrupted in a most striking way in 38.21–31. Now that the objects for which the metal was necessary have been described, we have a reckoning of the amounts of metal that were needed. It can hardly be doubted that here we have a quite secondary literary passage in which (v. 26) the use of the result of the census first narrated in Num. 1 is particularly out of place. The same is true of the reference to the special duties of the Levites under the direction of Ithamar, son of Aaron (v. 21), in which the regulations first reported in Num. 3 and 4 are anticipated. In addition, the beginning (v. 21) is formulated in a very turgid way, that is, if the text is not corrupt at this point (perhaps it originally read 'This is the result of the counting on the basis of the numbering of the community'), and further is overladen with a lengthy parenthetical clause (vv. 22 f.) about the work of Bezalel and Oholiab. Extraordinarily large quantities are quoted for gold (v. 24), silver (vv. 25–28) and bronze (vv. 29–31). In silver the quantity is in fact so great that it would be necessary to exact half a shekel from every adult male Israelite according to the total given in Num. 1.46. The amounts for gold and bronze stand in no rational relationship to the amount for silver. The use of the silver and bronze is still reported in summary detail, but this is not the case with the gold. Thus the section is not fully harmonized throughout.

[39.1–31] This section deals with the priestly dress on the basis of ch. 28. The pattern for it was obviously ch. 28 in its present form, the wording of which has mostly been taken over. Verse 1 forms the transition from the secondary passage 38.21–31 to the new theme, in which it is stressed that the items to be made out of the costly materials will now be enumerated. This transition with its plural subject is certainly the reason why, particularly at the beginning of some of the main sections (vv. 2, 3ab, 7 f., 22) the singular subject which has hitherto been customary has still been retained, but in most other places a plural subject appears. This transition has moreover replaced the transition passage 28.1–5. In what follows a note has then been inserted about the making of gold leaf to be woven into the costly fabric (v. 3a) as have the frequent references to the divine instructions given to Moses (vv. 5b, 21b, 26b, 29b, 31b), while on the other hand the references to the significance and use of the individual items of clothing (28.12b, 29, 35b, 38, 41, 42abb, 43) are omitted, as is the passage about the chains on which the breastpiece is to be hung (28.13 f.). It is remarkable that in ch. 39 silence is maintained about the 'Urim and Thummim' (cf. 28.30) which are to be put inside the breastpiece and that consequently in v. 8 there is also no longer any mention of the 'breastpiece of judgment' (so 28. 15) but merely of 'the breastpiece' (vv. 8ff.). The 'Urim and Thummim' (see p. 222 above) were apparently already completely foreign to the author of ch. 39. It is also remarkable that the details of 28.10 f. about the inscription of the two precious stones on the shoulder-pieces are omitted, perhaps because they seemed to be in opposition to the precious stones on the breastpiece, inscribed with the names of the tribes of Israel. Finally, presumably a better order has been chosen in ch. 39, in which of course the distinction between Aaron and his sons (i.e. the distinction between the High Priest and the ordinary priests) has fallen out; at the same time the addition about the priests' breeches which is manifestly such in ch. 28 has been worked into the whole. Thus v. 27 mentions 'coats' for Aaron and his sons (combination of 28.39a*a* and 40a*a*), but v. 28a mentions the turban (according to 28.39a*b* for Aaron) and the 'caps' (according to 28.40b for the sons of Aaron) without making any further distinction. Moreover there is mention of 'breeches' in v. 28b (after the addition 28.42a*a*) and finally in v. 29a the girdle (combination of 28.39b and 40a*b*). Right at the end (vv. 30–31a) comes the 'plate' (flower) of 28.36–37 without it being made clear that it was only a part of the turban of the High Priest. In a remarkable way the word 'plate' is glossed with the phrase 'the holy crown' (*nēzer*) (on this cf. pp. 225 f. above). It is not probable that the alterations mentioned have any real significance in the sense that the writer of ch. 39 slightly corrected the scheme of the P narrative in accordance with the actual circumstances of the post-exilic period. At best the omission of 'Urim and Thummim' could be understood in this sense; the omission of 28.30 was of course merely consistent, as the Urim and Thummim were not to be made but just to explain the use of the breastpiece. But the abandonment of the expression 'breastpiece of judgment', which is apparently bound up with this, is striking. We cannot, however, draw certain conclusions even from this.

[**39.32–43**] In the closing section 39.32–43 the whole work is now explained as completed (v. 32) so that now all the items for the maintenance of the cult, once again narrated in detail (vv. 33–41), are brought to Moses. He finds that all has been done well and so can 'bless' all those who have played some part (vv. 42 f.). It may be asked whether, in the general statements of vv. 32, 42 f., there is still the residue of a short account from the original P narrative, which said that the instructions given to Moses in chs. 25 ff. were all carried out correctly and well. The P narrative certainly must once have contained such an account.

7. THE FURNISHING OF THE SANCTUARY: 40.1 – 38

40[1] The LORD said to Moses, [2] 'On the first day of the first month you shall erect the tabernacle of the tent of meeting. [3] And you shall put in it the ark of the testimony, and you shall screen the ark with the veil. [4] And you shall bring in the table, and set its arrangements in order; and you shall bring in the lampstand, and set up its lamps. [5] And you shall put the golden altar for incense before the ark of the testimony, and set up the screen for the door of the tabernacle. [6] You shall set the altar of burnt offering before the door of the tabernacle of the tent of meeting, [7] and place the laver between the tent of meeting and the altar, and put water in it. [8] And you shall set up the court round about, and hang up the screen for the gate of the court. [9] Then you shall take the anointing oil, and anoint the tabernacle and all that is in it, and consecrate it and all its furniture; and it shall become holy. [10] You shall also anoint the altar of burnt offering and all its utensils, and consecrate the altar; and the altar shall be most holy. [11] You shall also anoint the laver and its base, and consecrate it. [12] Then you shall bring Aaron and his sons to the door of the tent of meeting, and shall wash them with water, [13] and put upon Aaron the holy garments, and you shall anoint him and consecrate him, that he may serve me as priest. [14] You shall bring his sons also and put coats on them, [15] and anoint them, as you anointed their father, that they may serve me as priests: and their anointing shall admit them to a perpetual priesthood throughout their generations.'

16 Thus did Moses; according to all that the LORD commanded him, so he did. [17] And in the first month in the second year, on the first day of the month, the tabernacle was erected. [18] Moses erected the tabernacle; he laid its bases, and set up its frames, and put in its poles, and raised up its pillars; [19] and he spread the tent over the tabernacle, and put the covering of the tent over it, as the LORD had commanded Moses. [20] And he took the testimony and put it into the ark, and put the poles on the ark, and set the mercy seat above on the ark; [21] and he brought the ark into the tabernacle, and set up the veil of the screen, and screened the ark of the testimony; as the LORD had commanded Moses. [22] And he put the table in the tent of meeting, on the north side of the tabernacle, outside the veil, [23] and set the bread in order on it before the LORD; as the LORD had commanded Moses. [24] And he put the lampstand in the tent of meeting, opposite the table on the south side of the tabernacle, [25] and set up the lamps before the LORD; as the LORD had commanded Moses. [26] And he put the golden altar in the tent of meeting before the veil, [27] and burnt fragrant incense upon it; as the LORD had commanded Moses. [28] And he put in place the screen for the door of the tabernacle. [29] And he set the altar of burnt offering at the door of the tabernacle of the tent of meeting, and offered upon it the burnt offering and the cereal offering; as the LORD had commanded Moses. [30] And he set the laver between the tent of meeting and the altar, and put water in it for washing, [31] with which Moses and Aaron and his

sons washed their hands and their feet; [32] when they went into the tent of meeting, and when they approached the altar, they washed; as the LORD commanded Moses. [33] And he erected the court round the tabernacle and the altar, and set up the screen of the gate of the court. So Moses finished the work.

34 Then the cloud covered the tent of meeting, and the glory of the LORD filled the tabernacle. [35] And Moses was not able to enter the tent of meeting, because the cloud abode upon it, and the glory of the LORD filled the tabernacle. [36] Throughout all their journeys, whenever the cloud was taken up from over the tabernacle, the people of Israel would go onward; [37] but if the cloud was not taken up, then they did not go onward till the day that it was taken up. [38] For throughout all their journeys the cloud of the LORD was upon the tabernacle by day, and fire was in it by night, in the sight of all the house of Israel.

[17] In the description of the furnishing of the sanctuary (v. 1–33) a clear distinction can be made between three parallel literary strata. Verses 1–16 contain a detailed divine command which is primarily concerned with the anointing of the contents of the tabernacle and the priests; there is a short explanatory note at the end. Verse 17 gives summary details of the erection of the tabernacle, in a passive form, which are nevertheless complete in themselves. The event is described once again, in full detail, in vv. 18–33. Now whereas the sections vv. 1–16 and vv. 18–33 presuppose the secondary additions to the P narrative, this is not the case with v. 17. This verse may therefore be assigned to P. In that case, the detailed instructions of chs. 25 ff. were presumably followed in P by a note, perhaps still preserved in 39.32, 42 f., on the carrying out of the necessary work (see p. 280 above) and a note on the furnishing of the tabernacle in 40.17. The temporal note in v. 17 is the first one given after 19.1 P. If we allow some time for Moses to go up the mountain and to receive and hand on the divine instructions, all the work on the sanctuary, which is here described as the 'tabernacle', after its chief feature (cf. 26.1), until its final completion, took about seven months.

[18–33] Of the two secondary sections, which occasional differences show not to derive from the same hand, the section vv. 18–33 must certainly be regarded as the older. It too takes up the basic features of chs. 25–31 and the additions made to them. Moses already begins to offer sacrifices (vv. 27a, 29ba) and in so doing anticipates the narrative of Lev. 8.9. The constantly reiterated reference to the divine command given to Moses (vv. 19b, 21b, 23b, 25b, 27b, 29bb, 32b) looks like a later substitute for a command of God which was originally missing; it is put in rather a clumsy way, as v. 18 shows Moses to be the chief subject of the whole section. The details of vv. 18–33 could stem from a later writer to whom the brief observation in v. 17 seemed insufficient and who took the material for his description from chs. 25–31. **[1–16]** In the same way—though more briefly than vv. 18–33—vv. 1–16 use chs. 25–31 as a basis for describing the furnishing of the sanctuary; this provides the basis for the attached narrative of the anointing and 'consecration' both of Aaron and his sons, and of all the cult items within the gate of the court. This anointing of the priests is treated in detail and appears to be the real purpose of this section. It is striking here that the act of anointing is described separately, first for Aaron (v. 13b) and then for his sons (v. 15a); here we may still see after-effects of the old tradition, which knew only an anointing for Aaron himself (see p. 230 above). In other respects this description of the anointing again anticipates Lev. 8; and already in this section the question arises whether it was not added only after the interposition of Lev. 1–7 had placed the continuation of the narrative in Lev. 8 at some distance. Perhaps even the division of the Pentateuch into 'books' had already taken place, so that the need arose to bring the theme of the furnishing of the sanctuary to an end of some kind at the end of the Book of Exodus.

[34–38] This question, presumably to be answered in the affirmative, arises all the more in view of the last section (vv. 34–38), for here too things are presupposed which are later narrated once again. The 'glory' of Yahweh, which manifests itself in the cloud (on this cf. 24.15b–18 P), by appearing over the tent of meeting (vv. 34a, 35a) —and in a mysterious way even in the tabernacle (on the parallel phrases vv. 34b, 35b cf. I Kings 8.10b, 11)—gave the sign of legitimacy and approval to the newly-built sanctuary and thus represented the proper conclusion of the whole work. If then it is further said in vv. 36–38, in anticipation of Num. 9.15 ff., but quite wrongly here, that the significance of the cloud concerns the departure or non-departure of the Israelites, it becomes quite clear that here a (secondary) ending has been achieved. In this way the Book of Exodus now ends with a look towards the progress of the history of Israel which primarily consists in the further journeys through the wilderness under the divine guidance.